THE ROAD OF SLAUGHTER

The Latvian 15th SS Division in Pomerania,
January–March 1945

Vincent Hunt

Helion & Company Limited

Helion & Company Limited
Unit 8 Amherst Business Centre
Budbrooke Road
Warwick
CV34 5WE
England
Tel. 01926 499 619
Email: info@helion.co.uk
Website: www.helion.co.uk
Twitter: @helionbooks
Visit our blog at blog.helion.co.uk

Published by Helion & Company 2023
Designed and typeset by Mach 3 Solutions (www.mach3solutions.co.uk)
Cover designed by Paul Hewitt, Battlefield Design (www.battlefield-design.co.uk)
Printed by Gutenberg Press Ltd, Tarxien, Malta

Text © Vincent Hunt 2023
Images © Vincent Hunt unless otherwise credited
Maps drawn by George Anderson © Helion & Company 2023

Cover: A tank-killer squad from the Latvian Legion's 15th SS Division marching in the blizzards in Pomerania, early 1945. (Picture courtesy of Latvian War Museum, Rīga. LKM 5-12947/1228-FT)

Back cover: The Road of Slaughter between Jastrow and Landeck now, as it would have been seen by Red Army artillery gunners at Wallachsee. Picture: Aivars Sinka, June 2023.

ISBN 9-7-81804512-59-3

British Library Cataloguing-in-Publication Data.
A catalogue record for this book is available from the British Library.

For details of other military history titles published by Helion & Company Limited contact the above address or visit our website: http://www.helion.co.uk.

We always welcome receipt of book proposals from prospective authors.

Contents

List of Maps

Acknowledgments

This volume is dedicated to the men who served as Latvian Legionnaires on the Eastern Front between August 1944 and May 1945 and who were interviewed by the author for this book between 2017–2022. Jānis Čevers, Laimonis Ceriņš, Žano Mūsiņš, Ēriks Rudzītis, Jānis Urpens, Talis Iskalns, Ziedonis Āboliņš and Henry Vītols came to Britain after the war. Harijs Valdmanis spoke on the phone from Norway on his 95th birthday. Arturs Grava was interviewed by Zoom from the United States on 20 July 2022, just four days before his 98th birthday. Their conversations have been transcribed from those recordings and correspondence. Most were in their mid–late 90s at the time, and I am grateful to them. Their eyewitness accounts form the core of this epic experience, which ended for 10,000 of these men in the UK. They are Latvia's Lost Legion.

This book is also dedicated to Daina Vītola, my translator, cultural guide and friend through six years of intense and seemingly-unending research. None of my three books about Latvia so far would have been possible without Daina. Her dedication, eye for accuracy and meticulous attention has been fantastic over what has sometimes been a nightmarish and complicated journey. The material deserves it: these accounts have never been published before in English. We winced together as she translated the gruesome story of the road to Landeck from the memories of Vilis Janums, Kazimirs Ručs, Zigurds Kārkliņš and Pauls Dzintars. This book is a tribute to her.

My search for Legionnaires to tell their stories led me to continue my association with Aivars Sinka of the Latvian Legion veterans' association Daugavas Vanagi. I owe an enormous research debt to him for his scouring of texts and research in archives, and his translations have added great depth and detail. His translation of Major Ķīlītis's experiences at Flederborn and Landeck truly tells of the horrific reality of war. I am grateful for the support of Daugavas Vanagi worldwide in this project and so have reproduced text and pictures from the 11-volume series known as 'the Green Books': *Latviešu karavirs Otra pasaules kara laika*: [*The Latvian Soldier During World War Two*]. The much-respected librarian at Catthorpe, Inese Auzine-Smita, kindly gave me a set. Daugavas Vanagi has prepared a webpage to help search for relatives affected by the war: <www.dvcv.org.lv/searching-for-relatives>.

The accounts of events in Pomerania by Colonel Janums and Major Kilitis are self-published, and, translated into English, have added important detail to this research. I am grateful to the central board of Daugavas Vanagi for their approval to use eyewitness accounts and images from these significant places. The stories of the veterans at the core of this book are accompanied by new maps drawn from these archive texts, giving precise military details of the operations. Arturs Silgailis' *Latvian Legion* has been a constant reference book.

As what happened at Podgaje-Flederborn became more significant, the National State Archives in Rīga allowed me to view and photograph the microfiche records of the 15th Division War Diary. Curator Ligita Saule tracked down specific orders and maps compiled for after-action reports which are reproduced here. Latvian War Museum curator Jānis Tomaševskis opened his archive for me and his advice and guidance has added greatly to this work.

The memoirs of Augusts Spilners, Imants Jansons and Brunis Rubess added yet more dimensions to the story of Latvian units retreating west as the German Army collapsed in Pomerania and Mecklenburg. I am grateful to Nora Spilners in Market Harborough, Jānis Jansons in Australia and Brunis Rubess's daughters Baiba and Banuta in Canada and Latvia for allowing me to use lengthy extracts and pictures from their father's diaries, and to John Čevers, Astrid Balodis, Kriss and Astrid Ligers and many more for enabling me to speak to the Legionnaires in this book.

Pauls Vanags, an Iron Cross winner and veteran of the Battle of More, was kind enough to talk to me on the phone from his home in Swansea at the age of 96, with thanks to his daughter Daina. Valdis Kuzmins, military historian and expert on the 15th Division, helped shape a re-thinking of this book's structure and emphasised the role of Lieutenant Eižens Bonoparts, killed at Domslaff.

Source material

Latvian Legion by Arturs Sigailis was lent to me by Russian Front veteran Jānis Čevers. I am sad I did not get to give it back to him. This book began life written around our conversations in Derby six years ago, fuelled by tea and biscuits.

My thanks go to Anta Brača at the Museum of the Battle of More (<http://www.moresmuzejs.lv/>) for the picture of the farmhouse *Mazratnieki*. The pictures of Legion chaplain Kazimirs Ručs are reproduced with the permission of the Latgale Culture Centre in Rēzekne (<www.Rēzekne.lv/en/latgale-culture-and-history-museum/>) with thanks to historian Kaspars Strods for his help and advice.

The Military Historical Office in Warsaw gave permission to reproduce the 1945 pictures from Podgaje-Flederborn; historian Maciej Maciejowski at the IPN in Szczecin added detail to the Podgaje-Flederborn story while Dr Marcin Owsiński at the Muzeum Stutthof w Sztutowie added expertise on matters relating to the Stutthof camp. Additional material on Stutthof comes from Latvian archives, translated by Aivars Sinka.

My thanks go to Arnold Koslowski for his contribution on Polish perspectives on Podgaje-Flederborn and for sharing his source material for use in this book. Modern images come from photographer Jim Donnelly, my friend and companion for a trip to Gdańsk, Hela and the forests of Kashubia.

My thanks go to those who translated additional Latvian, German and Polish stories and archives from the time. Patrick Howse translated from poorly-lit and difficult-to-read accounts in German of the disastrous action on the Flederborn to Landeck road from photographs of the microfiches of the 15th Division war diary in the Rīga National Archive. Tom Fane translated the story of the Kampfgruppe Hämel from the same source. Vic Thiele translated the frantic orders from the road to Landeck.

Janusz Korona and son Jan translated Polish accounts of the battles in Nakel [Nakło nad Notecią] given to me by museum director Tomasz Pasieka, as well as further accounts of those traumatic times in Podgaje-Flederborn and Słupsk. My fellow author at Helion, Wojciech Skóra, alerted me to several eyewitness accounts of this time, and I am grateful to Jan Sroka for permission to use Derk Steggewentz's brutal stories.

The pictures of wartime Toruń are used with the permission of the Muzeum Okręgowe w Toruniu [Toruń District Museum] with thanks to Justyna Gierad, Maciej Majewski and Natalia Rataj, my Town Hall guide during my visit there.

I am grateful to the following museums and remembrance centres for their guidance and advice: Dr Łukasz Nadolski, director of the Military History Department of the Land Forces Museum, Bydgoszcz [Muzeum Wojsk Lądowych w Bydgoszczy]; The Museum of the Second World War in Gdańsk, the District Museum in Piła, [Muzeum Okręgowe im. St. Staszica w Pile]; the Pomeranian Wall Museum in Wałcz [The Brickyard, or *Grupa Warowna Cegielnia*], the Muzeum Stutthof w Sztutowie in Poland and the IPN in Szczecin, Poland. I am grateful to Ireck Litbarski for allowing me to use a selection of images from his private RAD collection, with watermark retained. Izabela Jamrozik translated accounts relating to the battle of Jastrow.

In Latvia my thanks go to Lelde Neimane, Evita Feldentale and Professor Dr Valters Nollendorfs at the Museum of the Occupation of Latvia in Rīga; Edmunds Supulis, Kaspars Zellis, Mara Zirnite and Inta Meirina at the University of Latvia; and Inese Dreimane, Ieva Lešinska, Linards Muciņš and Indulis Zālīte, each very supportive over many years, with a special mention to the noted social anthropologist Vieda Skultans, whom I had the pleasure of meeting in Rīga.

In the UK through the Inter-Library Loan system I was able to draw on books from the British Library, UCL College Library and Wakefield Library, and my thanks to the staff of Didsbury Library, part of Manchester Libraries, for their help during the pandemic. My thanks go to Joseph Ford for accessing Legion commander Adolph Ax's account from Nakel through the British Library at that time.

I must acknowledge the influence of my uncle, George Hunt, who served in the war and whose books I inherited, my father Philip Hunt and mother Sylvia Christie.

I thank my colleagues for their ideas and inspiration, especially Dr Geoff Walton, Lawrence Brannon, Paul Clark, Peter Murray, Jeremy Craddock, Andy Dickinson, Jerome Read, Sam Heitzman and Rob Jones, and my musical friends who kept me sane: Rob Haynes, Howard Jones, Martin Bramah, John Paul Moran, Ron Higginbottom and Harry Stafford, with special thanks to the This and That Cafe, Soap Street, Manchester, for many years of sustenance.

Special personal thanks go to Nicola Sinka and my family and friends who lived with me on this journey: my sisters Alison Brammer and Christine Hunt and my son

Martins Vitolins-Hants, plus David Ford, Ian Muir, Dr. Doug Jeffrey, Dawn Bryan, Jane Drinkwater, Guy Nelson, Rick Roberts, Natalie Carragher, Louise Twelvetrees, Derek Ivens, Janusz and Agate Korona, Mike Brewer, Leigh Titterton, Neil and Julie Shaw, Mark and Ian Tilton, Laura Macmillan, Gunita Smirnova and Ugis Sarja, Daiga Kamerade, Professor Chris and Angela Young, Alistair Swiffen, Sue Keogh and – crucially – Biscuit at the Mac and PC Centre in Manchester, who saved my battered Mac many times and so made many digital transfers and conversations possible.

Finally, my thanks go especially to Duncan Rogers and the team at Helion, especially copy editor Autumn Brown, cartographer George Anderson and typesetter Kim McSweeney.

I am grateful to have a publisher who understands that oral history can be a powerful way of understanding better what happened in the past.

Vincent Hunt
Manchester
August 2023

Introduction

Legion veteran and historian Visvaldis Mangulis wrote of the Latvian 15th Division's experiences in Pomerania: 'In 50 days it marched 965 kilometres [600 miles] and fought 12 Soviet infantry divisions and a tank corps.'

At the core of this volume are the stories of men who were there, told to the author at their homes in the UK. They settled there after the war, having been offered work and unable to return to their homeland. I caught them at the end of their lives. These are the memories of the last surviving Latvian Legionnaires in the UK. I am grateful to them for telling me their stories.

The Eastern Front is known for its horror, and this book contains graphic descriptions of brutal violence, desperate choices and traumatic situations; of rapes and executions, and possibly several incidents for historians to explore further. The stories are ghastly: anti-aircraft guns blasting the 'human wave' of the Red Army, Latvian priests in trenches with Panzerfausts in 'kill or be killed' situations, Soviet T-34 tanks steamrollering refugee convoys, carnage and bodies everywhere. It is bloody, hopeless and exhausting, with chilling echoes of the war in Ukraine.

This book ends at the Oder but the story of the Latvian 15th SS Division will continue after this, telling of four separate endings: Colonel Janums' incredible escape from Berlin; the refusal by officers commanding a group of several thousand men to fight in the 'suicide positions' in Mecklenburg; the siege of Danzig, where more than 4,000 Latvians died and, described in the vivid translated memoirs of two of the very few Latvians who survived, the final battles of the heroic 'Recce' Battalion at Gestapo headquarters, Potsdamer Platz and Wilhelmstrasse in the Battle of Berlin. This is what happened in the seven weeks before that, from 22 January to 12 March 1945, told through the memories and diaries of people who came out alive. Their stories are strong stuff.

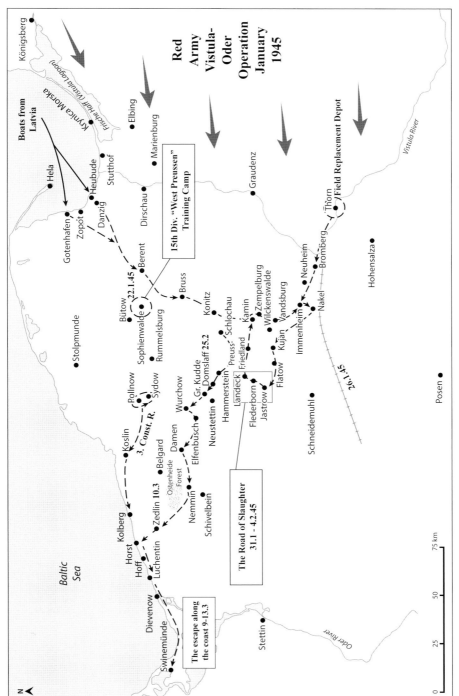

The journey of the Latvian 15th SS Division across Pomerania, January to March 1945.

Part One

The Beginning

1

The Russian Front

An elderly man sits on a couch with his feet up on a stool, hands folded in front of him. A pot of tea and three cups stand on a tray on a table nearby, with milk, sugar and biscuits. This is Jānis Čevers, born in Latvia and a veteran of the Eastern Front. The tea is for him, for me and for his son John. We have been talking for some time. He looks at me.

> I became like an animal. I had no human feelings any more. You see so many people killed, torn to pieces, wounded. It doesn't make any difference to you.
>
> As we were retreating we saw one young chap with both legs gone, sitting there pleading. We just gave him a grenade to kill himself. What can you do? You can't do anything, just run. No human feelings at all.

Jānis Čevers is rare. There are very few men left who survived the fighting on the Russian Front with the 15th Division of the Latvian Legion, and I have come to his home in Derby in the East Midlands of England to hear his stories. The 15th was one of two SS divisions formed in Latvia from 1943 onwards sent to strengthen Nazi units suffering mounting losses on the Eastern Front. Although the men of the 15th and its counterpart the 19th Division were described as volunteers, in reality the Nazis carried out a general mobilisation of men of fighting age. Because the Hague Convention of 1907 meant the Germans couldn't recruit nationals of other countries into their own army, they were assigned as 'SS'.

Russian Front veteran Jānis Čevers at his home in Derby, UK, in 2017. (Picture: author)

There were already Latvian units fighting in Russia before November 1943, but the bulk of the soldiers of the Legion were sent to the Eastern Front then: first to Staraya Russa and then on to the Velikaya River, where the 15th and the 19th Latvian Divisions served together in fierce clashes at Ostrova and Opochka in March 1944.

Both divisions suffered heavy losses. The 15th was effectively smashed as a fighting force by powerful Red Army attacks in summer 1944, retreating in disarray into eastern Latvia. There it was pulled out of the frontlines. All Latvian men born in 1925 and 1926 were called up to strengthen the division and sent to Pomerania – what is now Poland – to train. The idea was that they would be sent back to help defend their homeland once their training was complete but only about 1,000 were: most of the recruits were thrown into the fight to stop the Red Army's drive across the Vistula river. Very few of the survivors returned to their homeland due to the Soviet occupation: they formed the basis of today's global Latvian diaspora in Australia, Sweden, the United States, Canada, the UK, Belgium and Germany.

The second division, the 19th SS, fought a rearguard action to delay the Soviet advance on the Latvian capital Rīga, while the new recruits of the 15th and veterans of the Russian Front like Jānis Čevers were shipped west to Danzig [now Gdańsk] and Gotenhafen [now Gdynia] to regain fighting strength. Latvian civilians too were rounded up and loaded onto boats, sent to dig anti-tank ditches on the west banks of the Vistula to delay the vast numbers of Soviet T-34 tanks massing to attack. Soldiers lacking training, equipment or weapons were given shovels.

Mr Čevers is 94 when we first meet. He is very cheerful, and wearing the shirt of his local football team, Derby County. His son John brings a tray of tea, and I open my biscuits: custard creams and Jaffa cakes. Jānis takes a mouthful of tea. I switch my recorder on and he begins to talk.

> My name is Jānis Čevers. I was born a farmer's son in Varakļāni, Latvia, on 27 September 1923. I went to basic primary school then grammar school, a five-year course. I'd just finished the third year in 1943. I finished school in June and on 15 July I was called up into the 15th Division in Cēsis.
>
> We had experienced the Russians [in the Soviet occupation of 1940–41] but we didn't know anything about the Germans. We knew what Communism was and we were against Communism. We had experienced the atrocities from Russia in that year under Stalin.[1] Both my godparents and their families were sent to Siberia in June 1941. We went that day to the station and there were people shouting and screaming in the wagons, all locked in and sent to Siberia. When the Russians left, the Army officers went round villages rounding up men to help them. My brother Jazeps was taken; I wasn't. I wasn't 18. Jazeps had to dig holes while the police shot Communists, and then my brother had to bury them.

---

1   The 'Year of Terror' of 1940–41, when Latvia was occupied by the Soviet Union in the Molotov-Ribbentrop Non-Aggression Pact. Those considered political opponents of Communism, such as intellectuals, government employees and 'bourgeois nationalists' were murdered and 15,000 Latvians deported to Siberia.

There had been Jews in Varakļāni from 1784, and the town had the highest percentage of Jews per population in all Latvia. In the 1930s, the 952 Jews in Varakļāni made up nearly 60 percent of the population and ran 90 percent of all businesses. Most council members were Jewish, and Yiddish was sometimes used for council business.[2] Within days of the Nazis arriving in late June 1941, the intimidation began. Jews were ordered to wear yellow stars on their clothes and were moved to a ghetto. Those accused of collaborating with the Soviet occupation regime were shot by the local Self Defence Committee. Jānis' brother and sister watched the killing unfold.

> I had a sister two years older than me. One day in July Germans came in a lorry and collected all the able people, including my sister and brother. They drove them to Varakļāni and put them in the forest digging ditches. In Varakļāni there were a lot of Jews: more Jews than Latvians, because of all the shops. They were all collected in a big yard with walls all round. They were transported to the forest and all of them were shot. My sister and brother were standing next to the graves when the Jews were shot, then they buried them. Imagine? A girl of 18, 19. A baby in a mother's arms – they shot the baby first then the mother, on the grave's edge. And my sister had to bury them with a spade.
>
> They shot about 300 Jews that day in that forest in Varakļāni. I found out later there were a lot of Jewish girls from the grammar school I was at who were all shot that day. I had been teaching them some Latvian. Jews were always in business. They were never farmers or factory workers. Some people saw them as being richer than Latvians. We lived together and worked together but there was always a little bit of a division between Jews and Latvians. There was friction – because they weren't an industrial race, they were an academic race – but there were no atrocities, no pogroms.

Nazi propaganda blamed 'Jews and Bolsheviks' for the brutal year of Communist control and their demands for revenge found willing volunteers in the Arājs Kommando, a unit of Latvian irregulars led by Viktors Arājs, which was collaborating with the Nazi regime. Organised into auxiliary police units, the Kommando helped Nazi *Einsatzgruppen* death squads murder in the region of 3,000 Jews in Liepāja in summer 1941 and, in systematic mass killings, 26,000 Jews at Rumbula on 30 November and 8 December 1941. A further 20,000 Jews – 8,000 from Latvia and 11–12,000 from other European countries – and 15,000 other victims, including 10,000 Soviet prisoners of war, were killed at Biķernieki forest near Rīga.[3]

The Germans set up a Latvian administration and recruited 3,000 men into police battalions to support their invasion of the Soviet Union. Some of these units were sent to the Russian Front and some to police Belarus, which was fully controlled by

---

2 M. Meler, *Jewish Latvia: Sites to Remember. Latvian Jewish Communities Destroyed in the Holocaust* (Tel Aviv: The Association of Latvian and Estonian Jews in Israel, 2013), pp.410–414.
3 Meler, *Jewish Latvia*, pp.208–212, 300–303; Lumans, *Latvia in World War II*, p.241, quoting Ezergailis, *The Holocaust in Latvia*.

the Germans from September 1941.[4] The German units in Belarus, among them the unspeakably cruel and bloodthirsty Dirlewanger Brigade, were involved in operations suppressing partisan resistance and *aktions* murdering the Jewish population in vast numbers.[5]

The European Holocaust Research Infrastructure writes of this time:

> The main perpetrators of the murder campaign were members of *Einsatzgruppen* A and B and the Security and Order Police stationed in Belarus. Most of the Jews in Belarus were exterminated in two major waves: between the late summer and winter of 1941 and during 1942. As the scope of mass murder widened, the Germans increasingly relied on local collaborators and collaborating organisations. The last Jewish ghettos in Western Belarus were liquidated in the summer of 1942, while the Minsk Ghetto, one of the largest in Europe, was fully liquidated by October 1943. The percentage of Jews who perished in Belarus during the Holocaust is among the highest in Europe. The number of victims has been estimated to be at least 450,000 and may be in the range of 600,000, including Jewish refugees from Poland.[6]

Though the extent of the involvement of Latvian police battalions in these operations is still not definitive, their presence in Belarus at this time, plus the known participation of the Arājs group, have scarred the reputation of Latvians since. This scarring has also been fuelled by Soviet disinformation campaigns, such as the 1963 KGB-produced booklet *Daugavas Vanagi – Who Are They?* which falsely accused senior Latvian figures in the West of involvement in these war crimes. There are war crimes allegations against four of 42 Latvian police battalions, only one of which - the 18th - served in Belarus. The evidence presented at the Soviet-era trial of battalion members (and their subsequent execution) is highly questionable. However, there is no doubt about the involvement of the Arājs Kommando in the Holocaust-by-bullets in Belarus. The 1985 film *Come and See* directed by Elem Klimov is a harrowing and unforgettable portrayal of events there. It is considered an anti-war masterpiece, and can be seen with English subtitles at <https://www.youtube.com/watch?v=zjIiApN6cfg>.

The war became more vicious and revenge became an issue, Jānis Čevers remembers:

---

4   A. Silgailis, *Latvian Legion* (San Jose, CA: Roger James Bender, 1986), pp.10–16.
5   Oskar Dirlewanger's Special Commando of convicted criminals killed 30,000 civilians from its arrival in Belarus in February 1942. Dirlewanger's preferred method was to herd the population into a barn, set it on fire and machine gun anyone attempting to escape. His men later massacred 100,000 civilians in the suppression of the Warsaw Rising in August 1944. Source: T. Snyder, *Bloodlands – Europe between Hitler and Stalin* (London: Vintage, 2010), pp.241–243, 303–305.
6   European Holocaust Research Infrastructure website, Belarus country page, <https://portal.ehri-project.eu/countries/by>, accessed 8 December 2020.

No-one can deny the atrocities with the Jews: what Hitler did was terrible. But in every war there are atrocities. Once you get a gun, and you have the power, it changes your attitude. The Germans were very clever. They said 'We want the people in the [Latvian police] battalions to guard our frontlines with Russia.' That was a lie. They were trained policemen sent to Russia to fight partisans. The police battalions in 1941 were all volunteers. My friend was in one. He was sent to Poland. He told me they were ordered to shoot Polish girls. They were *ordered* to. They didn't want to do it. They thought they were guarding borders. The atrocities were all committed by battalion people, not the Legion.

In 1940–41 the Russians sent many Latvians to Siberia, so when the Germans came in, they [their families] had a vendetta against the Russians. That year of atrocities by the Russians meant that when the Germans came in there were reprisals. The police collected the Communists and shot them at night, and the civilians had to bury them. My brother was involved many times, my sister too. Mostly, those doing the shooting were all drunk.

The trouble with the Jews only started when the Russians came in. They [Jewish leaders] took over. They pretended to be Communists, and they ran Varakļāni. All the local leaders were Jews – they went straight to the top. That soured things a bit. When the Germans came in they were looking for Latvians who were nationalists and they set up this special Kommando to kill the Jews. I remember two of my friends from primary school were a little bit like Communists. The police went to their house, they were arrested, shot and that's it. No-one asked any questions. There were no court cases.

By 1943 Nazi progress on the Eastern Front had ground to a halt after military disaster at Stalingrad and an agonising, endless siege at Leningrad. Jānis Čevers and tens of thousands like him were drafted into the newly-formed Latvian Legion, given training and sent east to strengthen the frontlines.

There was basic training first, then we were transferred to Ventspils. I was sent on an NCO's training course there. We trained in the sand dunes in August carrying heavy machine guns in the sun – we were sweating like hell! We were training on old French First World War machine guns.

In early October 1943 we finished the course, were given a group [of men] each and sent to Russia – the whole division, through Jelgava and Ostrov. When we got to Russia they gave us the most modern weapons possible – the MG-42.[7] In my group there were nine of us. I was just above a private; a lance corporal or something. When I was called up I was 19, and just 20 as we left for Russia. We had a little Latvian badge on our arms and an SS badge. I was group leader for a heavy machine gun company. I had an MP40 machine pistol and a pistol. We were all Latvians in my company: we had some Germans in the head office.

---

7   Nicknamed the 'Bonesaw' as it could fire 800–1,200 rounds a minute and cut through anything in front of it.

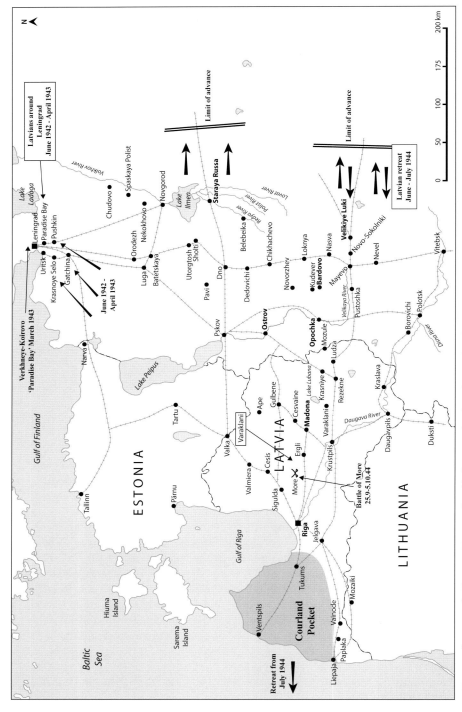

Latvian forces on the Russian Front 1942–44, first as police battalions, then from 1943 as the Legion. Thirteen Latvians won Iron Crosses for their actions at Verkhneye-Koirovo south of Leningrad in March 1943, which was dubbed 'Paradise Bay' because of the danger.

We didn't go to the front to start with. We were distributed around the villages, billeted to farmhouses with the old people. We had a few accidents because we weren't used to the equipment. The guns were going off while we were getting ready to fire them, that sort of thing. And it took us a while to calm the local people down. They were peasants and weren't used to this.

We were there for quite a few months, just guarding against partisans, in the area around Ostro Opochka and Velikie Luki. The partisans were attacking any foreign forces: Velikie Luki was known as a particularly bad place. Then we were moved nearer to the front to get used to the noise of the artillery. When we got to Ostro the train stopped a mile outside the station and we got down off the train into the mud, hearing all the shelling. I was frightened at first but then … well, you get used to it and accept it, like you accept anything in life. 'You're here. Do your best, try and survive.'

The Latvians were well-supplied before they were sent east.

We were in the Waffen-SS and we had very good clothing. Coats lined inside, boots lined inside: we could have slept in the snow, if we needed to. The Wehrmacht didn't get that in winter 1943! I was selected by Major Sproģis to take over food supply for the company. I got a month's rations from Battalion and I was responsible for the food rations. I dished out the schnapps in the evening, just a little shot, and gave my smokes to my mates. I didn't drink or smoke in the Army, not at all.

There was no action until we got to Velikie Luki in March 1944. The Russians were on the east side of the river and we were on the west, us in the 15th with the 19th [Division] on our left. In March there was a big offensive attack from the Russians. I was there on 16 March[8] but the big attack was on 26 March, and that was against the 15th, not the 19th. That's why the 19th escaped from Russia more or less full strength. We were all scattered.[9]

The river was frozen solid because it was winter. Usually the Russians always started at 06:00 with a couple of hours of bombardment before the infantry went into attack. You could set your clock by the two hours. Being shelled: it's nerve-racking. You just try to hide yourself during the bombardment, make yourself as small as possible. You know no-one's coming for you at that moment so you try and hide yourself as much as possible, but it's very scary. I was only two years at the front but I didn't get used to it. I'd always get butterflies in my tummy, but you can't do anything about it so you make the best of it. Try to survive, that's all. A lot of people didn't make it.

8   On 16 March 1944 the two Latvian divisions fought together for the first time, a date later used for the remembrance of Legionnaires' Day. This has been condemned by critics as 'glorifying fascism' and 'celebrating the killers of the Holocaust.'

9   Other veterans have said of this time: 'We were smashed up.'

Machine gun nest in the Bardovo area of Russia manned by the 34th Infantry Regiment of the 15th Division of the Latvian Legion. (Picture: Latvian War Museum [*Latvijas Kara Muzejs*], Rīga. Reference LKM 5-14225/1552-FT)

> We got letters from Latvia saying they could hear the artillery. [It went on] all day long. We were in bunkers in a forest, and the Russians were hammering for a couple of hours like they usually did, and those trees were just stumps – no snow, nothing – all gone. The company retreated three miles and there were a lot of casualties, naturally. Then six or eight German planes came to give them something back. That's the only time in the whole war I saw German planes!

I lean forward to take a sip of tea. 'What was it like being under that kind of attack?' I ask. 'All the shelling?'

> Some went a bit funny in the head, committed suicide. In my group one man put a hand grenade next to his head. He'd had enough, I suppose. I nearly went to pieces. That was the next stage, at Opochka, when the Russian steamroller on the Eastern Front started. The ordinary soldier at the front never knows what's going on beyond a couple of metres from where he is. Only the officers know and they never tell you anything. Our regiment retreated a couple of kilometres and a German SS unit came up to push the Russians back. They never returned. We stayed [where we were] and the SS unit never came out.

I lean forward, pour myself more tea and take a couple of Jaffa cakes and a custard cream. Mr Čevers takes a custard cream: his son John takes a couple of Jaffa cakes. Mr Čevers is getting into his stride.

In Velikie Luki I had two very close shaves. The first happened one autumn morning, nice and crisp, and we were in a village. I was walking with Sergeant Lauder, and the next second he disappeared. An artillery shell or a mortar must have landed right on top of him. He was torn to bits. There were bits of him everywhere. His head was 200 yards [183 metres] down the road. There was no flesh left on his ribs, like vultures had taken the flesh off. He was completely destroyed. And me – not a scratch. Just his blood on my uniform. We were walking side-by-side one moment, then the next he was in pieces. I was getting used to seeing people's bodies torn to pieces, and I was losing my human feelings. It didn't make any difference to me. I was becoming like an animal.

The other incident involved love letters from home. I was quite popular at school and I received a lot of letters from girls at home and I carried them all in my breast pocket. Well, you know the way the Russian bullets explode when they touch something?[10] The bullet must have hit the letters and exploded because there was a big black hole in all these letters, half an inch thick.[11] But the bullet didn't touch my flesh at all!

He takes a sip of tea and bites into his biscuit.

The most scary experience I had was in Russia, when we were in a village. Russian planes came over, attacking. I took the machine gun and rested it on the side of a wagon, standing up, firing at them. There was a chap next to me, feeding the ammunition. All of a sudden he got hit in the chest by a cannon shell which came out of his back. He said: 'Oh' – and that was it. The ambulance came, but there was nothing they could do. And I wondered if it was my fault, because the gun slipped – but he was shot before, my mate…

This is the first time Mr Čevers has admitted to having any feelings for those dying around him. I'm a little surprised. 'He was your *mate*?'

Well … we were together. I did wonder if I shot him, but I couldn't have done, from the angle…

---

10 Both Russian and German forces developed bullets which would explode on impact and detonate white phosphorous, so artillery spotters could adjust ranges based on the flash. The German version was known as the B-patrone, while the Russian version was the PZ. If they hit human flesh, the bullet would detonate inside the body with devastating effect. Source: American gunsmith Grant Cunningham, online at <https://www.grantcunningham.com/2014/11/the-exploding-rifle-bullets-of-world-war-ii/>.

11 About 1.25cm.

It seems odd to be drinking tea and eating biscuits while hearing such gory stories, but Mr Čevers has a wealth of tales to tell.

> After Velikie Luki we were shifted to somewhere near the Opochka area, somewhere in April or May [1944]. The frontline was stalemate. It was quiet a lot of the time, so some of the men were sunbathing on the bunker. They [the Russians] were preparing for a big push in July across the whole of the Eastern Front, so there was only the odd shell now and then.
>
> I was taken out of the line to sort out the wages for soldiers. I was a couple of kilometres behind the lines. Every month I took the wages to the front to dish them out. There was a little forest on the way to the front but it was full of partisans. In our battalion there were four companies and each company had a chap who did the wages. One of the men was caught by the partisans and they cut his tongue out. That scared me a bit. I didn't go through the forest on my own after that.
>
> Opochka was a very mountainous region. On our front we had bunkers dug in and at the bottom of the hill there was a lake. It's beautiful around there. I used to go fishing. I'd throw an anti-tank mine into the lake and all the fish would be stunned...

We all laugh, imagining that scene. He leans forward and puts his mug down.

> There was one incident in Opochka. We Latvians didn't have any tanks but the Russians always had one or two when they attacked with the ground forces. One day the tanks were in the field shooting at us and I was standing behind a tree. The tank fired and the shell hit the tree and exploded, and a long piece of red-hot shrapnel – sharp, shining steel – bounced off and sliced my leg. There was only a little bit of blood but I've still got the scar...

He lifts up his trouser leg to show me the scar.

> I was always scared of being blinded. Soldiers blinded – that's terrible. If something exploded close to you, like a grenade, you could be blinded by that. By the explosion, or from the pressure of the grenade exploding. That's quite a force. In the end I didn't care if I was shot dead. That would have been a blessing. But if you were wounded on the retreat and you were left behind, the Russians weren't very gentle with prisoners. There were all sorts of rumours. I suppose they had a reason because the Germans did bad things to them – tit for tat, I suppose – but you didn't want to get captured by the Russians. Oh no.
>
> One scorching day in July the Russians had launched a big offensive. We were fighting, retreating; fighting some more, retreating some more. There was a group of three of us boys who were friends: good mates. We were running to escape a Russian mortar barrage. The three of us took cover in a shell hole when

a direct hit landed among us. I was lucky, a second lad escaped injury but the third had both his legs blown off.

I could see the pain in his face and his blond hair was matted with blood. There was nothing we could do for him. We had to keep going. We knew what the Russians would do to him if they captured him alive. So we gave him a grenade and got going. A couple of minutes later we heard the grenade go off.

Even though I have heard many stories of combat in Courland, Normandy and in the trenches of the Western Front in the First World War, I am having to acclimatise to Mr Čevers' matter-of-fact eyewitness accounts of the savagery of the Eastern Front.

JC: I didn't think about it at the time, but now, of course … we were always thinking about how to survive.
VH: Did you lose many friends?
JC: From my group, four. And one was a very experienced machine gunner who was in Volkhova at the front in Russia. Oh, he was quick at doing his job. I was only four yards away. We were in a forest on one of those paths inside the forest. The Russians saw him and he was wounded in the stomach. There was no return. We had to move and someone said: 'He won't live. He's suffering too much.' And he [the wounded man] said to the first aid man: 'Give me your pistol. I want to end my life.' But he was already so weak, so the first aid man had to do it. And he was left there.
VH [astonished]: The *first aid* man shot him?
JC: Yes. That's nothing new. What else can you do? There's no chance to get out. There are so many nasty stories going round about what the Russians will do to you.
VH: People being run over by tanks…
JC: Yes, that happened in Russia as well. Wounded people on the ground – so many of them – and a tank comes along and finishes them off.

He reaches forward to take another drink of tea, his memory now active with stories of the chaos and carnage of the retreat from the Russian Front.

When the Russian push started the whole of the front exploded and there was fighting everywhere. The Russians were always drunk when they attacked. They ran towards us shouting in Russian: 'For country and for Stalin – *Urrāh*!' They said we were always outnumbered five to one.[12] But the Russians didn't value their soldiers' lives.

Within a couple of days we were disorganised. Our division was more or less annihilated. Germans, SS, Waffen-SS, Wehrmacht, Latvians – all mixed up. After Opochka there was chaos. Sometimes there was no time to dig trenches.

12 Often more. At the start of the Vistula offensive, Soviet superiority in infantry was 11 to 1 in some places, 7 to 1 for armour and 20 to 1 for artillery.

We were even fighting each other at one point – we thought they were Russians but they were ours. You don't know who's shooting. There could be a two-hour battle and then you find you're fighting your own men.

It was summer and it was warm so we were just sleeping in fields: no tents, no nothing. The whole of the Eastern Front was retreating. After July we didn't really fight any more. Where I was with the 15th, we had no officers, no nothing. There was no more command until we got to Latvia. We were like freelance soldiers. We just headed back to Latvia floating about, until we heard the order for us to collect near Madona.[13]

An account of the retreat from 1952 by Russian Front veteran 1st Lieutenant Arturs Brombergs in *The Latvian Encyclopaedia* makes for uncomfortable reading. It paints a picture of a quickly-worsening situation with the Soviets always one step ahead.

On 9 July, preparations for the retreat began; our service organs, transports and ammunition reserves were being pulled back. The Russians, whose observation planes often flew over our rear, found this out (or partisans operating in the German rear could have given the Russians that information). On the morning of 10 July 1944, the Russians opened a concentrated barrage by artillery, mortars and anti-tank weapons on a broad front; the fire was chiefly directed against the main roads [in our rear]. Many of our heavy weapons were destroyed before they could begin to return the fire.

Thus when the enemy, supported by tanks, began his assault, our troops began to retreat in a number of locations. The few rounds remaining for our weapons meant that the enemy could not be fought successfully.

Regimental and battalion commanders hurriedly attempted to organise resistance in the lines to which the troops were supposed to have retreated, and tried to halt the Russian assault by counterthrusts. These attempts were frustrated by pincer movements of Russian tank forces. Both divisions hastily dug in but could not hold the new defensive positions and fell back on the night of 13–14 July to the western shore of the Velikaya river, which was swollen and fast-flowing with rapid currents. The men had to wade or swim across or make improvised rafts to float across, as the Germans had already blown one of the two remaining bridges. The Latvians re-grouped and fought until 15 July, when all units fell back again.

The retreat of the 3rd Regiment was particularly tragic. The regiment (including the 1st Battalion of the 4th Regiment and a company of the 15th Sapper Battalion), had 500 men, as well as a German battalion of 240 men. The regiment, commanded by Lieutenant Colonel Kārlis Aperāts, on 15 July started to retreat in the direction of Pokrovskoye near Zilupe, east of Kārsava, on the Latvian-Russian border. The German battalion leading the march didn't have the right maps and, instead of Pokrovskoye, reached Kopin on the river Isa around midnight that night.

Since the bridge across the river had been destroyed, the force had to swim across, while beating off strong attacks by partisan forces at the same time. The group crossed the river by morning and continued to march north. At Stolbov the exhausted men rested until 13:00 then continued north in the direction of Mozuļi, annihilating a Russian battalion they met and capturing weapons, horse-drawn transport and trucks. At Peski 40 Russian tanks suddenly appeared over the crest of Mozuļi hill while a second group attacked the Latvians from the rear.

After a desperate five-hour fight, Lieutenant Colonel Aperāts' battle group was destroyed. Twenty-two Latvian officers, six German officers and 300 men

Lieutenant Colonel Kārlis Aperāts, who died at Mozuļi, pictured in Russia. (Picture courtesy of the Latvian War Museum)

were killed; another 300 were taken prisoner. According to reports, the critically-wounded Aperāts shot himself to avoid capture.[14]

One gruesome aspect of the battle at Mozuļi was the short shrift shown to prisoners and the wounded. Russian tanks smashed into the Latvian field-dressing station and crushed all the wounded under their tracks, according to this account in Volume Four of the 'Green Books', the Legion's official history.

14 A. Brombergs, *The Latvian Encyclopaedia* (1952), p.18, <https://www.cia.gov/library/reading-room/docs/BROMBERGS,%20ARTURS%20%20%20VOL.%201_0006.pdf>. Aperāts was posthumously awarded the Knights' Cross of the Iron Cross. One view is that Aperāts, through his 'selfless following of orders', according to fellow officer Vilis Hāzners, prevented the cutting off of multiple units and as a result prevented the Latvian region of Vidzeme falling much more quickly than it did. This bought time for the western region of Kurzeme [Courland] to be heavily fortified, which resisted until the capitulation in May 1945 and allowed hundreds of thousands of German military personnel and refugees to be evacuated.

It could be seen that enemy tanks drove into our field-dressing station, which was in a small wood to the west of Mozuļi. The enemy tanks shot at and drove right over our injured.[15]

This lack of mercy was to become a recurring theme of the fighting on the Eastern Front. As the battle died down, one Latvian commander who was to become famous for his ability, Vilis Hāzners, could only gather four officers and 60 men. All four officers and Hāzners himself were wounded. Believing themselves cut off, the group headed west on the night of 16–17 July, picking their way through swamps and forests until 40 survivors reached the safety of their own lines. Later it was established that the Aperāts battle group had been in the rear of an entire Red Army corps. Brombergs writes:

> Our soldiers, having gone several days without food, ill-armed, and lacking ammunition, had tied the enemy down for àn entire day, thus aiding the retreat of the German units, including that of the VI SS Corps. On 17 July, both Latvian divisions crossed the Latvian-Russian frontier east of Kārsava.[16]

Brombergs had been a policeman in Rīga between July 1941 and July 1943, when he transferred to the Legion as First Lieutenant. He fought with the 15th at Opochka, then joined the retreat back to Kurzeme. There, 'realising the Germans were sacrificing Latvian youth for their own ends', he deserted with his detachment and joined the partisans fighting the Soviets from the forests. He concludes his account:

> The retreat organized by the VI SS Corps had been poorly planned. The infantry was asked to do too much. Within the space of 24 hours, the soldiers had to take up more than two defensive positions; the unavoidable consequence of this was the mixing-up of units and the lowering of their capacity to resist. The organisation of the rear was unbelievably bad. For example, a section of the 19th Division's staff took over the direction of the regiment's supply vehicles. Due to incorrect orders, the vehicles were pulled back too far and could not fulfil their assigned tasks. The field kitchens of some battalions were in Kārsava, Rēzekne [in Latvia], and even near Rīga, while our forces were still fighting at Opochka and Krasnoye.
>
> The February, March and April battles on the banks of the river Velikaya, south-east of Ostrov, had caused us heavy losses, particularly as regards cadres. The replenishments of the gaps in our ranks [i.e., from the frontier guard regiments] could not replace the losses of officers and NCOs – neither in a

---

15   Osvalds Freivalds and Alfrēds-Jānis Bērziņš (Eds.), Latvian 'Green Books' *Latviešu Karavīrs Otra Pasaules Kara Laikā [Latvian Soldiers in the Second World War]*, vol. 4, (Västerås, Sweden: Ziemeļblāzma, 1979) p.226. Hereafter referred to as the 'Green Books.'
16   Brombergs, *The Latvian Encyclopaedia*, p.19.

tactical and technical sense, nor in morale. During the stabilisation period in the Kudevere position, the best NCOs and soldiers were sent to officers' schools and on NCO courses; they had not yet returned. This explains the relatively poor performance of the Latvian units during the retreat.[17]

For a man remembering events from more than seventy years before, Jānis Čevers' stories are incredibly detailed and vivid. But memory specialists say the more intense the experience – such as running for your life from Soviet tanks – the more detailed the memories.

> The Germans burnt everything – every house and farm. The sky was black and full of smoke. They lifted every sleeper [on] the railway lines, cut down every telephone post and burnt everything.[18]
>
> We were once in a cornfield, the corn was up to our waist, and we were told the Russians were somewhere ahead in an area of bushes. Some of us went to have a look. Once through the bushes there was a road and a Russian tank was coming. We were about two metres away. Usually there were soldiers riding on the tanks but they'd got off.
>
> We had one officer with us but he didn't give the order. We had Panzerfausts[19] – we could have liquidated the tank and shot them all! But I don't know why, the order wasn't given. Once a tank got isolated and surrounded by Panzerfausts, it didn't stand a chance. I had a drive in one we captured once: I didn't like it. They were like rolling coffins.
>
> Then we retreated about half a kilometre from that field and the Russians started shooting. There was a big German officer standing up waving his arms and shouting: 'Don't retreat! Do not retreat!' but the Germans kept running back. You could see one would fall, then another, hit by the Russian bullets. The place didn't have a name – it was just a cornfield near Opochka.

---

17 Brombergs, *The Latvian Encyclopaedia*, p.20. The US government file on Brombergs implicates him in the extermination of Latvia's Jews because of his membership of the police at the time of the Rumbula massacre. Brombergs left Latvia in 1945 for Sweden, becoming a CIA agent in Germany in 1951 helping identify and train spies to be dropped into Latvia. Later, by then working in the US, he had security clearance for covert operations with the codename CAMBARO-2 and was trained as an agent instructor, but when he went back as a spy in 1954 he was arrested by the KGB and sentenced to 25 years in prison. CIA notes dated 16 June 1972 assume he was under KGB control from 1957 and that KGB interrogators would probably have discovered the identities of all the agents Brombergs had worked with from January 1951 to May 1954. Brombergs' CIA secret files were released in 2003 and 2005. See bibliography for details.

18 The Latvian senior commander Rudolfs Bangerskis was forced to request that the Germans stop their scorched earth retreat in Latvia. Veterans say the Germans unintentionally flagged their plans to retreat to the Russians by setting fire to everything a couple of kilometres back from the frontline as they withdrew.

19 The hugely powerful shoulder-fired anti-tank bazooka became the scourge of Red Army tank units in Pomerania.

It was complete chaos. We were scattered and didn't know where we were. We ran from Opochka, retreating. There were Germans, Latvians, soldiers of all kinds. There was no more command. One tank came out into an opening and was firing, but our anti-tank gun got him. That tank was burning for four and a half hours that sunny afternoon, with the ammunition going off. None of the Russians got out.

We were attacked by partisans on the way back. There were a lot of partisans – Communists – loads of them. We suffered more from partisans than from Russians. The Russians were behind us and we were coming through the partisans – around Ludza, Kārsava – right through to Varakļāni. It's strange, isn't it? That's my birthplace.

Jānis' son John has gone to the kitchen to make more tea and is listening to the stories. He shouts through.

Dad retreated through his own village, and one of the gendarmes shouted to him: 'Can't you boys hold those bloody Russians back?'

We all laugh. I pick up the map of Russia I have brought with me to help trace his movements from Opochka back to Varakļāni. It's about two hours' drive by modern standards – about 160 kilometres. An hour of that would be from Opochka to the Latvian border. Mr Čevers continues his story.

I retreated through Varakļāni on a Sunday and went to see my family. We spent three or four days there. It's a Catholic part of the country so we went to church. It was full of Germans – there were hand grenades and machine guns everywhere.

There were thousands of refugees in the town. I met the director of my grammar school on the way. She was on one of the [refugee] wagons. She said: 'How far away are the Russians?' and I said: 'We last saw them three or four days ago, but we don't know. We've just run from them.'

We were so disorganised the Germans took over the defence to slow the Russians down. There was a big tank battle at Ērgļi. Most of Varakļāni was destroyed – all the wooden houses were burned down. A general order went out for the men of the 15th Division: 'Wherever you are, assemble at this collection point in Madona.' They collected what was left and we were sent to Limbaži. Some German SS there were sorting out all the war equipment – guns, cars, bicycles. We helped them for three or four weeks or so, then they sent us to Rīga.

What was left of the 15th and 19th Divisions re-grouped in the border area around Kārsava and Mērdzene. Both units had taken substantial losses, particularly in the infantry, and the regiments could muster no more than a few hundred men each. Neither the 15th or 19th artillery were fit for combat so those units were merged. The 32nd Grenadiers had been decimated. The remnants of the 15th turned over their weapons and equipment and were moved further west, re-organising as one regiment

Evacuation of the Latvian 15th SS Division to Pomerania. (Picture: Latvian War Museum, Rīga. Reference LKM 5-59573/2966-FT)

under Standartenführer[20] Kārlis Zēniņš, the commander of what had been the 34th Grenadier Regiment. This was now re-designated as a construction battalion, to be shipped from Rīga to West Prussia in late August, where the 15th was to re-group and re-build.[21] New recruits such as Imants Balodis from Rīga were drafted: he was 17 when he got called up in summer 1944.

> To boost the 15th, the call-up came for those born in 1925–26: 7,122 men altogether. In addition, those who up till then had probably been excused conscription because of their work were also called up, another 6,211 men. In July 1944 they boarded ships to Pomerania. The same year the call-up was received by those born 1927–28, including 3,647 boys, into the 'Air Force helpers'.[22] To begin with the training and service was in Latvia but by the end of 1944 almost all the boys had been sent to Germany to the air defence there. I was lucky. Together with a small group, we joined the Latvian Aviation unit, which in turn was part of the 15th Division.[23]

20 *Staf* – the equivalent of Colonel.
21 Silgailis, *Latvian Legion,* pp.101–103.
22 *Luftwaffenhelfer,* more commonly known as *Flakhelfer.*
23 Imants Balodis, recollections for the website <Latviesi.com>.

With other survivors from the Russian Front, Jānis Čevers was shipped from Rīga to Danzig that autumn.

> They sent us to the dock in Rīga and we were loaded onto a boat for Danzig in Germany, what was left of our 15th Division. That was in early October. There were a lot of youngsters from Latvia called up on that boat, very few of them in uniform. The Germans were catching people in the street and sending them to Danzig. There were lots of people drunk, and suicides too: people jumping over the side of the ship. The ships turned around to try and find them, but they never could.
>
> That short distance over the Baltic Sea between Rīga and Danzig took three days. English planes bombed us, about three of them, but there was no damage. We landed in Danzig and stayed there for a bit then we were sent about 20 miles south to a place called Konitz [the German headquarters in Pomerania, now Chojnice] and that's where we stayed training for a new 15th Division.
>
> When we got to Konitz there were only nine men left from my company out of 200. There was never that many, but it was supposed to be around that number. Three of us came in together – we were friends, and we had walked back together. I was a farmer's son, and we were country boys. They say the country boys were a bit tougher than the town lads; the walking and so on made their feet suffer. The townies couldn't walk anymore because of their feet bleeding and so on.
>
> VH: What was the mood like on that boat?
>
> JC: You get so accepting you don't bother about anything. You just take every minute as it comes. You don't think about war. You don't think about what happened yesterday or what happens tomorrow. You don't think any more. What can you do? You can't do anything, just run. No human feelings at all. It didn't make any difference if people were wounded, or screaming. No feelings at all.[24]

His son John comes in with a fresh pot of tea and puts it down on the table. 'More tea?'

---

24 Interview with author. Prompted by his son, Mr Čevers declined to 'tell the story about killing a Russian.'

2

Retreat from the East

The 19th Division spread out across eastern Latvia on a front covering the swamps around Meirāni, Barkava and Lake Lubāns. The aim was to hold back the Soviets and buy time for a mass withdrawal west to Courland and then onwards to Germany. The 42nd, 43rd and 44th regiments became battlegroups named after their commanders. The 42nd regiment was re-named Kampfgruppe [Battle Group] Galdiņš while the 43rd and 44th became Battle Groups Stīpnieks and Kociņš.[1] The defensive line was pulled back further on 9 August along the Madona to Gulbene railway line. Appeals went out for fresh volunteers to join up and defend the *Tēvija* [Fatherland] as the 19th fought to keep the roads to Rīga open. The entire VI SS Corps withdrew west to Nītaure on 19 September, falling back through Ranka, Jaunpiebalga and Vecpiebalga with the Soviets in close pursuit.[2]

Pauls Vanags was a Sergeant Major with the 19th Division, having served in Russia and fallen back to Nītaure with his unit. He was assigned to hold the homestead *Mazratnieki,* a large white farmhouse which made an obvious target for a Russian assault. In August 1944, to delay the Russian offensive against Rīga, *Mazratnieki* became the centre of a system of defensive trenches and bunkers around More. The main line of defence ran through the yard of the farmhouse. The Kupči family who lived there fled in September, shortly before the battles.[3] Mr Vanags earned an Iron Cross Second Class for what happened next.

---

1   Silgailis, *Latvian Legion,* p.101. Nikolajs Galdiņš was awarded the Knight's Cross of the Iron Cross in January 1945 for his bravery in Courland [Kurzeme/Kurland]. Taken prisoner by the Soviet Union in May 1945, he was shot by firing squad in Leningrad in October that year.

2   Silgailis, *Latvian Legion,* pp.109–120. Silgailis writes that the Corps fought off Soviet attacks during the retreat, but family stories from the area between Ranka and Jaunpiebalga tell of Legionnaires passing through farmsteads warning of an imminent battle, only for Red Army soldiers to appear suddenly the next day.

3   Correspondence with Anta Brača of the Museum of the Battle of More, May 2020. The Kupči family fled; first west to Courland as refugees and later to Germany and America. The daughter of the original owner, Ruta Kupcis, returned after independence in 1991 to find just an open field where the house had been, as it was destroyed in an explosion following the battles. She now lives in a wooden house built on the same family plot.

The farmstead *Mazratnieki* near More, Latvia, defended against Red Army attack in 1944 by Pauls Vanags. (Picture courtesy of the Battle of More Museum: <www.moresmuzejs.lv>)

I was given charge of the 3rd Battalion, 1st Company and the 2nd platoon. The company commander was Žagars, Herberts Žagars.[4] The defensive line stretched from Nītaure to More, and the fighting at More was very intense, hand-to-hand at times, and often went on for hours with trenches full of dead bodies. I can only tell you what happened at the homestead I was at, at *Mazratnieki* [slightly to the east of the main positions at More].

I didn't do anything special. I'm not a hero. After the first fighting my company commander Žagars came to talk to me and said: 'For what you have done, I would think you will get something.' Later, when I received the Iron Cross Second Class, I realised what he meant. I just led my platoon. Nothing special.[5]

4   Laimonis Ceriņš, another Legionnaire whose memories are included in this book, also served under Žagars. In declassified CIA files, Herberts Žagars is listed as a post-war intelligence source in the undercover cultural project AEMARSH, with the alias Herbert Kalniņš. The file states: 'The Institute for Latvian Culture (AEMINX) was established as a cover facility engaged in the preservation and development of Latvian national culture, collection of information on Latvian national life, and the safeguarding and preserving of physical, spiritual, and moral conditions of Latvians who were separated from their homeland. Alfreds Bērziņš, Aleksandrs Burmeisters, Jānis Cīrulis, Vilis Hāzners, Pēteris Janelsiņš, Freds Launags, Herberts Žagars associated with Project.' Source: <https://www.archives.gov/files/iwg/declassified-records/rg-263-cia-records/second-release-lexicon.pdf>, accessed 17 July 2020.
5   In fact, Mr Vanags single-handedly repelled a Russian attack without covering fire.

I decided to send a group led by Corporal Mednis to set up an MG-42 position on the lefthand corner of the homestead. That was on the forest side of the position, but the Russians had arrived, the mortars were coming down like rain and they couldn't dig in. So when the attack happened, we didn't have any support from there.

There was a small dip in front of us and the Russians were coming through that. On the other side of the depression there were a couple of houses. The Russians assembled there and shouted *'Urrāh! Urrāh!'* and were making a noise, so we fired over a couple of shots with our MG-42.

Mazratnieki was quite a modern homestead for those years and in the middle of the yard [was] a concrete bunker. I believe they were keeping fruit and milk in there and it was very well made, so that was my command point. After a bit of shooting I went to the bunker to have something to eat. We hadn't had a food supply for some time. I had opened a tin of meat paste and was eating that on a slice of bread. After a while someone rushed in and said: 'The Russians are here! Come out!' I thought something must be wrong. I ran out and as I went out of my bunker on my left, one of the machine gunners was running back from No Man's Land with his MG-42, so I saw that the situation must be serious. There was a bit of shooting around there for a while. In the house there was only Number One Platoon and over by the woods was Corporal Mednis.

I had a German machine pistol that I usually wore around my neck and two ammunition pouches on my belt, each containing three magazines. Soon we were out of our positions, without much help, shooting all around, mortars coming down like rain. We went past the next building, a cowshed made of stone, and then a barn. Running through there, I landed in a trench with Number Two Platoon. There was shooting all the time.

I noticed that there was what looked like an army greatcoat sticking out from behind some planks in the corner of the barn. That meant there must be someone standing there. It took me a while to figure out how to fire in that direction so I could hit him through the planks, and then I fired off quite a few rounds to try my luck. I waited for something to happen, but nothing did. I waited a little longer, then the man in the Red Army greatcoat suddenly fell out from behind the planks onto his face. It gave me pleasure to know that I had managed to get rid of him.

After a while there were several men in the platoon around me. We repulsed several attacks through the walls of the cowshed. Then some men from the second platoon came to help us. We managed to get to roughly the same position as we were before then I went to look at the man I had hit in the corner. It wasn't a greatcoat he had, but a big sack – and it was full of hand grenades. He was probably a specialist at throwing hand grenades. I had hoped he might have some light weapons I could use. We were always short of light weapons; pistols, machine pistols. That had been a problem since Volkhov [on the Russian Front] – a chronic shortage of weapons.

During this time the Russians entered the barn without me realising. The barn had a wooden roof and the walls were made of timber. There was a big door so you could drive in with a horse and cart, and I looked through the gap between the barn and the main building. I saw several Russians so close I could have touched them, either side of the door. I ran back to the second platoon and there was one of my men standing there by an MG-42. He was watching what I was doing, open-mouthed. I turned round and put the machine gun into the gap and emptied the magazine in their direction. I'm not sure I shot them all, but I went back and counted them later after we had recovered the homestead. There were 18 Russians dead there, plus the man in the corner.

We strengthened our trench defences and occupied the homestead again, setting up two-man positions in the living room and keeping watch on the road alongside the house from one of the bedrooms. That way one person could sleep while another kept watch. Not long after that there was an alarm. Tanks!

There was a self-propelled assault gun coming slowly down the road, a German *Sturmgeschütz*. On top of it were sitting about five or six German police, in a sort of green uniform, not the grey SS uniform. I ran downstairs and watched the *Sturmgeschütz* approach the barbed wire across the road, where it stopped. They looked a bit funny the way they were sitting and not moving, so I fired a few shots with my machine gun. I hit the gun but no-one moved. Then I realised: they were all dead, and they'd been tied to the gun which Russians were driving! The Russians twigged something was wrong and quickly reversed back down the road and disappeared into the woods.

I had set up a machine gun position at the side of the road with my Number One, Tomas, manning it. He reported that there was a General coming – actually his rank was something like Lieutenant Colonel – who came up to our machine gun position. He was dressed very well in a German officer's coat, a full-length rubberised coat to keep him protected from rain.

When Tomas challenged him, he tried to grab his pistol and jump into the drainage ditch at the side of the road. Tomas shot him. I went to see him. He was obviously dead: his chest was shot to pieces. But he carried with him a map – a map in Russian, with Russian writing round the edges, which was all covered in blood. I wiped the officer's blood off so I could see what the map said but I couldn't read it. I sent it back to the commander, [Major Gustavs] Praudiņš. He sent a message back saying it was a very important map and congratulating us on good work, and that our platoon would receive something for our efforts. I think maybe that officer was co-ordinating the attack on our positions.

Around this time my company commander Žagars was wounded and went back [for treatment] and the company commander changed. My official rank was that of a *junker*, with two white stripes on my epaulettes. When Lieutenant Adamsons was wounded, I was in charge of the whole company. The next in seniority was a sergeant from the second platoon who got drunk and wanted to kill Russians, and a group of eight men went with him. But you could hear them going across No Man's Land for miles around, and the Russians got them.

The trouble was he took a runner with him: a messenger who had all the secret codes, phone codes, things like that, which made things difficult later. The other messengers didn't know all that – and now the Russians did – and we had lost contact with the Battalion.[6]

The ferocious defence at More between 25 September 1944 to the Latvian withdrawal on 5 October – with a particularly intense five-day period of combat from 25 to 29 September – inflicted heavy losses on the Red Army and the attacks subsided. The fighting was so intense that *Mazratnieki* changed hands seven times: trenches across the area were so full of bodies that the survivors just filled them in. Latvian casualty figures record 190 men killed and 650 wounded, with Soviet casualties ten times that, based on the 1,986 dead in More War Cemetery and 750 in Nitaure Cemetery. The number of Red Army wounded is estimated at 9,576.[7]

One eyewitness account of the fighting in the region around Sigulda at that time comes from Jānis Kūliņš, later a postman in Turaida, then a 15-year-old. He collected the dead after the fighting and buried them, Russians first.

A machine gun or 'Bonesaw' was set up at the top of the hill. The Russians fired a pistol shot; that was the signal for attack. Now they are crossing the ditch, then the stream until they reach the barbed wire entanglement. The trenches are behind the wire but there are no Germans there because the machine gun oversees the trenches. The Russians approach the barbed wire, yell out *'Urrāh! Za rodinu!' [For the Motherland]* and throw their coats across the wire. They cross the wire, call out *'Urrāh!'* again and in a moment they are in the trenches. But the Germans have waited for this moment and after several machine gun bursts, they are dead. *Rat-tat-tat-tat.* They are all dead.[8]

On one trip to Latvia, I visited More and its museum. I had heard of a young Legionnaire from Jaunpiebalga who was at More and deserted, heading back to his family homestead and hiding in a barn. When the Red Army's post-war filtration of men reached his area he hid again, and, according to the family story, the soldiers took a man with the same family name instead, and shot him. The name of the man who deserted – and lived for another fifty years – is on the More monument as having been killed there. How could that have happened? The guide looked at me.

Many young men deserted. The fighting was very intense. The trenches were full of bodies; parts of bodies. It was too much for many of them. The trick was to find a dead Legionnaire and switch identity tags. That way no-one would ever come after you.[9]

6   Telephone interview with author.
7   Kovtunenko, *Battle at More,* p.77.
8   Jānis Kūliņš in Kovtunenko, *Battle at More,* p.102.
9   Conversation with author at More Museum, 2011.

Jānis Kūliņš suffered from a nervous condition for years as a result of clearing the battlefield as the Russians pushed towards Rīga.

> With the Germans it was easier. One of us would pass his shovel under one brace, the other under the second brace. With the Russians it was more difficult. They only had a belt. So we had to get the shovel under the belt and off we went. For those that had been killed in the last few days, we could grab them under their arms, but the others…[10]

The Germans used the time the blocking action at More bought them to re-group in Courland. The 19th Division was given the signal to withdraw from Sigulda on the night of 6 October to new positions at Džūkste, 60 kilometres west of Rīga. The 19th Division crossed the Daugava river at Mazjumprava, south of Rīga, on the night of 9–10 October, leaving the 15th Artillery to defend the western suburbs of the capital for another two days, then they pulled out too. At midnight on 12 October, after the last German and Latvian troops crossed the river, the two bridges across it were blown. Rīga was left to its fate and the 19th Division prepared to fight on in the bloody endgame of the Courland Pocket.[11]

At Džūkste, Pauls Vanags was wounded for a fifth time, but that injury would be his ticket to safety.

> The first time I was wounded in my back by mine shrapnel at More. I knew I was wounded but I didn't feel too bad. A British doctor told me comparatively late in life that I was carrying shrapnel. I needed some tests that involved a magnetic scan, and the doctor checked me and said: 'Good Lord. You've got shrapnel in your back!' Well, it's still there.
>
> After several more battles I had another wound in my back – which means I must have been running away! It wasn't very bad. It was only small and didn't affect me a lot. Then further on, during the retreat and already in Kurzeme I was wounded again by a landmine, this time in my right arm, in the back muscle, which still shows up quite well. After that I received notification that I had something like a medal, known as a 'three times.' I got a small round bronze wound medal for the wound at More. When I was three times wounded I should have got something but didn't. Instead I got a German medal for three attacks.
>
> Then came Christmastime [the battles at Džūkste] and I was wounded in the chest. All the previous times I had stayed at the front and the wounds had been treated there, but this time my lungs were shot and damaged. That was my fourth. That put me down for four months in bed. During that time, a Russian

10 Kovtunenko, *Battle at More*, p.100.
11 Silgailis, *Latvian Legion,* pp.118–124. Events in Courland between October 1944–May 1945 are covered in the author's first book about Latvia's war years, *Blood in the Forest: the End of the Second World War in the Courland Pocket* (Helion, 2017).

bomber came to bomb the hospital. In the room where I was, there were big windows from floor to ceiling. One of the bombs blew the window in. I was in bed and the glass from the window damaged my foot. It was bleeding and the Germans said: 'Oh, that's another wound!' and they noted it, and from there I was evacuated to Denmark, to Copenhagen, and [put] in hospital.[12]

The positions around More were part of the Sigulda Ring, a defensive arc to the east of Rīga designed to delay the Russian advance and buy time for the Germans to evacuate the capital and construct strong defences in Courland, which they did.

In the battles at More, *Mazratnieki*, Nitaure and the Kārtūži estate, the Legionnaires faced overwhelming superiority in numbers. At one point, three Red Army regiments were attacking positions held by one company. The attackers included men from penal battalions – the 270th and 271st Penal Companies – and Latvians from the 125th Soviet Latvian Rifle Regiments and 130th Rifle Corps. The fighting was akin to slaughter, with tanks mowing down rows of men and neither prisoners nor wounded being spared by either side.[13]

The fighting was particularly desperate on the Kārtūži estate, where Legionnaires built defensive positions in the cellars of the manor house as the upper floors and surrounding woods had been destroyed. Private Oskars Rozenbergs of the 318th Police Battalion described the scenes after the Latvians, with the help of German Tiger tanks, had fought off a Red Army attack.

> The Russians had attacked this sector the previous evening. They were faced by Latvian Legionnaires who suffered heavy casualties. They fought desperately all night to retain possession of Kārtūži. They were finally forced back, having to leave their dead in the trenches. They called for help all night until someone responded. But the enemy heavily reinforced the captured positions. Judging by the huge numbers of enemy dead, this morning's battle had been a real blood-bath for them. Our Latvian soldiers followed the tanks. Only some of them reached the trenches in the morning mist. The rest remained on the ground. But even having survived this terrible advance, they had the heaviest test ahead of them. They had to climb over piles of enemy dead that had been shot down by the tank machine guns. They finally recovered the bodies of their mates abandoned earlier. They were all naked: the Soviets had stolen everything.[14]

The confusion, destruction and chaos of war would leave a lasting imprint on the families of the dead.

---

12 Interview with author, 2020. Mr Vanags was still recuperating when the war ended. He became a prisoner of the British, eventually moving to Swansea in South Wales to work. Seventy-five years later, at the age of 96, he recalled his war service in several lengthy late-night telephone interviews with the author. He was awarded the Iron Cross First Class but never received the physical decoration. He died in 2021 aged 97 before this book could be published.

13 Kovtunenko, *Battle at More,* p.81.

14 Oskars Rozenbergs in Kovtunenko, *Battle at More,* p.59.

Now they [the dead] are being cleared and brought back here to Kārtūži estate, and laid out in their dozens along the pond, naked and disfigured. We walk along the rows in silence and in respect, trying to see whether we can recognise someone we know by their face or other distinguishing marks. Many have little signs with names, but there are many others that only God knows. Maybe a mother could recognise her son in some of these disfigured faces, but it is not always possible for their soldier mates. They will be buried as unknown soldiers. Mothers, sisters, wives will wait in vain. They will search the lists of the dead; they will seek news from others – all in vain. They will always live in hope that since they have not appeared in lists of fallen, they might return one day.[15]

Rolands Kovtunenko, a company commander at More who was awarded the Iron Cross First Class for his bravery, wrote in 2009:

It is possible that there are still some Latvian Legionnaires buried among Russian soldiers in trenches around *Mazratnieki*, which were filled in immediately after the battle because there were just too many to bury individually under the conditions prevailing at the time. These soldiers have not yet received their proper burial.[16]

The tactics used by the Latvians at More may account for the heavy casualties among those attacking, which included men from penal battalions alongside the 'worker-peasant' soldiers of the Red Army. Kovtunenko identified a difference in character between Latvians and Russians under fire.

Russians have a herd instinct. When they are in a large group, they can show a lot of heroism. Indeed, they can become quite belligerent. Individually, they lose all these traits. Therefore they can advance in a formation but when they arrive at the opposing trenches, where they have to start fighting individually, they break up into an uncontrolled mob. They are easy to eliminate at this stage in a piecemeal fashion.

He writes of the battles at More, and just before that at Lubāna:

Battles were won with infantry weapons. Attack and counter-attack were ultimately determined in hand-to-hand combat. During the Lubāna fighting, which preceded More, the enemy manpower superiority was even greater – of the order of 15 [to one] – but we still prevailed.[17]

15 Rozenbergs in Kovtunenko, *Battle at More,* p.59.
16 Kovtunenko, *Battle at More,* p.91.
17 Kovtunenko, *Battle at More,* p.79.

Former Latvian 15th Division artilleryman Laimonis Ceriņš, interviewed at his home in Derby, 2018. (Picture: author)

I'm sitting in the front room of a ground floor flat in Abbey Street in Derby with another man in his nineties, remembering his time in the war. His 'war' is the Eastern Front specifically between Danzig [Gdańsk in modern Poland] and the forests at Schwerin, just north of Berlin, between January and May 1945. The room is part-library, part-archive. There is a table, an armchair and a sofa bed, with every other available space occupied by stacks of books, piles of correspondence and heaps of newspaper clippings. Laimonis Ceriņš, like Jānis Čevers, settled in Derby after coming to work in Britain after the war. Thousands of Latvian men – former soldiers born between 1923 and 1926 – shared the same experience after surrendering to the Allies in 1945. They, and the Latvian women who came to the UK post-war as nurses and dental assistants, formed the core of the modern Latvian diaspora in Britain.

Mr Ceriņš has been one of the mainstays of the Latvian community in the UK for decades. He volunteered for the labour replacement scheme *Westward Ho!* which was offered to Eastern Europeans who did not want to return to their Communist-controlled homelands after the war ended. With him came 9,705 fellow countrymen and 2,126 women as former soldiers and civilian refugees, as well as 24,500 Ukrainian men and 4,720 women; 9,350 Polish men and 4,667 women; 10,000 Yugoslavs, nearly 6,000 Lithuanians and 4,000 Estonians.[18]

18 L. McDowell, *Hard Labour: The Forgotten Voices of Latvian Migrant 'Volunteer' Work*ers (London: Routledge, 2013), p.104 quoting Tannahill, *British Immigration Statistics*, 1958.

I am from Liepa, 12 kilometres north of Cēsis, on the way to Valmiera. There were three children in the family: me, a brother and a sister, Dad and Mum. I was born on 6 June 1926. I was the oldest – I think I'm a lucky one.

I was 18 when I joined the Legion on 6 August 1944. I got called up. The assembly point was not far from Valmiera. We found a neighbour with a lorry and went through Cēsis to Straupe but they said they were full up there, so we had to go to Brengule.

We knew what was going on with the Russians. We learned in school about what the Communists did in 1919 when they came in, and then the older generation told us what was going on the second time [in 1940–41].[19]

VH: So in the Free Latvia times [Latvia was an independent republic from 1918–1940], they taught you in school what happened in the 'Red Terror'?
LC: Oh yes. Oh yes. How the Communists shot our innocent people, or you had a landlord: 'Oh, that's it…'
VH: Shoot him?
LC: You have a bullet.
VH: There was this clear definition then? [of the Latvians the Soviets considered enemies]
LC: Oh yes, oh yes. Generally that's what's happened – that was quite clear.
VH: So the Soviets came again in 1940, and they left the next year [pushed out by the 1941 Nazi invasion of the Soviet Union, Operation Barbarossa] through your part of the country. Do you remember seeing the Red Army retreating?
LC: In my area it happened very quickly. They blew up the highest railway bridge between Liepa and Cēsis over the river Rauna. We lived near the main road between Cēsis and Smiltene, which was about 300 metres away from our house. We saw lorryloads full of Red soldiers going down the road. They didn't stop. Then there was a gap of about a week, and that time was very nasty sometimes. You never knew if you saw a stranger walking along the road. They could be Reds going east. The local Home Guard tried to organise themselves and keep watch. I remember going to the local government office and they were watching who was coming and going. Then the Germans came. You can't compare when the Russians came [in 1944] with the Germans when they came to Latvia. It's like day and night. People can call them Nazis or whatever. You can't say Germans were all Nazis. The ones I met, even soldiers, never talked about the war, or Hitler. Just family business. What his Dad or Mum did, or his brother in Germany. How you're keeping yourself, or whatever. Nothing about politics. I never met a German who talked about politics.

---

19 Mr Ceriņš was nearly 93 when we first talked. Liepa is in north-eastern Latvia, several hours east of the capital. There was a bloody wave of 'Red Terror' during the first Bolshevik government of Pēteris Stučka in Latvia after the First World War.

VH: The story goes that Latvians were greeting Germans with flowers when they came in?

LC: As far as I know that only happened in one place, and that was in Rīga. It didn't happen in our area. Oh no. Just keep watch when they're running from one place to another. We also learned in school what the Germans had done to Latvians for 700 years. And when the Germans came, the grown-ups said: 'It doesn't mean much. They may be going forward now, but they are not going to win the war.' And there were English spies – scouts – looking, watching too.

I ask him what he means. He tells me a story about an encounter after the war with a man working at the same engineering firm.

When I was working in Derby, a senior engineer, a reasonably old chap, came through our section. One day I was sitting by my bench, fiddling with an electric box, and this fellow came to me. 'Where do you come from?'

I said: 'From Latvia.' And he said: 'No, *exactly* where do you come from?'

So I told him. And he said: 'Do you know Valka?'

'Yes, I know Valka.' And he said: 'Valmiera?'

'Yes, I do.'

'Cēsis?' 'Yes.' 'Rīga?' 'Yes.'

Then after about half a minute's silence, he said: 'From Valka to Rīga took me one week to walk. To the posh area of Rīga – Mežaparks – and I met senior Latvian officers.' I think he mentioned one or two that I knew. I was surprised he came to me, when there were another three or four Latvians working at this firm, an old firm in Derby called John Davis Engineering.

And this funny thing happened in May 1944, a nice day. The commanding officer of the local Home Guards received a message saying there was a strange fellow sitting by a bush at the side of the road. Three Home Guards on bicycles went to that place. At that time there was a shop nearby. I was there.

They came in with that fellow. Very unusual leather boots, a thick coat, for that time of year; a cap. He was brought into the front room, and they start to talk to him. 'Who are you?' I think he said he was Estonian. He didn't understand Russian. Of course the local people didn't know Estonian. These Home Guards went into the office in the back, leaving me and this chap in the front. One of the Guards left his rifle in the front, say about two metres from this chap, with me here. They phoned headquarters in Cēsis to ask what to do with him.

I noticed he started watching that rifle. I went around the corner and grabbed it and put a bullet in it. He was so quiet, like ice: no emotion. Afterwards I was trying to find out what happened to him – nobody knew. It sticks in my mind that it was probably him. You see, he had served in British Army special units during the war. When the factory celebrated 100 years, there was a short story about him. Working behind enemy lines. You read about those men, in Italy,

France, Greece, Holland, but not there.[20]

I found an article once in the [British newspaper] the *Daily Mail* saying that these people were employed on the Eastern Front too, where the Germans lines were, to see what they were doing and where the tanks and artillery were. It struck me as being very unusual. And British people do not ask: '*Exactly* where are you from in Latvia?'[21]

On 16 August 1944, 29-year-old chaplain Kazimirs Ručs left Rīga with the Legion for Danzig on the boat *Warthe*, and wrote:

The whole of Daugavmala was full of people: fathers, departing Legionnaires, high school students, mothers, brothers, wives with children, relatives, brides … everyone cried and hugged during this parting. It was an incredible sight![22]

15th Division Catholic chaplain Kazimirs Ručs on his acceptance at Rīga seminary, 23 September 1936. (Picture courtesy of the Latgale Cultural Centre, Rēzekne)

Ručs was born in 1915 in Varkava in the predominantly Catholic eastern region of Latgale and grew up on a 35-hectare farm, poor but dreaming about becoming a priest. He studied at Aglona Gymnasium then in 1936 entered the Rīga Theological Seminary. Four years later he was drafted into the Red Army in the Soviet occupation and sent to Daugavpils to be mobilised. At the office 'a military man of Latvian origin' recommended he left the building to avoid that fate: Ručs did just that.

In the German occupation of 1941–44, Ručs became a priest and was made vicar of Cēsis Catholic Church as the country prepared to resist a Soviet assault. He was appointed as the chaplain of the 6th Corps of the 15th Legion Division on 5 June 1944 and travelled to Rēzekne, close to the border with Russia. There, he was appalled at

20 The author called John Davis Engineering to alert them to this story and see if more information could be found about this man's war record. Unfortunately, despite checking through the archives remaining after the firm was sold, this booklet could not be found.
21 Interview with author, 2018.
22 Kaspars Strods, *Garīdznieks Karavīra Zābakos* (2019). Daugavmala is the quayside on the Daugava river at Rīga, possibly near the castle. In his book *Dzīve ar Dievu*, Ručs says that Deacon Alberts Piebalgs raised his hand above the crowd, made the sign of the cross and blessed him and the ship.

Kazimirs Ručs pictured outside Cēsis Catholic Church on his way to the front in August 1944. (Picture courtesy of the Latgale Cultural Centre, Rēzekne. Reference LgKM 25254)

the sight of the Soviet bombing of the city: the area around the station looked 'like a ploughed field', he wrote.

As the survivors of the 15th Division fell back to Latvia in July 1944 after being smashed in Russia, Ručs fell back with them, through Madona, Cēsis and Sigulda to Rīga. The roads in Vidzeme were 'full of refugees,' he wrote. 'In the heat of July, the refugees on the [dirt] roads were covered in dust.' Ručs had a brother, Antons, who was also in the Legion. He was killed in the battles for Jelgava in July and early August 1944, a city Kazimirs had passed through on his way to the front.[23]

Born in Rīga on 21 December 1926, Brunis Rubess was a 17-year-old violinist in the city's Radio Orchestra when he was called up to the Legion

15th Division Legionnaire Brunis Rubess, later a successful businessman in Canada. (Picture courtesy of his daughters, Baiba and Banuta)

23 Strods, *Garīdznieks Karavīra Zābakos.*

and sent to Germany for training. In his autobiography he recalls his earliest moments as a soldier.

> It's 1 September 1944. Next to me two old chaps are talking, perhaps 25 years old. 'It's just going to be a mess in Germany. Our only hope is to get to Janums. The "Old Man" doesn't abandon his sons.' At that time I didn't know the famous story about how Colonel Janums, finding himself and his regiment 90 kilometres behind the Russian lines, managed to get his 'sons' out alive, out of the encirclement. 'To Janums? Who is he?'[24]

Fifty miles [80 kilometres] south of Derby, in a suburb of the city of Coventry, I am sitting in the kitchen of another Legionnaire, Žanis Mūsiņš, known by all as Žano. Even at the age of 95, he still has a commanding physical presence. He tells me he was a keen basketball player in his youth in Liepāja, before being called up in July 1944 and assigned to a unit of Legionnaires. The men were loaded into cattle trucks and sent to Germany for training. His diary, which he sent to me before our meeting, charts the journey there.

> 6 September 1944: Leaving the main railway station in Liepāja at 14:00 and heading into the unknown. By 16:00 we cross the Lithuanian border. We all sing the Latvian anthem even if we are slightly tipsy. As we slowly proceed through Lithuania we see many Russian tanks still smouldering after recent battles to force the Russian army away from the Baltic Sea.[25] We also notice that the railway tracks have recently been repaired.
>
> 7 September: We have arrived at Memel but do not stop until Königsberg railway station. Our lads find a German Army soup kitchen and get some German Army soup. We do not like it and when the trains move on, one of the crew throws the soup out through the wagon door, but unfortunately somebody was working by the line and got covered in the soup from head to toe! By some accident half of our train got left at Königsberg, but they caught up later on in Dirschau station. Next stop is Konitz station but we do not stop. By midnight we arrive at Sophienwalde station and unload.[26]
>
> 8 September: This morning I meet my cousin who is stationed at Sophienwalde before [he is] sent on a mortar course. Our target is Lendy village about 10 kilometres further on and we billet there.

---

24 B. Rubess and N. Ikstena, *Brīnumainā Kārtā: Stāsti Par Bruņa Rubesa Trim Mūžiem [The Autobiography of Brunis Rubess]* (Rīga: Nordik, 1999), p.73–74. Rubess emigrated to Canada and became a successful businessman. On his post-Soviet return to Latvia, he was appointed one of the governors of the Bank of Latvia. He died in 2009. Janums had a strong relationship with his men and was considered a father figure by many.
25 To open up the land route to Germany.
26 Königsberg was then the capital of East Prussia and is now Kaliningrad, under Russian control. Returned to Poland after the war, Konitz is Chojnice while Sophienwalde is now Dziemiany.

The 15th Division on the way to Gotenhafen in Pomerania 26 August 1944 on the boat *Sumatra*.
(Picture: Latvian 'Green Books', permission of Daugavas Vanagi)

10 September: The army drills start early and they try to teach us how to shoot, stab or blow up Russians. We are dressed in German uniforms with SS insignia. We do not like them but because they mean we receive better catering, we put up with it. From then on, all goes into daily routine. Our squad is formed specially for heavy machine guns as it is slightly select from the rest of our squaddies. We lived a bit dangerously because one of our lads had a crystal radio in a matchbox. We listened to the BBC news so we knew what the situation was at the front – until one day our CO arrived at our billet and demanded to have our radio, with the warning that we could have been shot for this.

There's nothing special to report after that until the beginning of December, when army gossip reaches us that we will soon be returned to Latvia to support the other [19th] Latvian Division which has been holding back the 3rd Russian army in Kurzeme.[27]

Loaded aboard a ship, Brunis Rubess and his fellow soldiers are about to leave Latvia:

On 9 September 1944, we are on the ship in Rīga's harbour. My class teacher, my relatives and my Mirdza have come to see me off. We – plucky young boys and grizzled veterans – sing the Latvian national anthem *Dievs, svētī Latviju* [*God Bless Latvia*] as we slip down the Daugava to the sea. A day and a half later, we

27 War diary of Žano Mūsiņš, given to author.

get off at Gotenhafen harbour. We stand next to each other in a sort of half-civilian line. Other 20-year-old men in uniforms – corporals and sergeants – while looking at some paperwork, walk past us, counting: 'One, two, three … forty seven, forty eight – the 33rd Regiment.' So I join the second company [*rota*] of the 33rd Regiment. It takes a week for some more knowledgeable lads to tell me that this is Janums' regiment. My wish has come true. I am amazed.

We come to the Libuš region.[28] There we are billeted in a farmhouse that is managed by a tall, thin German with a pointed hat. Very soon he gets the nickname Fau-Divi (V2) after the rockets that the Germans are shooting towards England. We sleep in the top part of the cowshed and, of course, we get treated like new recruits. We are badly supplied, but we have to lie down, stand up, run – all the training of the new recruits is aimed at increasing stamina and breaking individual will.

The commander of the 33rd Regiment of the Latvian 15th SS Division, Colonel Vilis Janums, had a reputation as a Houdini-like figure who could get his men out of tight situations. He went on to mastermind the incredible escape of 900 men to the Americans at the Elbe. Pictured here in Russia, 1944. (Picture: Latvian War Museum, Rīga. Reference LKM 5-8237/597-FT)

A soldier has to learn to do all sorts of pointless things if he is ordered so to do. One of the orders designed to break one's will is: 'Take the bucket and go to the well.' I go to the well, fill it with water and take it back. The water is poured on my head. 'I never told you to get water…'

The distance between a new recruit and the regimental commander can't be measured in kilometres: perhaps light years would do. Sometime in December, the day arrived when our company was visited by Colonel Janums. Interesting. A bit frightening. But you can't see much. Short thin chap. With an officer's straight back. Small moustache, with a wise bird's eyes. Very different from the war heroes that we saw in German films.[29]

---

28 The Latvianised name of Lippusch as it was known in German, now Lipusz.
29 Rubess and Ikstena, *The Autobiography of Brunis Rubess*, p.74.

In Coventry, Žano Mūsiņš and I have skipped forward three months.

> 12 December: Today we received the order for our Battalion to be transferred to Kurland. Unfortunately there are 16 of us who are not going, but are kept back for the formation of a new Battalion from our lads coming out of German [RAD] work units. I was in tears because I was looking forward to going back to Latvia, but in the army you go where you are told.
>
> 14 December: The new recruits arrive and unit formation is started. Quite a few are from Rīga, because to [go to] University you had to serve one year in a German Works Unit [*Reichsarbeitsdienst*, or RAD]. All the commanding staff is new too. Everything starts again from scratch![30]

Brunis Rubess has just made a decision even he can't work out, but it will be one that saves his life.

> Though my uncle Gustiņš once told me sharply that a soldier is just a civilian in a uniform, I slowly realised that my civilian skills were of no special use to me here. However, some bits are. We constantly didn't have enough to eat. It seems that Fau-Divi played the piano in the evenings and, having discovered that I played the violin, he asked me to play along. He had a half-decent violin left over from his student days and a love for student songs, that I had also heard. Like *Ich hab' mein Herz in Heidelberg verloren*.[31] While we served the muse, the lads from the company stabbed a pig to death with their penknives. The pig squeals loudly and I play and sing louder. Art for one, meat for another. When the local police come looking for the evidence, it has long gone into our stomachs.
>
> When I talk about fate, I often think about my schoolmate Gunārs Ozoliņš. We were together in Janums' 2nd Company. We spoke often. Gunārs helped me, a completely impractical person, with advice and practical help. We had both agreed that as soon as there was an opportunity, we'd apply to a unit that was going back to Kurzeme. Gunārs' parents were there, my Mirdza was there. But on a nice December day, our company 'mother' – First Sergeant Kažoks – asked if there was anyone who would like to volunteer for *Gasschutzunteroffizierschule* – a gas defence instructor course in Bromberg. Nobody regarded this opportunity as attractive, because you'll have to run, lie down and jump while wearing a gas mask. For that reason I have no idea to this very day why I applied (and was mocked for such volunteering). Was it a guardian angel? Fate?[32]

Laimonis Ceriņš was among a group of new recruits taken to Rīga, loaded onto a ship to Danzig around 20 August, then taken to the 15th Divisional headquarters at Sophienwalde, 85 kilometres inland.

---

30 Žano Mūsiņš war diaries.
31 *I Lost my Heart in Heidelberg*, a German hit song from 1925, which also became a musical and a film.
32 Rubess and Ikstena, *The Autobiography of Brunis Rubess*, p.76.

We didn't have uniforms at that time. Nothing. No uniforms, but drill: marching. There was a lake: we went to swim and wash in that. One day our platoon was marching towards the railway station, about a kilometre away, with a white house where the gendarmerie were. Ten men had to take bread loaves out of the railway carriage. In charge there was a German fellow. Towards us was coming a Corporal, a gendarme. What the Germans wanted, if you marched anywhere, you had to sing. Always. Never silent, always singing. Now, there is a nasty song: 'We will make a German dance on hot bricks.' This chap marches up and says to us in Latvian: 'Stop, stop!' And we say: 'A German, speaking Latvian?'

He says: 'Who is dancing on hot bricks?'

We had a Corporal in charge of us, and so this German was asking who our commanding officer was, where we were staying and so on. Then he said: 'From now on, I don't want to hear anything about hot bricks.' He was a Baltic German. But he let us go.[33]

When I was in Sophienwalde there was a Captain Bergs, sitting down in a field telling us about war. I met a Sergeant Major who was in his unit in Daugavpils in the 1930s, just before the Baltic Germans received their 'invitation' to return to Germany. That chap told me what happened. The Baltic Germans went home, but Captain Bergs didn't. Everyone knew he was a Baltic German. This Sergeant Major asked him when he was going back, and Captain Bergs said: 'I'm going nowhere. I was born here in Latvia, I was educated here. The Latvian Army gave me a job: I'm staying here.' He was in Zedelghem too. And Colonel Skaistlauks.[34]

As part of his training, Mr Ceriņš was asked to volunteer to go to artillery school in Leitmeritz in Josefstadt near Prague, the capital of [then] Czechoslovakia.[35]

We got our uniforms just before we left: standard German Army uniform with black patches, but they tried to give us Italian boots they used in the desert.

---

33 The song is an ancient anti-German folk song, as the Germans were the lords of the manor. It details what a serf would do if he found the money to buy Rīga castle with all its Germans: *'I would do to the Germans, as the German did to me. I'd make the German dance on hot bricks.'* The Baltic Germans were for centuries the ruling elite in Latvia but also one of the largest ethnic minorities and a significant economic force. Around 50,000 of 62,000 Baltic Germans in Latvia were sent back to Germany in a mass 'repatriation' conducted over several weeks in October 1939 after the Non-Aggression Pact signed between Hitler and Stalin. Queues formed at the House of Blackheads in Rīga for those leaving, shipped from Rīga, Ventspils and Liepāja, to be settled in the Warthegau, an area of West Prussia ceded to Poland after WWI and re-occupied in the Nazi invasion of 1 September 1939. Another 11,000 Baltic Germans were 'repatriated' in the spring of 1941. (More details at <https://eng.lsm.lv/article/culture/history/after-700-years-in-latvia-baltic-germans-vanished-in-a-matter-of-weeks.a297470/>)
34 15th Division artillery commander and Iron Cross First and Second Class holder Voldemārs Skaistlauks. Zedelghem is the camp in Belgium where Latvian servicemen were held after the war, designated by British Field Marshal Montgomery as 'disarmed enemy forces'.
35 The former Jewish Quarter of Prague, and birthplace of Franz Kafka. Now Josefov.

We said: 'What happens when it starts raining?' So we had to wait. We had a Signals unit with us too. The training was at a really high standard: classrooms like I've never seen before, how to use wireless equipment and telephones; how to use the 105mm howitzers. There were five men on each gun. The man aiming it, the man firing it, the loader, the man who fetches the ammunition and the guy who arms the shell. We learned all the jobs, and also how to defend your position if the enemy gets through to your gun. We had two to three days with experts in infantry fighting; chaps who already had experience at the front. How to defend your gun depends on the situation you are in: with standard rifles, or hand grenades. We had standard five-cartridge Czech-made rifles, made in the Škoda factories which were taken over by the Germans. They were really good rifles. In the last stage of the war I had a ten-cartridge semi-automatic rifle.[36]

At this stage of the war, even before facing the ferocity of the Red Army's Vistula to Oder offensive, the German military was short of equipment. Mr Ceriņš laughs.

We didn't have helmets. We didn't have bayonets. In February I found a helmet by the roadside that was the right size for my head. Someone had chucked it away, but it was a good one. According to the rules, you needed a pistol. I should have had one because I was in charge of paying the wages and supplying food for 180 men. But no pistol. Even the ammunition was short. You had to be very sensible how you used it.

We didn't have SS badges. Latvians couldn't be SS. Only German-born could be SS. The 19th had the swastika on their collar. In the 15th we had the Rising Sun. One day a German officer said he had a very important order to read us. He said it came from Berlin: 'Sorry, you can't be SS, because you are foreigners.' That was officially said. Then we were issued with soldiers' ID cards, and you need a photograph for that. How do we do that?

So we took empty tin cans of soup with shiny metal inside and we cut out SS collar flashes and put them on a jacket. Only one. We took a photograph and then passed on the same jacket to the next man so he could have a photograph. That was probably November, in Czechoslovakia. On either 1 or 2 January 1945 I was told to go to the office to collect the identity signs, the Rising Sun insignia. That's how we got our official identity. We had Latvian arm badges too. I've still got mine.[37]

---

36   There is a detailed discussion about the artillery school at Litoměřice/Leitmeritz on the Axis History forum at <https://www.forum.axishistory.com/viewtopic.php?f=38&t=196414>.

37   The 'fire cross' or *Pērkonkrusts* (thundercross) collar patch was introduced for the Latvian Legion in March 1943 to replace the SS runes (Silgailis, p.230). Latvian military units used the 'thundercross' swastika from the early 1920s, but the symbol can be found in Latvian settlements from the fourth and fifth centuries. The swastika was carved above the door to a home to protect it from lightning. Source: website <Latvians.com> at <https://latvians.com/index.php?en/CFBH/Zimes/zimes-00-sheet.ssi>.

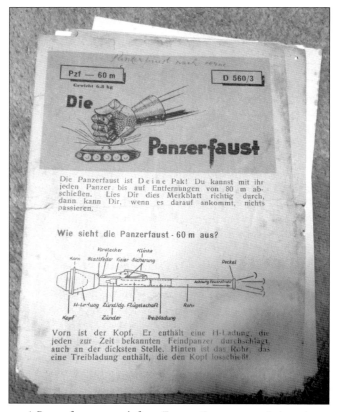

A Panzerfaust manual, from Eastern Front veteran Laimonis
Ceriņš' box of memories.

He rummages through his box of mementoes to find it. I notice a small pamphlet. It's
a leaflet explaining how to arm and fire a Panzerfaust. I laugh.

> VH: Is that an instruction manual … for a Panzerfaust?
> LC: (laughs) Yes, it is.

He reaches into the box and lifts out a thick pile of paper, wrapped in plastic.

> This here is everything about the 15th Division. My own stories. How I left my
> home.[38]

The telephone rings and interrupts us.

---

38 Interview with author, Derby, 2018.

3

Arrival in Danzig

There's a buzz in the summer air in Gdańsk Old Town at night. People are eating in open-fronted cafes and restaurants or strolling along the riverside, chatting and laughing or admiring the 17th-century architecture. Mock Spanish galleons with modern engines chug up and down the Motława river on sightseeing tours.

The Long Market, Gdańsk's main thoroughfare and tourist attraction, has been the city's main artery since the Teutonic Knights conquered it in 1308. The most prominent of citizens and even monarchs laid their heads to rest in the tenements lining the colourful 'Royal Route'. The history is amazing. The ornate fountain of the sea god Neptune with his trident dates back to 1615. The Town Hall with its elegant narrow tower pre-dates it by half a century: tourists gather to enjoy its 37 charming, chiming bells.

Most visitors to Gdańsk come to see the Golden Gate, a 17th-century arch into the centre of the city decorated with figures representing values considered desirable in its citizens – Prudence, Justice, Piety and Harmony. The gate was badly damaged by Soviet shelling in the Second World War but restored to its former glory afterwards, though when Danzig became Polish in 1945 and took the name Gdańsk, many of the German influences were removed.[1] One German inscription from Psalm 122 which remains on the gate is an ironic comment given the events here at the turn of 1945.

> May those who love you be safe! Peace be within your walls and security within your towers![2]

Danzig was the entry point for many of the Latvian Legionnaires who arrived in Pomerania from August 1944 onwards, as the Nazi military machine re-grouped after its mauling on the Russian Front. A vast base covering an area of 700 square

---

1   Gdańsk tourist information online at
    <https://www.Gdansk.pl/en/for-tourists/tourist-attractions, a,12042>.
2   City of Gdańsk website at <https://www.Gdansk.pl/en/for-tourists/the-upplands-gate-the-highland-gate-and-the-golden-gate,a,12128>.

Gdańsk at night, August 2018. (Picture: author)

kilometres was created in Pomerania to train Waffen-SS soldiers, including the Latvian conscripts.[3]

Known as the *Truppenübungsplatz Westpreußen*, the land was taken from local farmers: they were despatched to a labour camp at Potulice near Nakel [Nakło nad Notecią]. The prisoners from there and camps at Stutthof and Bruss [Brusy] were set to work to build it, part of a network commanded by SS Obersturmführer Otto Neubauer, head of the central building commission of the Waffen-SS and Police Danzig/Westpreussen. There were satellite camps at Brusy, Lipush, Chelmach Wilich, Lesno and Dziemiany [Sophienwalde]. Also held there were 500 Jewish women prisoners originally from the Kaiserwald concentration camp in Rīga, transferred from Stutthof to Sophienwalde or held at the monastery in Brusy.[4]

Farmers were turned into slave labourers overnight, finding themselves and their children subjected to Nazi medical experiments. One example is the Kacmarczyk family, farmers in a village near Stargard until 1942. In June that year, a German farmer was given their land and they were sent to Potulice, where the father was put to work in the forest, dying shortly afterwards, apparently from the rigours of the hard work. The family suspected he was injected with phenol.

In an article by Miroslaw Piepko titled *The Mystery of Sophienwalde* his son, Zdzislaw, described how a group of fifty boys aged between 16 and 17 with blond hair and blue eyes were selected for 'unusually thorough medical examination' and 25 were then sent to Sophienwalde, where they were given injections in their spinal area. Zdzislaw described the process:

> First a long needle was pushed into the spinal area and then some fluid was put into the hole made by the first needle. Shortly afterwards their hands swelled enormously and the skin on their arms, right up to their shoulders, turned violet and yellow. The colour lasted a few days. The same procedure was followed several more times, always with a few days in between. Similar or perhaps the same injections were given to a group of young Jewish girls.
>
> After a month the 25 boys were summoned again. This time they were forced to ejaculate and collect the sperm in test tubes. While they were thus occupied

---

3   Many Latvians left their homeland as refugees because their children had been sent to Germany. The consequence was to increase the negative impact on the viability of the Latvian nation after the war.

4   M. Orski, *The Jewish Camp at Brusy-Dziemiany* (Yad Vashem Studies, Volume XXII, 1992). The camp was evacuated in January 1945, with 500 women sent west on a death march. The 100 women who remained were shot in Lesno on 10 February 1945. (G. Labuda, *Historia Pomorza*, 1–3, Poznań, 1969–2003). Around 5,000 Poles, Jews, Germans and Belorussians died at Potulice in the decade between 1939 and 1949. The Nazi camp, known as UWZ Lager Lebrechtsdorf-Potulitz, was a holding camp for Polish children who were used to provide slave labour to move building materials and load and unload freight at the railway station. Of the 1,296 people who died there between 1941 and 1945, 767 were minors. After the war, the Polish authorities used Potulice to hold German prisoners and Poles from the Home Army. Some 2,915 Germans died there between 1945 and 1949, mainly due to typhus and dysentery epidemics.

they could hear the screams of the Jewish girls nearby. The girls were apparently undergoing different experiments.[5]

Of the 25 boys brought to Sophienwalde from Potulice, only three survived. The majority died in the gas chamber at Stutthof. While the descriptions of what happened here are vague, Piepko says one prisoner was ordered by the SS to carry the 'excised wombs' of Jewish women out of the base and bury them in the nearby forest. Sophienwalde was a tough place: Kacmarczyk's camp had 1,300 men to start with, but only 300 survived.[6]

By the turn of 1945, a total of 3.8 million Soviet troops were waiting for orders to strike westwards across the Vistula river, with Berlin the ultimate goal. They would be led by the 3rd Belorussian Front commanded by Marshal Ivan Chernyakovsky, veteran of Kursk, the battle for Belarus and Operation *Bagration*, the clearing of German forces from Lithuania and Latvia in summer 1944.[7]

Marshal Konstantin Konstantinovich Rokossovsky's 2nd Belorussian Front was to thrust towards the Baltic Sea from the south, cutting off German forces in East Prussia and the main port of Danzig while covering the right flank of the advance on Berlin. Further south, the 1st, 4th and 2nd Ukrainian Fronts would launch attacks into Silesia, Slovakia and Austria as the Soviet Supreme Command, the STAVKA, landed a sequence of staggered and powerful blows on the German defensive line, keeping them off-balance.

Hugely outnumbered, reinforced with the old men of the *Volkssturm* milita and often using horses to transport equipment and weapons, the German defences reeled under the force of the offensive launched on 12 January 1945.[8] Eastern Front historian David Glantz noted: 'It is no wonder that those divisions were oftentimes simply vapourised by the Soviet assault.'[9] The German chief of staff Heinz Guderian repeatedly asked Hitler for more reserves to shore up the defensive lines in north-eastern Poland, but Hitler refused.

Guderian's view was that the Eastern Front in that region was like 'a pack of cards. If the front is broken through, at some point all the rest will collapse, for twelve and a half divisions are far too small a reserve for so extended a front.'[10]

The Red Army would pay a heavy price too: it's estimated that half a million Soviet soldiers died in combat in the Second World War on the territory of present-day

5   Miroslaw Piepko, 'The Mystery of Sophienwalde' translated from the Polish by Eric Schneider. From the magazine *Jewish Monthly*, circulated by Gertrude Steiner, discovered in the Andrew Ezergailis archive at the Museum of the Occupation of Latvia, Riga, 2022.
6   Piepko, 'The Mystery of Sophienwalde.'
7   N. Davies, *Europe at War 1939–1945: No Simple Victory* (London: Pan Books, 2007), p.123. Chernyakovsky was to die shortly after the operation started, on 18 February 1945, from wounds received in the assault on Königsberg.
8   C. Duffy, *Red Storm on the Reich: The Soviet March on Germany, 1945* (New York: Da Capo Press, 1993), pp.26–29.
9   Glantz (1986, p.507) in Duffy, *Red Storm on the Reich*, p.51.
10 Guderian (1952, pp.387–388) in Duffy, *Red Storm on the Reich*, p.62.

Sophienwalde church [now Dziemiany], one of the main towns for the Latvians deployed in Pomerania. (Picture: author)

Poland: 800,000 became prisoners of war. There are 638 registered Red Army cemeteries and isolated graves across the region.[11]

The Latvians of the 15th Division were billeted in villages around the West Prussia training camp: Bütow, Sophienwalde and Berent.[12] The Legion's second-in-command, Arturs Silgailis, noted the harsh conditions endured by soldiers stationed there.

> There were no barracks. Units were accommodated in villages and many of them were forced to live in quarters not suitable for winter conditions, such as stables, barns, home-made bunkers etc. Many lived in tents until the late Fall. There was also a lack of firewood … only sufficient for the preparation of meals. The cutting [down] of trees was strictly forbidden.[13]

They were mostly raw conscripts, in some cases teenagers rounded up from the streets, who had been drafted into the Legion in the summer and autumn of 1944. Stories from the time tell how off-duty Legionnaires had to be watchful of 'honeytraps' on their nights out: some were lured into alleyways by local women and murdered by the Resistance. Only the officers and non-commissioned officers had any real experience of the kind of combat they were about to face, having fought the Russians at Opochka and on the Velikaya River.

Although the 15th Division had been re-grouping in Pomerania since August 1944, its state of readiness for an encounter with the combat-hardened troops of the Red Army was not good. One teenager, Talis Iskalns from Ozolnieki near Jelgava, had been called up into the Labour Battalion [*Reichsarbietsdienst* or RAD] and sent by boat from Rīga to Gotenhafen where he became part of the 15th Division.

> I was born on 9 February 1926. I had a brother, Ivars – but the Russians killed him. They sent him to Siberia and he died within six months. He was only a student: 18 years old. He'd done a little bit of protesting, like youngsters do. And they rounded them all up and sent them to Russia where they all died. That was in 1940. He was one of the first. I was 14, otherwise I would have been with him. Then unexpectedly the war started. The Germans attacked the Russians. I was quite glad about it because they got the Russians out of our country within a few days. They just ran away. They were so surprised they didn't know what was happening. They didn't even fight back as far as I could see. The main road towards Russia was full of cars and trucks heading back to Russia with equipment. Then the Germans arrived.

The first Germans he saw were some soldiers cycling with their sleeves rolled up, and the Russians were running away from them. Control of Latvia changed hands within a matter of two or three days: the Germans were in and the Russians were out.

---

11 E. Ochman, *Post-Communist Poland – Contested Pasts and Future Identities* (Abingdon: BASEES/Routledge series on Russian and East European Studies, 2013), p.125.
12 Bytów, Dziemiany and Kościerzyna today.
13 Silgailis, *Latvian Legion,* p.154.

Former Legionnaire Talis Iskalns at his home in Catthorpe, Leicestershire, UK, December 2017. (Picture: author)

We were quite happy to see the Germans because they knew we didn't like the Russians. They were quite friendly and let us do whatever we wanted. We had our own government although there was a German in charge. Of course the Communists were rounded up. I was at school, so we just carried on as before.

The first people to fight were the volunteers. They had lost their families and they hated the Russians, so they volunteered. Later the Legion was created. They called it *freiwillige*, voluntary, but it was nothing like voluntary. It was either go into the Legion or be sent to a concentration camp. For me that was later because I was 14 when they came in; still at school, at a gymnasium, the middle education.

At that time in Germany the German youth all had to go into a thing called *Reicharbeitsdienst* [RAD] which was a bit of Army training, discipline and marching. Instead of a rifle you had a spade. It came to us as well. We were asked to go to Germany to do this *Arbeitsdienst*, and if we wanted to go from the gymnasium to university we had to do it. My time came when I was 18 so I volunteered to go to Germany. It wasn't that bad – it was good training, actually.

Before we could go we were all rounded up in Jelgava and the Gauleiter said goodbye to us and wished us luck. We went to the station and got on a train. As we were waiting to leave, Russian bombers appeared for the first time and started dropping a few bombs, so we got off the train and took cover in the park. After that the Germans changed their minds and told us that we could stay in Latvia and do our service on the Russian front, so we went about 60 kilometres out of Jelgava and that's what we did, digging trenches and things to stop tanks. It didn't work and it was all for nothing. The front came nearer and we had to walk back to Rīga. In Rīga we were told: 'Now you're in the Legion. You're not in the *Arbeitsdienst* now.'

Being in the Legion meant being sent to the front. Talis and his group were loaded onto a boat and despatched to Pomerania.

We were sent to Gotenhafen. We were supposed to do some training, live in tents. We didn't have any rifles so instead we used sticks. At that point towards the end of the war the Germans were very short of everything: short of food, equipment. We had to wear our old *Reichsarbietsdienst* uniforms but they wore out pretty quickly. We couldn't get any new boots so some people had to stay in their tents all day because they couldn't walk without boots: we got there at the end of summer and it was starting to get cold and wet and we couldn't walk in the mud without boots.

There was one German in charge but otherwise it was Latvian officers and instructors, who had to do what the Germans said. It was very uncomfortable in cold weather in the tent – there was nothing in it, so we were just sleeping on the bare ground. We collected some tree branches from the woods and put them on the ground to sleep on with just a blanket over us. It was wartime and Germany was short of everything. It was us in the 15th Division in the village and the barracks, and there was a lake in the woods and some men made huts to sleep in out of the trees, huts with three shelves, one for each man.

By that time it was already very cold and freezing hard with not much snow, about half an inch. There was no water and no facilities to wash so we had to go on the frozen lake and try and get ourselves clean by rubbing ourselves with frozen snow to get the dirt off. We had a little stove inside the hut. With all these people inside I suppose it was warm enough but the snow was landing on the roof and dripping through.

There were about 30 of us in that hut, all from the *Arbeitsdienst*, turned into soldiers, alongside proper soldiers; we were there to get some training but without any weapons to train on. Nothing at all. Then lice started appearing from somewhere in those huts. At first we were laughing and joking about it, but soon we were all covered in lice and it was horrible.[14]

Ziedonis Āboliņš was 18 when he was called up into a labour battalion. The son of farmers from the Pūre region near Tukums, he was allowed to stay and bring in the harvest because he was the only male in the family. Then the Germans came back for him.

In October 1944 they called me a second time, but this time to join the Legion. What choice did you have? You either joined the Legion or you went into the woods.[15]

The police went looking for you if you didn't turn up, and really at that age you want excitement, to see places, and you're not afraid of many things. We all

---

14 Interview with author, Catthorpe Manor, 17 December 2017.
15 As a fugitive. Mr Āboliņš was born on 21 March 1926, and died a few months after this interview.

Eastern Front veteran Ziedonis Āboliņš with wife Ināra at their home in Catthorpe, December 2017. (Picture: author)

went. I don't think many tried to avoid it. You had to go, so we went. The writer and dramatist Harijs Gulbis and I both went to the gymnasium in Tukums.

We sailed from Rīga on 4 October to Gotenhafen in Germany. From there, we were sent to the training ground at Sophienwalde. I was in the 33rd Regiment and that was located in a small village called Lippush, near Sophienwalde. I was in the first *rota* and the commander was Lieutenant Bonoparts. Not Napoleon! He was Latvian, a fantastic chap. I don't remember much about that time except being hungry all the time. The supply was very chaotic. We were sleeping in barns so it wasn't very pleasant.[16]

The remnants of the 15th Division gathered in the training area in West Prussia between Bütow and Berent, their ranks swelling with the inclusion of those born in 1925 and 1926, many of whom had been in Germany already with the *Reichsarbeitsdienst* labour battalions. One of these men was Jānis Urpens, another Legionnaire who came to the UK after the war.

16 Interview with author, Catthorpe Manor, 17 December 2017. A gymnasium is like an English grammar school. A *rota* is the equivalent of a company. Bonoparts' first name was Eižens.

I was in the *Arbeitsdienst* for ten months which I joined to escape from joining the Army. Most of the time I was on the island of Silte, on the North Sea coast of Germany. We were mending roads and digging sand, planting grass. The *Arbeitsdienst* was meant for young Germans before they joined the Army, like military training, but most of it was 'any jobs that needed doing'. I was there until the end of August 1944 and then I was 'voluntarily mobilised' – that was the expression they used – into the Army.

Then we were sent to a camp at Konitz for two months training and then we went to Lauenburg [Lębork] to a school for NCO training. But we couldn't finish the course because the Russians came and we were sent back to our division.[17]

Another RAD recruit turned Legionnaire was Arturs Grava, who emigrated to the USA after the war. From his home in Cleveland, Ohio, four days short of his 98th birthday, he emailed his memories of joining the Legion, and of the NCO school in Lauenburg.

As opposed to most Legionnaires, I spent most of my service under direct German command or close to Germans. With that, I gained an understanding of German attitudes to Latvians and of the attitude of the ordinary soldier to the war, which will not have been gained by most Legionnaires.

Being born in 1924, I received the conscription order at the moment the Legion was founded. I was a student in the final year of secondary school and I took the opportunity to finish my schooling by applying for German work service (RAD). About 40–50 Liepāja secondary school students did the same. The call-up into the RAD was planned for later; due to factors that weren't under our control, it was delayed until the autumn. I departed for Germany at the beginning of October 1943.

Work service for us was by the airports in Mecklenburg, at first with German boys doing intensive military training near the towns of Neustadt-Glewe and Parchim. After three months, the Germans were called up into the army, while the Latvians were combined with Latvians in other units. My new place was Schwerin airfield (*Fliegerhorst*). We worked mostly on roadworks, also travelling out to other locations. For a while we were cycling out to the other side of the city to build shelters in tunnels dug into the hills.

When that was done, we were sent to a Waffen-SS training camp at the town of Bruss in East Prussia. Right by there were Latvian training camps, but the huge influx of new recruits and the shortage of instructors meant they couldn't take us in. On the other hand, the Germans willingly kept soldiers-to-be in their control, who were subjected to them anyway.

During training it was made clear to us that they couldn't demand from us the German soldiers' oath, only a promise to be faithful in the fight against Bolshevism. As the basic training finished, we went through specialist sapper,

---

17 Interview with author, Fenstanton in Cambridgeshire, UK, 2019.

sniper and gas fighting training, before we were allotted to various Latvian units. Those who had finished grammar school were given the opportunity to apply for instructor [*Unterfuehrer*] training. At that time the Latvians were very short of instructors.

The longest journey, around 1 November 1944, was to the Lauenburg Instructor School. There were two companies of us Latvians there, about one kilometre from each other. The school's leadership was pretty arrogant, demonstrating German superiority, but the instructors seemed acceptable to us. Some were even friendly. It was also explained to us that we weren't members of the SS but just Waffen-SS grenadiers and that we didn't have the right to any SS privileges.

Lauenburg was very much an extension of basic training, including discipline, obedience, marching, commands, military command structure, etc. Every morning we had a half-hour run around the campus. The food was OK initially, inadequate near the end.

In addition to that we had a lot of weapons training – machine guns, pistols, hand grenades, flamethrowers, mines. Theory of weapons' capabilities. Much time was devoted to anti-tank defence – not guns, but Panzerfaust, Panzerschreck, T-mines, foxholes. Attacks on bunkers. I remember marches to distant training grounds carrying weapons and boxes of ammunition. And singing during the marches.

For the field: some sandbox instruction, camouflage, use of binoculars, signalling, distance estimation, orientation, crossing of waters, attack formations and tactics, patrols, night exercises. About once every two weeks we went by train to a large training area to the north – possibly Stolp – for a two-day field exercise.

Political education [*Unterrichte*] was about once a week, explaining the essentials of National Socialism. About every two weeks we received a Sunday pass to go to the town of Lauenburg.

The instructors, on average, were fair. Initially, there were some bullies; we had been drilled enough and resented their attitude. Intellectually, we were more than their match and learned to resist. The nicest guys were a few non-commissioned officers, several times wounded and exempted from frontline service. I met one of them – wounded again – on my way to the *Kriegslazarett* [field hospital]. He told me that the commanding officer of my company had been captured by the Russians.

All trainees in SS military schools were put under the direct command of Himmler. Our training at Lauenburg was expected to be completed at end of January. However, the front collapsed and we were sent away on a very cold day in unheated boxcars, on about 20 or 21 January. The instructors travelled in a separate car.

After a day or two at Pasewalk, Mecklenburg, without disembarking from the train, we began returning to Westpreussen. We stayed at a party school in Pomerania for four to five days, had some Panzerfaust training, then continued our voyage and reached Schlochau on about 9 or 10 February. The train was very slow, halting and waiting for hours every 20 kilometres or so; our escort consisted of Lauenburg officers and *Ushas* [*unterscharführers*, or junior squad leaders]. At Schlochau we were turned over to the 15th Division.[18]

Around ten minutes' drive from Gdańsk Old Town, in the Maćkowy district, is the site of a now nearly-forgotten SS punishment camp. Construction began in October 1939 using Polish prisoners from Stutthof, closely guarded and forced to sleep on straw thrown on bare earth. *SS-Kaserne Danzig-Matzkau* developed into a facility with 45 separate buildings – half were barracks, half were administration buildings, with a canteen, kitchen, hospital, warehouses and an armoury. There was a sports hall, swimming pool and a gas station to fuel the 100 or so vehicles based here.

Until autumn 1940 it was used as a barracks, then for the next year as a transit camp for ethnic Germans repatriated from the Baltic states. In 1941 it was converted into a punishment camp for SS men and military police convicted of desertion, insubordination or homosexuality. The first 347 convicts arrived in January 1942, and by the end of the year the population had risen to 1,858. Most stayed between six to nine months before being released to serve the rest of their sentence in penal battalions. Among the inmates were members of the SS penal unit Dirlewanger, notorious for their cruelty during the suppression of the Warsaw Uprising. Many prisoners were sentenced to death and executed here: among them was a war reporter and former employee of the Rīga Ballet and Opera, Jānis Oļģerts Teteris, who was killed between 7 and 9 October 1944.

Jānis Teteris was born in Rīga on 3 January 1907 with a last listed address at 27 Ernestines iela in Āgenskalns. He was an Oberscharführer in the SS Standarte Kurt Eggers, a propaganda unit, and he was attached to the 6 *Lettische SS-Kriegsberichter-kompanie*.[19] His records note that he was a member of the Latvian Army Reserve Press Corps – officially a squad leader in the Waffen-SS War Correspondents – but there are no further details of his service or the crime for which he was executed. The Matzkau camp was evacuated in February 1945 and the inmates moved to other camps at Nuremberg and Mosbach.[20]

⌒ — ⌒

I've driven to West Bridgford in Nottingham to meet Henry Vītols, a remarkably sprite 94-year-old man. He is friendly and sharp-witted and appears young beyond

---

18 Arturs Grava, memories of Lauenburg. Sent to author 20 July 2022, trans. Aivars Sinka.

19 The 6th Latvian SS War Reporter Company. Kurt Eggers was a war reporter and editor of the SS magazine who had been killed in the Third Battle of Kharkov in 1943. Teteris' file at the International Tracing Service includes the note that the information was given by Latvian soldiers in the same camp who 'have had the opportunity to observe what was happening in the camp'. Source: ITS file passed to author by grandson John Teteris.

20 Marzena Klimowicz-Sikorska,'SS men were punished in Gdańsk', 22 February 2010, <https://www.trojmiasto.pl/wiadomosci/W-Gdansku-karano-SS-Mannow-n37085.html>, accessed 11 July 2020. Captured by the Soviets, the NKVD used it as a camp for prisoners too. It later became a dairy, but is now closed.

his years, wearing a T-shirt and check shirt like a man half his age. His real name is Henrijs Teodors Vītols: 'Henry' is his English name. He is now a full-time carer for his wife, who is confined to bed in the back room after having had a stroke on their 60th wedding anniversary. Despite visits from health workers four times a day to help, this is a demanding workload for someone his age. He's in good spirits though.

> HV: I'm from Rīga, born 23 May 1925. We lived in 4 Valdemara iela, *dzivoklis* [flat] 8. We rented it. My father was a watchmaker trained in Hamburg, and he came home, worked hard and opened a shop, selling watches and crystals. But he lost his business when it caught fire. We weren't insured. After that we all slept in one room.
>
> I was called into the 15th Division in August [1944]. After the medical we were put on a train and sent for training as soldiers. Then all of a sudden we were turned around and put on a ship on the Daugava. My father came to the ship and gave me a gold half-sovereign. He said: 'What shall I give you?' And I said: 'A bottle of vodka!' He gave me a big piece of bacon, and I swapped some of it with a German sailor for a bottle of vodka.
>
> It was a bit scary with alarms going off all around but we went to Germany. The alarms were [because of] submarines. Then we were sent to Bütow. We were supposed to train to fire light artillery but all of a sudden we started to move. The Russians were behind us all the time. For a young-ster – aged 18, 19 – it was something new. We walked and walked and walked. I fell asleep and was nearly left behind.
>
> VH: Did you go to Sophienwalde to train?
>
> HV: Yes, we did. We were marching, and if you didn't do it properly the Germans were shouting: 'Down. Run. Down. Run.' Press-ups and run. And then we had to go.[21]

Augusts Spilners was another Legionnaire in Pomerania who came to the UK after the war, and his family settled less than 20 miles [32 kilometres] away from Henry, in Melton Mowbray in Leicestershire. His daughter Nora translated the diary he kept throughout these years and has sent it to me. It is incredibly detailed, dramatic and vivid and demonstrates a deep underlying religious faith. This is how Augusts remembered the emotional turmoil for many when his unit was sent from Courland in Latvia through the port of Ventspils and then by boat to Pomerania.

> October 8: Orders come that the whole regiment will continue to march to Ventspils. We are being sent to Germany. Many boys disappear and we will have to decide whether to go. Maybe it will be better. So now there are long lines of Latvian soldiers who begin the march to Ventspils. The sick are taken by train.

---

21 Interview with author, Nottingham, May 2019. He joined the 33rd or 34th Regiment. He couldn't remember exactly. As he ended the war with Colonel Janums, it was probably the 33rd.

When night comes we find somewhere to stay, eat dinner and go to sleep. I am tired.

October 9: We continue to go on, coming ever closer to Ventspils. The terrain [between Rīga and Dundaga] is forest; sandy and poor. Thirsty. Cannot get any water. Our stop comes close to the woods of Ventspils. The evening is clear and the night will be cold. This will be the first night under an open sky. We are looking for twigs to light a fire so we can boil coffee to be a little warmer.

October 10: At noon we go to the port but many boys have run away, they do not want to go by sea. We are going. We are not going to flee the fighting and danger, but hope to go back to Latvia with training

Augusts Spilners, pictured in 1947, who kept a detailed diary of his Eastern Front experiences. (Picture courtesy of his daughter, Nora Spilners)

and weapons. In the evening we board the ship. I am calm. With us are many soldiers. With the words 'God bless Latvia' we leave the dark Latvian coast hoping to return soon.

October 11: The sea is calm, the weather is overcast and foggy, and nothing can be seen. A few times a day there is an alert, but luck is with us. We will get to the port tomorrow.

October 12: [In front of our eyes] a foreign land glides by, buildings and port equipment. German warships and submarines are entering the port. In the evening I step off the ship: my first step in a foreign land. God give me strength to withstand. In the evening we go to Danzig where we have accommodation at a school. The night is cold.

October 13: We go to the station that will take us to our positions. At the station we are stripped of all ammunition and weapons that still exist. We climb on the train that will take us into the unknown.

October 14: Travel all day. The weather is foggy and we see nothing. We go through the former Poland and at all the stations and cities there are German flags. At one station we meet Legionnaires who are ready to be placed for training. Food and clothing is very poor. No cigarettes. The Germans show great distrust towards the Latvians.[22]

22 Diary of Augusts Spilners. Courtesy of Nora Spilners.

Latvian civilians were shipped to Pomerania too. Aina Urpens was 16 when her parents decided to leave rather than live under the Communists again. The family left home on a horse and cart and initially sought refuge with farmers in Courland [Kurzeme] before being ordered by the German authorities to go to Ventspils to be evacuated.

It was autumn 1944 when the Russians were quite close to Rīga. On no account were we going to stay with them so we got a horse and cart and went over to Kurzeme which was still free, and we stayed there with some farmers. There were masses of us. There were so many people who just left everything behind.

It was very crowded. We spent about two months sleeping on a farmer's floor. The Germans used to come round and keep an eye on us and how we lived. We lived very dangerously. In our group there were about 15 or 16 people. There was one poor elderly lady: we used to put straw around her and cover her with a blanket and leave her to sleep all day. One day our mother and father told me and my brother to take a horse and go to town to buy food. I never knew why until later, when my father told me the Germans came looking for deserters. The people who worked for the farmer and lived in the house had a son who was a deserter from the German Army, so they hid him under that old lady. Can you imagine? We would all have been shot! That's why my parents sent us out that day.

Then one day the Germans came and said: 'Every able-bodied person must go to Ventspils on this day and get on board this boat,' so we went. My father said: 'We shall go, even if it's not what we want.' Many people went into the woods. From the other farm some men jumped out of the windows and ran into the woods, but the Germans shot them. They probably thought they were deserters. We saw them being shot. So we went to Ventspils, and after 18 hours on the boat we reached Poland. The boat was so full there was standing room only.[23]

Sarmīte Ērenpreiss-Janovskis grew up in a wealthy suburb of Rīga, the daughter of a well-known bicycle manufacturer with a factory in the Jugla district to the north of the city.

I can remember my childhood in Latvia when the Germans were there. They were very polite, but I guess that depends on who you were. If you were a gypsy or a Jew or a mentally ill person, you were done away with, but they could be gentlemen. Not so the Russians.

We had a Russian general, his wife and his mother-in-law parked in our house in Baltezers [a very desirable district to the north of Rīga]. They took over the ground floor, while my father was in hiding. My mother had four young children in the house and she said he had gone abroad to buy steel for the bicycles. It was horrible for us because this man had a pistol, and every morning he'd go out into the big garden with pine trees. Four gardens down there was a wooden house which they [the Soviets] took over and tortured and murdered our people there. They were all found there later with their hands tied behind their backs with barbed wire and their eyes stabbed out. There's a cross on the roadside to this day commemorating that. When the Germans came in people received them with joy, because all the terror was gone for us.

We fled from Latvia on the last day of July 1944. My father had to stay behind to keep the factory working for the Germans. They didn't make bicycles then but ammunition, and we thought that at any moment the Allies would win and we could go home. My mother, us four children and our nurse went from Rīga harbour to Königsberg by ship. We were very privileged: we had packed everything up in boxes which were sent ahead. Our firm was supplied with steel by a German man who had three factories in the Ruhr, where all the electro-power stations were, in the mountains – a beautiful area. They'd spent plenty of summers in our villa in Baltezers when we were small, and they'd said: 'War is coming and if you need shelter, come to us.' As it turned out, when we did turn up we weren't particularly welcome, but that's how it is in war. But we had an address to go to.

We were waiting for a train at Königsberg station, completely dark. My mother was afraid of losing us so she tied us together with a piece of rope. We were there for two days and two nights and then on the third day a train slowly came into the station. There were people hanging off it from everywhere, hanging out of the windows. Then it stopped and a station porter cut the rope holding us together and started stuffing us through the windows. I don't know why but I got separated and fell into another compartment from my mother, my three siblings and my nurse. It was completely full. There were people up on the luggage racks, in the seats, on the floor – and there were wounded soldiers. As a kid I'd never even been in a train or on a bus because my father had seven limousines. And it was frightening. Suddenly you're there with bloody heads, people with no legs or no arms, all sitting there filthy ... filthy. I was going to cry but then I said to myself: 'I'm my mother's child and I'm not going to cry.' I was seven.

Someone said: 'What's your name?' I said, 'Sarmīte Ērenpreiss.' And they laughed and laughed and held their heads. They were laughing at my name. There was no other Ērenpreiss in Latvia: it's like saying 'Elisabeth Windsor'. That made me cry. They asked me in German but when I started crying they said in Latvian: 'Don't cry, little girl. Where are your parents?'

I said: 'My mother's here somewhere – I don't know.' I didn't know you could walk through a train, so one man who could walk put me on his shoulder and we pushed through the carriage to find her and my nurse, and I put my head in my nurse's lap – she always smelt of Nivea and had a starched pinafore – and then I started crying again...[24]

24 Interview with author.

In Derby, Jānis Čevers recalls his arrival in Danzig after many months of combat in Russia.

> We came in by boat to Danzig, right on the sea front. There was a big *lazarett* [field hospital] of wounded German soldiers on the beach – thousands of them. That was the beginning of August when we arrived in Danzig. Hot days, thousands of wounded. We may have stayed in Danzig a couple of weeks before we moved on to Konitz. The whole Division was spread around the region in little villages. Then more recruits came from Latvia; youngsters to be trained. I was a Corporal by then so I didn't have to go to training any more. I stayed with the officers.
>
> My responsibility was ammunition, and the [artillery] training was with live ammunition. You know what youngsters are like – miscalculated, fallen short, didn't explode. To me they were all youngsters. I had to look after them and make sure their guns were cleaned properly.
>
> My job was to go on the ranges and collect the shells that hadn't exploded from the field – and I hadn't had a day's training. I chucked one I couldn't take care of down a well for drinking water once. That was a bit naughty. What happened when somebody cleaned the well after the war?
>
> Then I was put to work with a German SS Sergeant and we sorted out the ammunition together. We were there until the end of January 1945 with the Division until the Russians broke through the German lines at Nakel.[25]

Soldiers from all corners of Hitler's Greater Germany re-grouped in this part of Pomerania to resist the Red Army hammer blows in January 1945 against Nazi front-lines the length of the Eastern Front, from the Baltic Sea to the Danube. The regional Nazi administration had its headquarters in Brusy with its own garrison.[26]

The 700-square kilometre West Prussian training ground, which the Latvians talk about as 'Sophienwalde' or 'Konitz', was more like a region in the Pomeranian countryside. They gathered in Lauenburg: some were sent south to Toruń, others to Bruss [now Brusy] and Konitz. The size of the New Forest in Hampshire in the UK, the training ground had a vast perimeter, on the other side of which lurked danger.[27]

Sections of the surrounding forests were controlled by, or were bases for, an array of partisan units and Resistance cells including the Gryf Pomorski group around Brusy, led by the Colonel and Roman Catholic priest Józef Wrycza. The Home Army and the Armija Krajowa [AK] also operated in the area. The Home Army was in regular radio contact with the exiled Polish government in London with an established courier route for smuggling prisoners of war and secrets out of the country. As historian Norman Davies writes:

---

25 Interview with author, Derby, 2018.
26 Tenhumburg family website at <http://www.tenhumbergreinhard.de/1933-1945-lager-1/1933-1945-lager-b/bruss-Sophienwaldee-brusy-dziemiany.html>, accessed 10 November 2021.
27 The New Forest is slightly larger, at 753 square kilometres. (from <https://www.newforest.gov.uk/>)

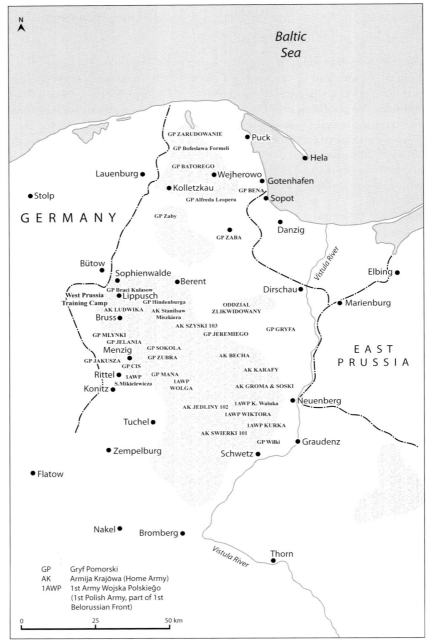

Polish partisan groups operating in Pomerania (now Poland) in the region around Danzig (now Gdansk), 1939-45. Areas under their control are shaded in grey. Partisans from various groups operated from camps across eastern Pomerania from 1939–45, and the Latvian bases at Sophienwalde, Lauenburg, Konitz and Toruń [Thorn] brought them into close proximity.

The extraordinary feat of intercepting, dismantling and delivering the entire working parts of a German V2 rocket shows just how sophisticated the link between England and Poland had become.[28]

There was partisan activity across the Gdańsk region, concentrated to the west of Gotenhafen and Danzig, particularly between Gotenhafen and Lauenburg. Further south, to the east of Bütow and Schlochau and directly in the path of units moving south-west from Danzig was an intense grouping of partisan units stretching from the Vistula to the outskirts of Konitz at Rytel [Rittel].

The Polish partisans and Resistance attacked from their camps in the forests, with around 500 fighters and strong support locally. The Resistance gathered vital intelligence on the V1 and V2 rocket programmes which was fed back to the Allies. The SS struck back to stop disruption to supply lines and troop movements. Local history holds that Latvians were responsible for the deaths of some of these partisans, although they did not arrive here until later. Several of the bunkers in the area used by partisan groups destroyed in SS attacks have now been restored.

One such site is at the Green Palace at Wielkie Chelmy [Gross Chelm], which was attacked by the 35th *Ersatz* [Replacement] SS Battalion commanded by Fritz Nordmann in March 1944.[29] A sign at the site tells the story of what happened here:

On 21 March 1944 Waffen-SS divisions and Jagdkommando units from nearby Wielkie Chelmy surrounded the Green Palace, covered by units in the hills. The men were from the 35th SS Battalion, consisting of the remnants of a 15th Latvian Waffen-SS volunteer team which had been annihilated in the USSR and transferred to Pomerania on 1 November 1943.[30] They secured the SS West Prussian training ground [perimeter] around Gross Chelm up to Sophienwalde.

The training camp was commanded by SS Standartenführer Fritz Nordmann, who at the same time commanded an elite detachment of the Jagdkommando to fight partisans in the surrounding Tuchola forest. They used specially-trained dogs to track down the guerrillas and successfully liquidated the partisan group CISA. Jagdkommando units were also located in the Wielu, Tuchola and Szlachcie forests. They murdered local villagers for helping the partisans, killing children too and often entire families, for example in Wielun and Baku.

The Wehrmacht soldiers stationed in Brusy were used in this attack too. A total of 300 soldiers were used against nine partisans. Despite this, two partisans managed to escape during the night, for which the German commanders

28 N. Davies, *Heart of Europe – the Past in Poland's Present* (Oxford: Oxford University Press, 2001), p.58, sourcing J. Garlinski, *Hitler's Last Weapons* (1978).
29 Nordmann became Commandant of the West Prussia SS training camp in November 1944, and was in charge when the Soviets crossed the Vistula in January 1945.
30 This is problematic, as the Latvian Legion wasn't sent to the Russian Front until 12 November. It's possible, if this claim is accurate, that this could have been men from the 2nd Latvian Regiment wounded on the Russian Front who had been sent back to Pomerania to recover and were then re-deployed. Latvian sources do not believe this claim is accurate, though.

A cross commemorating the partisans killed by German forces in March 1944 at the Green Palace, Wielkie Chelmy [Gross Chelm]. (Picture courtesy of Pawel Bukowski)

had to vigorously explain themselves to Berlin. The Germans lost 13 dead and many wounded. After leaving this area at the beginning of February 1945, the 35th SS Battalion fought near Kołobrzeg [Kolberg] and Berlin. The survivors surrendered to the Americans in May 1945. Released from captivity in 1946, many left for new lives in the USA and Canada.[31]

In February 1945 the Red Army captured Konitz after heavy fighting in which 800 men were killed and the town was extensively damaged. On 21 March Gryf Pomorski

31 Information boards at Wielkie Chelmy, translated. There are issues about the reliability of the information at this site, which has been considered by several historical researchers with insight into the Latvian Legion. The 35th was a German rather than Latvian unit, so the soldiers would be unlikely to go to live in the USA or Canada. The Latvians of the 15th did surrender to the Americans and many did go to live there after the war: it's possible the writer has confused the two units. One photograph at the site shows a group of Latvian soldiers from the 19th Division in front of the palace: the 19th were not in Pomerania. One possibility is that the photograph on the information board is a composite. Rytel District Council did not respond to requests for further information about its sources.

was dissolved and its weapons surrendered to the Soviets. However, some leaders were executed and others sent to the gulag.[32]

A series of photographs gathered by collector Irack Litbarski gives an extraordinary and poignant insight into the world of the RAD teenagers in Pomerania. This selection of six images shows an RAD troop at a base in Schivelbein – captured by the Soviets in March 1945 – and at Groß Tychow [Tychowo], 20 kilometres south-east of Belgard, which was also home to the notorious prisoner of war camp Stalag Luft IV.

The RAD unit presents arms.

---

32 Tenhumburg family website at <http://www.tenhumbergreinhard.de/1933-1945-lager-1/1933-1945-lager-b/bruss-Sophienwaldee-brusy-dziemiany.html>, (accessed 10 November 2021. Having resisted the German invasion of September 1939 valiantly, in the absence of any support from the Western Allies, and having killed or wounded 50,000 Wehrmacht troops in doing so, Poland 'ceased to exist' as Soviet Foreign Commissar Molotov put it when the Soviets moved in on 17 September, and was divided between Hitler and Stalin. An agreement in the German-Soviet Treaty of Friendship signed on 28 September 1939 allowed their security services – the Gestapo and NKVD – 'to take joint action against the expected Polish Resistance'. The NKVD moved in, filtering out professionals or state employees and deporting them to Gulags in Arctic Russia, Siberia or Kazakhstan: two million people in all. Half were dead within a year of their arrest. (Davies, *Heart of Europe*, pp.56–58.)

RAD recruits march in full equipment from Schivelbein.

RAD troops take part in a funeral march at Lauenburg [Lębork].

An RAD guard of honour for a dead comrade, at Lauenburg station.

Basic military training with rifles, Gross Tychow.

The changing of the camp guard.[33]

33 All pictures used with permission of Irack Libarski. See more at: <https://www.flickr.com/
photos/94791180@N06/albums/72157683659953494>.

4

Inside KZ Stutthof

I drive south-east from Gdańsk for about an hour to the holiday town of Krynica Morska on the Vistula Spit, a sandbar linking West Prussia along the Frisches Haff lagoon to what was once Königsberg, the capital of East Prussia, and the port of Pillau.

It is a beautiful place to spend a sunny summer weekend and a good starting point for my journey west in the footsteps of the Legionnaires, but the contrast between now and 1945 couldn't be more polarised. Then, this picturesque strip of sand, bars and pizza joints was the scene of unimaginable suffering, terror and death for hundreds of thousands of people in blizzard conditions: just like more or less everywhere both east and west of here.

The Spit is a popular holiday destination for Poles, and Krynica Morska is its main town. The one road along it is choked with traffic. I stay in a pleasant hotel bearing the town's German name: Kahlberg. It's truly a lovely setting. There are endless sandy beaches for children to play on and ice cream shops, restaurants, supermarkets and stalls selling buckets and spades – everything needed to keep a family fed and happy on holiday – plus the chance to snatch romantic moments watching the sun set or admire the lights twinkling at night. At the far end of Polish territory a red lighthouse warns shipping of the presence of the Spit, and this serves as a natural destination for those wanting to stretch their legs away from the hustle and bustle of the stalls selling inflatable rings, soft toys, plastic AK-47s and holiday tat.

I am one of those people. As I walk up to the lighthouse I find a small Second World War remembrance garden next to it. It's not a big garden and something about it feels a little compressed. That's because this is a place of lost souls. A lot has been fitted in here: inside the boundary hedges stands a statue of a Soviet soldier, PPsh submachine gun slung across his chest, amid other memorials and plaques. Perhaps what explains the strangely claustrophobic atmosphere is that this garden is a graveyard too. There are 240 Soviet soldiers buried here, in 42 mass graves in the space of 300 square metres. Of those 240, only 39 could be identified. The fallen soldiers were exhumed from burial sites around Krynica Morska and re-buried here in a six-year operation from 1945 to 1951. The words chiselled in stone into the base of the figure read:

Praise to the heroes of the Soviet Army

A statue to 240 Soviet soldiers who fell in operations around Kahlberg, now Krynica Morska, buried in 42 mass graves in the Garden of Remembrance at the lighthouse. (Picture: author, August 2018)

The advance west by the Red Army from late 1944 generated understandable anxiety in the population of East Prussia. Reports of atrocities by Red Army soldiers at Nemmersdorf in October 1944 spread rapidly: this was just 120 kilometres east of Königsberg. The stories were of unspeakable crimes: sexual violence, mutilation and cold-blooded, sadistic murder. East Prussia emptied in panic as civilians ran rather than risk falling into the hands of an army whose soldiers would do such things.

What happened at Nemmersdorf has been controversial ever since, as the number of dead reported – 72 men, women and children killed in horrible ways – has never been substantiated. Testimony from soldiers arriving in the town is of much lower numbers, although the savagery is unquestionable. German newspaper reports on 28 October 1944 gave the number of dead as 26, and made no mention of naked women nailed to barn doors. Historian Peter Clark quotes research by Bernard Fisch from 1997 which put the dead at nineteen locals and between four and ten people who were passing through Nemmersdorf.[1] The contemporary reports, whether deliberately inflated for propaganda reasons or naturally exaggerated from the telling, served to terrify East Prussians.

The drama of the moment was amplified because everyone had known for a long time that a Red Army attack into Germany across the Vistula was coming, but Nazi Gauleiters like Erich Koch, the Mayor of Königsberg, would not evacuate their towns until catastrophe was upon them. Only days before the attack, thousands of civilians fled. Peter Clark writes in *The Death of East Prussia*:

> Either as a result of spontaneous flight or organised evacuation roughly half a million people, or twenty percent of the population, had left East Prussia by the time of the final Russian offensive in January 1945. Another estimate puts the figure higher, at 650,000.[2]

Stalin wanted cold weather before launching his attack. He couldn't risk the thousands of tanks he planned to unleash against Hitler sinking in the swamps of Poland. When a heavy frost set in early January, Stalin named the second Friday – 12 January – for the start of the attack.

The Soviet supply machine clicked into action, as did Stalin's political educators. Tanks, artillery and aircraft parts sent to Stalin in vast numbers on Allied supply ships arrived from Vladivostok, Odessa and Murmansk. Troops were brought in from Mongolia and the Caucasus to strengthen the frontline infantry units. By night they were told of the cruelty, death and suffering of Leningrad, Kharkov and Stalingrad, atrocities carried out by the fascist imperialists they were about to attack.

The scale of the operation to cross the Vistula was vast. Around 200 Soviet divisions lined up for the move west along a front stretching 600 kilometres from north

---

1   P. Clark, *The Death of East Prussia: War and Revenge in Germany's Easternmost Province* (Chevy Chase, MD: Andover Press, 2013), p.100.
2   Clark, *The Death of East Prussia,* p.102, quoting Scheidler *Dokumentation der Vertreibung,* vol 1, part 1, pp.12–13 and Meindl, *Ostpreussens Gauleiter,* pp.434–35.

to south. Facing them were 70 German divisions. The Red Army had overwhelming superiority in numbers: Soviet infantry outnumbered the Nazis eleven to one, they had seven times as many tanks and twenty times the number of artillery guns.[3]

On 12 January intense artillery barrages softened up German defences before a ferocious Red Army assault began, supported by ground attack aircraft and bombers. Tanks rolled towards Nazi lines laden with infantrymen. The ten thousand anti-tank ditches, six metres deep and seven metres wide, dug by forced labourers in the past year – which stretched from Königsberg through the Masurian Plains, Elbing, Marienburg and from the Frisches Haff lagoon south to Toruń – did not slow them down.[4]

Defying orders to remain in the towns, civilians took to the roads to try and outrun the Red Army. Lorries and heavy wagons carried women, children and the elderly along roads not built for this scale of traffic. Some refugee convoys were caught in the fighting as the Red Army tightened its noose from Königsberg south to Elbing along the Frisches Haff, a theatre of war known as the Heiligenbeil Cauldron. The port of Pillau, with a harbour that could take ocean liners, submarines, torpedo boats and minesweepers, offered a way out by sea, but the only other escape route was across the Frisches Haff lagoon; 70 kilometres long, 10 kilometres wide, frozen over and covered in snow.[5]

The stories of flight and tragedy along this route are painful to read. Long convoys of trucks and carts trundled down these icy roads and through choked towns, with Soviet fighters machine gunning and bombing the columns as the people fled. Horse breeders attempted to get their prized animals away amid chaos and carnage.[6]

The debris of war lay all around: abandoned wagons, baggage and dead horses; stacks of furniture, sewing machines, grandfather clocks, chests, boxes and even sacks of oats dumped at the roadside to lighten the loads. Across the ice, risking and often losing everything, hundreds of thousands of people abandoning East Prussia made their way across the frozen lagoon from 26 January to 4 March towards Elbing and Danzig in the hope of escape. Many were caught on the ice as Soviet fighter planes attacked: countless numbers were killed in a hail of bullets or drowned as the ice gave way.[7]

To make matters worse, German units began running short of ammunition within days of the start of the Soviet attack. Entire units were encircled in rapid advances by Soviet tanks. In blizzard conditions, the German Fourth Army fell back west to find the Soviet 48th Army ahead of them. The Red Army's rapid pincer movement in late January had cut off East Prussia from the rest of Germany.

3   Clark, *The Death of East Prussia,* p.103.
4   Egbert Kieser, *Prussian Apocalypse – the Fall of Danzig 1945.* Trans. Tony Le Tissier. (Barnsley: Pen and Sword Military, 2011). Originally published in German as *Danziger Bucht 1945. Dokumentation einer Katastrophe* (1978), pp.3–5.
5   Kieser, *Prussian Apocalypse,* p.56.
6   See Patricia Clough's *The Flight Across the Ice* for further details of the fate of the Trakehner horses.
7   Kieser, *Prussian Apocalypse,* pp.64–67.

The Germans broke through and joined up with the 7th Panzer Division to fight a rearguard action against the 2nd Belorussian Front at Elbing, a town founded by the Teutonic Order in 1237. After three weeks of fierce fighting, the Soviets took the town on 10 February and then set it alight: the fires destroyed 65 percent of the town and all of the medieval Old Town. Elbing lay in ruins with its population of 100,000 long gone.[8]

Cut off in the Heiligenbeil Cauldron, a rump of coastal territory 50 kilometres wide and defended by 15 divisions of the Fourth Army, the German troops kept the lifelines open for refugees on the Frisches Haff for two months. Destruction and desperation was everywhere. Vast numbers of refugees and wounded soldiers and the columns of concentration camp inmates and prisoners of war being marched west merely added to the already considerable depths of human misery.

With Königsberg surrounded and besieged, an intense military operation against the Germans stepped up in mid-March, which would leave 93,000 dead and 46,448 as prisoners in a period from 13–28 March, together with vast amounts of tanks, field guns and aircraft lost.[9]

Königsberg held out until late April, amid terrible scenes of death, destruction and hunger. There were reports of hamburgers made from human flesh being sold on the black market in the late winter. When doctors verified the reports, police began to investigate accounts of women and children being lured into ruined buildings and murdered for their flesh.[10]

Leaving the Spit on a weekend is much easier than visiting it. Traffic is queueing on the one road into Krynica Morska from soon after breakfast, while it takes me only a few minutes to reach Sztutowo, once Stutthof, a few kilometres in the opposite direction. The dark, ominous gates of the Stutthof camp, one of the first of the Nazi concentration camps, stand in sharp contrast to the candy floss, pizza and beer I left behind so recently.

I am here because Stutthof was a camp that many Latvian civilians and soldiers passed through during the war in one capacity or another: most as prisoners, some as guards; as participants in the brutal 'death marches' when the camps were cleared ahead of the Soviet advance. The veteran Latvian journalist Frank Gordon likened one account from Stutthof to experiences at Auschwitz, and what happened here had a significant bearing on Latvian history.

One of the prisoners held at Stutthof was Konstantīns Čakste, son of the first President of Latvia, Jānis Čakste. As chairman of the Latvian 'underground government' – the Latvian Central Council, or LCP – Čakste was part of the intellectual resistance to Nazi rule during the Second World War, but was arrested by the Gestapo in 1944 for signing a letter calling for Latvia to have an autonomous government in

---

8   Clark, *The Death of East Prussia*, p.131; destruction figures from <https://www.triposo.com/loc/ElblC485g/history/background>.
9   Duffy, *Red Storm on the Reich*, p.206.
10 Clark, pp.337–338. Peter Clark's *The Death of East Prussia* and Christopher Duffy's *Red Storm on the Reich* give detailed accounts of this grim chapter.

The gates at the Nazi concentration camp KZ Stutthof near Danzig, where new arrivals were whipped. (Picture: author)

the occupation. In September 1944 Čakste and other leaders of the LCP were transferred to Stutthof.

In the summer of 1943 Čakste, as head of the LCP, had asked Vilis Janums through his old friend Captain Kristaps Upelnieks to draw up a list of weapons to arm the nationalist military group led by General Jānis Kurelis – the *Kurelieši* – which the Nazis had intended to use against the advancing Russians. This was the first step towards a rebel military force to turn on the Germans and seize stretches of the Kurzeme coastline ahead of a British intervention. Upelnieks was Kurelis' second-in-command. The list of arms was smuggled to Sweden. The weapons shipment was to be arranged by the Latvian ambassador in Sweden, Voldemārs Salnais.[11]

Salnais and the Latvian Consul General in London, Kārlis Zariņš, had developed good working relations with the MI6 station in Stockholm run by Harry Carr, and through it, to London.[12] The LCP had encouraged resistance against the Nazi occupiers, established channels of communication through diplomatic bags to London, and prepared for a military uprising by joining forces with General Kurelis and his men. But with the Red Army approaching, the Germans moved quickly when the LCP publicly announced a new independent Latvian state on 9 September 1944.

Their camp was surrounded and Kurelis was arrested. His 1,360 men were disarmed and a group sent to Stutthof camp. General Kurelis was transferred to Latvian HQ in Danzig. The original go-between, Upelnieks, was one of eight officers taken to Liepāja's Karosta prison, court-martialled and shot.[13] One of three officers pardoned, Lieutenant Colonel Eduard Graudiņš, was sent to Stuffthof, but died in the death march of February 1945.[14]

The go-between for the Latvians with the Swedish was Leonīds Siliņš, one of the senior figures in the LCP during the war. He gathered the original German documents from Stutthof relating to the *Kurelieši* for his 2003 book *Latvians in the Stutthof Concentration Camp 1942–45.*

The orders from the time reveal that the *Kurelieši* numbered about 1,000 men living in forest camps and villages in Kurzeme. A large number of deserters from the Latvian Legion were discovered in the round-up, as well as former members of Latvian police units, Estonian and Latvian aircrew and Russian and Dutch prisoners.

Legion regimental commander Colonel Janums visited Stutthof in November 1944 to have talks with the *Kurelieši*. The Colonel was accompanied by a German deputy commandant while he was in the camp and was not allowed a general meeting with the Latvian prisoners. One of the inmates at the camp, Bruno Kalniņš, an established political leader and democracy campaigner, described the meeting to Janums'

11 J. Leitītis, *Pulkvedis Vilis Janums. Raksti, Stāsti un Atmiņas*, trans. Aivars Sinka (Toronto: Daugavas Vanagi Central Committee, 1986), p.51–52.
12 G. Swain, (2009) *Latvia's Democratic Resistance: a Forgotten Episode From the Second World War,* European History Quarterly, 39 (2), pp. 241–263.
13 G. Swain, *Latvia's Democratic Resistance,* pp. 241–263 (2009). Kurelis died in Chicago, USA, in 1954.
14 Military Heritage Tourism webpages, online at <https://militaryheritagetourism.info/en/military/stories/view/261?1>.

biographer Jēkabs Leitītis in correspondence forty years afterwards. The men agreed that LCP [Latvian Central Committee] chairman Konstantīns Čakste would represent them. Kalniņš wrote of the meeting:

> We had a very positive impression about this visit because it meant we hadn't been forgotten. Janums had asked for us to be set free. I should add that Janums collaborated with the LCP and was our military advisor. Neither Colonel Silgailis nor Miezis visited us.[15]

Four days later, an order from Stutthof camp commandant SS-Obersturmbannführer Paul-Werner Hoppe noted:

> Some of the Kurels are not deserters at all, but joined General Kurelis in the belief he would fight against Bolshevism. They must be forwarded to Konitz for inclusion in the 15th Latvian SS Division. (It has already happened; these men are no longer here at Stutthof).

Hoppe wrote that 356 Latvians and Estonians were sent to the SS camp at Mackowy near Danzig, plus a further nine who were held by the Liepāja *Einsatzkommando*, who could not be housed at Stutthof. A second order the same day was marked 'Urgent' and addressed to Fritz Katzmann, then a Waffen-SS Major General in charge of the Danzig area and responsible for the liquidation of the Stutthof camp and its 105 sub-camps.

Hoppe warned Katzmann that there may be up to 3,000 Latvians and Estonians coming from Ventspils in Latvia to Mackowy from that region in the near future.[16] The 331 *Kurelieši* from Stutthof along with Estonian and Latvian police and air force personnel were sent to the SS collection point at Hemitz where 244 were assigned to the 15th Division or an Estonian Legion unit and 87 went into labour battalions.[17] Another thirty-four men shipped to Stutthof at the same time were not freed and

15 Bruno Kalniņš correspondence with Jēkabs Leitītis, in *Pulkvedis Vilis Janums. Raksi, Stāsti un Atmiņas [Colonel Vilis Janums. Writing, Stories and Memories]* 'Miezis' is probably Jānis Miezis, a civil servant in the Latvian Self Administration based in Berlin. Stutthof had held 454 men from the round-up of *Kurelieši*, but 89 had already been transferred to the Legion.

16 Telegram 1775 from Hoppe to Katzmann, dated 20 November 1944 in Siliņš, *Latvians in the Stutthof Concentration Camp* (2003). Katzmann was one of the most brutal and callous of the senior Nazis, responsible for genocide in Wroclaw, Katowice, Lwow, Danzig and in Operation Reinhard in Galicia. The Katzmann Report detailing the extermination of around 430,000 Jews in Galicia was one of the most significant documents of the Holocaust and was used as evidence at the Nuremberg Trials. He oversaw the installation of the gas chambers at Stutthof and then closed down the camp system as the Russians approached. He disappeared at the war's end and lived in Darmstadt under a false identity until his death in 1957.

17 Siliņš, *Latvians in the Stutthof Concentration Camp*, p.121, quoting security police orders 16.11.1944. Online at <http://www.periodika.lv/periodika2-viewer/view/index-dev.html?panel:pp|issue:/g_001_0303029454|article:DIVL515|page:121|block:P121_TB00002|issueType:undefined>, accessed 30 October 2020.

were sent to work camps: they were considered politically untrustworthy, deserters from special assignment battalions or members of the Communist partisan group *Sarkanā Bulta* [*Red Arrow*] caught in the Nazi round-up.[18]

The idea of using Stutthof as a holding centre for enemies of the Nazis was being planned three years before the war started in September 1939. Within hours of the invasion, Polish opponents of the Nazis were transported here. At first Stutthof was used for imprisoning and eliminating Polish civilians, mostly anti-Nazi intellectuals, then in 1941 it became a 'labour education' camp and in January 1942 a concentration camp: *Konzentrationslager [KZ] Stutthof.*

The largest group among Stutthof's 110,000 prisoners were Jews but men, women and children from 28 countries were held and died here: Lithuanians, Latvians, Russians, Hungarians, French, Germans. Of those, 65,000 died through overwork, disease, malnutrition, bad treatment and abuse; around half were Jewish. Stutthof was at the centre of a 39-camp system including Potulice, Toruń and Bydgoszcz in which 57,056 people were held prisoner as of 5 November 1944.[19]

One Jewish prisoner at Stutthof, Edith Suefert, had been transported by train from Stuttgart to the Rīga Ghetto as the killing of Jews *en masse* began in Latvia. From Stutthof she was moved to Toruń before being marched west ahead of the Red Army offensive in January 1945. Liberated by the Russians, she later made a statement about her wartime experiences which was among the evidence collected for the trial of the Latvian Nazi collaborator Viktors Arājs, whose Arājs Kommando assisted the mass killing of Jews. Amid her positive identification of Rudolph Seck and Maximilian Gymnich she reveals the cruelty shown by the Nazis towards their captives.

In October 1944 I came to Stutthof. We were transported by boat. At least three persons died from hunger on the way. We were 3,000 persons (together with Kaiserwald)[20] in the lowest hold of the ship. The transport was the worst that I have experienced. Nearly no water, we were not allowed to go on the decks and I only received one kilogram of bread during six days and no other food besides it.

In Stutthof we were guarded by habitual criminals … Daily I was beaten with a whip by SS supervising women. I do not know the names of any of the female supervisors. They were SS women and Polish female prisoners. I do not know any more the name of the camp commandant. I further recall a Scharführer [squad leader] with red hair who was particularly brutal. I do not know his name. We were fenced in by live electrified barbed wire. Daily at least three to four women ran into the wire in order to commit suicide. Frequently we had to parade for roll call, standing for ten hours with half a portion of food.

From Stutthof I went to a camp near Thorn [Toruń]. We were accommodated in tents. I do not know any names of this camp. Up to 15 women died there per

---

18 Silgailis, *Latvian Legion*, p.233; Leitītis, *Pulkvedis Vilis Janums*, p.51, trans. Aivars Sinka.

19 Stutthof Museum website at <http://stutthof.org/historia/>.

20 A concentration camp in Rīga used from 1943 to hold Jewish prisoners from across Latvia, from the Vilna Ghetto [Vilnius] and later from Hungary and Łódź in Poland.

day. I was there till early or middle of January 1945. Then we had to march to Korowna [Krone] owing to the Russian advance. 250 sick women were shot by the SS (Lithuanian SS) in the camp. We went to the penitentiary at Korowna and were liberated on the next day by the Russians.

I still have to add the following.

I have seen at Stutthof how naked women only wrapped in a blanket were led into the gas chamber.

There was a typhoid epidemic at Jungfernhof in 1941 and 1942. I myself was afflicted three times with para-typhus.[21]

I have seen at Stutthof that SECK administered 25 blows on the naked buttocks [of] prisoners with a truncheon.[22]

What remains today at Stutthof are the boundaries of the 120-hectare site, the administration buildings, one or two huts where prisoners were kept, the gas chamber, the gallows and a series of information boards bearing witness to what happened here. There's a vast field where the barracks for prisoners were: for Jewish women, Aryan women, sick prisoners, 'superior' German prisoners – sickeningly efficient, clear cut and separated.

A plan of the camp extension after 1943 – the New Camp – makes for chilling viewing. Surrounded by barbed wire and high voltage electric fencing and overlooked by guards in watchtowers, there were 40 blocks for prisoners of various categories: 'functional' prisoners, superior German and Polish prisoners, Danish and Lithuanians, as well as Aryan and Jewish women. Outside the Danish block was a gallows. Quarantine blocks were used to house Jewish prisoners after June 1944, and prisoners in the last stages of life were separated out.

21 Jungfernhof was an overflow concentration camp for Jews from Germany and Austria at Mazjumprava Manor near Šķirotava railway station, three to four kilometres east of Rīga, which operated between December 1941 and March 1942. Trainloads of Jews from Württemberg, Hamburg, Lübeck, Nuremberg and Vienna were murdered after being sent to Jungfernhof: only 148 people survived of around 4,000 making the journey. A mass grave containing the bodies of 800 Jews who died of typhus, malnutrition or were executed was discovered in summer 2021. A memorial is due to be unveiled in 2024.
22 Staff sergeant [Oberscharführer] Rudolf Seck (1908–1974) was the commandant at Jungfernhof camp near Rīga in Latvia. A close associate of the main SS chief in Latvia, Rudolf Lange, Seck oversaw the shooting of trainloads of Jews from Europe at Biķernieki and Rumbula in 1941 and 1942. Survivors later testified that Seck, who kept an office at Gestapo headquarters in Raiņa Bulvāris in Rīga, was known to visit the Gestapo clothing depot at Peterholm Street to help himself to the jewellery and belongings of murdered Jews. Seck would have been evacuated with the surviving Jungfernhof prisoners shipped to Stutthof. He was convicted of crimes against humanity in Latvia by a West German court and sentenced to life in prison. Maximilian Gymnich was a brutal Gestapo adjutant and driver for the Rīga ghetto commandant Kurt Krause, who punished the slightest contravention during inspections with 'brutal beatings, hangings and shooting'. He committed suicide while in British custody in May 1948. Statement of Edith Suefert in British military archive files relating to Viktors Arājs, held at the Public Records Office, Kew, London. Accessed September 2021.

There were workshops for repairing weapons, for tailoring and metalwork, shoe-making, dressmaking and saddling. There was a furrier and an area for growing vegetables and flowers. The vegetables fed the SS guards in the camp, and the flowers were sold in Danzig and surrounding villages. There were production halls where 120 inmates made parts for Focke Wulf aircraft, specifically the Ta-152 fighter. In another hall, 100 inmates made components for submarine production.

The Ta-152, a high-altitude variant of the Focke Wulf 190, was pressed into service from January 1945 from various bases, including Mecklenburg in Germany. Lack of quality control and a shortage of spare parts meant the plane was unreliable and came too late in the war to be effective. However, the seven kills registered by Ta-152s in the short amount of combat time the plane did get suggest it was more than a match for the Allied Mustangs, Thunderbolts and Tempests. A recurring theme in the closing stages of the war was the hampering of new Nazi aircraft by a lack of proper testing and shortages of parts.[23]

New arrivals at Stutthof were given a special 'welcome' at the main gate with its watchtower above – a whipping. They then spent two to four weeks learning the rules of the camp, marching in rows of five, lining up and conducting roll calls, learning their numbers and recognising commands in German. After this they were allocated to work teams. Anyone who broke camp regulations by smuggling food, smoking at work or trying to escape was dumped in one of six 'bunkers' in a barracks hut. These were tiny rooms, some without windows, where inmates were given just bread and water. Any prisoners who died were taken to the morgue by special collection teams – the *Totenkommando* – where gold teeth were removed and the body disposed of.

Stutthof's displays focus on the human belongings that made the Nazi extermination policy so personal: in one room there is a collection of shoes worn by the people murdered here. The shoes form a small, sad pile in front of a large photograph on the back wall showing a huge mound of similar shoes. There is a soldier pictured by the mountain of shoes: it stands taller than he is. Nazi doctors also conducted medical experiments here on prisoners.[24]

One of the most notorious chapters of Nazi activity surrounds claims that the bodies of prisoners who died at Stutthof were used by Dr Rudolf Spanner at the Gdańsk Medical Institute to produce soap. This episode was described in 2006 as 'one of the darkest pages in the Second World War' by Witold Kulesza, the director of the Main Commission for the Investigation of Crimes against the Polish Nation.[25]

23 Jeff Ethell, *Ta 152 – Monogram Closeup 24* (Sturbridge, Massachusetts: Monogram Aviation Publications, 1990), pp.33–34. The National Air and Space Museum in the United States has the only remaining example of a Ta-152, which is being restored in workshops in Maryland. More details at <https://airandspace.si.edu/collection-objects/focke-wulf-ta-152-h-0-r11/nasm_A19600317000>.
24 Information boards and camp visit, Stutthof camp. Author's visit August 2018.
25 Auschwitz-Birkenau Museum webpages at <http://auschwitz.org/en/museum/news/human-fat-was-used-to-produce-soap-in-Gdańsk-during-the-war,55.html>.

Historians at the IPN, Poland's National Remembrance Institute, spent four years looking into Spanner's activities and decided it was true: the soap Spanner produced was used to wash autopsy rooms and dissection tables.

> Witnesses testified that it had an unpleasant smell. This led to almond oil being added to it. The investigation found that Spanner's personnel produced somewhere between 10 and 100 kilograms of soap from corpses. Investigators tracked down some of the soap produced by Spanner. Samples had been used as evidence of Nazi war crimes between November 1945 and October 1946, during the Nuremberg trials. A jar containing the soap is stored, along with the rest of the Nuremberg trial documentation, in the archive of the International Court of Justice in The Hague.[26]

Railway wagons at KZ Stutthof were converted to mobile gas chambers to kill sick Jewish women. (Picture: author)

The far end of the camp is particularly sombre. There is a small brick gas chamber, a gallows and a crematorium. Prisoners could be executed here out of public view and their bodies burned in the crematorium next door. The three ovens used are still here. The memorial boards tell of sick Jewish women being shot in the head here, burned in the ovens and their ashes dumped in a pit nearby. Among the exhibits is a canister of Zyklon-B, the gas used in the chambers opposite. It's a desperately sad scene in a

---

26 Auschwitz-Birkenau Museum webpage at <https://www.auschwitz.org/en/>. Interrogated after the war, Spanner denied using bodies from Stutthof and said the soap made from human fat was only used to inject into ligaments. He escaped punishment and worked later as a physician in Schleswig-Holstein. He died in Cologne in 1960.

place of such cruelty: there is a designated 'beating place' and on the far side beyond the Jewish camp, a pyre for burning corpses.

There are also some railway wagons. One of these was a mobile gas chamber, which would be loaded with sick and elderly Jewish women. A cylinder of Zyklon-B would be dropped inside. The train would travel for one or two stations down the narrow gauge railway and then return to unload its cargo of dead directly into the crematorium.[27]

The Red Army advance in January 1945 prompted the wholesale evacuation of concentration camp populations west, and the force-marching of thousands of sick, weak and ill-treated prisoners turned into a disaster. The commandant at Stutthof, Paul-Werner Hoppe, had drawn up detailed orders for the evacuation and management of the 69,000 prisoners there and from nearby sub-camps. He issued a map showing the route the columns should follow; first west to the town of Nickelswalde, then to Lauenburg. He specified the order of march, the times the column left Stutthof and the numbers of guards with them. He gave specific instructions for the bodies of prisoners who died along the way to be buried in one place.

Prisoners were issued with 500 grams of bread and 120 grams of margarine, but none had clothing to protect against the bitter winter conditions: many were barefoot. Exhausted from forced labour and weakened by years of poor diets, some prisoners didn't get the chance to set foot outside the sub-camps, succumbing to the harsh weather before the day of the evacuation. Others were shot, or killed by lethal injections of kerosene, strychnine or Lysol, a disinfectant.

Konstantīns Čakste was among the prisoners who left Stutthof on 25 January 1945 for holding camps at Kramp [now Krępa Kaszubska], Gans [Gęś], Dombrowa [Dąbrówka], Goddentow [Godętowo], Lanz [Łęczyce] and Gross Boschpol [Bożepole]. There were thousands of prisoners, POWs and military personnel on the move in blizzard conditions.

Čakste died in Gęś on 21 February 1945. He was buried there the next day in an individual grave. After the liberation of Poland in March 1945, the prisoners who died in these camps were exhumed and brought to Krępa Kaszubska where they were re-buried. There are nearly 800 former Stutthof prisoners from many nations in this cemetery: Čakste's body is believed to have been re-buried at Krępa in 1951, and he is commemorated there.[28]

The Lithuanian poet and dramatist Balys Sruoga had been arrested by the Nazis as a political hostage and was a prisoner for six years at Stutthof. He was with Čakste when the march reached the village of Gęś, about 12 kilometres south of the coast at Łeba, where the prisoners set up camp in a former RAD barracks. Sruoga wrote:

27 Information boards at Stutthof camp, author's visit, August 2018.
28 Correspondence with Dr. Marcin Owsiński of Muzeum Stutthof w Sztutowie, 15 July 2019.

The camp itself was small and shabby, nestled against a good-size hill and bordered on the other side by a huge impassable swamp. The barracks were seedy and [as] squalid as rabbit hutches – or no, too mangy even for that. At the beginning of this journey there had been 1,600 men in our column; barely half remained. Some had been scattered along the way, others were shot.[29]

Already half-starved, the prisoners lived on scraps of horsemeat and watery soup, and epidemics start to spread. SS men were sent out to find farmers willing to sell them food – the prisoners were the last in line. Sruoga noticed a strange habit among the Latvians, who declared that they would die 'in three days' if they developed a temperature of 38.2C (100F) – and then did. This happened to Čakste. Sruoga wrote:

> Towards evening he's begun to make good on his promise. From time to time he loses consciousness, comes to and passes out again. When he's awake, he's telling his friends his last will and testament. And again he faints away. He eats nothing, understands no-one. During the night he's hallucinating. The next day and the following night, he's in the throes of some strange convulsions. His face is twisted. His hands trace circles in the air. His feet pedal as if he were riding a bike. He doesn't regain consciousness … And then what? Exactly three days after this promise, Konstantīns died – of some strange, unknown, unintelligible disease.[30]

Sruoga and his fellow prisoners knew who Čakste was, so they set up a wake, which was also attended by Latvian SS guards with them, then buried him. But the German in charge of the march column demanded that Čakste be dug up again in case he had been buried with his gold teeth. Shortly afterwards, the Russians caught up with the march, the SS scattered, and the prisoners were rescued.[31]

The prisoner columns which had left towns such as Thorn, Marienburg, Elbing, Graudenz and Kulmsee to save themselves from death or captivity at the hands of the Red Army moved on to Rieben and Putzig, then south along the coast to Gotenhafen, where they could get out by sea.[32] Thousands did: 7,000 from sub-camps in Gotenhafen on 25 March; 3,300 from Stutthof on 25 April; another 1,060

29 B. Sruoga, *Forest of the Gods* [English edition] (Vilnius: Vaga, 1996), p.305.
30 Sruoga, *Forest of the Gods*, p.313.
31 Sruoga's nightmare did not end then. He was arrested and interrogated at the Russian screening camp in Toruń until pressure from Lithuania's writers had him returned to his country, where he wrote *Forest of the Gods* in several months before dying in 1947 aged 51. The censors would not allow publication of the memoir until 1957. The English edition was published in 1996, translated by his grand-daughter Aušrinė Byla. It is a very good read, and highly recommended.
32 In modern Poland: Toruń, Malbork, Elbląg, Grudziadz, Chelmza, Rybno, Puck, Gdynia.

two days later. But thousands also died along the way from fatigue, hunger or diseases picked up in the camps, as well as many who were shot by their SS escorts.[33]

While the death marches are a chapter of horror in their own right, one name – Palmnicken – stands out in this history of savage and unspeakable behaviour. Thousands of prisoners had been evacuated from camps east of Stutthof as the Soviets advanced, with Königsberg as their destination. The city was already surrounded and besieged so a group of around 5,000 women were diverted to Palmnicken (now Yantarny), a town on the coast. Escorting them were 30 SS men with 120 other guards, including Ukrainians, Latvians, Lithuanians and Estonians, as well as men from the labour battalion Organisation Todt.[34]

Only around 2,500 to 3,000 women arrived. They were weak, hungry and close to collapse after not eating for days, dressed in rags in bitter winter conditions, marching and sometimes running in deep snow. The route they took was littered afterwards with the bodies of dead prisoners: around 1,500 died or were executed on paths through the forest and along the streets of towns in a gruesome final 24 hours. One of the guards on the march had the nickname 'The shot-in-the-neck Commissar'. On the final two kilometre stretch of road between Sorgenau and Palmnicken 300 bodies were found the next day.[35]

At Palmnicken the SS guards wanted to seal the survivors up in a mine but the local *Volkssturm* commander Hans Feyeraband, who had been an artillery officer in the First World War, refused to allow that. Palmnicken's Mayor Kurt Friedrichs was also the local Nazi Party boss. He responded by posting Feyeraband and his men to new positions out of town, prompting the veteran officer to shoot himself. In a series of massacres over several days between 31 January and 5 February, the guards marched women along the beach then machine gunned them, amid terrible scenes. Only around 200 of the 5,000 women who started the march survived. Some escaped

33 Information boards, Stutthof, author's visit. Translated. The survivors made it from Gdynia and Hel on the boats *Elbing* (25 to 29 March 1945) and *Zephyr* (25 March to 2 April 1945) to Hamburg, Kilonia and to the concentration camp at Neuengamme. The boats *Wolfgang* and *Vaterland* docked first at Stutthof, then the small coastal village of Nickelswalde [Mikoszewo] to the east of Gdańsk and then at the harbour on the peninsula at Hel on 25 April. They made it west to Sassnitz, Stralsund, Warnemunde and Neustadt by 3 May. The *Kwarantanna* arrived on 5 May at Eckenforde after calling at Stutthof, Nickelswalde and Hel on the same day, 25 April. Another boat loading that day – known to Polish historians as 'the fourth barge' – sailed to Lauterbach and Klintholm, arriving on 5 May 1945. The last boat from Stutthof, Nickelswalde and Hel was the *Ruth*, on 27 April, which set sail for Flensburg.

34 Blatman, *The Death Marches – the Final Phase of Nazi Genocide* (Cambridge, Massachusetts and London: The Belknap Press of Harvard University Press, 2011). (Originally published as *Les Marches de la Mort*, 2009), p.119.

35 Blatman, *The Death Marches*, p.120 and Kossert, 'Endlösung on the Amber Shore: The Massacre in January 1945 on the Baltic Seashore — A Repressed Chapter of East Prussian History', *The Leo Baeck Institute Year Book*, Volume 49, Issue 1 (Oxford: Oxford University Press, January 2004), pp.3–22.

along the way while others who survived the massacre on the beach were given shelter by local people.[36]

⟨⟨ — ⟨

The old road south lies almost directly opposite the main gate at Stutthof. A two-hour drive will take me to Toruń, with a short stop along the way for the impressive and dream-like medieval castle at Marienburg, now Malbork. It is an incredible sight: the largest brick-built castle in the world; a UNESCO world heritage site.

This seemingly impregnable medieval fortress was built by the Teutonic Order in the 13th Century to honour Mary, the mother of Jesus. The heads of the Nazi leaders span with desire when they saw it, and they used it for their annual camps indoctrinating the Hitler Youth.

In January 1945 Soviet generals brought the curtain down on that episode of history. The castle was badly damaged in the assault and repairs have taken decades. I visit on a sunny afternoon to find modern day Teutonic knights in costume willing to trade blows for a handful of zloty. The medieval theme continues with jars of ancient honey and mead offered for sale on the trestle tables lining the castle walls and tempting bottles of strong dark ale with recipes dating back centuries.

I carry a couple of bottles of ancient ale back to my car and drive through the town to find one of the vehicles involved in the Soviet campaign, identified on the military memorial website *Traces of War*. In front of a military training college, an ISU-122 self-propelled gun stands on a concrete plinth in a square. The plaque in front of it reads:

> *To the heroes of the Red Army on the 20th anniversary of the liberation of the residents of Malbork on March 17, 1965.*[37]

Driving south out of town there is a further reminder of the human cost of those times. I stop to walk around a small but neatly-maintained graveyard to the Soviet soldiers who fell here. A plaque by the gate records the names of the fallen, buried in mass graves. These small graveyards with their simple acknowledgment of the sacrifice of so many men will become familiar to me as I journey west across Pomerania.

Now I am heading for Toruń, Nakel, Kolberg – places every Legionnaire of the 15th Division knew. I feel that I need to see these towns to understand the wider context of this story properly.

---

36 Blatman, *The Death Marches*, p.124. Mayor Friedrichs escaped to the west on 15 April and was imprisoned by the British in Neuengamme a month later. He was released in October 1947 and granted a pension.

37 Author's visit, August 2018. Online at <https://www.tracesofwar.com/sights/28619/Liberation-Memorial-ISU-122-Self-Propelled-Gun-Malbork.htm>.

Malbork Castle, known in 1945 as Marienburg. (Picture: Gregy. CC BY-SA 3.0 pl, online at <https://commons.wikimedia.org/w/index.php?curid=21824061>)

An ISU–122 self-propelled gun used in the battles for Marienburg stands in front of a military academy in the town. (Picture: author)

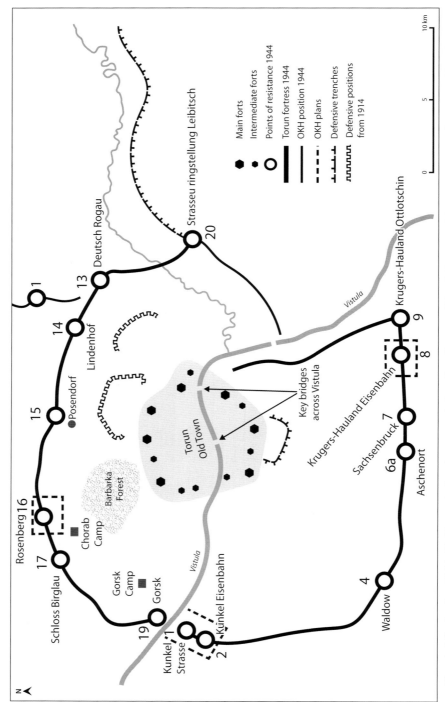

Toruń's defensive ring, 1944–45. Composite based on originals from 'Fortifications of Vistula Pomerania Toruń Fortress Fortifications 1944-45' by K. Tomczyk, W.Grabowski, Jakub Franczak, Tomasz Iwaszkiewicz, Tomasz Kowalski, Paweł Pilarski and Mariusz Wojciechowski, published by SGK Tomasz Kowalski, 1st edition, Grudziądz 2018 and 'Toruń Fortress, Map of Fortifications and Garrisons'. Ed: Jacek Biesiadka. Pracownia JB72 Jacek Biesiadka, 2017.

5

Toruń

The medieval walled city of Toruń in modern Poland is a lovely place. Considered one of the marvels of the Middle Ages, it was home most notably to the astronomer Nicolaus Copernicus and has a well-deserved reputation for producing delicious gingerbread. The centre has an easy-going feel punctuated by the passing of time announced by charming musical clocks, as tourists eat and drink at the many outdoor bars in the centre, surrounded by beautifully-preserved period buildings.[1]

Toruń hugs the contours of the western bank of the Vistula river tightly, essentially unchanged over eight centuries. The river is wide and impressive here, a natural barrier to foes. Tourists throng to stroll through its 13th century streets and admire the Gothic city walls, Old Town, impressive town hall and ruined castle. By the time I arrive in the late afternoon every parking place in the centre has gone so I park down by the river. There's a wide double-level promenade along the banks of the Vistula with food stalls, souvenir sellers and entertainers, and lots of boats offering pleasure trips: river cruisers, a small paddle steamer, a Viking longboat; even families chugging along in what look like small bathtubs with canopies and outboard motors.

Toruń city was founded in 1231 by the monks of the Teutonic Order as a stronghold to protect commercial Hanseatic League trading routes along the Baltic coast with western Europe and to defend the spread of Christianity across Eastern Europe. UNESCO World Heritage experts regard Toruń as offering 'an exceptionally complete picture of the medieval way of life' and consider the planning and construction of the town among 'the highest achievements in medieval ecclesiastical, military and civil brick-built architecture', ranking it alongside Krakow.[2]

These medieval streets have been witness to tumultuous and violent events. The city was conquered and occupied by the Swedish in the mid-17th century then annexed by Prussia at the close of the 18th century: Toruń was a garrison town for Napoleon on his way to Moscow and was later heavily fortified by the Prussians.

The city has always been closely connected with Polish identity, and with independence in 1920 Toruń became the administrative capital of Pomerania. It was an

1   Toruń is also known as Thorun, Thorn and to the Latvians, Torna.
2   UNESCO World Heritage Centre online: the medieval town of Toruń at <https://whc.unesco.org/en/list/835>.

Traffic crossing the frozen Vistula at Toruń after the bridge was cut in the German invasion of Poland. (Picture: Kurt Grimm, from the District Museum, Toruń. Website at <www.muzeum. Toruń .pl>. Ref: A.1762)

important military garrison, transport hub and centre of political and cultural life, but on 7 September 1939 the Nazis occupied the city. After just a matter of weeks the prisoner executions began in the Barbarka forest. The city's Jewish population was removed and 16,000 Germans re-settled in the region.

The leather-coated sadists of the Gestapo set up a base for their terror and torture in Chopin Street in the Old Town. Concentration camps opened in a prisoner-of-war complex based in fifteen forts around the city. From the earliest days of the war, British soldiers captured in Norway and in the fighting in France at St-Valery-en-Caux, Calais and Dunkirk in 1940 were transferred here. Among them was British officer and later politician Airey Neave, who was moved to Toruń in February 1941. He was transferred to the officers' camp at Colditz Castle after an escape attempt, and broke out of Colditz the following year.[3]

Other British officers to escape from Toruń were the Commando officer Tommy Macpherson, a Scot famous for his operations with the French Resistance, later knighted and awarded the Military Cross with two bars, and Battle of France and

3   Neave was the first British officer to escape from Colditz. In March 1979, while he was Shadow Northern Ireland secretary for Margaret Thatcher's forthcoming government, Neave was killed by a bomb attached to his car in the House of Commons underground car park by the paramilitary group the Irish National Liberation Army [INLA].

Toruń under German occupation, December 1943. (Picture: Kurt Grimm, courtesy of the District Museum in Toruń. Reference: A.1038)

Colditz DSO hero Group Captain Brian Paddon, who broke out of the cells at Stalag XX-A while being court-martialled.

Also held at Toruń briefly was Frank McLardy, a Liverpool-born fascist-supporting soldier who volunteered to fight for the Nazis and was part of the British Free Corps of SS volunteers.[4] After 1941 thousands of Soviet prisoners were moved to Toruń, with 33,000 prisoners of various nationalities held at Stalag XX-B in nearby Marienburg. American POWs, Australians, Canadians, New Zealanders and South Africans were spread across camps in Eastern Europe and the East Prussia region as the war progressed.[5]

Toruń became strategically important towards the end of 1944 as Germany prepared its defences against a Soviet offensive across the Vistula. Thousands of prisoners were forced to dig anti-tank ditches. Latvians were rounded up on the streets of Rīga and sent there to do that, as were newly-drafted teenagers without the equipment or training to be much use in the frontline as soldiers. Among the draftees was Augusts Spilners, sent from Danzig to the Field Replacement Depot in Toruń, where the construction regiments were digging anti-tank ditches.

> October 15: Stepped off the train at Posendorf station [now Łysomice], not far from Torna. Do not know how it will be. We see many civilians who are digging tank trenches. Some lads mention that we will have to do that. That is true. We are housed in plywood tents and there are no beds so we sleep on the ground, on straw.
>
> October 16: At the training site we hoped for weapons, but got spades. We have to dig trenches. Some lads dig hard, but I look at this work with the utmost indifference. I did not come here to dig fortifications; I came to prepare to defend the homeland, but that cannot happen – so I will make the best of it. Lunch is brought to work: a litre of thin soup. Evening. Half a kilo of bread is issued, with a few grams of margarine. I think the food will be bad. In the following days the boys are wandering around looking for potatoes in the fields. In the morning we go to Possendorf. Every day we go to work. We work until four in the afternoon. Gradually camp life becomes routine. At the barracks more Latvian conscripts arrive.
>
> The days go by, and on 28 October we have to go to Posendorf station. We will be taken to a new place of work. The trench work is going at a fast rate, although we Latvians make very little progress. This work does not interest us, and we did not come here to do it. However we believe it will fill our time. On the front situation we do not know anything because we do not receive any newspapers. We are fully isolated from the outside world, and we are not free to leave.

4   More details about Frank McLardy can be found at <https://www.liverpoolecho.co.uk/news/local-news/waterloo-born-traitor-who-fought-6958022>.
5   There is now a memorial to those who were prisoners in the Marienburg camp in a corner of the Municipal Cemetery at Malbork [Cmentarz Komunalny w Malbork].

Latvian 15th Division 'Digger' camp, winter 1944. The men of the construction regiments were based in camps outside Toruń Old Town. Note the round tents. (Picture courtesy of the Latvian War Museum, Rīga. LKM 5-14383-1580-FT)

The grim reality of the approaching war could not be ignored, as Augusts Spilners notes in his diary for December 1944.

December 18: Today we carry the wounded from the hospital train to other transport because the front is approaching. Wave after wave of wounded comes in. It is an unpleasant sight. Many arms and legs are just bloody rags. How sad for these people. What life will they have without arms and legs and how many people will be unhappy? But their faces are the hope of life, and the main thing is they are left with life.

December 21: Going to work in the trenches. The weather is cold and the ground is frozen, so we have to work with pickaxes. The work is not producing anything. So as not to freeze we make bonfires. We have to work until 13:00. When we get home it is already 15:00. We eat soup and some lads buy one kilogram of bread for 25 marks. In the evening we go to bed early. It is cold.

December 24: Christmas Eve. Today we come home from work early. Washed and shaved. In the evening we go to Torna church where the Latvian soldiers have a service around the Christmas tree. Peace on earth and goodwill towards men. Candles shine on the branches of the green tree. The pastor makes a touching speech, and there are tears in everyone's eyes. Peace, but there is no peace on earth yet. Death follows thousands of people. It is a land of exile and wandering folk.

Men of the 1st Rīga Police Regiment (1st Construction Regiment, 15th Division) digging anti-tank ditches several metres wide as part of the Toruń defences. (Picture courtesy of the Latvian War Museum, Rīga. LKM 5-54470 2652-FT)

All eyes are lifted up in prayer with folded hands. Lips whisper of pain and despair. God give peace and pour his love into human hearts. Each company's tree is burning.[6] Our company commander speaks to us, and wishes that next year we will be home. One after another we light candles on the small tree.[7]

By 1945, Toruń was one of the major Nazi fortresses in Poland, with thousands of Latvians there too. Some 10,000 men had been shipped out of Rīga to West Prussia. At this late stage of the war, overall SS commander Colonel Georg Martin could not gather enough weapons, ammunition and military supplies to arm the equivalent of two battalions of men in Toruń and a third in Pomerania, so they were designated as *buvpulki* or construction battalions, earning the nickname 'The Ditchdiggers of Toruń' [*Tornas grāvrači*].[8]

The Latvian battalion in Pomerania was commanded by Colonel Teodors Brigge. Brigge's group was 70 kilometres east of Kolberg when the Russian attack began: he quickly took his men to the port and got out by ship to Stettin before the city was surrounded.[9]

6   Latvians describe the lighting of candles on the Christmas tree as 'burning the Christmas tree.' It's a tradition that continues today.
7   War diary of Augusts Spilners.
8   I. Kažociņš, *Latviešu Karavīri Zem Svešiem Karogiem 1940–1945* [*Latvian Soldiers Under Foreign Flags*] Trans. Aivars Sinka. (Rīga, Latvijas Universitātes žurnāla 'Latvijas Vēsture' fonds, 1999), p.182.
9   Kažociņš, *Latviešu Karavīri*, p.182.

Gunārs Janovskis, later a popular novelist, wrote several books about his experiences in Pomerania. (Picture: courtesy Sarmite Ērenpreiss-Janovskis)

The two battalions in Toruń were commanded by Lieutenant Colonels Osvalds Meija and Nikolajs Rušmanis. The men were without weapons, and uniforms and clothing were in a bad state. Unfit for combat, they were a drain on the fighting resources and food supplies of the 15th, so were used to reinforce defences in and around Toruń.

One soldier in Pomerania, Gunārs Janovskis, who later became a well-regarded novelist, was an interpreter for the German Army. He described conditions in Toruń in his book *Pie Tornas [At Toruń]*:

[The ditch] stretches over fields, along the side of a wood. It's not particularly deep or wide. The walls of the ditch are strengthened with pine tree branches. Every now and then there are dips for munitions. At certain intervals nests for machine guns have been built. The ditch has been dug by the main road. Big ideas are taking place here: the ditch goes under the main road, deeper and wider, so when the Russian tanks approach we just have to blow it up. But there are 1,000 cubic metres of soil that have to be dug out and thrown over the side.

The whole battalion has worked here for over a week now and we are basically still in the same spot. We haven't got any further. To plan is one thing: to carry out that plan is another. The men are not happy. Yesterday the food transport simply did not arrive. At least the thin soup warms your stomach. Sometimes at the bottom you might find a little bit of something but today we even had to do without that. And no bread.[10]

The influx of so many foreigners had an impact on wartime Toruń. Janovskis writes:

The city by the sea started to sound foreign. Latvian could be heard everywhere. Life revolved around *Northern Front* brand cigarettes and extremely strong potato vodka, bacon and money – which lost its value within a day. A packet

10 G. Janovskis, *Pie Tornas*, trans. Daina Vītola (Vasteras, Sweden: Ziemeļblāzma, 1966), p.101.

of cigarettes was the fastest way to a girl's heart. The Central Station was full of people on their way to the west. The local trains going in the other direction, to Toruń and Bromberg [Bydgoszcz] were for soldiers' use. The officer in charge in Toruń was called Colonel Punduris.

The Latvian group headquarters was in an old damp school by Toruń park. The Germans called it an *ersatz* group. Strictly translated that meant 'Army reserves' but the more popular translation meant 'surrogate' or 'incomplete' – a temporary replacement. The *ersatz* group consisted of construction battalions, pilots without planes, the remnants of Border Guard units, groups of policemen, prison guards, prefecture employees, the wounded, waifs and strays, stragglers from disappeared headquarters, commissions, committees and departments: all were commanded by Colonel Punduris.[11]

The Colonel's career shows our nation's changeable fate in the past 50 years. He had [with many other Latvians] diligently served the Tsar, and after that gave an oath of allegiance to the red rag/flag of the revolution; served in democratic and authoritarian regimes,[12] then again under a Russian master and in the end looked quite respectable in a German uniform. In his varied life the Colonel had one basic motto: if you have to serve foreign masters, do it well.

The Latvians are living in plywood huts, 45 men in each, sleeping like sardines. If one turns during the night, everyone has to. There's a stove in the middle of the hut and a man on duty to keep it going round the clock so they are warm. Once a day they get some soup. If they're lucky there might be a piece of meat with it: otherwise a circle of fat floating on the surface and a few blue potatoes at the bottom. We get given some dry food. We don't have weapons: instead we have spades. The Germans called them 'weapons of honour.'

Every morning we have to walk five kilometres and dig tank defences when we get there. At 13:00 we go back and the next shift comes. We don't have targets to meet but we are standing around in the cold, and we need to keep moving. Those who don't have footwear or have hidden their boots so they didn't have to go digging – we called them 'barefooters' – stayed in camp but had to chop firewood or peel potatoes. There is a potato field nearby and sometimes we find a potato to put in the stove to stave off hunger.

Some Latvians have made contact with the Poles but they don't give anything for money; only in exchange for useful items, like woollen socks, knitted jumpers or underwear. Once a fortnight we get taken to the sauna but it's too far and coming back many catch cold. We live on the edge of the forest: there's a station nearby but trains in the morning and late evening only. It's a long way to town. We write to our loved ones: 'Do you have any socks to spare? Mine have had it. Please send.'[13]

---

11 Janovskis, *Pie Tornas*, p.7.
12 In Latvia's interwar independence period under Kārlis Ulmanis.
13 Janovskis, *Pie Tornas*, p.51 and p.29.

Motley crew. Soldiers of the 3rd Construction Regiment of the Latvian 15th SS Division in Toruń dressed in a range of ill-fitting uniforms. (Picture courtesy Latvian War Museum, Rīga. LKM 5-13647-1422-FT)

Life was not easy for these men. Without transport, getting food was difficult. Living accommodation was dire and medical help was not easily forthcoming, but cultural events were organised. The Kurzeme Construction Regiment, stationed in Toruń, had a men's choir. A violinist, A. Lindbergs, gave performances.[14] Also in Toruń was Roberts Zuika, later one of Latvia's pre-eminent choral conductors, who formed an Army choir in Bulduri during the retreat to Kurzeme. A concert planned for 5 February 1945 didn't happen because of the Russian advance.[15]

The vast influx of personnel into Toruń brought increased demand for accommodation, refreshment and other services. Laimons Sakne was a Cēsis-born Latvian from the 15th Division in Toruń who was captured by the Russians and conscripted into the Red Army. He managed to avoid fighting in the Battle for Berlin, was jailed but escaped and then surrendered to the Americans. He later emigrated to Australia

---

14 Latvian Legion webpages at: <https://latvianlegion.org/index.php?en/history/level-040-conclusion.ssi>, accessed 24 January 2019. The conductors were P. Dreimanis, A. Tulgis and T. Kenins.
15 Zuika formed choirs in the Latvian forces and Displaced Persons camps in the west after the war, which performed 170 concerts in two years. He went on to conduct choirs at several Song Festivals post-independence. He died in 2015, aged 102. (Obituary, Baltic News Network, 06 February 2015 at <https://bnn-news.com/brilliant-conductor-roberts-zuika-passes-125147>). Zuika's brother Kārlis became Latvian Minister in Manchester in the 1960s.

On parade: the 2nd Construction Regiment ready for inspection, 18 November 1944, Toruń. The original caption identifies in the centre of the picture Pltn. A. Liepiņš and Pltn. R. Muizzemnieks. (Picture: Latvian War Museum, Rīga. LKM 5-51559-2416-FT)

where he wrote his memoirs *Liktenis Rotaļa [Game of Fate]*, which included this portrait of life in Toruń.

> Like in any big town Toruń had its pubs, hotels and 'open houses' where Polish women work. Nobody is forcing them to do this job – it's a free choice. And the choice is: long hours in a factory and a bowl of thin soup or an easier life in a brothel. A lot of beautiful German-speaking Poles choose the latter. But beauty is only one of the necessary qualifications. You have to be fit for the job.
>
> In the German officer clubs, gendarmes keep order. But the place is meant for soldiers and frequented by Germans and Latvians. Winter is very hard, with snow, and the brothel hours at the weekends when the soldiers can get time off are long, with long queues of soldiers waiting outside in the snow. You could get permission for time off. In the foyer there was a no-nonsense German woman selling tickets, and the price included three glasses of alcoholic drink and maybe a girl. The profit stayed with the Germans.
>
> If you have the right coupons in the big hall you can get stuff to eat – 'nibbles' –perhaps something cold. You couldn't choose the girls. They chose their own partners. At the beginning the order was given to choose from the wounded who were 'on holiday' from the front. Then if time permits, or the norm hasn't been exceeded, that's the time for the rest. So wounded first.
>
> The girls pull straws for the visitors that remain. They can choose. Finding out on the grapevine about this internal order – the way things are – very soon

the Latvians stand in the line with bandages on their heads or with their arms in a sling, or leaning on a crutch or a walking stick. The girls very quickly realise what's going on but they are friendly to the Latvians. The Iron Lady taking tickets at the door didn't realise what was going on, and neither did the Germans who went home without being serviced: they had to go home without.[16]

The process of evacuating Allied prisoners from camps in Lithuania started during summer 1944. Thousands were moved in July from Stalag Luft VI at Heydekrug near Memel in East Prussia [now Klaipėda in Lithuania] to Stalag XX-A at Toruń or Stalag Luft IV at Gross Tychow in Pomerania, where there were 7,000 American POWs, 866 British and around 200 Australians, Canadians, New Zealanders and South Africans. Some of these men had been prisoners of the Germans since 1940.[17]

As the Red Army approached in July 1944, they were packed into a cargo ship heading for Swinemünde. When they disembarked they were forced to run to the camp at Stalag Luft IV being beaten with rifle butts and slashed with bayonets by fanatical young Kriegsmarine cadets. This 'run up the road' left more than 100 prisoners with serious cuts and wounds – one died – but it became a regular feature for new arrivals. The camp became a byword for brutality, even in the later stages of the war.[18]

In Toruń, priorities turned to survival. The sounds of battle could be heard in the distance. Latvians in Toruń were advised by the military officers to prepare one bag containing essentials.

Any gold you've got, jewels, morphine … in Toruń the chaos is not too bad yet. Tomorrow get some men, promise them a bottle each and get them to take your stuff to the station. The trains are still taking luggage. Will it arrive at its destination, will you ever see it again? That's a different question…"

Those who could flee did, in cold, unheated wagons, on the ice and in snow-storms, with their belongings … [trying] to get to Danzig in endless columns of horses, tractors, of wagons covered with waterproof groundsheets. Many were on foot with sledges, belongings thrown on haphazardly. There they mixed in a rag-tag group together with refugees from the Baltic countries, together with 25 surrounded and practically unarmed divisions.

This is the first time in this war the Germans get to see the real bloody face of war, not just to listen to speeches of praise and read beautifully formulated magazines … The repatriated Baltic Germans had been dispersed in the Warthe area [the Warthegau area of Poland annexed by Germany]. For these people especially, Polish soil started burning under their feet. They gathered in large

16 *Laikrasts Latvietis*, Nr. 132, 16 February 2011, p.15 at <http://www.laikraksts.com/raksti/raksts.php?KursRaksts=1077>, trans. Daina Vītola, accessed 20 January 2019.
17 Now Tychowo, south of Koszalin. Report by the International Red Cross, October 1944 at <http://www.stalagluft4.org/luft%204%20reports.html>, accessed 24 January 2019.
18 J. Nichol and T. Rennell, *The Last Escape – the Untold Story of Allied Prisoners of War in Germany 1944–45* (London: Penguin, 2003), pp.24–28.

numbers in stations and on overcrowded trains and fled to the West ... The hierarchy of the previous order was abandoned. One Adjutant's wife demanded: 'Have you ordered a car? What do you mean – I have to carry my own luggage? What about our silverware and our paintings?'

At that time, Toruń station was not particularly crowded. Those who could were urged: 'Go to Toruń and get on a train west – anywhere!' The doctor in the camp wanted a pneumonia patient taken into hospital, but the hospital refused. 'We are only taking the badly wounded from the frontlines,' they said. 'If you bring him, we'll have to turn him away.'[19]

It was on 20 January 1945 that the order was given for all divisions to retreat, but the order didn't reach the Ditchdiggers. They waited and waited as the sounds of battle got closer, but still no order arrived. Eventually they couldn't wait any longer so as dusk fell, they left. The word spread among the soldiers was: 'Make your way to Janums. He can work wonders.'

A sharp freeze began that day as the Ditchdiggers still in Toruń began to march west in snowstorms. Several times on the journey to Zempelburg [Sępólno Krajeńskie] Soviet tanks caught up with them and made short work of the unarmed soldiers. In one incident near the village of Neuheim, soldiers of the 5th Battalion of the 1st Construction Regiment were passed by a column of Red Army tanks, which they mistook for Germans. The Russians stopped and opened fire on the unarmed Latvians. Those who tried to surrender were lined up and shot: some men ran into a school but the tanks pursued them and destroyed it, reducing it to ruins and killing anyone who surrendered. More than a hundred Latvians died in the incident. Ernests Šperliņš was an eyewitness:

> The evening came, it got dark. The men waited idly for the time to set off. It was less freezing and a full moon was shining. At 21:00, the fourth platoon left the house, stood in a double line on the road and waited for the company to join up behind the third platoon. Immediately three platoons of the company appeared on the farm access road and behind them the horses and carts. The platoons walked in pairs in a column, came out on the big road, and walked on towards the school. The fourth and second platoons had already passed when the sound of tanks was heard. As the third platoon passed, the first tank also appeared. It had a German cross on its side and riflemen on top.
>
> One followed after another. It was a whole column that slowly drove past the company. To the commander of the fourth platoon, however, these tanks with German markings seemed suspicious. German tank guns usually have a flame suppressor at the end of the gun, but they didn't. In a defensive instinct, he stepped into a deep ditch, but it was uncomfortable to stand in a ditch when the whole platoon was standing on the road. It felt awkward to raise the alarm, because all the officers of the company also saw the tanks.

19 Janovskis, *Pie Tornas,* pp.257–262.

Plagued with doubt, he got out of the ditch, but then immediately the sound of the first tank machine gun was heard at the school. The platoon commander did not have to suppress his alarm. With a shout, 'Russians! Behind me!' he ran to the nearest yard. The whole platoon followed as a mob.

The road that had the houses ran perpendicular to the main road. The platoon did not flee along the street, but from one courtyard over the fence to the next, until the village houses ended. While running away you could hear that the machine guns of all the tanks were firing. However, while they were running through the yards of the house, those escaping were never visible to the tanks, and it seems that the tanks did not pay attention to the runners either, because the whole company, three platoons, was on the other side of the road, i.e., in the opposite direction.

The houses ended in a river gully. The platoon jumped in there and felt reasonably safe. After a while the shooting died down, but then there was the sound of two cannon shots and, after a while, more machine gun firing, which ended soon after. Everyone waited to see what would happen next.

Suddenly a group of people approached along the river bank. The men flattened themselves to the side of the gully and froze still. As the group got closer, a conversation was heard, which, when they got closer, turned out to be Latvian. It was a relief and a surprise. They were soldiers of the battalion headquarters with the battalion commander. The HQ-men joined the men in the river gully and waited for further events. Finally, the tanks left. The battalion commander asked for three volunteers for reconnaissance. They volunteered and returned to the scene of events, cautiously because they could not know if all the Russians had left. They could also have left guard posts in the village. The full moon shone. The air was full of a strange smoke or fog.

Everything looked very unusual. Upon arriving on the main road, an unimaginably terrible view was revealed. They were all dead. Some who were fallen on the road had been flattened by tanks. Others lay on the side of the road, but most of them were in a ditch, where they had tried to escape; to hide from the bullets. On the road lay the circular parade hat of the assistant company commander. He was the only one who had one like that. The horses were also lying on the ground, shot.

Nothing was spared. The first company had not yet managed to stand to for the march on the road when the tanks approached. The soldiers had tried to stay in the school. They had not complied with the Russian order to come out, so the tanks fired two cannon-rounds at the school, which exploded inside and destroyed everything.

Many died or were injured in the rubble. The survivors came out. They were lined up and shot. They lay in a line in the light of the moon in varying positions. The moans of the wounded and cries for help were also heard from the school building. The three soldiers felt like they were in a bad dream from which they cannot wake up. With a heavy step, they went back to report on what they saw.

The survivors came to the scene of their fallen members as if it were a farewell. They also saw that the Russians had frisked the fallen. Everyone was deprived of their personal documents, the so-called 'Soldbuch'. Presumably, they received badges of honour for doing so. Probably everything else that was useful to the Russians was taken. Even in the carts, all the backpacks had been cut open and the contents searched.

The battalion commander gave the lieutenant a special order to take some men and care for the injured in the school building, but the rest, some 70 people, each took a blanket over their shoulders and followed a compass direction straight across the fields and woods towards Zempelburg.

In Neuheim there remained some 300 fallen soldiers, for whom you could apply the usual phrase 'missing in action.' The list of soldiers' names in the company was left in the cart with the dead horse.[20]

Those who survived pressed on to the safety of Zempelburg where the 15th Battalion Task Force vowed revenge. The unit tracked down the Russian tanks to Immenheim [Mrocza] and destroyed them, as well as freeing captured soldiers from the 2nd Construction Regiment. The next night about 1,000 men from the 2nd Battalion were surrounded at Immenheim but broke out.[21]

On the snow-filled roads of Eastern Europe at this time nearly 240,000 Allied prisoners of war were being force-marched west by their Nazi captors, 100,000 in the north where the Latvians were. Most of the Allied prisoners involved were moved from their camps in the blizzards of late January, with temperatures down to minus 25 Celsius.

Bombardier Alfred Gray kept a diary noting the remarkable distances covered by the POWs. Having left Toruń at 03:00 on 20 January, the march covered 32 kilometres to Schulitz before he slept in a field of snow. At 06:00 on 21 January the prisoners covered 41 kilometres to Bromberg where he slept in a garage. The next day was 32 kilometres to Immenheim then 14 kilometres on 23 January to sleep in a fire station; four kilometres the following day to Vandsburg and on 25 January – with the Russians by now not far away – 40 kilometres to a big farm outside Flatow. By the end of the month, with his feet skinned and frostbitten and the boys 'all in' they were still covering 40 kilometres a day on hilly roads thick with snow and no hot food. On 1 February, having covered 20 kilometres to rest in a barn, he wrote: 'Hope terrible ordeal will soon be over.'

Alfred had to survive for another two months on very little food, covered with lice, with only the clothes he was wearing, marching west as Allied bombers flew

---

20   Ernests Šperliņš, recollections in *Atmiņu Stāsts Tornas Grāvrača Atmiņas –Testimony: Memoir of a Thorun Ditchdigger*, from *Laiks* numbers 90 and 91, November 1989. Trans. Aivars Sinka.
21   By the end of the month, the survivors had reached Hammerstein [now Czarne] where they stayed until 19 February, re-grouping. This town too had dark secrets. Hammerstein housed the prisoner of war camp Stalag II-B, first used for political prisoners of the Nazis, then prisoners from the blitzkrieg in Poland and France, then Russians, with 38,000 captured Soviets held here. Tens of thousands of prisoners died here.

Men of a tank-killer unit of the 15th Division Latvian Legion in blizzard conditions in Pomerania. (Picture: Latvian War Museum, Rīga. LKM 5-12947/1228-FT)

overhead. His group crossed the Elbe on 21 March and reached the safety of Hanover on 16 April, where the survivors were fed, de-loused, bathed and issued with new uniforms, before being flown home in a Stirling bomber on 22 April.[22]

Another prisoner at Stalag XX-A, Jack Stansfield, had been captured in Belgium in 1940. When the camp was evacuated on 21 January 1945, Jack and some other prisoners were towards the back of a long line of prisoners beginning the march west. They hung back, then hid in a snow-filled ditch before finding other prisoners hiding in the cellars of buildings hoping to be liberated by the Russians. When the advance units of the Red Army arrived their lives were saved by a Polish boy who convinced the soldiers they were British. Six Germans taken prisoner were not so lucky – they were shot dead in front of the group.[23]

22   Diary of Alfred Gray, part of the BBC WW2 People's War online at <https://www.bbc.co.uk/history/ww2peopleswar/stories/53/a2759853.shtml>. Article ID: A2759853. Contributed on 18 June 2004.

23   Stansfield family story at <http://wartimeguides.blogspot.com/2015/05/thanks-this-trip-weve-discovered-new.html>, accessed 24 January 2019. The Stansfield family visited Toruń and were shown around by two English-speaking guides, Hania and Pawel Bukowski, who arrange tours and gather information on wartime Toruń and the camps in the area. Their website is at <http://wartimeguides.blogspot.com/>.

Gunner Henry Owens of the 51st Highlanders had been transferred to a sub-camp of Stalag XX-B at Camp 210, a metal fabrication factory in Langemarke Strasse, Elbing, as the Germans prepared to move the prisoners west. There were eight other British POWs with him and they quickly readied themselves for the journey, stuffing as much tinned food as they could carry into their Army kitbags. Henry wrote:

As we entered the main road in Elbing, there was evidence of the Russian penetration. Bodies lay about in the snow and German troops dressed in all-white uniforms and heavily armed were moving east past us. It would appear that the Russians had attacked under cover of darkness, shot up the town and retreated again.

We rendezvoused with other British POWs who had been in prison camps in the Elbing area, and were marched out, apparently making for the Baltic coast. After marching for some time, we came across a long column of civilian refugees, who had been travelling in high-sided horse-drawn wagons loaded with all their worldly possessions. The column was at a standstill. Apparently they were held up because the crossing over the river Vistula was for the use of military traffic only. How long they had been there I do not know, but many had frozen to death still in their wagons. Other bodies lay at the side of the road. They looked like wax dummies.

We helped ourselves to any food we could find in these wagons, marched on and crossed the Vistula towards Danzig. It was on this section of the march that I faltered. I felt terribly tired, with a sinking feeling, as if the cold had affected my stomach. I sat on one of the abandoned carts and rested. Several comrades pleaded with me to carry on, otherwise I would freeze to death or be shot. After a short while I recovered my strength, and from that moment, I did not falter for the rest of the march.

We marched nearly all of the first night, eventually stopping at a barn, where we lit fires and melted snow in our dixies, adding dried milk (Klim) to provide a hot drink (no rations were provided by the Germans). The next day we marched on again, with the sound of Russian artillery in the background. As the packs on our backs were too heavy, most of us used makeshift sledges to pull our possessions along. As the days went by we got weaker; the built-up stock of food reserves had gone, we were plagued with lice and dysentery, and frostbitten limbs turned gangrenous. We were sometimes bundled into barns at night, but on at least one occasion we spent the night in an open field with no food at all.

It was not only British POWs on the march. It seemed that the whole of the civilian population of the Baltic states and East Prussia was fleeing from the Russians, some no doubt collaborators who feared for their lives. There were also Russian, French, and POWs of other nationalities. This all added to the food problem. Rationing had obviously broken down, and the Germans could not provide for themselves, even less for the refugees and POWs: these were low priorities.

It was tragic to see POWs who had survived the horrific march into captivity from Dunkirk and St. Valery four and a half years previously going down with dysentery, gangrene and frostbite, and having to be left behind to die or be shot.

There was no back-up transport to take away the sick; you just left them behind, hoping they would survive, perhaps in a Russian hospital.[24]

The marches tested human stamina and endurance to the limit. Many prisoners survived marches of 800 kilometres [500 miles]; some covered 1,500 kilometres [900 miles]. Hundreds died on these marches, which sometimes lasted several months. There were three routes west. Around 100,000 POWs in the north were heading for Stettin, then Fallingbostel and Lübeck; 60,000 prisoners in central Poland were moving west from Stalag Luft 7 to Lamsdorf, Gorlitz and Luckenwalde, and in the south 80,000 prisoners, including an estimated 25,000 Americans, were marching from Stalag VIII-D at Teschen to Nuremberg and then Moosburg in Bavaria.[25]

On 28 February, the Red Cross passed on details gathered by its delegate Robert Schirmer to the American Legation in Bern, Switzerland. The Legation sent a telegram to the US Secretary of State, which read:

> Northern Line of March: About 100,000 prisoners are moving along the northern German coast to the west. The great mass of prisoners are now resting in the area between Anklas, New Brandenburg, Demmin and Swinemünde. The rearguard is still on the roads west of Danzig, between Stolp and Lauenburg. The prisoners will continue their march westward until they reach the region of Hamburg, Bremen and Lübeck. The southern edge of this group reaches to Schwerin and Oustrow.
>
> The prisoners, German officers and guards are eating the same rations; which consist of approximately one quart of hot water and three potatoes daily, plus 200 grams of bread every four to five days (when available). The prisoners are selling everything they have in order to obtain food, but with little success. Eighty percent of them are suffering from dysentery, which is apparently contagious. The information in this telegram … was obtained by Schirmer, personally.[26]

Toruń is a lovely place to spend a couple of summer days exploring the city and its fantastically preserved history, from Copernicus to more recent events. It's warm

---

24 Henry Owens' diary, from the 51st Highlanders' archive, online at <https://51hd.co.uk/>. In four months these men had one hot meal, not daring to take their boots off in case they couldn't get them back on again. Eventually the column reached Bitterfeld near Halle, where the Americans had reached German lines. After a march of 1,000 miles [1600 kilometres] from Danzig through Stolp, Koslin, Stettin and Swinemünde, then through Wismar, Wittenburg and Magdeburg to Halle, the men were handed over, fed and flown first to Brussels in an American Dakota then to the UK where they arrived almost exactly five years after being taken prisoner.

25 A.J. Kochavi, *Confronting Captivity: Britain and the United States and their POWs in Nazi Germany*. (Chapel Hill, NC: University of North Carolina Press, 2011), p.68.

26 Stalag Luft 4 website, quoting telegram at <http://www.stalagluft4.org/Paules%20and%20Lunsford.html>.

Toruń Old Town, summer 2018. (Picture: author)

and dry in the late summer so I can eat outside, stroll along the Vistula, admire the architecture and absorb the tourist buzz. My final night in Toruń is a balmy summer's evening and the Philadelphia Boulevard along the riverside embankment throngs with couples and families promenading.

I take the last boat trip of the evening for a gentle chug down the wide river past this remarkable walled city and under the two bridges that almost define its boundaries, but I still haven't managed to work out how Toruń escaped the fury and destruction visited upon places like Elbing and Graudenz. Over coffee outside a café I strike up a conversation with a woman who tells me that Toruń was traditionally a German town.

Before the coming of the Nazis, most prominent citizens were either German or Jewish. The Nazis started killing Toruń's Jews in the Barbarka forest soon after the occupation, and the Gestapo moved their headquarters to Chopin Street, with a centre for torturing their victims at the Collegium, just a short distance from here outside the town walls. These days, she says, people think of Toruń as Krakow's little brother: not as big and not as busy, with visitors coming to spend money and have a good time – they don't think about the rest.

But there were 60,000 PoWs here, including British soldiers taken prisoner in France and at Dunkirk. There were thousands of Latvians here too, digging ditches – but I can't find any evidence of those Latvians or where those anti-tank ditches were. The only memorial I can find in the Barbarka Forest is to Polish Scouts who were

Toruń and the river Vistula, summer 2018. (Picture: author)

shot there by the Nazis. Despite several inquiries, it's clear that the town's information centre would prefer the focus of tourists to be on more cheerful matters, such as gingerbread.

It's not until a while later that I discover the answers to these questions, thanks to the Wartime Guides Hania and Pawel Bukowski. They were away while I was in Toruń, but Pawel fits several missing pieces into the historical jigsaw from Polish memories, including a twist that I was not aware of: some Latvian soldiers in the area before the Legion arrived between October and November 1944 were apparently used as guards in the camps for Jewish women.[27]

From the end of January 1945, the Germans gradually lost their hold on their strongpoints on the eastern bank of the Vistula. Marienburg with its famous castle was lost on 29 January, Elbing fell on 10 February and resistance at Graudenz ended on 6 March.[28] Toruń itself was captured largely undamaged by the 70th Soviet Army of the 2nd Belorussian Front after virtually all the German defenders withdrew west, leaving only pockets of resistance. Although the physical damage to the city was minimal, the war changed the fabric of Toruń, Pawel writes:

> Toruń was occupied by the Germans on 7 September 1939. From the very first days the Germans started the *Intelligenzaktion*; that is, arresting Polish activists who could be leaders of resistance: lawyers, medics, priests and so on. They

27 It's possible these men were from the disbanded Arājs Kommando of Latvian collaborators (see footnote p.116). Their involvement in the Holocaust has been a stain on Latvia since, and their whereabouts at this time has not been established.

28 Duffy, p.175.

imprisoned them in Fort VII and Fort VIII in the city, and executed 1,000 people in the Barbarka forest. The rest were sent to concentrations camps.[29]

At the same time the Germans moved all the Jews to the ghetto in Łódź. Having 'cleaned' the city they moved in Germans from Ukraine and the Baltic countries as part of their programme for a new society: *Heim ins Reich*.[30] Poles who did not sign up for German citizenship were moved from their property or city to other regions. My grandfather Antoni and his family were moved from their home and sent to a farm, where he worked with British PoWs.

Toruń was a very important railway hub and used as a big storage depot and hospital when the German Army attacked the Soviet Union in 1941. There was also a PoW camp for around 50,000 Allied soldiers. It was part of the *Stellung* defence line which started in Slovakia in southern Europe and stretched north to the Baltic Sea: a network of fortified lines called 'breakwaters,' ready to stop a Soviet counterstrike.

Toruń was declared a stronghold city in March 1944, and Nazi area commander Heinz Guderian gave the order on 27 July 1944 for the city and positions around it to be fortified.

The core of the defence line was around 10–15km from the town centre, based on trenches, anti-tank ditches and reinforced pillboxes. Much of this can still be seen in the terrain.

Needing more labour, from 28 August 1944 the Germans organised two sub-camps of the Stutthoff concentration camp for Jewish women: Baukommando Weichsel and Baukommando Ostland. The guards in these sub-camps included Latvians, according to family tales handed down in Poland.[31]

In Baukommando Weichsel – the Vistula Construction Command – there were around 5,000 women from Auschwitz, Kaunas and Rīga. This camp was part of a sub-camp system which had its headquarters was in Bocień near Chełmza. It was closed on 18 January 1945, and most of these women were either killed or died during the evacuation.[32]

Baukommando Ostland was organised along the same lines, with around 5,500 Jewish women in small sub-camps. Germans were forced to work with them, as well as civilians from the villages nearby, like my great-grandfather Alexander. He worked at Lisak sub-camp digging ditches. He survived, but a lot of people died there. To build fortifications around Toruń itself, the German set

---

29 More than 100,000 Poles were murdered in the *Intelligenzaktion*, designed to remove opposition to the Germanisation of Poland before eventual absorption into the Reich.

30 'Back home to the Reich' – a policy of including ethnic Germans to become part of a Greater Germany.

31 These men would not be Legionnaires, but earlier recruits to the SD.

32 The concentration camp was known in German as Bottschin. Chełmza [Kulmsee] had been cleared of Jews from the beginning of the German occupation and Poles forced to join the *Volksdeutsche* lists.

up two camps for women prisoners in Korben [now Chorabie] and Gorsk, both to the north of the town.[33]

There were so many prisoners sent into this area to work on these defences that the Nazi military engineering company Organisation Todt set up a headquarters in Toruń. Three train transports brought women from Stutthof on 24, 25 and 26 August 1944. The first 1,700 worked in villages around Brodnica; another 1,700 in villages near Toruń, including Korben and Gorsk, with the remaining 1,600 in Bocien, Wideopas and Grodno. The prisoners were forced to dig anti-tank and drainage ditches, to camouflage concrete bunkers and shovel soil onto their roofs to hide them. They did this wearing light dresses and slippers, with some working in bare feet, overseen by guards with guns, dogs and riding crops who beat them regularly.[34]

At Korben, a sub-camp of Stutthof in the forest near Toruń, women were housed in flimsy barracks from August 1944 and forced to dig ditches. They worked from 05:00 to dusk on starvation rations day-to-day, living in groups of sixty in plywood huts with no floors, with branches from trees scattered on the ground as a buffer from the freezing earth. Bedding was scarce. Breakfast was a piece of bread with margarine and a cup of black cereal coffee. Dinner was a soup of carrots or cabbage. Local people gave them onions to help stave off famine.

The camp was guarded by around 140 soldiers from German forces in the area, including about 60 from Lithuania, Latvia and Estonia who had previously served at the Potulice camp, historian Tomasz Ceran wrote in a 2017 newspaper article.[35] Camp commander Antoni Willi often fired random shots at prisoners during drinking sessions. Women prisoners were forced to engage in sexual favours for the guards, and any who got pregnant were taken to the forest and shot. They died from hunger, the freezing conditions and disease – there was a typhus epidemic – and from the sadism of the guards. Marianna Ulawska was a 11 year-old girl at the time, and saw the Jewish women going to work.

> They had wooden shoes on their feet – clogs. They were dressed in something grey, like blankets. The guards were all SS men. Some wore black uniforms; others were in lighter brown or yellow uniforms guarding the women. Dad said that the [men in] lighter uniforms were Latvians: they were said to be worse than the German guards. If a guard was kind, they sometimes let the women come to us to drink water. Mum cooked potatoes for the women to eat.

33 Correspondence with Pawel Bukowski, 2019. There is a memorial stone at the site today, commemorating these women.
34 Ardanowski, J.K., and Sztama, P. *I call you from the depths* (Brodnica: Wszechnica Edukacyjna i Wydawnicza Verbum, 2014) pp.138–142.
35 Based on evidence given in the 1949 trial in Toruń of SS-Hauptsturmführer Hans Jacobi, former commandant of camps in Argenau [Gniewkowo] and later Korben [Chorabie].

Another eyewitness, Maria Pouch, was a girl at the time. Her father Andrzej Białecki worked in the forest and helped save prisoners who survived the execution after the camp was evacuated

> People sometimes tried to throw food to the women but the Germans wanted to shoot Poles for it. There was an insatiable aggression in these SS men.[36]

Legionnaire Harijs Blezūrs left Latvia for Gdynia on 12 October and after a circuitous journey, arrived in Posendorf. His group was then sent to a camp they shared with men of the Arājs Kommando. In a transcript of an audio tape recorded in 1997 and passed to the author, he said:

> Our weapons were taken away and we were given shovels. We had to go and dig ditches, tank ditches. We lived in a kind of round tent. During the day we went off on foot singing – you had to sing – and then we went to dig ditches. There were only Latvians there. There was also at that time that Arājs company. That was the unit that shot Jews. At that time, we were in the same camp. They were in a different location, but it was quite a big camp. I remember that everyone said: "That's Arājs."

On 18 January 1945 the order was given for the Korben camp to be cleared. A group of 180 women too weak to march west was lined up for execution and shot. Around 28 women survived by hiding in the pile of bodies: 152 corpses buried in an anti-tank ditch were exhumed after the war and re-buried in the cemetery at ul. Grudziądzka in Toruń.

At Grodno, prisoners were selected for the march west on the basis of whether they could complete a '20-metre run'. Those that couldn't were taken to the nearby Grodno Lake and murdered. Excavations there in 1971 discovered a gruesome mass grave. This took 80 soldiers three days to uncover and revealed the skulls of 720 victims, all of whom had been killed by hand, using batons, rifle butts and pickaxes.

The women who did pass the test as fit to march set off in columns heading north and west. If a woman was unable to continue, she was killed: bayoneted or bludgeoned with a rifle butt. Of the 900 women who left Bocień and Grodno, only 300 survived. About 1,300 Jewish women from Korben marched through Bydgoszcz to Koronowo. Only 997 of them met up with the Red Army and the Polish People's Army.[37]

---

36 Article by Tomasz Ciechoński, 13.06.2017: *They commemorated the victims of the German Jewish camp* at <https://Toruń.wyborcza.pl/Toruń/7,48723,21956357,upamietnili-ofiary-niemieckiego-obozu-dla-zydowek-zdjecia.html>. The Latvians involved would not have been Legionnaires as they were in ditchdigging camps. Most probably they were men from the SD under orders from their German masters. This would include the notorious Arājs Kommando, who wore lighter coloured uniforms, and the testimony of Harijs Blezūrs places them in Toruń at this time. This is an area that bears further research.

37 Ceran, T. *The Economics of Extermination* (02.03.2020) online at <https://przystanekhistoria. pl/pa2/tematy/obozy-koncentracyjne/62142,Ekonomia-i-Zaglada-Podobozy-KL-Stutthof-w-okolicach-Toruńia-1944-1945.html>.

In May 1949 former Korben camp commander SS-Hauptsturmführer Hans Wilhelm Robert Jacobi was sentenced to six years in prison but died in hospital the same year. He had been praised by the court which tried him in Toruń for showing a 'human attitude' towards his prisoners, in contrast to his successors SS-Hauptsturmführer Antoni Willi from Szczecin and SS-Hauptsturmführer Wilhelm Bendig (Bendinger) from Elbląg. The latter men were never captured.[38]

So how come, despite being one of the centres of this ring of Nazi sadism, with a German garrison and a natural defensive feature in the Vistula river, Toruń was not shelled to rubble by the Soviets like many of the cities that resisted? Pawel Bukowski from Wartime Guides has an answer.

> The evacuation of civilians and POWs from Toruń started in January 1945, part of a plan codenamed 'Roland.' The Red Army laid siege to the city but apart from a few skirmishes did not attack the city centre. When the German garrison realised their frontline was a long way from Toruń and they were isolated and unlikely to get help from outside, the commander ordered an immediate withdrawal.
>
> During the night of 31 January–1 February 35,000 German soldiers escaped from Toruń, destroying two bridges to delay the Soviet soldiers. The worst casualties happened by accident on the left bank of the Vistula river when a cattle truck loaded with ammunition exploded, killing 200 people and destroying civilian houses nearby. The Soviets came into Toruń unopposed in the early morning of 1 February 1945.[39]

The chief of the German Army General Staff at the time, Heinz Guderian, had another explanation. In his 1952 memoir *Panzer Leader*, he said Himmler ordered the evacuation of Toruń, Kulm (now Chełmno) and Marienwerder (now Kwidzyń) without the approval of the OKH [German Army High Command, or *Oberkommando des Heeres*.] He wrote:

> By reason of the independent decision of Himmler's the Vistula line was lost without a fight.[40]

Toruń was spared because the Germans withdrew. The Red Army would stay in Toruń until July 1991. When Poland returned to post-Communist independence, a monument commemorating Polish gratitude to the Red Army for the liberation was dismantled and stored in the yard of a concrete-cutting company. The sociologist Ewa

---

38 Ceran, *The Economics of Extermination*.
39 Pawel Bukowski, Wartime Guides in Toruń, correspondence with author, 29 May 2020.
40 H. Guderian, *Panzer Leader* (Middlesex, UK: Classic Penguin, 2000), p.405.

Ochman visited the site and photographed it for her book *Post-Communist Poland – Contested Pasts and Future Identities*. She wrote:

> The demolition of the monument in 1997 triggered protests as the removal of the obelisk also entailed the exhumation of the remains of Red Army soldiers. Graffiti sprayed on the monument read: *People rest here! Poles as well. And you spit on them. You? Catholics?*[41]

For a city celebrated for its medieval past, there is a lot to assemble to tell the stories of Toruń's more recent but extremely painful Second World War history. Gingerbread will only cover up so much of such a dark, disturbing past.

The airfield seized by the Germans in September 1939 and used throughout the war remains, as do the military barracks, hospitals and warehouses. A former lard factory in the centre of Toruń, a camp known as Szmalcówka, was used between 1940 and 1943 as a re-settlement camp for Polish families held prisoner by the German occupiers. Of 12,000 prisoners, 1,199 died at Szmalcówka from starvation, lack of health care, sickness and brutal treatment by the guards. Nearly 400 children were among the dead.

At the cemetery Cmentarz Komunalny Nr. 2 there are memorials to those who died at Szmalcówka near to where the factory stood at Grudziadzka 139. Close by is a monument to 539 Soviet soldiers who died in 1945. Although the city was spared the obliteration experienced in Schneidemühl and other places that resisted, another cemetery – Cmentarz ul. Wybickiego – contains a mass grave of 188 Soviet soldiers who fell in the fighting for Toruń in 1945. There are also 21 Soviet forced labourers buried there.[42]

This is not the cheerful history that Toruń is known for.

---

41 Ochman, *Post-Communist Poland,* p.148.
42 At Traces of War website, online at <https://www.tracesofwar.com/sights/5445/Soviet-War-Graves-Cmentarz-ul-Wybickiego.htm>, accessed 21 June 2020.

6

First Contact

Vast reserves of fuel and ammunition had been stockpiled to keep 25,000 artillery pieces and mortars firing and 3,800 tanks rolling once the Red Army attack across the Vistula began on 12 January 1945. Marshall Chernayovsky attacked Königsberg the following day but dogged German resistance meant it was ten days before he could lay siege to the city. By then the hospitals were overflowing with wounded soldiers and the city was choked with refugees from the countryside. One of the few ways out was through the deep water port of Pillau [Baltiysk], on the northern end of the Vistula Spit. It became a key stopping point in the vast German seaborne evacuation of Operation Hannibal, as more than 450,000 refugees passed through Pillau before the town was captured in late April.[1]

On the western side of the Vistula Latvian Legionnaire Žano Mūsiņš could sense a change in mood, and wrote in his war diary:

> 16 January 1945: Corporal Veiss and I are sent to the Regiment's warehouse to receive armaments and ammunition for our Company. Going through some village Corporal Veiss shoots down some Polish sausages from drying frames in a farm. As always, we are half-starved from army food.
> 17 January 1945: We are still in the village, but there is some sort of feeling in the air that something is going to happen.
> 18 January 1945: We are testing our MG42 machine guns with real ammunition and adjusting all the sights so we can hit something smaller than a barn door!
> 19 January 1945: I am on guard duty during the night and had to exchange a few shots with unknowns after midnight.[2]

---

1   P. Clark, *The Death of East Prussia,* p.167. An estimated 2.5 million German soldiers and civilians were shipped out of East and West Prussia and Danzig in Operation Hannibal between mid-January and 8 May 1945.
2   Diary of Žano Mūsiņš, supplied to author.

In Toruń, preparations were being made to evacuate the town ahead of the Soviet offensive. The only way out was to head west. Augusts Spilners and his fellow soldiers gathered as much kit as they could carry.

> January 15: Our old group splits. They are taking men who have been fighting before. We are issued new clothes, boots, underwear and all accessories. Regiment commander speaks to the whole battalion and wishes good luck to us fighting soldiers and happiness. We leave tomorrow.
> January 16: We are waiting for the departure order. Today we have to go and dig trenches. Maybe the fighting will not come. I am redeployed to the fourth battalion of the 16th Company.
> January 19: We no longer need to go to work … Hear that the Russian tanks are only twelve kilometres from Torna [Toruń]. The battle is starting behind us. We are given tinned food and a loaf of bread. Everything goes topsy-turvy. We start to leave and lots of property is left behind because we cannot take it with us. I will have to carry my backpack. In my bag are two loaves of bread, two pairs of underwear, two [pairs of] socks and two blankets. The bag is heavy. The boys have found some boards to make a cart, so three or four men have put their bags on it. However, the material is weak and the cart breaks many times. Want [them] or not the belongings are sent flying in the ditch. Laughter as men look for their documents; if lost there is strict punishment from the Germans. We go through Torna and across the bridge over the Vistula river toward Bromberg.
>
> A tank is positioned on every street corner. Russian intelligence planes fly in the sky. It is sad to be leaving Torna; we have lived here for more than two months. The day [turns to] evening. We are sliding like eels; some pull sledges, others carry bags. We have only gone a few kilometres but already I feel the bag hurting my shoulders. However, I do not want to throw anything away; everything is needed. It is starting to get dark, and the weather is cold.
>
> While I am walking [I am] sweating; when resting [I] feel the cold. The snow sticks and then melts on my boots. They are new and let the moisture through. My legs are getting wet. We have already walked twenty kilometres but have to go further. The area is not inhabited, and we do not stay in the woods. I am tired. A few are dragging their bags in the snow. After a further five to six kilometres we rest. I wanted to rest after one kilometre!
>
> It is midnight yet we go on further. No houses so the regiment can't settle. We see refugees who have made a fire by the roadside and are resting. Cold, freezing young children and infants crying. Terrible. How far will these people go in the frost and snow? I am infinitely tired, in pain every step of the way, but to stop means to die. In the morning we [find] a mansion where there will be rest. We are sent to a loft where the wind whistles through so we cannot even light a fire. Took off my wet socks, put them underneath me and fell into a deep sleep.[3]

3   Diary of Augusts Spilners.

Months of camp life, harsh conditions and poor diet were taking their toll on soldiers like Ziedonis Āboliņš.

By this time we were all eating *ersatz* food because of shortages of everything, and soon we were suffering for that: most of us developed yellow jaundice. The lucky ones were put in hospital where there was decent food and a decent bed and it wasn't too bad. Everyone was hoping to get yellow jaundice! Then at the beginning of December [1944] I did.

I was sent to a German SS *lazarett* [hospital] in Konitz and that was fantastic. Oh, the food! It was meant for the real, proper SS; not chaps like us. They discharged me just before Christmas 1944 but by that time my unit was already fully trained and they were sent to the front, so I was placed in Berent for the Christmas and New Year. Everyone who was not properly trained went to Berent, [which was] like a reserve camp. There were quite a lot of civilians and refugees there too.

So in January 1945 I was digging anti-tank ditches for a couple of weeks and also working in the forest chopping down trees. At the end of January or the beginning of February 1945 – I can't remember exactly – I was sent to a unit that was formed from all these people that were hanging round and sent to the front. But I never really saw any Russians, because we were retreating all the time, all that February.

There was no real supply and by that time all the farms were empty. All the people living there had gone. We had to eat so we were living off whatever we could find on the farms. Our uniforms were summer uniforms so we were terribly cold in the snow as well. It was more or less up to us to find something to eat. One day we came across some English marmalade: it was fantastic.

Our unit commander was Captain Schimolunous, a Lithuanian. We were retreating all the time. You could hear the Russians, hear the battles and the shooting, but I never saw any. There were people who couldn't walk any more: I don't know what happened to them. There were refugees everywhere too. Horses and carts, mothers with children, civilians. It was chaos. I was very lucky to have had jaundice and been in hospital because otherwise I would have been caught up in the fighting – in that lot. Instead I had four very, very good weeks in the hospital. Another thing was that while I was in there they came and did the blood group [tattoo] and I didn't get that either. At least I was ahead of the Russians.

After a while I was declared cured, so I had to go back to that horrible place again. How they discovered you had yellow jaundice was by taking you to a dark bunker where the doctor was, and he took a lamp and looked in your eyes. If your eyes were getting yellow he sent you straight to the hospital. I came back and the doctor didn't remember that I'd been anywhere, so after a while I went back and said to him: 'I've got yellow jaundice.' He looked at my eyes and sent me back to the hospital. The head nurse at the hospital remembered me and said: 'What are you doing back here – I thought you were cured?' So I quickly made up a story about a heart problem and said: 'The doctor didn't send me back here for nothing – my heart's bad.'

The German doctor asked me some questions and let me stay. He was only a young man and he didn't want to send me back to be shot. The nurse was protesting but he said I could stay. Then I caught flu and that decided it. The Russian front came nearer and nearer and I thought I would definitely be sent back to the fighting, but the doctor gave me documents to go in the other direction, back to Germany, and away from the front. I managed to get on a train with a lot of other wounded German soldiers and I went where the train went. I ended up in a town called Schwerin. The hospital was in a school, named *Adolf Hitlerschule*.[4]

By then Augusts Spilners had reached Bromberg.

January 20: Along the road are many civilian refugees all fleeing the enemy. How I would like to rest, but we have to go on as each minute is precious. The Russians are already in Posen [Poznan] where we were meant to go. In the evening, we go through Bromberg. The boys bring sausages from culled cattle. I am not interested. My neck starts to hurt severely and my legs are frozen from walking in the snow.

Bromberg is abandoned. All the German units have withdrawn and the bridges are prepared for detonation. A wave of Russian tanks has begun to roll from the east, flowing unstoppably forward. Along the road [west out of] Bromberg are huge lines of refugees. Carts drawn by animals block the road, and we have to get off the road into the deep snow. Many boys are left behind; they cannot keep up. No-one cares about the sick. It's everyone for themselves. With anguish I am holding on. I do not want to stop and die.

At ten in the evening we come to a German mansion. The Germans have already left; [the only people] here are Polish workers. We will be able to settle in an empty house. The door is locked but [we] soon open it. The lads are looking for food the Germans have left. Our group finds a jam pot and we share the jam together. Eating jam with bread. Others boil potatoes they find in the cellar. Then the boys find pigs and geese in the barn. Our group kills a pig and we start cooking and eating. No-one thinks about sleeping. I am tired and am lying on the hay which has been brought in to the room. Tonight we will be warm sleeping.[5]

---

4   Interview with author, 27 November 2017. In later life Mr Āboliņš enjoyed a high-flying career as an architect and was a key figure in Latvian choral circles both in the UK and Latvia. The author interviewed both Mr Āboliņš and Talis Iskalns on the same day in their neighbouring homes in the Latvian community in Catthorpe in Leicestershire. Both had jaundice at the same time in 1945, were in hospital at the same time and missed the SS blood group tattoo because of their illness. They were probably on the same boat to Gotenhafen from Rīga on 4 October 1944.

5   Diary of Augusts Spilners.

Legionnaires of the 2nd Battalion of the 32nd Regiment of the 15th Division, who volunteered to return to Latvia to fight the Red Army in Courland [Kurzeme]. 670 men were shipped back to the western port of Liepāja from Danzig. Picture from January 1945. (Courtesy of the Latvian War Museum. Reference: LKM 5-16347/1652-FT1-2)

The 15th Division had a strength on paper of 19,000 men but when it was sent to the front in January, it had to leave one-third of its men at the training camp because there were only enough weapons for two-thirds of the division.[6] Numbers had been swollen by an influx of teenage recruits, possibly as many as 700, from the RAD (*Reichsarbeitsdienst*). German officers took over training while the Latvian officers were sent to learn specialist military skills, but efforts to deliver efficient fighting units were hampered by a lack of equipment. Fighting strength was further weakened when a unit of 670 volunteers and four officers under Captain Jānis Lanka was created as the 32nd Regiment reserve battalion and sent back to Courland to reinforce the frontlines against the Soviet offensive there (pictured above).

Reinforced by 330 men from the Field Reserve, the 32nd Regiment was reformed into two battalions with 39 officers, 234 NCOs and 1,490 soldiers, one battalion led by Major Alksnītis and one by Major Siliņš. They were armed with two infantry cannons, six mortars, 27 machine guns, 75 automatic rifles, 63 submachine guns, 1,179 rifles, 427 Panzerfausts and 180 Panzerschrecks.[7]

6   A rump of 456 men left behind at the camp under the command of Majors Šmits fell back unarmed later in the month to Danzig, where they were pressed into service resisting the Red Army encirclement.
7   Archive of Arvīds Krīpēns, Latvian War Museum, Rīga.

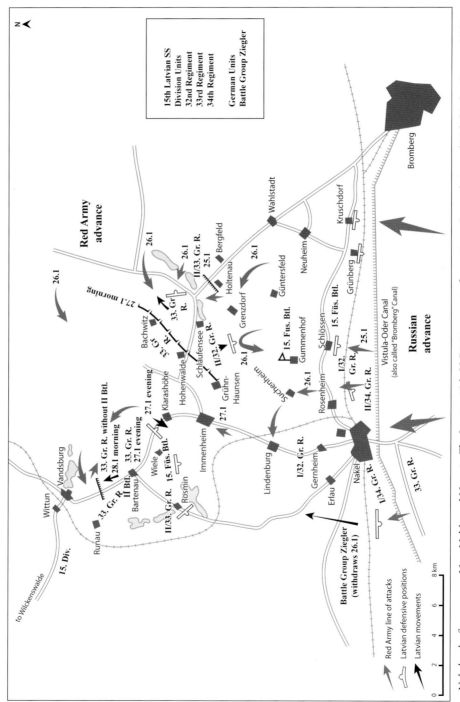

Nakel – the first contact. Now Nakło nad Notecią. The Latvian 15th SS Division saw its first action at Immenheim and Nakel in late January 1945, suffering heavy casualties. The men were in almost constant retreat after that until crossing the Oder in March 1945.

Equipment was moved using horse-drawn carts as there were few cars and trucks, and fuel was scarce. There was a shortage of boots and winter uniforms, and not every man had a steel helmet. Legion historian and deputy chief Arturs Silgailis judged that the division 'was far from combat readiness' when it was ordered to move through Konitz and Vandsburg towards Nakel on the night of 21–22 January.

The immediate objective for the Latvians was to defend the Vistula-Oder canal and to link up and join forces with the German garrison at Bromberg further east.[8] Under the overall command of Lieutenant Colonel Pauls Celle, they were sent into action at Immenheim on 22 January 1945.

In his diary for that day, Augusts Spilners writes:

> We go to Nakel but the Russians are already ahead of us, so we look for a detour across roads full of snowdrifts. Just the same as yesterday the roads are full of refugees, and it is harder to walk. At twilight we come to a mansion where the people lived luxuriously. The rooms have beautiful furniture and everything is left [as it was] when the owners fled. The remaining Poles feed the cattle. We think we are going to stay the night, but after an hour we go on. We would like to rest, but cannot. Going through the snow which has drifted across the field road is hard going.
>
> The moon shines and lights the sky. At 22:00 we arrive at a hamlet: we will rest here. The weather is brutally cold. For an hour we stand in the field waiting to go in. Then we go to a house and look for wood to light the oven. The lads find a bottle of wine and have a good time. The minute we rest we are almost doomed, because Russian tanks come driving down the street [into the hamlet]. Everyone is scared and we do not know what to do. Then thoughts begin to focus gradually, and our commander decides to withdraw from this position. Some leave their bags and flee, but Elmārs and I cut through the side roads. We've lost [our friend] Valdis. Russian tanks signal to each other that the coast is clear. [Then we are spotted] and the Russians start firing at us with machine guns. Bullets are flying over our heads … luckily there are no victims.
>
> The wind starts to get up and now there is a snowstorm. We have to go across the fields and around the village to escape the tanks. We rest, and throw many items out of our backpacks, keeping only [what is] necessary. We walk all day. I am tired and use all my strength to keep going. Many vehicles and carts have been left either on the road or by the side of the road. Having gone twenty kilometres, we come to a house. We are shown a small room where we can go in. It is just 'standing sleeping.' The lads who were left behind arrive one after another, including Valdis. I have become increasingly ill, have not eaten anything and cannot eat. The pain in my throat is burning, and I cannot sleep.[9]

8   Silgailis, *Latvian Legion*, pp.154–155.
9   Diary of Augusts Spilners.

Legionnaire Žano Mūsiņš at his home in
Coventry, May 2018. (Picture: author)

Žano Mūsiņš' diary entry reads:

> 22 January 1945: We started to
> move after midnight and have
> moved through Konitz and just
> now are close to Immenheim. You
> can feel that battle lines are close.[10]

As we talked at his home, I asked him
what he meant by that.

> ZM: In the Army, you just know. It's
> like an animal. You don't actually
> see or feel anything, but suddenly
> the whole system is working differ-
> ently and you know something is
> going to happen. You can't tell but
> the whole relationship in the Army
> between officers and instructors
> [NCOs] and the men … it seems to
> filter down.

VH: How do you feel being a 21-year-old in a German uniform? All around
you you're hearing stories about the Eastern Front. Do you sense that something
bad is going to happen?
ZM: I was always brought up very patriotically and seeing what the Russians
did to our country in 1941, I was prepared to do anything to stop them coming
back – and this was part of it. That was one of the reasons the Germans didn't
have much trouble calling us up, because we didn't want the Russians coming
back.

It wasn't so much the Russians themselves, it was the system. The Russians
couldn't have done anything to us if it hadn't been for the Latvian Communists.
They were the ones who had all the information and did all the damage against
our people. Imagine: on 14 June [1941] they just arrested and deported all of
the Latvian intelligentsia – the ones who did something.[11] All of a sudden you

---

10 Diary of Žano Mūsiņš.
11 The date of the first mass deportation of Latvians by the Soviets, when 15,000 were sent to
Siberia. A second mass deportation in 1949 sent a further 43,000 Latvians to labour camps in
Siberia.

think there's something wrong. [Vilis] Lācis,[12] [Jānis] Kalnbērziņš,[13] [Alfons] Noviks[14] – they were the later ones. There was a part of the Latvian intelligentsia that was left-wing. Lācis wrote beautiful books, patriotic books – but it turned out he was a deep-seated Communist and all of a sudden he was Minister of the Interior, and they threw our government out. He was one of the guilty ones.

We heard about the atrocities, of course we did. As soon as the Germans came in they opened up all the Cheka places. There were dead bodies everywhere, like in the *Zilais brinums* in [his home town of] Liepāja.[15]

We felt it in the college. 1940 was my last year but I wasn't allowed to finish college because I wasn't a member of the Communist Party. They said: 'It's needed for the faithful.' Even from the beginning in 1940 when things changed I felt they added a bit of pressure trying to get people to join 'the Red Corner' – a sort of Pioneer group with a Communist trend. I always got out of it by making excuses saying I had to go out to sea to carry out trials [he worked in a shipyard] … and I think eventually they decided that was it.

In 1944 we wanted to go to the Army anyway. They were coming to our border. Anything we could do, we would try to stop them. We knew it wouldn't be any better than the first time.[16]

The first unit to leave the training camp was the 15th Fusilier Battalion led by Sturmbannführer [Major] Vilis Hāzners, which reached Immenheim at noon on 23 January to find it in Soviet hands. He attacked, and by 14:00 the Latvians had re-taken the town, freeing 1,000 men from the 2nd Construction Regiment taken prisoner by the Russians as they retreated from Toruń unarmed. They also captured 30 Russians.[17]

Regimental veterinarian Lieutenant Augusts Ķikāns was with Hāzners: like many men he had wanted to return to Kurzeme to fight there in January but his boss had refused permission.

12 Writer whose 1933 novel *A Fisherman's Son* was a bestseller, and which remains the most translated Latvian literary work. Maintained links to the Communist underground during the independent Latvia interwar period, then became First Minister of the Soviet Republic until 1959. Signed orders in 1941 and 1949 deporting 58,000 fellow Latvians to Siberia, including Kārlis Ulmanis, four times Prime Minister and, following a coup, President from 1934–1940. Ulmanis' government had funded Lācis' writing and a film version of his book.
13 Communist Party boss in Soviet Latvia 1940–41 and 1944–1959. Former Red Rifleman and underground Communist Party organiser in the Latvian interwar period.
14 Soviet-era KGB boss, known for his cruelty, use of torture and execution of political prisoners. Convicted of genocide after Latvian independence was restored.
15 The 'Cheka' is the Latvian name for the internal security police, at various times the NKVD and KGB. Communist regime police killed 18 prisoners at the *Zilais brinums* in June 1941. (See author's previous book *The KGB and Latvia* for more details.)
16 Interview with author, May 2018.
17 Silgailis, *Latvian Legion*, p.162.

Soldiers of the 3rd Battalion of the 32nd Grenadier Regiment of the 15th Division of the Latvian Legion on their way to Immenheim. From the left: Purlans, Corporal Buks. Rear: Zemītis. (Picture: Latvian War Museum, LKM 5-13771/1453-FT)

It was very cold, about minus 22 degrees, as we moved out to the front on 22 January. We didn't have winter clothes, the carts were overloaded: we didn't have enough carts or enough horses. The horses weren't shod for winter either: they slipped and slid on the ice and it was a shame to watch them pulling the carts.

The squadron reached Immenheim. Because of [the] battles we were forced to leave it on 27 January. The inhabitants, mainly Poles, were very unfriendly. In the evening we reached Wilckenswalde. Food wasn't available, the horses hadn't had oats for days. On 31 January I went in to see the Division's [chief] vet Dr Wahl. I told him we were surrounded, and asked where I could get hay, straw and oats for the horses.

He said I needed to find hay and straw wherever I could, and to hand in a written request for oats as aeroplanes would drop supplies. I couldn't laugh in his face, so I made my way out.[18]

The records from Immenheim of the 15th Division Sapper Battalion, translated from the official history in the Legion 'Green Books', give an insight into German command methods in Pomerania. On 23 January the sappers were approaching the town:

At 14:10 the battalion stopped about 1 kilometre before Immenheim, which had recently been taken by the Recce Battalion. Here the battalion received its first battle orders, to clear out Immenheim. At 15:15, the battalion entered Immenheim.

Most of the 3rd Company hadn't yet arrived, so the 1st and 2nd Companies were ordered by the Divisional Commander [von Obwurzer] to shoot all the men found in the village, for the reason that they had supported the partisans who had offered resistance to the Recce Battalion. In discussions with the Recce Battalion and 34th Regiment commanders, who also had arrived in Immenheim, it was decided not to fulfil this order, but instead to warn all civilian men to leave the town. This order by the Divisional command had actually been aimed at the town's Polish inhabitants, but it was hard to separate those out from the Germans.

The men of the battalion carefully searched all the houses, as a result of which they succeeded in gathering quite a lot of Russian, Polish, English and French prisoners, who had been in the town's POW camps but who had, during the Russian attack on the previous day, escaped and hidden in the town's private houses. All the prisoners were put back into one of the POW camps, putting guards in place. In searching the houses, there was some resistance and one soldier from the 2nd Company fell.[19]

18 Ķikāns, 'Green Books,' vol. 6, pp.140–141.
19 Legion 'Green Books,' vol.6, p.256. The order is given so casually to shoot all the men in the village as partisans that one might wonder if that was routine.

Men of the 3rd Battalion of the 34th Regiment six kilometres north of Immenheim in late January 1945. Snow camouflage was not issued, so soldiers improvised in blizzard conditions, described in the original caption as 'carnival costumes'. (Picture: Latvian War Museum)

Many men of the 15th Division would experience combat for the first time at Nakel. Having been away on a gas mask instructors' course in Bromberg, Brunis Rubess finally caught up with his unit to find that many of his former friends were now dead.

> When our company is sent to the front on 22 January, we still haven't received winter clothes. In summer jackets, the boys go and fight the Russians. I stay behind, because I have to look after the anti-chemical weapons equipment for the company. After two weeks I come to the front with a supply unit. We stop near a field dressing station. It's full of wounded shot-up soldiers. Some have had their legs or arms blown off – others have lost limbs to frostbite. They moan and shout and there's nothing you can do to help them. The few doctors don't have enough strength or medicine. It's like an ante-chamber of hell.
>
> In the morning I meet Lieutenant Neilands. I quickly say to him: 'Lieutenant, sir, Private Rubess reporting for duty for the 2nd Company.' Neilands replies: 'Son, there's no such company anymore.'
>
> Of 150 in our company, perhaps twelve are left. The rest are either shot, frozen [suffering from frostbite] or taken prisoner.[20]

20 Rubess, *Brīnumainā Kārtā,* p.77. Atis Neilands would later play a significant role in the Recce Battalion's defence of the centre of Berlin in late April-early May 1945.

Rubess' decision to apply for the gas instructors' course saved and changed his life. He missed the boat taking the volunteers back to Courland, where survivors of the savage fighting were executed or sent to labour battalions in Estonia, Siberia and Kazakhstan; he escaped the fate which befell his company colleagues, and, because he didn't have the SS blood group tattoo, he avoided the subsequent stigma of being '*fucking* SS'. He wrote:

> As these tattoos were only given to SS soldiers, after the war it made it most likely that you would be persecuted. An American in Occupied Germany after the war would not care or know about their history. A little 'bird' (i.e., the tattoo) in the armpit of a young Latvian boy meant just one thing: '*fucking* SS' – a damned SS man, who would receive the requisite treatment. A kick up the arse. Eviction from the camp. Trouble in getting permission to leave the country. Whatever is appropriate at the time.

In his memoir he reflected on how powerful fate was, and concluded that sometimes thinking about that was 'too frightening.' Then some good fortune came his way.

> Neilands remembers the reference I received for supposedly having good German and suggested to the battalion commander that I be a messenger. Major Lazduzieds agrees: 'Present yourself to the regiment's headquarters and stay there until I give you further instructions.' That was his clearly unclear order.[21]

Also sent out from the training camp *Westpreussen* to slow the Soviet advance was an 'alarm unit' of men from the 31st SS Division; Hungarian Germans who had seen recent action in Hungary. They would fight alongside and under the command of the Latvians through some of the darkest days ahead. On 22 January they took up defensive positions around Flatow [now Złotów]. That night, three companies of another unit with them, Kampfgruppe [Battle Group] Joachim, commanded by SS Hauptsturmführer Helmut Joachim, were ambushed in woods controlled by Polish partisans and suffered heavy casualties. Withdrawing to Immenheim, the unit was placed under the command of the 15th Division and fought alongside the 15th Fusiliers defending the area around Immenheim until 28 January.

Here, the scale of the slaughter and the desperate situation the Latvians were about to become embroiled in becomes apparent. At 02:00 on 27 January, Divisional commander Wulff sent out 42 lightly-armed 'volunteers' from the Supply Regiment to scout out the road to Zempelburg: only three came back. By now down to 80 men, the 32nd Regiment was sent to positions north and south of the road into Flatow, with orders including the words: 'Anyone retreating into the town will be shot.'

With the 31st SS covering the withdrawal further west from Flatow and stragglers boosting numbers, Major Alksnītis reached Jastrow on 1 February, with four

21 Rubess, *Brīnumainā Kārtā*, pp.77–78.

makeshift companies of around 60 men each. In the period between 22 January–4 February 1945, when the 32nd Regiment reached Landeck, Alksnītis lost between 1,000–1,500 men – an average of 100 men a day.[22]

This account of the retreat of the Reconnaissance or 'Recce' Battalion to Jastrow shows how close and sudden the combat could be.

> On 29 January at 01:00, the command of the Reconnaisance Battalion was again taken over by SS-Hstuf. Pomrehn. His adjutant was Lieutenant Jurgens. The battalion had repeatedly received an order from the commander of the Division to hold the occupied positions to the last, even in cases [when] their neighbours had been pushed back and communications had been lost. At 10:00, when the enemy lauched a tank-supported attack on Sypniewo, the Battlegroup Joachim retreated.
>
> The enemy in the sector of the battalion operated with cavalry reconnaisance units, and shelled the battalion with sparse mortar and anti-tank cannon fire. The reconnoiters found large enemy formations moving along the road from Zempelburg to Kujan in the rear of the battalion: cavalry, artillery and battle-supply wagons. This movement was being observed the entire day. According to information received later, the enemy was in the rear of the battalion in a depth of about 30 kilometres. A pullback began at 17:00. Along forest paths, sometimes completely without roads, the battalion bypassed all inhabited places. The guide was a local resident.
>
> Upon reaching the Pr. Friedland-Kujan highway, the commander of the battalion and commanders of the companies entered a homestead to ascertain the location and gather information. Entering the yard, they met a group of Russian commanders entering the yard on horseback from the other side. The distance was about 10 metres. To their call: 'Our boys, Russians?' our commanders replied 'Our boys.' Several shots followed, and the Russians fell out of saddle. Help for them rushed in, and our commanders pulled back to their units in the coppice.
>
> Following this incident, the Russians surrounded the homestead and burned it down. The next objective was to cross the Pr. Friedland-Kujan highway and to reach Flatow across the lakes. Russian battle-wagons and infantry were moving along this highway. When the last Russian units had passed, the battalion crossed the highway and continued its march.
>
> On 30 January, at dawn, the battalion reached Friedrichsbruch. From there, large Russian units could be seen moving parallel to the direction of our march. From local residents we learned that Flatow is still ours. The battalion then proceeded to Stewnitz for rest, setting up defense posts. The commander of the battalion went on to Flatow to establish liaison. At 18:00, the battalion received

---

22 R. Pencz, *For the Homeland, The 31st Waffen-SS Volunteer Grenadier Division in World War II* (Mechanicsburg, PA: Stackpole Military History Series, 2009), p.235 and Alksnītis in Latvian 'Green Books', vol. 6, p.74.

an order to proceed to Flatow, promising rest there. The threatening situation of the Division, however, did not permit any rest. The battalion received a new assignment to take new positions east and west of Gursen by 05:00 to secure the retreat of the Division through the town, and then cover the retreat of the Division to Jastrow.

On 31 January, the battalion set out on the march to Gursen and reached it at 03:00. During the period from 06:00 to 12:00 the units of the Division passed through. During this period, the battalion had several fierce skirmishes with the enemy. At 12:30, the battalion received orders to retreat to Jastrow.

When the last units of the Division left Gursen, the commander of the battalion dispatched the supply platoon subordinated to the battalion on the road in the direction to Flatow. On contact with the enemy, this platoon was dispersed, and the battalion received no warning about the approaching enemy. The staff of the battalion was surprised in Gursen by the attacking advance company of the enemy. The 3rd and 4th Companies ran into a critical situation when the enemy cut off their retreat routes.

In close combat the 1st Company succeeded in stopping further advances by the Russians, and the envelopment from the right side. In this way, the 3rd and 4th Companies could pull back and join the rest of the battalion. Following the arrival in Jastrow, the soldiers received their regular meal and rest for the night.[23]

Kazimirs Ručs was the 15th Division's Catholic chaplain during this time. He saw the intensity of the combat as the Latvians tried to hold back the Soviets.

During this time the Latvians were facing two Red Army divisions with a huge number of tanks and artillery with orders to overcome the Latvians and destroy them. They fought in very difficult conditions. Pomerania was the place the Red Army went through to get to Berlin.

In January 1945, having crossed the Vistula, the Red Army attacked Pomerania. Everything that could be used was used against the oncoming Russians. Supplies of weapons and equipment sent from Berlin were destroyed by the Russians. Many men went to the front without a coat, only a rifle. There was no heavy weaponry, and not enough ammunition to withstand the Red Army artillery and tanks. In the encirclement at Landeck the Legionnaires fought hand-to-hand against the Russians. The blink of an eye could change everything. One person had to fall. Who is more scared and slower? A man could be shot or stabbed in the blink of an eye.

In war training it was emphasised that the enemy had to be bayonetted in the stomach. The slightest hesitation and you paid with your life. Fate is decided by survival instinct, not an ideal. The vast snowy battlefields were soaked in blood.

23 Freivalds, *The Latvian Soldier,* p.189. Trans. Arturs Grava, sent to author 20 July 2022.

Across them the cries of the wounded could be heard, suffering and in agony. It was a dreadful sight.

As the encirclement grew closer, the fighting zone was pushed together. In places the enemy is only 300 metres away, and you shot deliberately. You had to follow military training, which taught you not to panic. Don't get up where you've thrown yourself as the enemy will have aimed at that place. You have to move a step or two to the side, then get up. That way the enemy bullets shouldn't hit you. Take only a few steps, then fall back to the ground. Only with those sorts of jumps can you retreat. Thousands of Latvian Legionnaires died in the Landeck encirclement. They were basically grammar school boys mobilised in Latvia.[24] Some were barely 17 years old.

About 7,000 Legionnaires were drafted into the Legion after very basic training; the others were left in reserve. Those who didn't fall in battle were captured by the Russians, particularly those in the Reserve. I have to say that in Pomerania almost all the grammar school generation mobilised were killed. Few reached the West.

Many young men deserted and made their way to Danzig, where they were usually caught by the heartless German gendarmerie and hanged without trial as 'traitors to Germany'. How can the hopes of these young people for their homeland and their beliefs be described when, without a word and without honour, their dreams end at a German town's lamp post.[25]

---

24 In higher education, i.e., aged 17–18.
25 Ručs, Extract from *Dzīve ar Dievu* (2004) in Daugavas Vanagi Mēnešraksts Nr. 3 (01 July 2010).

7

Nakel

Modern day Bromberg – Bydgoszcz – doesn't feel like the eighth-largest city in Poland, but it's a nice place, built in a head-spinning number of styles from brick gothic to Art Nouveau to modern. Timber-framed granaries line the Brda River behind the sculpted figure of a tightrope walker crossing the water that has become the town's modern signature. There is, of course, a disturbing recent history.

Bydgoszcz was occupied by the Nazis soon after the Second World War started, and almost immediately the *Intelligenzaktion* began here – the systematic rounding-up, imprisonment or murder of those resistant to Hitler's plans. There were mass executions in the Market Square. Jews were sent to concentration camps or murdered. Slave labourers toiled in appalling conditions at an explosives factory in a forest on the edge of town called DAG Fabrik Bromberg, which is now a grim monument to their memory known as the Exploseum. DAG [*Dynamit Aktiengesellschaft*] was established in the 19th century by Alfred Nobel, the famed Swedish chemist and inventor of dynamite.[1] There was a workforce of 40,000 forced labourers – Polish, Russian and Ukrainian prisoners – at what was one of the largest Nazi explosives production bases.[2]

I spend a morning looking round this cold and miserable site charting Nazi efforts to manufacture nitroglycerin, and the efforts of secret Polish Home Army cells in the workforce to sabotage that. The Polish Resistance ran an extensive network here which helped smuggle back home Allied aircrew shot down over eastern targets.

It's a beautiful day so I eat a sandwich in a sunny city park to combat the chilly damp of the concrete corridors of the Exploseum then look around town, full of reminders of the horrors of the Nazis. I drive west alongside the Bydgoszcz Canal towards Nakło nad Notecią, known in 1945 as Nakel. Built 175 years previously, the canal at just 25 kilometres long was short but important, linking the Vistula with

---

1   Press release *Exploseum: Former German explosives factory turned into interactive museum* dated 01 February 2016 at <https://ec.europa.eu/regional_policy/en/projects/poland/exploseum-former-german-explosives-factory-turned-into-interactive-museum>, accessed 29 October 2019. Exploseum website at <http://www.exploseum.pl/>.

2   Bydgoszcz city tourism website at <https://visitbydgoszcz.pl/en/explore/what-to-do/2522-exploseum>, accessed 29 October 2019.

the Elbe. During the war, the Nazis used it to move bulk goods into the city and so keep the railways free for war materials. I follow its path until I reach the outskirts of Nakło, the scene of the first real action for the Latvians.

The 34th Grenadier Regiment captured most of the town on the evening of 24 January. Sporadic street fighting continued overnight. To the east, the 32nd Grenadier Regiment dug in at Schlossen while Vilis Hāzners and the 15th Fusilier Battalion took up positions north of the canal at Kruschdorf.[3]

Žano Mūsiņš was a rookie Legionnaire in that force and kept a diary of his memories.

> 23 January: We engaged some advanced Soviet troops but as they were without tank support, with our machine gun fire we chased them back towards Nakel. It is a peculiar feeling that you have to shoot at another human being for no apparent reason except that he is shooting at you. A few bullets whistled past my ears! It was a strange elated feeling but no fear, almost like being in competitive sport.
>
> 24 January: We have advanced to the town of Nakel and taken some of it, but the Russians received reinforcement with the help of tanks, and that stopped us dead. We had no artillery or tank support![4]

Russian Front veteran Jānis Čevers also saw action at Nakel and discovered the ways of the war here.

> We didn't have winter uniform in Russia, but when we got to Nakel in Poland we would march through a village and men would take bed linen, cut a hole for their heads and cover themselves with it. The Poles stripped their beds! There was no official camouflage. We had a darker blue uniform. A little bit darker for SS. I think the Wehrmacht [uniform] was lighter. We were thrown in even though the youngsters weren't fully trained. The Russians broke through and we were sent to push them back. We pushed them back 12 kilometres and stayed in Nakel with them sitting outside.
>
> The Russians first started going at Nakel with tanks but in towns tanks are no good, especially with those Panzerfausts. We liquidated all those tanks and they didn't come in any more. You can hide behind corners and then fire the Panzerfausts.
>
> The Polish hated the Germans, and when we pushed the Russians back a lot of Russians stayed there, hiding in the cellars. One day a Polish man says to us: 'My wife will make dinner for you,' so three or four of us went to his house, sat around the table and we put our guns on the table. He says: 'Oh, no need for them.'
>
> As soon as we started eating the Russian soldiers opened the door. It was a trap. Naturally we ... you know ... we shot them. We threw some grenades into the cellar and we got out of there. We escaped the trap.[5]

3   Now Ślesin and Kruszyn, just west of Bydgoszsz.
4   Diary of Žano Mūsiņš, given to author.
5   Interview with author.

Nakel town centre, summer 2018. Now Nakło nad Notecią. (Picture: author)

The street fighting in Nakel lasted until the morning of 25 January. As the Red Army captured Bromberg and moved west, Žano Mūsiņš and his fellow Latvians braced themselves to resist from positions east of the town.[6] His diary of those days reflects the pressure the Latvians were under.

> 25 January: We are trying to hold our positions but it becomes very difficult because the Russian anti-tank guns shoot very precisely and our heavy machine gun positions have to be changed every five minutes or so. We manage to hold out till the night closes in…
>
> 26 January: Russian troops [launch an] all-out attack with the support of tanks and heavy artillery fire. We are pushed back too because the [German] army unit on the flank of our battalion has withdrawn without us being informed, so we are in danger of being surrounded. There is no more connection with our command point and all units are in a state of disorganisation.[7]

6   *The Latvian Encyclopaedia*, 1952, p.28, from de-classified CIA files.
7   One theme occurring regularly in Legion stories is of German units withdrawing without informing the Latvian units left holding their positions. In this case, Battle Group Ziegler to the west pulled out. Commanded by SS Brigadeführer Joachim Ziegler, Battle Group Ziegler was part of the 11th SS Nordland Division. The division was shipped to Pomerania in January 1945 after three months of fierce defensive fighting in the Courland Pocket in western Latvia from October 1944. Ziegler's division then broke the siege of Arnswalde in Operation *Sonnenwende* and destroyed 197 tanks between 3–18 February in the defence of Stettin,

The men firing at Mr Mūsiņš were probably from the 889 Artillery Regiment and 328 Infantry Division, and most of the Soviet tanks in Nakel were from the 9th Guard Tank Corps.[8] At his home in Coventry 75 years later, we discuss the range of feelings Mr Mūsiņš experienced during these days.

> We were supposed to make a stand in a certain place but we met the Soviets halfway. If they had been expecting us I think we would have had a good thrashing, but they weren't. The observers spotted them first so we more or less jumped on them, and they were so surprised they couldn't hold out. They had a couple of those Maxim machine guns, with the little wheels on a carriage, so they had to drag them. They didn't have anything like the MG-42 that you could throw over your shoulder and put two little legs down and start firing. And they couldn't match the firepower of the MG-42. Whatever was in the way was simply swept down. We called them the Chainsaw or the Bonesaw.
>
> When we were in those showers it was no joke, but you overcome your fright because you've got a job to do. You just concentrate on that, and you ignore the bullets whizzing around your earholes all the time. Really, the biggest fright starts after it all calms down and you've got time to think back, and usually you're scared to bloody hell, and you think: 'How the hell did I get in there?' But before that you haven't got time to think because you've got things to do.

Mr Mūsiņš is a tall, well-built and clearly once-powerful man, around 1.9 metres.[9] Although now a little unsteady on his feet at the age of 95, he has very definite opinions about his experience on the Eastern Front.

> Nakel was sheer hell. There's no worse fight in war than in towns, where people live. It's terrible. Every corner, everything: you don't know what is where. You don't know where to shoot. You turn a corner and you could run into one man or a dozen. You don't see something until you're onto it. That happened a lot. The real front units – the sappers – had already broken the front of it. We were on the north-east side of Nakel, on the town side of the railway: we crossed that when we were pulling back.

---

for which he was awarded the Knight's Cross with oak leaves. Ziegler and the Nordland's Danmark and Norge regiments ended up defending the south-eastern approaches to Berlin in April 1945 alongside Latvian, Spanish and French SS men. Ziegler tried to break out from the city but was badly wounded by shellfire and died from his injuries on 2 May 1945. Source: Beevor, *Berlin,* p.383 and Traces of War website for medal details at <https://www.tracesofwar.com/persons/21310/Ziegler-Joachim.htm>.

8   Correspondence in September 2021 with Dr Łukasz Nadolski, director of the Military History Department of the Land Forces Museum, Bydgoszcz [Muzeum Wojsk Lądowych w Bydgoszczy] and author of three books in Polish about this action.

9   In old British measurements, 6 feet 3 inches.

He looks at the map.

> I can't really recall too much of it. It was a bit of a surprise, my first taste of war. You take care of other things, not really thinking about where you are. It was my first action: what they call 'christening by fire.' It was hell.
>
> Our biggest problem was the Russian anti-tank weapons. They were our biggest enemies. You'd take a heavy machine gun with a stand and go up in a house on the first floor with a view from where you can fire. You let off three or four bursts of fire but then you'd better move! You'd only have a minute or so to move to another place, or you'd had your chips. Because those Russian anti-tank guns! They could shoot from five miles away through a window. Christ – the precision! After about a minute … straight through that window … BOOM!
>
> I learned that in Nakel. I was on the third floor, overlooking the river and it was ideal. All of a sudden there was a big *boom!* underneath us on the floor below and the squad commander shouted: 'Get out of that window! Go elsewhere!' No sooner had we got out than *Boom!* in there. If he hadn't said anything that would have been us all finished.
>
> They were bloody terrors. And you learned to judge it, because your life was in your own hands. They'd have you. They were really precision instruments. If you didn't move off, you'd had it. You had to keep changing your positions from one place to another, and they'd chase you to hell and back. The best thing to do was to move from that building to another. All the time you had to be on your toes, and that's very stressful.[10]

The Latvians were on the receiving end of new Soviet methods of tackling defensive positions. The experience of street fighting in Königsberg earlier that month had prompted Marshal Bagramyan to call on his officers to find new tactics for urban fighting. One approach was to take out the upper floors of buildings first, as observers used the height to direct defensive fire. After taking out the 'eyes' of the strongpoint, the focus was directed at the lower floors, basements and cellars.[11]

Encirclement was another feature of combat on the Eastern Front. Red Army commanders surrounded towns like Nakel and divided them into manageable sections, using heavily-concentrated fire to overwhelm and grind down defensive positions. Detachments of about 400 men in a mix of infantry and machine gun companies supported by tanks, assault guns, artillery and mortars would then storm and overcome any resistance remaining.

On the night of 25–26 January 1945, the Russians broke through the Latvian frontlines on a wide front at Nakel, Hohenberg, Schlossen and Kruschdorf. The 34th Regiment pushed them back and, with German reinforcements but taking heavy losses, the 15th Fusiliers re-captured Kruschdorf. Soviet tanks moved up, and with no heavy weapons, the Latvians fell back north to positions between two lakes at

---

10   Interview with author, 2018.
11   Beloborodov, 1978, in Duffy, *Red Storm on the Reich,* p.354.

Schlaufensee [Słupowo]. A further Red Army breakthrough at Schlossen left the flank of the 34th Regiment exposed and put pressure on Immenheim further back. To make things worse, an attempt by the 15th Fusiliers to break through the encirclement thrown around them ended with almost all the officers being killed or wounded.

Among the wounded was battalion commander Vilis Hāzners, a Russian Front veteran decorated with the Iron Cross for his bravery who became a significant figure in the post-war history of the Latvian Legion. He was badly wounded at Immenheim and shipped to hospital in Denmark, where he spent the rest of the war.[12]

The 32nd Regiment left many dead behind too. Two companies led by Major Alksnītis fought at Nakel, two companies under Major Fridrichs Rubenis fought at Schlossen – Rubenis having replaced Lieutenant Colonel Pauls Celle, who had suffered a nervous breakdown – and three companies under Major Siliņš fought at Schlaufensee. Having suffered heavy losses, the survivors fought their way back in small groups to Immenheim, which they held until 27 January, before retreating through Kujan to Flatow.

The 33rd Regiment fought on and stopped the Red Army working round the left flank of the division. The 15th Artillery blew Soviet roadblocks open and under the cover of a snowstorm slipped through the Russian lines to the village of Wittun, about three to four kilometres west of Vandsburg.[13] But here, the divisional commander SS-Oberführer Herbert von Obwurzer and his interpreter Untersturmführer Putniņš disappeared. Stories varied as to how this happened, but they were presumed dead. Command passed to SS-Oberführer Adolf Ax, whom Legion historian Arturs Silgailis describes as 'an elderly man with little ability to command.' The Red Army eventually forced German and Latvian forces out of Nakel on 27 January.[14]

⌒ – ⌒

12 Hāzners biography at <https://latvianlegion.org/index.php?en/accused/Hāzners/level-05-bio.ssi>, accessed 02 June 2020. Hāzners was a founder of the Daugavas Vanagi veterans' benevolent association at the Zedelghem camp in Belgium and emigrated to the United States in 1956. In 1979 he was the first Latvian officer accused of war crimes when the US Immigration and Naturalisation Service brought a denaturalisation case against him based on falsified KGB documents, notably Paul Ducmanis' 1963 booklet *Daugavas Vanagi – who are they?* which named him. Imants Lešinskis, the KGB agent who oversaw production of this propaganda and circulated it among western visitors to Latvia, admitted it was made up when he defected. The case against Hāzners collapsed due to lack of evidence. An appeal by the Office of Special Investigations [OSI] was rejected and a judicial review criticised the prosecution for presenting vague and conflicting witness statements and for coaching witnesses. Further detail, including extracts from the lengthy proceedings, can be found at <https://latvianlegion.org/index.php?en/accused/Hāzners/level-00-case.ssi>.
13 Silgailis, *Latvian Legion,* p.162. These towns are now Witunia and Wiecbork.
14 In one story, von Obwurzer was last seen riding a white horse towards the frontlines after mentioning 'family problems'; in another – by Ax – he was ambushed and killed by a Red Army reconnaissance unit, while a third version has him surviving the war before living in Berlin. Ax led the unit until February 1945 when he was replaced after the disaster along 'the Road of Slaughter'. He was then put in charge of the 32nd SS Volunteer Division '30 January' which fought and was mostly destroyed at Halbe. Ax survived.

Memorial to the liberation of Nakło nad Notecią in the town centre. (Picture: author)

My visit to Nakel happens in summer, when this part of Poland seems like a very agreeable place. It's part of a network of medium-sized long-established county towns with good road connections past fields bursting with crops. At Ślesin, I stop and look on my map to see how the Soviet advance played out. The silvery-green Bydgoszcz Canal, lined with anglers and their rods, runs straight west below the town. Once over the canal the terrain is flat and exposed up to a tree line a couple of kilometres north. These are farmers' fields – there's no real cover. Advance Soviet units would have had to cross this wide stretch of open ground then fight their way uphill to the railway line and a key road and rail bridge. After that, the road leads through Ślesin village up to the main road east and west at the top. Buildings overlook the road all the way, and many could be old enough to be the originals – it looks like a tough slog.

⁐ — ⁌

I drive on and park in the centre of Nakło, feeling a little strange. This is where Žano Mūsiņš was, facing tanks; where Jānis Čevers was, escaping deadly traps. In the centre of the town square there's a monument to the war. It's like the broken end of a sword, a tall thin shard of concrete with a complex geometric twist as it rises. There's a stone block carved with figures around a metre and a half from the ground, with the date *1945*. The scene is one of celebration, with a young woman giving flowers to a Polish Red Army soldier. A child rushes to greet another soldier while a local youth waves the flag of Communism cheerfully. Perhaps ominously, the officer in the centre of the scene seems to be observing everything carefully. There are fresh flowers – plenty of them – around the base of the column.

This one memorial alone sums up the complexity and difficulties of Polish history since then. The monument signals gratitude to the 1st and 2nd Polish Armies, created in the USSR in 1944, which fought as part of the Red Army offensive liberating Poland from the Nazis. The officers were often either Russian, or Polish Communists. There was no love for either Stalin or Communists in Poland, with many Poles deported to Siberia between 1939–1944, along with Lithuanians, Estonians, Latvians and many other ethnic groups. In 1941, General Anders formed a separate Polish army in Russia at the request of the Polish government-in-exile in England, which fought with the Western Allies against the Nazis in Italy, notably at Monte Cassino.

It is the Communist soldiers commemorated on this statue, but the flowers are for Polish Army Day on 15 August, the week before my visit. This celebrates Polish victory over Lenin's Bolsheviks in 1920 which halted the export of worldwide Communist revolution from the Soviet Union. Polish history is no less complicated than anywhere else.

I walk to the south-facing edge of the square and check my map. Along the road stretching away ahead of me – Hallera – the Red Army tanks and infantry moved in towards Nakel. When the battle was lost, the Germans and Latvians pulled out to the north, behind me, heading for Mrocza – then Immenheim – along Mrotecka Street. Many Poles stayed in their basements and waited for the battle to end.

Mannequin of Soviet soldier at Muzeum Ziemi Krajeńskiej, Nakło nad Notecią. (Picture: author).

Nakło looks like a thoroughly nice place. Although there's been human settlement here since the 10th century, the centre has the feel of a 1920s period county town, with local government buildings, a library and a town hall built around a main square, where the war memorial is. Just off the square is a local history museum in a half-timbered wooden barn-style building with a huge solid wooden door. I knock on it, more in hope than anything else. To my surprise it's answered by the museum director, Tomasz Pasieka, who not only speaks English but also gives me a guided tour.

Tomasz tells me that the war years brought uncertainty, fear and death to Nakło, and his museum contains a potted history of that. In glass cases around the walls, equipment abandoned by the retreating German troops is displayed. There are petrol tanks, gas masks, grenades and ammunition cases. Standing at the far end of one glass cabinet is a mannequin of a young and rather traumatised-looking Soviet soldier in a quilted jacket and trousers with a showroom condition PPSh sub-machine gun slung around his neck.[15] He has felt boots and his hands are bare, but what's most noticeable is the thousand-yard stare that's coming from under the felt cap with the red star. It's a model, but this youth does not look much older than 20, nor does he look well-fed or at ease. The effect is quite poignant.

Another cabinet is dedicated to one of Nakło's most celebrated personalities, the athlete Klemens Biniakowski. Born in 1902, Biniakowski was Polish sprint champion 22 times and raced at the 1928 Olympic Games in Amsterdam in the heats of the 400 metres. He went to the Berlin Olympics in 1936 as Poland's flagbearer, and ran a stage in the 4 x 400 metres qualifying round. In August 1939 he was mobilised and fought in the September campaign against the German invasion. During the German occupation he became a target for the *Selbstschutz*, the right-wing Self Defence militia which sprang up to support the Nazi administration. After escaping several militia traps, Biniakowski headed for the Swedish island of Gotland through Lithuania. Captured and arrested by the Germans, he was sent first to the Sachsenhausen concentration camp, then in 1942 transferred to Neuengamme, near Hamburg.[16]

In a cabinet on one display table there is a model of the Potulice concentration camp, seven kilometres east of here, which was used by both the Nazi and Communist regimes as a place to hold prisoners. It was set up by the Nazis as a forced labour camp making wings for the Messerschmitt Bf 109 fighter and Bf 110 bomber. Estimates are that 25,000 prisoners passed through Potulice, which came to specialise in using Polish children separated from their parents as slave labour, loading wagons at the railway station or moving building materials. They were badly treated, underfed and abused and many became ill: of the 1,296 people who died there in the Nazi era, 767 were children.[17]

---

15 Known to the Latvians as 'Pay-pay-shah'.
16 Biniakowski always managed to outwit those trying to kill him, and lived until the age of 82. He died in March 1985.
17 From *Forum Bydgoskiego Stowarzyszenia Miłośników Zabytków 'BUNKIER'* at <http://forum. bsmz.org/viewtopic.php?f=9&t=284>, accessed 29 October 2019, translated. With Nazi defeat, the camp was used by the victorious Communist authorities between 1945 and 1949 as a detention centre for 34,932 Germans, prisoners of war and anti-Communist Poles from the Home Army [Armija Krajowa] first by the NKVD Soviet security police and later by the Polish Communist-era

Nakel resident and Polish champion sprinter Klemens Biniakowski [centre] was a target for local fascist groups. He always got away. The other athletes are probably friends from Towarzystwa Gimnastycznego Sokół [Falcon Gymnastic Society] in Nakel, Biniakowski's first sport club. (Picture courtesy of Tomasz Pasieka)

The frontlines of the war swept through Nakło leaving not only death and destruction in their wake but also stories of lucky escapes, courage and humanitarian gestures. Tomasz gives me a booklet of stories from the war written by people from the town. One remarkable account comes from Henry Adamczyk, who was a babe-in-arms as the Germans prepared to flee from the Soviet advance.[18]

In the final days of January 1945, Nakło was a place of intense warfare. The Nazis were fleeing [west] and coming to the town. As happens at such times, the magnitude of the tragedy was compounded by the very severe winter.

Food was beginning to run low, so my grandma and mother went to family living in nearby Paterek in search of food. I was a toddler then, 18 months old, and looked after by my aunt Basia (who was a bit older than me) and uncle Tadeusz (who was a bit younger than her). We were three little terrified children. In the city the battles started for real and shells were exploding nearby. Aunt Basia realised that it was not safe in the apartment, so she took me by the hand and with her younger brother Tadeusz, left to search for a safer place.

My mother and grandma, now re-supplied with food, were trying to return to Nakło from Paterek, but with a group of about a hundred people were stopped at the edge of the village on the way to Nakło by a Red Army artillery unit. The barrels of their guns were pointing at the town, ready to fire. When they heard there were still civilians there, the commanding officer decided not to shell Nakło. My mother and grandmother came upon us by chance as we were looking for shelter in the cellars of buildings at ul. Bydgoska 47/49, where there were other people also using it as a shelter.

One man saw soldiers wearing white snow capes, thought it was the Russians and hung the Polish flag on the building. That was not a good decision. The soldiers turned out to be Latvians, fighting together with the Nazis in SS formations.[19] Everyone was ordered into the yard and the men were lined up against the wall, with the intention of being shot. Horror and despair descended upon us. Then through the gate from the Bydgoska road, Nazi soldiers arrived on a motorcycle, shouting to flee, because the Russians were right behind them. We

Ministry of Public Security. Hunger, overwork and lack of medical facilities meant epidemics of typhus and dysentery were rife. Estimates of the death toll at the camp vary between 2,915 and 5,000. Source: *Centralny Oboz Pracy w Potulicach (1945–1949)*, a report for the project *Potulice – jedno miejsce, dwie pamięci* [*Potulice – one place, two memories*] at <http://www.geschichtswerk-statt-europa.org/media/projekte/Die Broschure.pdf>, accessed 29 October 2019, translated.

18 Some readers may consider these accounts a fraction too remarkable and point to them as Soviet mythmaking of hero soldiers who saved Poles to deflect from the deportation and killing they perpetrated against the Polish themselves. As one Latvian remarked: 'Elements of the story may well be true but taken as a whole it sounds embellished. I have read a lot of Soviet-written history and general propaganda and it fits the bill.'

19 Author's note: See Jānis Čevers' earlier comments that the Latvians had not been issued with snow camouflage, and were stripping bedsheets from houses as they retreated to blend into the winter fighting conditions better. The picture of the Legionnaires at Immenheim some days earlier [p.130] shows them wearing bedsheets.

were formed into columns and marched along the Pocztowa road in the direction of the railroad crossing, a protective shield for the soldiers.

Bullets were whistling above us. We stopped at the last building on the right (currently a garage and workshop) to shelter from the heavy gunfire. We were put into two lines, me in my mother's arms. I was getting hungry and started to cry loudly. A soldier ordered my mother to silence me. I don't know why, whether because of my lack of German or because of my perverse character (certainly not because of my heroism), I carried on crying.

Such insubordination was too much for the Nazi. He hit her on the chest with the butt of his rifle. Mother fell to the floor with me in her hands. Grandma came running up with Aunt Basia and Uncle Tadeusz. They helped Mum get up and hide from the Nazi. Grandma managed to quieten me down. We were formed into columns again, still as a protective shield, and driven towards Mrocza. At the railroad crossing the Nazi who had assaulted my mother got hit with a stray bullet and fell to the ground. As she passed him, my mother surreptitiously spat on him.

When we reached the next village the Nazis suddenly left us. We debated what to do next. Grandma, Aunt Basia, Uncle Tadeusz and some others decided to go back to Nakło. Still carrying me in her arms, my mother was intent on going to my other grandmother in Minikowo, where my father was supposed to be heading. As it turned out, Father tried to reach Nakło through Ślesin but was caught by the Nazis and locked up in a barn that was going to be set on fire. Somehow he managed to escape – but that is a different story. Mother continued her heroic march in the snow and freezing temperatures, wearing shoes without socks and still carrying me. We were getting more and more cold in the frost and snow, and there was no way of warming up.

Finally we finally reached Minikowo [east of Nakło]. The Russians were stationed in the village, concentrating their troops before an attack on Nakło. When I arrived, I was practically an icicle and my mother couldn't stretch her arms from the cold. One of the Russian soldiers stationed in my grandmother's apartment took me in his arms and began to warm me with his body and rubbed my body intensively with spirit. To the great delight of my close relatives and the soldier who took care of me, I began to come back to life. Many times the soldier took me in his arms, cradled me and hugged me, humming lullabies under his breath. Someone noticed tears in his eyes…[20]

Suddenly the order came for the soldiers to leave the village for Nakło. My guardian picked up his equipment, hugged me and set off to free my hometown

20 It turned out he had a child Henry's age 'back home': a sentimental story full of horror, fear and jeopardy, with one or two holes – but forefronting the humanitarian, caring actions of the Red Army soldiers who came to the rescue, saving not only the boy's life but the lives of everyone in the village and freeing them from the Nazis. It's a perfect story for a pro-Soviet audience.

from Nazi occupation. Unfortunately, I never knew his name or whether he survived the war. [21]

Another story is that of Alfons Kubicki, who was born in Nakło in January 1929. His father worked at a meat plant and was called up when the war started, then taken prisoner and sent to a POW camp. From there he was sent to work at the *Dynamit-Aktien Gesellschaft* [DAG] Fabrik Bromberg explosives factory, one of three arms factories built by the Nazis to produce nitro-glycerine.[22]

> There was an explosion at Legnow [the DAG factory] on 24 June 1944 which killed German engineers, some prisoners and a few Poles, among them my father. When the detonation happened he was either in the bunker, or near it. The cause has never been fully explained. Some say it could have been a suicide attack, or a work accident.[23]

Alfons had been sent to work on a German-owned farm in Gromadno, 20 kilometres south-west of Nakło after his father told the German authorities the family wanted to remain Polish rather than join the Nazi *Volksdeutsche* list, despite the privileges Greater German citizenship brought. Alfons witnessed the liberation of Nakło.

> The Russians arrived from three sides; from Mrocza, Bydgoszcz and Paterek [four kilometres south of Nakło]. The battles took place on the night of 26–27 January 1945. It was heavy winter. I remember the next morning there were six tanks on the street destroyed; burned-out houses, the road and railway bridge was in ruins, there were barges sticking up in the frozen river and lots of debris. After the liberation the cleaning and re-building began, getting the factories back to work and organising co-operatives. The event I remembered the most was the community funeral for the people who were executed in Paterek. Military cars carried the coffins to Nakło cemetery.[24]

Before I leave the museum Tomasz gives me directions to the cemetery, about a mile out of town above the railway line. I drive there to look round it. The 500 Red Army men who died in the battle for Nakło were laid to rest here in their own dedicated section. There is a column with a red star on the front which is in good order and has

---

21 From *Zeszyty Historyczne Muzeum Ziemi Krajeńskiej* Nr. 5 (Historical Notebooks of the Krajeńska Museum) in 2015. Trans. Janusz Korona.

22 Part of the DAG Fabrik factory is now the award-winning Exploseum museum, mentioned earlier.

23 Kubicki, A., 'My memories of the war in Nakło' in *Zeszyty Historyczne Muzeum Ziemi Krajeńskiej nr 5* (Historical Notebooks of the Krajeńska Museum, 2015). Trans. Janusz Korona.

24 Between October and November 1939, as part of their action against the Polish intelligentsia and community leaders, the Nazis murdered 218 people from the area around Paterek and Nakło, among them 46 priests and religious officials, including two nuns.

Red Army memorial at Nakło nad Notecią cemetery, summer 2018. (Picture: author)

been painted recently. The graves are clean and well-maintained, but they are bare plots, dusty and unmarked. There is something missing. It takes a few moments for me to realise what is absent, and then it dawns on me. It is love.

The graves of local people are tended carefully and fresh flowers have been laid on many of them. There are watering cans and trowels on some of the plots, and people obviously come and spend time with their dear departed. That's not the case with the graves of these soldiers, who came from the various corners of the Soviet republics and gave their lives in the battle against Hitler.

It's a strange message to digest. These men died freeing the town from the grip of the Nazis, but they were not from here, and – in a way, understandably – no-one mourns their lost lives at this spot any more. While their graves are neat and tidy, there's no evidence that anyone actually cares about them as people. Maybe that's just what happens after 75 years – almost everyone who lived through that time and knew anything about it is dead as well. And why would Poles who lived through the Communist times mourn nowadays for foreigners who wore the uniform of their next oppressor?

A monument to the 178 people killed by the *Selbstschutz* local fascist militia stands in a separate section of the graveyard. This was the gang that could never catch the sprinter Biniakowski: if they had, his name would have been on this monument too. These were such twisted, deadly, treacherous times.

SS-Oberführer Adolph Ax wrote an account of events at Nakel in a 1947 report, published in a difficult-to-find book by Terry Goldsworthy called *The Waffen-SS in Allied Hands, Vol 1 – Personal Accounts from Hitler's Elite Soldiers*. Ax wrote the report without reference to his notes or any of the Latvian commanders who were there, and admits that the dates of the action described may have been one or two days earlier than estimated.

Ax arrived in Deutsche Krone on 22 January 1945 as Chief of Staff of the VI SS Corps HQ, taking orders from the HQ in Furstenburg of Operations Staff, Baltic Sea.[25] Under the direct command of Army Group Vistula, his orders were to defend the Nietze sector between Schneidemühl and Bromberg [Piła and Bydgoszcz]. The division consisted of:

- The 15th Waffen-SS Latvian divisional HQ and map reproduction section.
- The 32nd Infantry regiment with two battalions of four companies each.
- The 33rd Infantry Regiment, with two companies of four battalions each.
- The 34th Infantry Regiment with two battalions of four companies each.
- An anti-tank company with nine 75mm anti-tank guns and caterpillar tractors.
- The 15th motorised signal battalion with one motorised telephone company and one motorised radio company.
- The 15th Engineer battalion with two companies.
- The 15th Reconnaissance Battalion with four motorcycle companies.
- Task Force Joachim, with six rifle companies.
- A supply battalion.
- The 1st Battalion 15th Artillery Regiment with three batteries of four 105mm howitzers.
- The 48th SS Panzergrenadier regiment.
- An artillery battalion.
- Two motorised rifle companies from the SS NCO's officer school at Lauenburg and the security detachment committed in the Nietze sector.[26]

As 15th Division commander von Obwurzer was away, Ax inspected the regiment. His first impressions were not good. Ninety percent of the men in uniform were hopelessly inexperienced and untrained replacements, some of whom had not fired live ammunition before. There were few heavy weapons, no winter equipment and the artillery had been sent elsewhere, but Ax describes the personnel as of 'excellent calibre', in good health and with morale generally high, though he adds: 'the fighting quality was doubtful due to training.' Hatred of Russia was deeply rooted and rein-forced during the Soviet occupation, he noted, with the Latvians regarding fighting against Russia as 'a national duty.' Of the political attitude of the Latvians in the division, Ax wrote:

25 Operations Staff *Ostkueste*.
26 Ax, in T. Goldsworthy, *The Waffen-SS in Allied Hands, Vol 1 – Personal Accounts from Hitler's Elite Soldiers* (Newcastle upon Tyne: Cambridge Scholars Publishing, 2018), p.216.

They were Latvians first and foremost. They strived for national independence. Confronted with the alternative of having to choose between Germany and Russia, they decided in favour of Germany because they desired to ally themselves with Western civilisation. To be subject to German control seemed to be the lesser evil.[27]

On 24 January, Divisional HQ was moved to Vandsburg and the 34th Regiment was sent from Konitz to Nakel with an advance detachment with orders to take the town. Progress was slow as the roads were icy, covered in snowdrifts and blocked with refugees heading north. In his report, Ax is critical of the commander for moving too slowly and cautiously, despite the fear of enemy tanks in the area and the lack of weaponry to defend against them.

By 15:00 the Latvians had taken Immenheim but reported slow progress and fierce enemy resistance in the direction of Nakel. The attack was postponed to 25 January when Nakel was taken in fierce house-to-house and street-by-street fighting. A motorcycle squad was sent to Bromberg to make contact with the German garrison but was fired on in the forest and failed to get through. The Bromberg garrison then fought off a Red Army attack as reports came in of a big build-up of Soviet vehicles, including a number of tanks, in the Lebrechtsdorfer forest south-east of Nakel.

A thaw on 26 January meant the roads were already barely passable for wheeled vehicles, then heavy snow fell, bringing all supply traffic to a standstill. Soviet tanks were spotted advancing from the south-east at Bergfeld. Without artillery or anti-tank guns, the Latvians could only defend themselves with light weapons. They decided to wait for nightfall then attack, but were themselves attacked during the afternoon from the Lebrechtsdorfer forest. This attack was thrown back, and the Latvians counter-attacked unsuccessfully at 02:00 on 27 January.[28]

Ax also offered his thoughts on the mysterious disappearance of Divisional Commander Herbert von Obwurzer, whom history has recorded as talking of family problems before disappearing out toward the frontline on a horse, never to be seen again. Of his final moments, Ax wrote:

> At noon [on 27 January] the division commander SS-Brigadeführer von Obwurzer was reported missing. He had been at the CP [Command Post] of the 34th Regiment and from there drove to the CP of the 33rd Regiment in a small Volkswagen car. He did not arrive there. The escorting motorcycle messengers were unable to follow the car because of the deep snow. They could see the commander's car drive through a group of farmhouses some distance away and heard several shots.
>
> When they advanced on foot they received fire. The farms were located behind our own lines. It was presumed that along the drawn-out front a Russian

---

27 Ax, in Goldsworthy, p.218.
28 Ax in Goldsworthy, pp.220–224.

patrol had infiltrated into the main defensive area. The division commander was probably killed.

Ax continued:

> SS-Brigadeführer von Obwurzer was a regular officer of the former Austrian Army. As a result of his excellent leadership abilities and his thorough understanding of the problems of the Latvians, he was well-liked by the division.[29]

That afternoon the Russians entered Nakel and street fighting began. Further attacks came from the east at Hohenberg, and the division was scarcely able to withstand the pressure, fighting without winter clothing in temperatures of 14 degrees Fahrenheit (minus 10 degrees Celsius). Hohenberg fell that evening, then reports came in that Deutsche Krone had been taken. The decision was taken to evacuate Nakel that night. Ax concluded that without heavy weapons, artillery support or protection on the flanks, the 15th SS was no match in open terrain for the fast, mobile Soviet troops with tanks. The troops were not trained for situations needing 'considerable manoeuvrability', he wrote, adding:

> In issuing orders and transmitting messages, a detrimental factor became evident, namely that the division personnel did not speak German and consequently everything had to be translated.

In addition, the Dutch 48th SS Regiment could not be sent in time to help because there was no transport and nine anti-tank guns were not enough to defend the entire division. Considering the subsequent bad feeling between Ax and the Latvians, he praises their performance in this difficult situation.

> The troops had to endure extreme hardships because they were not equipped with winter clothing. The worst factor was the lack of felt boots. Most casualties were the result of frostbite. The personnel of the division fought with valour. They proved their merit particularly during an attack.
>
> No concentrated tank attack was launched. Such an attack directed against the flanks of the 15th Waffen-SS Grenadier Division would have dealt the division a deathblow.[30]

---

29 Ax, in Goldsworthy pp.223–224. Von Obwurzer was posthumously promoted to SS-Brigadeführer. While few Latvians have words of praise for Obwurzer – who fought in Latvia in the anti-Communist pro-Baltic German irregular force the Freikorps Iron Division during the 1919 battles of independence, he would certainly have been better liked by them than Ax was.
30 Ax in Goldsworthy, pp.225–226.

The graves of Soviet soldiers who died in 1945 at Nakło nad Notecią cemetery, summer 2018, untended. (Picture: author)

The intensity of the fighting at Nakel is described by the Latvian commander Jūlijs Ķīlītis in his memoirs of his service in Pomerania with the 34th Regiment of the 15th SS Division, translated here into English for the first time. This was some baptism of fire for the young recruits. Ķīlītis wrote:

> ...Major B. phoned me and warned me to be careful, that three enemy tanks had suddenly crossed the front in his sector, and they were driving round the town. Just a couple of minutes later, something stopped by our house, roaring loudly and suspiciously, opposite the shuttered window. When I looked at it, I saw the barrel of the machine gun and the turret with a red star on it. It was an enemy tank: a T-34. Sitting on the tank were four enemy soldiers, each armed with machine guns. Immediately, we lay down, but as the enemy didn't fire, we rushed out through the kitchen into the yard, taking Panzerfausts with us. It was quite a surprise. By the time we realised what had happened, the tank roared ever stronger and rolled further down the road, deeper into our rear.
>
> The tank had driven over to this side of the railway line and, to get back, it had to come past here a second time. We quickly put traps around everywhere on both sides of the crossing and started to wait. If the tank had seen us in this little house, it would simply have knocked it over on top of us. Together with

the Adjutant and Lieutenant I., we stood on one side of the crossing and decided to have a go together.

We didn't have to wait long, when the tank, roaring angrily again, came nearer from behind, down the only road. It had probably driven through the town and having found it empty, was going back to look elsewhere. We got ready for the fight. Our nerves were taut, like violin strings, because it's not as easy as it sounds to shoot up a tank and, additionally so, one with infantrymen sitting on top looking all around for someone to kill with their machine guns. They were the tank's bodyguards and eyes.

There's a moment where you have to stand eye-to-eye opposite the enemy and everything depends on who is nimbler and uses his weapon better. The tank appeared round the corner of the street and neared the crossing. It turned sideways towards us. You couldn't choose a better location. I was already aiming but the railings on the crossing were in the way of a direct shot. I waited for the tank to move forward just a metre … At this moment there was a *whoosh!* in the air, and the characteristically bright explosion showed that someone had got there before us. The tank slid forwards another 10 metres, then stopped and lit up like a flare.

Corporal Spuldzenieks, my runner, who stood twenty or so metres nearer the road, had shot off his Panzerfaust and hit it in the right place. All the infantrymen on the tank, except one left lying on the body of the tank, poured off it into the ditch. Then the hatch on the turret burst open and, one after the other, the tank's crew jumped out.

My lot, seeing that the tank was on fire, all jumped out of their hiding places and stood up with their guns in their hands, hunting the enemy soldiers. The machine gun positioned by the crossing, which the tank hadn't noticed, now angrily opened fire. The tank was completely surrounded by my guys and it was a wonder that they didn't shoot each other. I then ran out onto the road and tried, by shouting, to stop the firing, because I wanted to get at least one live prisoner. However, the shooting didn't stop until the enemy stopped moving. One man holding an automatic was so carried away, that having positioned his gun on the back of a colleague, like a living stand, blazed away wildly. The fighting spirit was excellent, and the routines gained in training came in very useful.

A long shout of *Urrāh!* rent the air, when the flames were followed by a thick blanket of smoke, which climbed high in the sky to signal victory over this monster. For many of them, it was their first meeting with a tank and they were very happy with the excellent capabilities of the Panzerfaust. It created a trust in one's weapons and oneself. A few men wanted to get closer to the tank. I called them back, because you could shortly expect explosions in the interior of the tank, where there would be signal rockets and ammunition and similarly, all weapons would be loaded and as the tank got hotter, they might fire by themselves.

And so it happened: first of all the rockets exploded, then the ammunition and finally the cannon, which had been loaded, shot for one more time.

Multi-coloured flames shot out of every gap. Once the explosions died down, one could assume there would be no further incidents.

We gathered up the documents from the fallen and after looking through them, sent them on to the regimental headquarters. The enemy soldier who was left lying on top of the tank had literally roasted there and the smell of burning flesh on the wind hit our nostrils. After about four hours, the flames died down. Now the tank looked like a blackened ghost.[31]

Ślesin's Soviet cemetery officially commemorates 211 Red Army soldiers who died in the fierce combat. However, around 2010, eyewitnesses told historian Łukasz Nadolski of the Muzeum Wojsk Lądowych in Bydgoszcz the remains of dead Latvian 15th Division Fusiliers were buried there as well. Attempts were made to exhume the Latvian fallen around 2015 but the Russians did not give permission, apparently fearing that the cemetery would be destroyed.

Ślesin's Soviet cemetery. (Picture courtesy of Łukasz Nadolski of the Muzeum Wojsk Lądowych, Bydgoszcz)

31 Ķīlītis, *"Es karā aiziedams…" Mani raksturīgākie piedzīvojumi Otrā pasaules karā*, pp.149–151, trans. Aivars Sinka.

8

Vandsburg and Jastrow

The Latvians withdrew from Nakel with their wounded but left many dead behind. The 33rd Regiment, 15th Fusiliers and Battlegroup Joachim fell back initially to new defensive positions to the north of Immenheim between the Weilensee Lakes.[1] From here, near Klarashöhe, the Latvians could keep the road to Vandsburg open for as long as possible and tackle Soviet troops advancing from both the south and east. Their plan was to let the Soviets get close then unleash a hail of fire to maximise casualties, blunt the attack and buy time for further withdrawal. Initially, the plan worked: Red Army advance units fell back with heavy casualties after their first attack. But they came back after dark to try again, and fighting for control of villages in the area continued through the night.[2]

Because trucks were scarce, horses pulled their two artillery guns, slowing down the retreat and meaning the Latvians were harried constantly by the Russians. Žano Mūsiņš describes these days in his diary.

> 27 January: Our unit withdraws towards Vandsburg. There are constant skirmishes with Russian troops. We have to be very careful of them using all sorts of tricks to trap us…
> 28 January: They have managed to trap us in a small corner. But thanks to our CO we manage to fight our way out towards Jastrow.
> 29 January: We hold off [the] Russian offensive by trapping two of their tanks and destroying them. Lull in fighting for a bit.[3]

I ask Mr Mūsiņš to explain more about 'the tricks' the Russians were playing with them.

> ZM: They formed small units in German uniforms. Not all of them spoke German, but one of them might ask for directions and then they'd say to

---

1 Latvian military historian Aivars Petersons describes Battlegroup Joachim as 'an unstable Yugoslav (Croatian), Ukrainian, Russian and German mixed formation.'
2 Silgailis, *Latvian Legion,* p.163.
3 Žano Mūsiņš' diary.

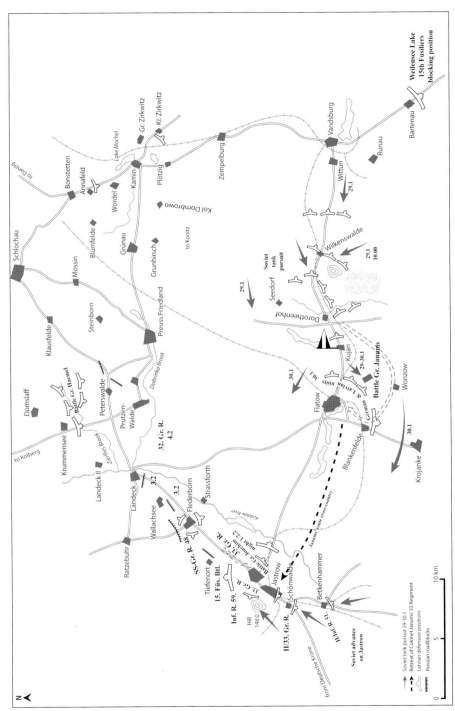

Operations 27–31 January 1945. The retreat from Vandsburg to Jastrow, the prelude to the slaughter at Flederborn and Landeck.

us: 'You shouldn't be here, you should be over there' and they'd baffle us and confuse us, try to split us and disorganise us. Their main trick was to send a man in dressed as a German general, with his arm tied up as though he's injured, and they'd play hell sometimes. I suppose war is war.[4]

VH: Who was your CO?

ZM: This was a unit the size of a company, and our commander was a man called Lieutenant Bruno Dombrowskis. I kept in touch with him after the war. He went to Canada – he's dead now. His father was an official in the Latvian Embassy in London in the Latvian independence time in the 1930s and his mother was an English teacher at one of the Rīga girls' schools. He spoke five languages fluently. He got shot up later in the war. He ran into a machine gun and it ripped all his guts to bits. A couple of hundred metres behind us there was an Army medical unit and one of the surgeons opened him up in the snow, there and then.

They took about three metres of his intestines out because he was ripped to bits. They sewed him up, put him on a sledge, took him out with a horse and got him to hospital. And he survived! You'd be surprised. He still had the scars on his right arm and hand, but he almost got ripped in half, and that scar didn't heal. The scar across his stomach was like a great big groove right across the muscle. Where the bullets went in on the left-hand side there was a little dot but where they came out on the right-hand side they were the size of half a crown [a pre-decimal British coin about five centimetres across] where they didn't heal over. He had a scar almost from his neck to his navel, but he survived. He died about 2003 in Canada.

Mr Mūsiņš stands up and goes into the kitchen to make another coffee. When he returns I read out extracts from his diary to him:[5]

1 February: Trying to form some kind of defence in front of Flatow. Digging foxholes for machine guns, but we are short of defence against tanks. Local actions but nothing more.

2 February: Getting quite hot, fighting resumes with full force. Twice we manage to stop Russian advance with infantry.

3 February: The Russian tanks break through our lines and scatter our units. As we have no defence we withdraw out of Flatow in nearby forest and make

---

4   See chapters 2 and 11 for examples of Red Army soldiers in German uniform as wounded generals.

5   While both the memory-stories of Mr Mūsiņš and his diary notes give vivid descriptions of the action he was involved in, the dates he has put against some events feel slightly out, a situation historians might describe as 'the unreliability of memory.' The Latvians had withdrawn from Jastrow by 1 February and between 2–3 February were caught up in the calamity on the Flederborn road. The dates have been retained here for their human sense of chronology: the events they describe are possibly a few days earlier.

a stand here against their infantry. We have suffered heavy losses in the action and are in a sad state.

He puts the coffee down and continues:

We did get a bit shot up. We took the lightly-wounded with us but there was nothing we could do for the badly-wounded. We had medics with the units but those who couldn't move by themselves had to be left. There was no choice. Usually they had pistols and they did what they…

He leaves the sentence hanging. It's obvious what he means.

ZM: Later on we managed to catch a couple of Russian prisoners. They said: 'Whatever you do don't give up, because when they catch Latvians they shoot them dead straight off.' That was the first news we had about the drastic situations.

VH: Were you surprised?

ZM: Well … no, not really. It gives the impression that all Russians were bad, which really is the wrong thing. It's only the few of them that were. And as the Germans said: 'The Latvians were no angels either.'

VH: What happened to the prisoners?

ZM: I don't know. They were sent back to HQ usually, and what happened was they sent somebody to accompany them down there. They would take them somewhere quiet and shoot them, and then say they were shot while running away. Probably that's what happened. But I don't think I could do that. Not to an unarmed person. I don't think I've got it in me.

VH: What about the waves of Russian attacks? What was that like?

ZM: The Russian Army's not like an ordinary army. They all come standing upright: crowds of them, walking. Imagine what it's like with an MG-42? It's like a broom, sweeping them down. But there are thousands of them coming. I'm not surprised they say they lost 20 million in the war. They never fought like an army. We ducked, we dug in; we only stood up when it was absolutely necessary. Otherwise you don't survive. But they came with their political bloke with a gun behind them.[6] It was absolute slaughter. Like old Peter the Great said when Charles XII of Sweden milled his men down: 'What does it matter? It's only 100,000 men. Russia has plenty more.' Obviously that attitude has survived until now. War is a terrible thing.[7]

VH: So it was tough?

6 The NKVD political commissars.
7 A reference to the Great Northern War of 1700–1721 and possibly The Battle of Narva of 1700, a crushing defeat for Peter the Great, when the Swedes defeated an army three or four times stronger.

ZM: We took heavy losses. It was terrible – hell on earth. All of a sudden the line lit up and then came the order: 'Right. Take it.' And that's when we had to go in and do what we had to do. You don't feel very friendly towards them then. But there's nothing you can do.

VH: What about the tanks?

ZM: Tanks don't do much to ordinary people. They go looking for support points like heavy machine guns or whatever to pick out, but [the problem is] the infantry that follows. Tanks don't go far without the infantry because they become vulnerable to Panzerfausts. Tanks can run over anything and take positions but they can't hold them: they need the infantry supporting them to do that. Once you stop the infantry you stop the tanks, and usually they pull back. So, I'm dug in a foxhole with an MG-42 going left and right, left and right. I'm here and there are thousands who aren't.[8]

The conditions for the Latvians were challenging. They were trying to move quickly in freezing conditions cross-country, wading through chest-deep snow on open ground while taking as many weapons and as much equipment as they could. *The Latvian Encyclopaedia*, published in Sweden seven years after the war, says of this time:

Although lacking proper clothing and weapons, in great cold and snowstorms, our young men fought tenaciously against an army much stronger in numbers and equipment.[9]

At this point, the Latvian military historian Valdis Kuzmins believes, the 15th Division commanders made a serious tactical mistake. A better option strategically given the blizzard conditions, lack of equipment and poor transport was a withdrawal to Konitz, but reports of Soviet tanks near Zempelburg possibly swayed the commanders away from this choice.[10]

Kuzmins believes one option should have been going north to join up with German units south of Danzig. Fighting their way through Soviet lines would have been tough, but there was the possibility of evacuation west. The decision to go cross-country meant the Latvians would have to fight their way through a two-pronged Soviet attack cutting across them in both directions, denying access to possible evacuation from a big port city like Kolberg. The escape plan to go through Vandsburg, Flatow, Jastrow and Flederborn would lead to disaster – and to the fields and forests around villages like Wilkenswalde, Dorotheenhof and Landeck being stained with much Latvian blood.

8   Interview with author. Mr Mūsiņš was an excellent raconteur and his recall of detail was amazing. Occasionally he would say: 'Don't forget I'm 95. My memory is lacking. Whatever's in those notes I wrote down at the time. At my age, memory plays tricks sometimes.'
9   *The Latvian Legion* from *The Latvian Encyclopaedia*, published in Sweden, 1952, p.29, from de-classified CIA files.
10 Silgailis, *Latvian Legion,* p.163.

The 1st Battalions of both 33rd and 34th Regiments fell back to Vandsburg to cover the retreat west with the aim of linking up with the 32nd Regiment at Wilkenswalde, 10 kilometres to the west. The 33rd Regiment arrived there on the afternoon of 28 January without their two remaining artillery guns after a fighting retreat hampered by fuel shortages, in blizzard conditions and with biting winds. Colonel Janums checked on his men marching in columns, and noticed that one man's ear had frozen and was completely white:

> I stopped the column and order the soldiers to check each other, to see if anyone else has frostbite in their nose or ears. I actively participate in these checks and I find another soldier with a frostbitten nose. I tell him to immediately rub his nose with snow. Then I start to shame him, saying: 'Hey, you're a young lad but you haven't noticed that your nose is freezing off!' The lad, having taken a handful of snow, rubs in the snow and pulls a face. I stand next to him and show him how to do it. Finally, the lad can't hold back and says: 'Sir, your nose is white as well!'
>
> I touch my nose and can't feel it at all. I had no choice but to rub my own nose with snow. It turned out that more than thirty men in the column had frostbite. Those men who had rubbed their extremities with snow before they went into warm premises had no after-effects.[11]

The 34th Regiment dug in two to three kilometres east of Wilkenswalde and fought off a Russian tank attack that evening. Here, Latvian accounts tell of a stand-up row between the battle group leaders, the German SS Hauptsturmführer Helmut Joachim and the Latvian 33rd Regiment commander Colonel Vilis Janums. Janums' men had been given a night's rest after their fighting retreat, with the perimeter manned by Joachim's men. Joachim apparently invented an attack by twelve Russian tanks to get Janums's men to replace his own in the trenches, going house-to-house and ordering the Latvians out at gunpoint. Janums faced Joachim down and he backed off, after which Janums checked the positions and found no tanks. The Latvian Legion history 'Green Books' record that Janums reached the conclusion after the incident that:

> Based on all the signs, the Joachim Battle Group's men show a strong tendency to seek out more comfortable and peaceful positions.[12]

The next morning the tanks were back with infantry, and by 10:00 had broken through the lines held by Joachim's men, who retreated. Janums sent his 2nd Battalion to stop the Russians. They destroyed a tank before the ammunition ran out and then had to flee for their lives, running across open fields for the shelter of the forests east of Dorotheenhof [Dorotowo]. The withdrawal was covered by the 31st SS but casualties

---

11 V. Janums, *Mana Pulka Kauju Gaitas* [*My Regiment in Battle*] (Sweden: Daugavas Vanagi, 1978), p.162.
12 Janums, in Legion 'Green Books', vol. 6, p.164.

Latvian Iron Cross winner and artillery commander Aleksandrs Mateass, killed at Wilkenswalde, January 1945. (Picture: public domain)

were very high. Among those killed at Wilkenswalde was the artillery commander Aleksandrs Mateass, a long-serving police battalion and Legion officer with the rank of Waffen-Hauptsturmführer. Cēsis-born Mateass had won the Iron Cross Second Class in 1942, one of the first Latvians to be so highly decorated.[13]

But the fight was not over. Soviet tanks found the edge of the defensive lines to the north and drove down the forest firebreak roads to attack the supply and logistics teams gathered deep in the woods. Panic ensued as they fled towards Flatow, leaving the rest of the men out of contact with divisional HQ at Kujan. They began to make their way west in small groups, avoiding the main roads. At this point Colonel Janums stepped in to restore order and take charge of the retreat, which involved a night march through chest-deep snow and thick forest south of the Flatow road navigating by compass and map. Eventually, exhausted, they reached the garrison at Flatow early in the morning of 30 January.[14] The 1st Company, commanded by Lieutenant Eižens Bonoparts, did not arrive for another 24 hours. The 'Green Books' note:

13 Silgailis, *Latvian Legion,* p.163. A former Scout leader, Mateass was tasked with developing the Latvian version of the Hitler Youth, the Latvian Youth Organisation or LJO [*Latviju Jaunatnes Organizācijas*]. Latvian boys aged 10–13 were told they could 'shake off all the disgraceful doctrines Communist rule had tried to inject into them' and prepare themselves for the struggle against 'the blood enemy of our people: Bolshevism and Judaism'. Latvian sources say the youth organisation was a struggle between Nazis who wanted a Hitler Youth and the Latvians, led by Alfrēds Valdmanis, who wanted to build a future 'free Latvia.' A centralised youth organisation was seen as a step in that direction. It was a struggle which the Latvians appeared to win, at least while Mateass was in charge. Mateass stayed in contact with the anti-Nazi underground and was pushed out, presumably, for being too pro-Latvian.

14 Silgailis, *Latvian Legion,* pp.164–166.

On 1 February, the 1st Company returned to the regiment. Three enemy tanks had blocked their way at Dorotheenhof and blocked their retreat. When Lieutenant Bonoparts had shot up one tank, the other two hurried away and the company could continue its retreat without hindrance. Going through enemy-held territory, the company had a number of brushes with the enemy. Only thanks to Lieutenant Bonopart's outstanding orienteering skills and bravery, the 1st Company, even in the most difficult of circumstances, always ends up with victory. This company returned to the regiment armoured with Russian-type machine guns.[15]

The Red Army was not far behind. The town was surrounded. Short on ammunition, without anti-tank guns or heavy weapons and carrying many wounded, the roads west to Jastrow or north-west to Landeck looked like the best option for the Latvians and the German units with them. After discussion, the decision was made. Janums' 33rd Regiment, a German anti-aircraft battery and some of the guns from the 15th Artillery would hold Jastrow as long as possible while all the other units moved out.

The 34th Regiment, with the remnants of the 32nd Regiment and two of the 15th Artillery guns, would move north to Flederborn. There they would relieve the 48th SS Grenadiers who were holding the village. The 48th Grenadiers would then clear the road to Ratzebuhr [Okonek] – a left fork off the road at Flederborn.[16] The Latvian Encyclopaedia paints a bleak picture of the situation, and doesn't pull any punches when it comes to apportioning blame.

> During the night of 30–31 January the remnants of the 15th Division retreated to Jastrow. There, it was found, Russian mechanised forces had already encircled the Division, and the ring was constantly tightening. The Division had lost its anti-tank guns during the previous battles; our motorised transport capacities, already reduced, were overtaxed with more than 500 wounded. The 15th Division's battle strength had been sharply reduced … During this time, the divisional commander [Adolf Ax] was an incapable old gentleman who lacked will power.[17]

What followed would be a fateful and fatal four days, and the result would be carnage.

꣐ ⸺ ꣐

Seventy-five years later I'm driving down the same roads. Just out of Mrocza [Immenheim] the road cuts through a forest and climbs a ridge where a huge

15 'Green Books', vol. 6, p.172.
16 Silgailis, *Latvian Legion,* p.166.
17 'The Latvian Legion' from *the Latvian Encyclopaedia*, 1952, p.29, from CIA files de-classified in 2005 under the Nazi War Crimes Disclosure Act.

motorway runs along the horizon. A vast multi-billion euro decade-long road-building programme means many places are like this at the time I'm in Poland.[18]

Around here – I've just passed through the village of Szczutki – the fields beyond the forest are open and wide, dotted with hayrolls and red-roofed farmhouses. Barns nestle amid the gentle slopes of the countryside. Further out from Mrocza the landscape suddenly opens up to enormous fields, stretching for kilometres at a time. The blades of the wind turbines on either side of the road whirr busily as I drive past. This is real farmland with visibility for kilometres: the only safe place to be in a war here would be in the forest.

On a hot August afternoon it's a nice drive, but the Latvians were here in temperatures of minus 20 degrees Celsius with heavy drift snow, shelling, fast-moving tanks, constant alerts, equipment and weapons to carry, plus little or no food, lack of sleep and wounded to move. I know I am very far indeed from experiencing the true conditions of January to March 1945 in Pomerania, but it's good to see the lay of the land. I look up the places I'm passing through: Chmielewo, Smolary, Szczutki. There is little information about them other than they are villages in the administrative district of Gmina Sicienko, and their distance from Bydosczcz. It appears that in this modern world, these towns have no other history.

I reach Mrocza's market square and stretch my legs in the late afternoon sun, admiring the cheerful peach and pink buildings in the centre of town. A stage has been set up in the middle of the square for a concert in the evening. It's a charming place; the central hub for the villages in the region, but I can't see any memorial to what happened here in 1945. The winds of misfortune and evil certainly blew through this town, and the buildings around this square have seen more history than they will admit, but maybe people just want to get on with their lives as they are now, untroubled by the past.

A short drive brings me to another impressive town centre, that of Więcbork. In the Second World War this was Vandsburg, an important link in the Germany military network in this region. This too is a lovely place on an August afternoon. There is a big open square with a splashing fountain and a beautiful church on the far side. This is the Catholic Church of the Assumption of the Blessed Virgin Mary and Apostles Simon and Juda Tadeusz, which has been here since 1772. Beyond the church, a slope leads down to a large lake ringed with trees. Two small sailing boats in the distance are being powered across it by a refreshing breeze.

The church looks too important not to look inside. The interior is rococo; all ornamental curves, scrolls and frescoes with altars. There is a baptismal font from 1780, a pulpit from the 1870s and confessionals dating from the late 18th century. Outside, on either side of its doors, a series of stone plaques remembers places of great suffering

---

18 April and August 2018. Article from 05 February 2020 *Poland's Expensive Highways* by Jacek Krzemiński at <https://www.obserwatorfinansowy.pl/in-english/polands-expensive-highways/>.

Modern day Mrocza. In 1945 this was the German military centre of Immenheim, which the Latvians were ordered to defend against Soviet attack. (Picture: author)

Więcbork's picturesque centre. In 1945 this was the German military centre of Vandsburg. (Picture: author)

in Poland during the Second World War: Katyn, Potulice, Stutthof; the Warsaw Rising.[19]

Next to the church is an area to sit and chat as children and the occasional dog play in the water jets of the fountain. Information boards display photographs showing the pace of life in Więcbork from the turn of the century onwards. There's one picture from 1938 showing the church and the path down to the lake I have just walked along. It's almost unchanged as the backdrop for the grim scenes that played out here in late January 1945.

At Vandsburg, Jūlijs Ķīlītis was ordered to hold the town against a massed Red Army attack as the HQ retreated on 28 January, an impossible task without artillery. Ķīlītis writes that he thought that '…he was expected to die a hero's death.' His men spent the night in a burning manor house at Wilkenswalde.

When he and the remains of his men arrived at Kujan, he was treated coldly by divisional commander Wulff and given a written order as proof in case he refused to take a battalion plus two companies and hold Kujan at all costs. He counted the men available and reached a total of 60 before going back to Wulff and angrily requesting that he amend the written order, changing the word 'battalion' to 'incomplete company.' At this point, Ķīlītis's relationship with Wulff was completely ruined.[20]

Even the chaplains were given Panzerfausts and sent into the trenches to hold back the Red Army, as Catholic minister Kazimirs Ručs wrote in his memoir *Life with God*:

> Little is written about the 15th Division in Pomerania, which was sent to the 'frontlines of death' – and me with them. I too had my blood group tattooed so it could be seen immediately which blood group I needed if wounded. Terrible.
>
> Before the dreadful battles of the Landeck encirclement was the siege of Vandsburg, a town of about 30,000 inhabitants. The front was about 500 metres outside the town. The Red Army soldiers attacked in repeated waves screaming *Za rodinu, za Staļina!* [*For the Homeland! For Stalin!*] That made the Legionnaires more angry. They fought even more fiercely and repulsed the Russian attack. The frontline was re-established about one kilometre distant from the town. I was in the trenches with the [Lutheran] minister, Jūlijs Straume.

---

19 Diocesan website, translated, at <http://diecezja.bydgoszcz.pl/2009/02/21/wicbork-wniebow-zicia-nmp-i-apostoow-szymona-i-judy-tadeusza/>. Church furnishing detail from Roman Catholic parish website, quoted in Polish wikipaedia at <https://pl.wikipedia.org/wiki/Kościół_Wniebowzięcia_Najświętszej_Maryi_Panny_i_św._Apostołów_Szymona_i_Judy_Tadeusza_w_Więcborku>. Both accessed 02 August 2019. The NKVD execution of 22,000 Polish Army and police officers and members of the intelligentsia at Katyn in April and May 1940 on Stalin's orders following the annexation of eastern Poland by the Soviet Union was denied until the Gorbachev era. On 13 April 1990 the USSR admitted responsibility for the massacre and expressed 'profound regret.'

20 J. Ķīlītis, *"Es karā aiziedams…" Mani raksturīgākie piedzīvojumi Otrā pasaules karā* [*I Go to War: My Most Characteristic Adventures in WWII*], trans. Aivars Sinka (Self-published, Ottawa, Canada:1956), pp.157–168.

Russian tanks appeared behind the lines and threatened to attack. All the Legionnaires still in the town were ordered into anti-tank positions. All the reserves and even lightly-wounded men were sent to the trenches. Panzerfausts were given to me and Chaplain Straume: I put an anti-tank bazooka on my shoulder and took up a position at the rear. This time the tanks didn't attack but went on towards Landeck. The anti-tank grenade has to be fired from about 30 metres away, if you're not shot first. When it explodes, the grenade reaches a temperature of about 1,000 degrees. It melts the steel side of the tank, drills into it, ignites the petrol, blows up the ammunition and the tank begins to burn dreadfully. It's not possible to describe the feeling when this is happening.

There was a medical point at Vandsburg School. The wounded were operated on without anaesthetic. The corridors were overflowing and the smell of blood hung in the air. Not only was there blood all over the floors but the walls were spattered with it too. At the moment that I went into the operating room, Major Vilis Hāzners was lying on the school table. He, also without painkillers, was having a bullet removed that was stuck in his body. Outside wounded Legionnaires waited their turn. The bloody queue wound its way around the streets almost right up to the frontline.[21]

Latvian Red Army Captain Jānis Grīnvalds was also in Vandsburg, but in the period immediately after the 15th Division was forced out. For some Red Army soldiers, the battles would now have a bitter edge – the thirst for revenge after one of their commanders was killed. On 1 February, Grīnvalds wrote:

The Latvian SS men have killed Major Ostrowski – the deputy commander of the 3rd Guards Cavalry Division – from behind. They attacked from a hide-out this side of the frontline. In revenge for Major Ostrowski, the Cossacks won't take any Latvian SS prisoners.[22]

I leave Więcbork along General Jozef Haller Street, lined with offices and administration buildings and named after the 'Blue General' whose blue-coated soldiers fought off the Bolsheviks in the Polish-Soviet War between February 1919 and October 1920. General Haller moved his troops into Pomerania to claim it for Poland in 1920 as part of the Versailles Treaty after the First World War. In front of tens of thousands of cheering onlookers at Putzig, he rode his horse fetlock-deep into the Baltic Sea to perform the ceremonial 'wedding to the sea' ritual to celebrate the return of the Polish Corridor and with it, Polish access to the Baltic for the first time in 138 years.[23]

21 Dr K. Ručs, extract from *Dzīve ar Dievu* (2004) in *Daugavas Vanagi Mēnešraksts Nr. 3* (01 July 2010). Online at <http://periodika.lv/periodika2-viewer/?lang=fr#issue:217835>, accessed 20 May 2021.

22 J. Grīnvalds, *Kā Es Redzēju Tās Lietas [As I Saw Those Things: The diaries of Jānis Grīnvalds.]* trans. Aivars Sinka. (Rīga: Preses nams, 2002), p.280.

23 *New York Times* article, 'Poles symbolise union with sea' dated 13 February 1920 at <https://times-machine.nytimes.com/timesmachine/1920/02/13/118261587.pdf>, accessed 21 January 2020.

In the late afternoon sunshine it's a pleasant drive west from Więcbork to the county town of Złotów, formerly Flatow, past mostly open fields with occasional woods and lakes. The woods become real forest – properly managed forest, with firebreaks and timber processing plants and the smell of wood burning in the air. It's picturesque. I pass through a country village nestling along a tree-lined road with a bridge across a river, then the forest returns with farmhouses dotted here and there.

Złotów itself is a big place, with a population of 18,000 and railway connections to Piła and Chojnice.[24] There are lovely parks, town squares and lakeside walks, and it's impeccably clean. There's a monument acknowledging the gratitude due to the Polish and Soviet soldiers who took part in the battles at Flatow, which ended on 31 January 1945. After the war Flatow reverted to Polish rule, took a Polish name – Złotów – and the remaining German population was expelled.[25]

A few kilometres further on, I reach a road bridge across the river Gwda towards Jastrowie, where the next stage in the journey of the men of the 15th Division was to unfold.[26] There is a memorial stone on the bridge marking where the Polish and Russians crossed the river on 31 January–1 February 1945 in the operation to breach the German defensive line at the Pomeranian Wall. To my left, there is what looks like a railway bridge. It's twisted, almost ruptured, but still intact. It has slipped towards the water but isn't in the river. It's an odd sight and I can see people there, so I pull up at the nearest safe point and walk back.

It was once a railway bridge but is now an informal tourist attraction. The Germans blew it to slow the Red Army advance, but not well enough to destroy it completely: that's why it's so twisted. It remains as a slightly hazardous curiosity for passers-by.

I drive on into Jastrowie, once a thriving 19th century German horse-trading town. In the Second World War Jastrow was a significant part of Germany's Pomeranian Wall defensive fortifications, known to the Nazis as *Die Pommernstellung* and to the Poles as *Wał Pomorski*. At the centre is a spired church: substantial two and three-storey buildings hug the road through the town. One house on a bend has an enormous black-painted wooden balcony jutting out over the pavement. I'm reminded of several war stories from Jastrow told to me by Legionnaire Jānis Čevers. One of his duties while here was to send out official notification to families whose sons had been killed in action: the 'death letters.'

> I was writing to the families of the dead, sending them letters [that their loved ones had written but not posted] with maps of where they were buried. The letters were brief: 'Due to enemy action, your son has been killed. He is buried here etc., etc.' All because I could type. That field hospital [*lazarett*] was in Jastrow.

---

24 Two of the big cities of the region: then known as Schneidemühl and Konitz.
25 Złotów town website at <https://www.zlotow.pl/history_of_zlotow.html> (accessed 25 June 2022). Złotów was liberated by units of the 11th Infantry Regiment of the 4th Division J. Kiliński.
26 The Germans and Latvians knew the Gwda river as the Küddow. Both versions of the name have been retained as that is how they are referred to in the original texts.

Memorial on the road bridge over the river Gwda near Jastrowie commemorating the start of the successful assault by the Polish army to breach the Pomeranian Wall. (Picture: author)

A monument to the Second World War: the ruined railway bridge over the river Gwda [Küddow] at Jastrow, blown by the Germans to slow the Red Army advance, never restored. (Picture: author)

He has another memory from that time that could well have been his last.

> I don't know why but in Poland I was always behind the lines with officers even though I was a Corporal. I was involved with German officers and our officers, who gave me certain responsible jobs like evacuating the *lazarett* in Jastrow.[27]
>
> I was in a village behind the lines. I went by myself, walking in the street. Suddenly I feel something on my shoulder and there's white powder. [What happened was] a Polish man in an upstairs window had dropped a home-made bomb on me but it hadn't gone off. Naturally I opened the door of the house a little bit and you could say gave him some of his own medicine.[28]

Jastrow's key strategic position in the defence of Pomerania is illustrated by two things I notice as I pass through. The first is a monument to the Pomeranian Wall on the road leading to Podgaje [known to the Latvians as Flederborn]. The second is a road sign in the centre of the town, pointing in both directions.

27 See Chapter 11.
28 Interview with author.

Modern Jastrowie. The turning for the road to Podgaje-Flederborn and Lędyczek-Landeck.
(Picture: author)

To the left the road leads to Piła and Wałcz [Schneidemühl and Deutsche Krone], both important cities high on the Soviet list for capture or destruction. Schneidemühl, given the status of *Festung* [Fortress] with the consequent requirement for it to be defended to the last, was more or less obliterated in the battle between the Red Army and its Nazi defenders: three-quarters of the town was destroyed and there was barely a building left standing in the city centre.[29]

Deutsche Krone was an important link in the Pomeranian Wall with defensive bunkers and camouflaged gun positions dotted around it. A vitally important railway line brought in supplies and reinforcements to keep resistance going. Heinrich Himmler, when appointed commander of Army Group Vistula, set up headquarters here on his train. But neither the defences nor Himmler – soon exposed as not being anywhere near up to the job – could stop the Russians and Poles for long, and the town fell on 14 February.[30]

To the right the sign points to Koszalin and Człuchów: in German times Köslin and Schlochau. Köslin had been one of the early regional production centres for the V2 missiles fired at London from launch sites further west along the coast at Peenemünde. Prisoners of war were used to make the rockets to the specification of programme chief Oberst Walter Dornberger under the technical direction of Werner

29 From Carl von Ossietzky Universität, Oldenburg webpages at <https://ome-lexikon.uni-olden-burg.de/orte/schneidemuehl-Piła>, accessed 25 July 2020.
30 A. Beevor, *Berlin – The Downfall 1945 (London: Viking-Penguin Books, 2002), p.91.*

von Braun, and a Long Range Missile School was established in the town under Oberst Gerhard Stegmaier to train troops to handle and fire these new weapons.

Radio transmissions to Stegmaier's command post in Köslin – *Kommandostelle Sigfried* – were intercepted by the code-breaking specialists at Bletchley Park in England in May 1944. The messages when cracked revealed the team working on the V2 project. Köslin was captured by the Soviets on 4 March 1945, and the Red Army and a 'trophy battalion' seeking out Nazi secret technology reached Peenemünde on 5 May, only to find much of the launch site destroyed. Von Braun's team of scientists had abandoned it in early 1945 for Bavaria, hidden their documents and then on 2 May surrendered to the Allies.[31]

In the opposite direction to Köslin, Schlochau had been a Hitler Youth training centre and a strongpoint in a line of 800 bunkers in the Pomeranian Wall, stretching from Schneidemühl and Deutsche Krone through Rummelsberg and Bütow. The road to Schlochau lay directly in the path of a powerful Soviet thrust to the Baltic Sea that in the weeks to come would decide its fate and that of Konitz, Neustettin, Baldenburg and, closer to the coast, Stolp and Kolberg.[32]

The chief of the German General Staff at the time was Heinz Guderian. His memoirs give a glimpse into the speed of the German collapse in Pomerania:

> Feb 2: Fall of Toruń
> Feb 3: Enemy bypassed Schneidemühl and entered Outer Pomerania
> Feb 12: Graudenz lost
> Feb 15: Konitz and Schneidemühl lost
> Feb 28: Schlochau, Hammerstein, Bublitz and Baldenburg lost
> Mar 1: Neustettin lost.[33]

The Latvians re-grouped in Jastrow briefly – more or less overnight on 30–31 January – after the escape from Flatow, having been hassled, harried and ground down by the pursuing Russians. Battalion commander Jūlijs Ķīlītis only arrived in the morning, having led his men on an overnight march from Flatow. As his memoirs reveal, there was a brief moment of joy before the bleak realisation that they were surrounded by two divisions which had orders to destroy them.

> When we saw the first houses of the little town of Jastrow in the distance between the trees, it was already 08:00 and the last day of January. A fresh morning breeze blew towards us. The snow crackled lightly under our feet, hinting at the coming thaw. We spent the whole of the previous night marching from Flatow

---

31 C. Campbell, *Target London: Under Attack from the V-Weapons During the Second World War,* chapter 26 (London: Hachette UK, 2012) and S.J. Zaloga, *V-2 Ballistic Missile 1942–52* (London: Bloomsbury, 2013).
32 In modern Poland these towns are Piła, Wałcz, Miastko and Bytow; Chojnice, Szczecinek, Biały Bór, Słupsk and Kołobrzeg.
33 Guderian, *Panzer Leader,* p.418.

A ceremonial photograph from 1938–39 of Major Jūlijs Ķīlītis, commander of the 34th Regiment of the Latvian 15th Division. (Picture: Latvian War Museum, Rīga, LKM 5-14234/1561-FT)

to Jastrow. Yesterday evening, when we were still in Flatow, the news about the enemy's attacking moves and directions depicted a disconcerting scene: we were in danger of being surrounded again. Still, ever the optimist, this time too I hoped for the best. I remembered my friend Ikše saying: 'You'll win this war! Just always be wary and unrelenting.' And, as people in war always try to believe in something, and to follow some star of fate, I thought about how and where we could get out. And so, now, thinking about the events of the last few days and nights, a thought flashed into my mind: what happened to my friend Pēteris Balodis? There has been no news from him since he went into the forest with the battalion the day before yesterday. I hope that nothing has gone wrong for 'Špuchtiņš' ['Pipsqueak']…

At the first houses I climbed out of the car and started to walk. The beautiful houses round here interested me. They were all private dwellings and must have belonged to well-off people. Not a soul could be seen, so the people have probably already run away. At a bend on the road, a small group of our people came towards us and at the head of the group, dressed in a white towelling swimming gown and with a long black beard, Peter B. himself was marching! The friend that I had almost been crying over was here again! Then everything will be fine. We happily shook hands. There wasn't much opportunity to talk and explain, because Major B. wanted a quick drink and a sleep. He hadn't slept for two nights. They had all worn themselves out, marching across snowy fields and through woods, until, after a number of clashes, they reached the road to Jastrow. I packed my friend into my car so that he could sleep and, pleased at the outcome, I walked on.

According to my superiors' orders, my battalion and I needed to stay and rest in the town square and the nearest road by the church. There we were

Oberführer Adolph Ax, the German commander of the Latvian 15th SS Division during the disastrous encirclement at Flederborn and Landeck in February 1945. (Picture: Latvian 'Green Books')

supposed to get lunch, or some food that passed as such. As the big fighting retreat began, we didn't receive food regularly. We didn't distinguish between the names of meals any longer but instead used the principle that 'Eat what you can get, when you can get it, as much as you can.' A big help in this was the care that German households had taken – the full cellars with 'veka' jars containing poultry, meat and boiled fruit. With that help, sustenance wasn't too bad, except in situations where other diligent 'auditors' had got there before us.

Having put the battalion where ordered, and having arranged the lunch, I went to a nearby house. The houses here weren't as grand or as well kitted-out as on the outskirts, where we had entered that town. But as I had spent the night marching without any sleep, I stretched out pleasurably on an old couch.

After about an hour, the regimental commander Lieutenant-Colonel Vīksne arrived and in a quite pessimistic tone said that we are in a fair amount of trouble and that this is probably the end. According to the information we had received, our whole division was surrounded by two enemy divisions, whose orders were to destroy us. There was bewilderment written on the regimental adjutant's expressive face. All the routes out had already been captured by the enemy.

Ķīlītis continued:

We will shortly be given the Divisional Commander's orders about what to do next. As the reader [of his memoirs, written in 1956] will already know, at the head of the Division was a weak man with an ability to think that was as short as his surname – Over-Colonel Ax. I still clung to the hope, quietly, that the head of the *štābs* [HQ], the German Major Wulff, would be able to do something and provide the appropriate influence on his weak commander, so that the old 'General HQ-ist' could show his class. For reasons unknown to me, that didn't happen. For this weakness, Wulff paid with his life. Three days later he fell at Landeck.

After a while, the regimental commander returned and informed me that the Division had decided to break through to Landeck. On the other side of the encirclement, supposedly, is the 32nd Pomeranian Division, which will then help us. The distance we would need to cover is about 15 kilometres. Having taken up the area survey map, I started to investigate it, using coloured pencils to identify uneven ground and watercourses. German wartime maps were bad in this regard, because they were printed in just one colour and were hard to read. The direction towards Landeck looked like a fairly good prospect, covered in forest. Only at Landeck itself was the route crossed by a small river. I liked the area, because the forest would act in our favour.

After lunchtime, the regimental commander came a third time and said that I should get my battalion ready and reinforce it with the regiment's other units, because today, I would have a special task. I muttered quietly to myself that 'again they have found an emergency button to push at a difficult moment'. But, as I hadn't done anything special the previous day, I kept my mouth shut. I ordered the battalion to stand-to just outside the house and I counted them, to see what exactly was left after the recent battles. The scene was pretty sad. Though the situation with the rank and file soldiers was not too bad, there were enormous gaps in leadership positions. None of the companies still had its commander.

The 1st and 2nd Company commanders were injured at Vandsburg; there as well, the commander of the 3rd Company died a hero's death, and the commander of the 4th, Over-Lieutenant Z., was injured at Flatow. Each gap was filled by new replacements, and only two of them were of officer rank. The tough fights behind us, like at Nakel, Vandsburg, Wilkenswalde, Kujan and Flatow had each taken their toll, and the shortage of experienced fighters was growing.

While I sorted things out and put the units together, the battle orders arrived. My battalion and I would – today, by the time darkness fell – reach an inhabited place called Flederborn, where we would take over its defence from some German battalion. Flederborn had to be held at all costs until the Division was able to pass through as part of its breakout.

Flederborn was about nine kilometres from Jastrow, on a road that went on to Landeck. Looking at the map, on the left, just outside the town, some hillocks rose quite high; whereas on the right the area was open and flat. Nearer to Flederborn was forest. That was all I knew and saw at the start. The rest I would find out later on the way, or once I reached my objective.

I sank into my thoughts, trying to make the decisions about how to fulfil this order, trying to foresee the blockers that could get in my way. The regimental commander encouraged me to get moving, as there would be time to think things through *en route*. I ordered the battalion to stand-to. I made clear to my men that each time we had fought successfully in response to the tasks that we had been given. Now the time had come to fight for ourselves, for our lives. Our fate – whether we get out of the encirclement or not – would depend on the way that each of us fulfilled their tasks and sacrificed themselves for their colleagues. I was sure that we could get out, if everyone listened to my orders. And now … may the Almighty protect us!

I picked out the vanguard company, gave them the order and at about 14:30 we set off. I sat in my car and slowly set out in front, to take the column out of Jastrow and on to our marching road. Later, I decided to follow in the gap between the vanguard company and the core of the battalion. Behind us would follow Major B. with his threadbare battalion and one battalion from the 33rd Regiment. After about 20 minutes, we reached the edge of the town, where our required route was signposted.[34]

While Major Ķīlītis moved out of Jastrow, Latvian units were still finding their way there. This excerpt from the Latvian 'Green Books' describes how one unit caught in the chaos at Dorotheenhof had to hide out and wait for nightfall then fight their way into the town. The fighting spirit and leadership qualities of Lieutenant Eižens Bonoparts are again highlighted.

1 February 1945: In the morning we entered an abandoned homestead: following the difficulties endured during the march we had no desire to stay in the forest. At dawn, we found out that we are only a small distance from the road. From the three captured Ukrainian prisoners in the neighbouring homestead we learned that Flatow is already in enemy hands and that all our forces have retreated to Jastrow.

Since the house was only some 300 metres from the road on which the Russian forces were moving, we made no fires during the day. Since we had little rifle ammunition, we left our rifles and armed ourselves with captured Russian submachine guns. At dusk, we began moving to Jastrow.

Upon reaching the Flatow–Jastrow railway, twelve horsemen and a sled passed us. When the sled had gone some distance from us we raised the company and crossed the road in a line. On the road, the line stretched out, and a Russian column moved out of the [nearby] estate and approached within a few steps. The column stopped and somebody asked in Russian: 'Who's there?' The man nearest did not reply and the Russian fired a burst from his sub-machine gun into air. We got down and opened fire on the column.

The enemy retreated to the estate. Under heavy enemy fire, in darkness and fog, the remaining part of the line crossed the road, and the company vanished. The enemy, obviously, was fooled by our white camouflage covering our clothing and insignia, and because most of us were armed with their sub-machine guns.

---

34 Ķīlītis, *I Go to War*, pp.169–172.

Our automatic riflemen returned to the company in several hours. By continuing our march we arrived at the main road. Everybody had caught a cold. Since the men were coughing, we could not approach the road. The enemy transport columns were moving on the road without a break.

The company carried their wounded, and many had frostbite. We had to get across the road, one way or another. The column had moved past us for about an hour when a space appeared. Taking advantage of this, Corporal Melkus began firing at the column that had passed with his machine-gun fire. This caused confusion in the column. Taking advantage of this moment, we ran across the road into the forest. We continued our march through the forest, past villages in the direction to Jastrow.

2 February 1945: We approached Jastrow not knowing if our forces were still there. We let a man on a watch post come close, and then yelled: 'Who are you?' It turned out that he was a German, and that our forces are still in Jastrow. We entered Jastrow at 05:00 and took a rest until 08:00. We then arrived at the regiment headquarters and as soon as 10:00 took defence positions with the Battlegroup Joachim.

In the forest we destroyed a patrol whose men were Polish, but in Russian uniforms with the Polish eagle on their caps. At 16:00 before a menacing enemy penetration, Colonel Janums ordered us to repel the enemy and hold out until the next order. Lieutenant Bonoparts with his 27 men and forces collected launched a counter-attack and expelled the invaders. Corporal Kasmins was wounded in these battles. At 19:30, an order to retreat arrived. The company arrived at Flederborn during the night.[35]

While the centre of Jastrowie looks like it may have done before the war, the road to Podgaje-Flederborn leads past a series of three-storey flats with a concrete Communist-era feel about them. They're painted pink with deep peach balconies, each with a satellite dish and a parking space outside. There are more of these flats further out of town, slotted into gaps between more traditional buildings. There's an odd disjunct about this: a clash of styles.

The modern road out of Jastrowie is quite fast, with stretches of dual carriageway; a far cry from February 1945 and horse-drawn carts laden with wounded Latvian soldiers, steered by men like Jānis Čevers and surrounded by refugees, under fire and caught in an apocalyptic traffic jam. What happened next was slaughter – and history as it stands does not acknowledge this properly.

My journey along this road will take me through one of the darkest weeks in the history of the Latvian Legion – their 'Golgotha' – in harrowing detail. But what brought me here initially is an incident that is still controversial today – the massacre of 32 Polish prisoners at Podgaje-Flederborn.

---

35 Writer unknown, Latvian 'Green Books', trans. Arturs Grava, sent to author 20 July 2022.

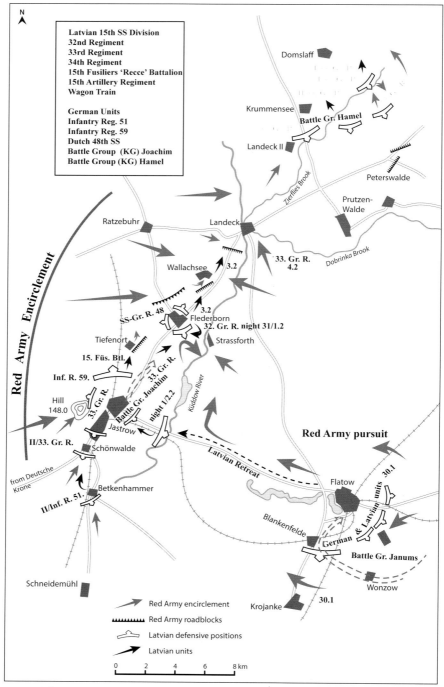

The encirclement at Flederborn and Landeck, 31 January–4 February 1945.

Part Two

The Road of Slaughter

9

The Road of Slaughter 1: Jastrow to Flederborn

The story of what happened on the road between Jastrow and Landeck is an episode of war at its most brutal. It is considered by many Latvians as the darkest 48 hours in their nation's military history. Soldiers, wounded men and refugees were trapped in a murderous traffic jam after the Red Army surrounded the column, blocked the road ahead to Landeck and the escape route west to Ratzebuhr and then blasted every living being with machine gun fire, artillery shells and Katyusha rockets. The result was slaughter, leaving – at a very rough estimate – five and a half thousand Latvians dead in a space of ten kilometres. The exact figure may be much higher if Russians, Polish, Germans and refugees are included.

What happened there, and especially at the village of Podgaje-Flederborn, can be told in English through revealing eyewitness accounts gathered by the author from interviews with veterans in the UK, coupled with translations of memoirs from the official history of the Latvian Legion, from entries in the 15th Division's war diary held in the Latvian National Archive, and from personal stories published in the post-war Latvian press-in-exile. There are contributions from Latvians fighting with the Red Army and from Poles researching these events themselves. The accounts are graphic and bloody, often stomach-churningly so. The picture that emerges is of the wholesale slaughter of civilians and defenceless wounded men, with the Red Army as perpetrators.

Pauls Dzintars was one of the 15th Division's regimental doctors, who arrived in Jastrow late on 30 January 1945, having retreated from Flatow.

> Flatow turned out to be a complete 'promised land'. All the inhabitants had been evacuated only that morning, nothing had been looted. The house where we were staying had abundant reserves of food and drink. We drank champagne from tarnished bottles, peppermint liqueurs, wines. In a neighbour's letterbox, I found a key to a seven-room flat. Everything had been left in perfect order. I changed my underwear but otherwise left everything as it was, taking only a pen. There was a tremendous booze-up that night but at 04:00 the order came to move on. That was accompanied by a lot of swearing but many men weren't

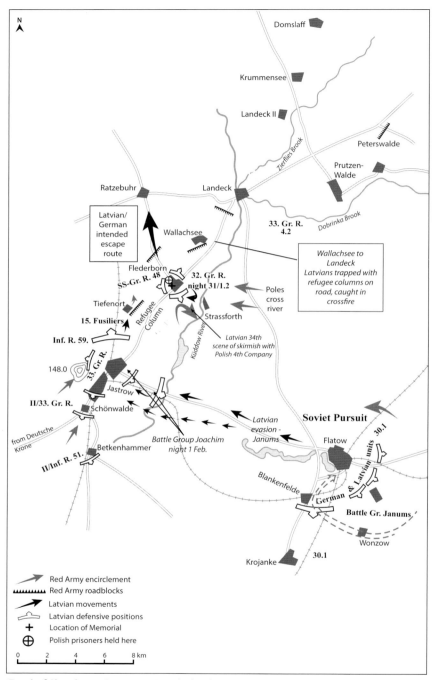

The Road of Slaughter – Jastrow to Landeck. The Latvian advance up the encircled road between Jastrow to Landeck through Flederborn is described by one survivor as 'the 15th Division's Golgotha'.

capable of moving anywhere. They were tossed on carts and those who could walk went on foot. The carts were full of the 'spoils of war'. Late in the night, after a long journey, we entered Jastrow. The town had been half-deserted but there was still electricity. I felt ill, my throat hurt. I was afraid of diphtheria. I ordered an injection of serum for myself.

Dawn came on 31 January and with it news that we were completely surrounded. There was now a medical company in Jastrow with 500 wounded who couldn't be transported to the rear. I felt better and the division doctor Vollrath ordered me to take over the post of 32nd Regiment 3rd Battalion doctor, as Dr Punnenovs and his assistant had apparently stayed with the Russians. The first task was to find the wagon drivers, who then became fighting men, together with a motley assortment of provisions men, accountants and those with frost-bite or feet rubbed raw. We amassed 136 men. The same happened in other units and in the late afternoon about 1,000 men set out to break through to Flederborn.[1]

The 1st Polish Army attacked the Latvians as its units swept towards the Pomeranian Wall. The Poles had been in action since the battle for Lenino in Belarus in October 1943, and their job was to safeguard Zhukov's flanks and breach the Pomeranian Wall. This ran in two sections: *Pommernstellung d1*, running from Stolp to Neustettin and down to Deutsche Krone. The second section, *Pommersche Seenstellung d2,* ran from the Kolberg fortress on the coast through Körlin to Landsberg an der Warthe.[2]

Polish historical researcher Arnold Koslowski has studied the battles of the Pomeranian Wall and translated into Polish the memoirs from the road to Landeck of the Latvian commanders Colonel Janums and Major Ķīlītis, as well as the accounts of many Latvian soldiers. The full story has not been told so far, he believes:

> It is a story full of simplifications, myths, half-truths and silences about the fallen Polish soldiers. There are no stories about ordinary Germans, Latvians, Estonians. There are no stories of civilians, of refugees. There are few stories about the 'places whose names no-one remembers.'[3]

On the morning of 31 January, led by the German Hauptsturmführer Hans Pomrehn, the Latvian 15th Fusiliers 'Recce Battalion' moved out of Jastrow to clear resistance at Tiefenort, in the hills to the west of the road to Flederborn, which the German 59th Infantry had failed to hold. The 34th Regiment led by Lieutenant-Colonel Vīksne set out for Flederborn, a small village held by the 48th Dutch Waffen-SS. In support was the one battalion that remained of the 32nd Regiment, led by Major Alksnītis. Their

1   Dzintars, Pauls: article in *Daugavas Vanagi Mēnešraksts*, Nr.5 (01 September 1999) online at <periodika.lv>. Trans. Daina Vītola.
2   In modern Poland, Słupsk to Szczecinek and Wałcz; Kołobrzeg to Karlino and Gorzów Wielkopolski.
3   Arnold Koslowski, correspondence with author.

184 THE ROAD OF SLAUGHTER

orders were to hold Flederborn so the Dutch 48th SS could then clear the road to Ratzebuhr and open up an escape route to Neustettin. Crucially, this road had been cut the day before by Soviet units.

In addition, the Red Army had got ahead of the Latvians and encircled them, setting up firing positions at Wallachsee in the high ground west of the road from Flederborn to Landeck. As a result the column was caught in a trap, and the Red Army blasted the road with shells, Katyushas and machine gun fire. As the eyewitness accounts relate, the refugees and the wounded men on wagons were sitting ducks. Pauls Dzintars described the scenes – and the combat readiness of the Latvians – as they set out from Jastrow:

> The break-out attempt was carried out by four battalions from the 32nd and 34th Regiments. Janums' regiment [the 33rd] stayed to defend Jastrow because the division HQ and special units were still there. Our combat qualities were highly questionable. The units had been formed in such a hurry that the leaders didn't know their subordinates. Many soldiers had never been in battle. With us we only had about 15 horse-drawn carts with ammunition and my cart with dressings. My medical orderlies were Jevelevs and Ameriks.[4]

Lieutenant Augusts Ķikāns, a veterinarian for the 34th Regiment, had been assigned to the baggage train taking both munitions and wounded from Jastrow through to Landeck. He described the scenes in his memoirs:

> In the evening of 29 January we reached Jastrow. We were meant to stay there even though the Russians were hard on our heels. We couldn't understand why the carts full of badly-wounded were kept by the battle units. On 31 January we were surrounded. The division constantly suffered severe shortages of ammunition. A fierce battle started in the town on the morning of 1 February. The wagons were standing on the road ready to move. The breakout was planned in the direction of Neustettin via Flederborn, but we stood there the whole day and night.[5]

As the Polish and Russian units moved to isolate Schneidemühl and Deutsche Krone to strike north and west towards the Pomeranian Wall, their men advanced through a series of small rural villages in the Polish countryside on the way to Jastrow, among them Deutsche Fier [Piecowo] 11 kilometres west of Flatow; Freuden Fier [Szwecja] 12 kilometres north-east of Deutsche Krone, which was captured by the 4th Infantry Division, and nearby Stabitz [Zdbice], a fortified

---

4   Dzintars, *Daugavas Vanagi Mēnešraksts,* Nr. 5 (01 September 1999) online at <periodika.lv>. Trans. Daina Vītola.
5   That route involves taking a left turn west towards Ratzebuhr at Flederborn, a road which had been cut by Soviet advance units.

strongpoint in the Wall defences.[6] It's possible the civilians at Flederborn were villagers from here, who had abandoned their homes to flee north away from the fighting – only to walk into the fatal encirclement in the forests at Flederborn, Wallachsee and Landeck.

Corporal V. Irbe from the 15th's 1st Medical Company described the situation in Jastrow as the Latvians prepared to move towards Flederborn.

> There was chaos. Lots of soldiers and refugees were there and numerous injured filled not just the large school to overflowing, where the main first aid dressing station was, but also the hospital. The Division lost a lot of men but in the last few days it hadn't been possible to transport the injured away from there. It was said that more than 700 injured Legionnaires were in the town. All the Division's horse-drawn vehicles were handed over to the medics for transporting the injured. The most heavily-injured were put into motorised ambulances and the more lightly-injured on horse-drawn carts; some sitting, some lying down.[7]

Battalion commander Jūlijs Ķīlītis went out a short way from Jastrow to scout the road ahead and was dismayed at what he saw.

> I stopped the car, got out and let the vanguard company past. Just there, not far ahead at a bend on the road was a small copse through which you could see fields, but on the left were pretty steep hillocks. When the vanguard company had gone through the copse and I was already thinking about getting back in my car I could see small figures on the left of the road in the hillocks. I stopped and raised my binoculars. On the hillocks, about a dozen men were setting something up. The distance to them must have been about two kilometres.
>
> After a short while, from the hillocks, there was the sound of a quiet shot and two shells exploded just by the copse, which was followed by a couple of bursts of distant machine gun fire. I got a sudden feeling in my chest that again, things would not be good. We Latvians are not having a successful time of it. Again! Having left my car behind, I ran to the copse so that I would have a better overview of what was happening. Something had to be fixed or changed here because, if the enemy was already on those hillocks, then to march a battalion along an open road would mean suicide, or at least heavy losses. Attacking that high ground would mean diverting from my objective and not fulfilling today's orders.
>
> I frantically started to look around for some cover in the landscape, some way out; something to save my battalion from the threatening danger. From

---

6   By way of comparison, the 2021 populations of these villages shows Piecowo, 212; Swecja 800 and Zdbice 150.

7   V. Irbe, Article in the periodical *Daugavas Vanagu Mēnešraksts,* Nr.1 (01 January 1982) online at <periodika.lv>. The carnage on the Jastrow to Landeck road lasted from 31 January–4 February 1945, and Irbe left Jastrow at 10:00 on 1 February.

the effort of concentrating through the binoculars, my eyes started to water, which hindered my view. The company at the front, which was already some way ahead, gave the agreed signs that there was enemy ahead.

Ķilītis stopped the main force by the copse and the men went into sheltered positions and took cover in the ditches. A messenger arrived from the company at the front and asked what to do next. There had been no directs hits yet, but that could change at any minute:

> My brain worked overtime, looking for a way to carry out the orders I had been given. We have to get through! We had no other choice. Mixed in with these thoughts was my seething anger about the speed at which the leadership wanted to push us out onto this march, without giving us time for review and reconnaissance. Just here, almost mechanically, I noticed that on the right of the road was a flat strip, like a drain. The road, on an embankment, will probably partly hide the strip from the enemy. At least it will be a bit further away [from the enemy] and that could be something in our favour. I said the same to the messenger, who then headed back down the road to his company.
>
> The commander of the vanguard company had already split his men into groups and, after receiving the sign, I saw that they slowly drifted to the right and down into the sunken strip. This was just the beginning, I thought – the test would come later. According to the map and the landscape, I reasoned that we will be diverting to the side for a bit, but later, once we are in the wooded areas, we'll be turning back to the route. This manoeuvre visibly protected us from enemy fire.
>
> When the vanguard company moved into the fields, what I saw satisfied me. The time came for the core of the battalion to turn into the field. Now there was no scope for me to go by car and, leaving my effects and the car with the driver, I moved forward on foot. Snow-covered fields can be pretty deceiving and can hide all sorts of surprises, especially in an unfamiliar location, which is why I decided to go to the vanguard company, so that with them I could see in good time what would happen next.
>
> The snow in the open country was fairly thick with a frozen crust which broke underfoot when marching. This slowed our tempo. After about half an hour's intensive marching, I caught up and marched with the vanguard company. It wasn't great going cross-country, because it was crossed by ditches every 100 metres or so. It was a nightmare when the carts followed across the open ground. Very soon the axles broke and the carts just stopped. We had to pick the most urgent materials and weapons and carry everything over our shoulders. The carts (i.e., sleighs with horses) we left for those following to look after, hoping they'll come back to us after being fixed.

The thick snow and the warmth of the thaw slowed the company's progress – steam was rising from every man. To hinder progress, the Soviets began to shell the Latvians.

The first shells were quite near, but went over our heads. Then a shell hit our route just in front of a small group of men. My first thought was: 'That's the end of them.' But only one man was left lying in the snow – the rest just kept going on, quietly. Other shells weren't as accurate and, as far as I could see, didn't cause us any losses. Later, seeing that they weren't being particularly successful, the enemy tried long-range machine gun fire, but as our distance from them increased, that also wasn't successful.

Here I stopped at a small area of raised ground, from where it was possible to have an overview of what was happening on the road and behind us. A smallish group of my men were determinedly sticking to the roadside ditch and pushed on, ignoring that they were under fire. Our surroundings now took us into a small valley, where a couple of our forward units were already heading. Suddenly I was surprised by the buzzing of bullets, like a swarm of bees.

Just as I was going to throw myself forward into the safety of the valley a long burst of bullets hacked at the path a couple of steps in front of me. Instinctively I fell to the ground, but in such a position that I was completely exposed in the open. The snow was hard on this small piece of raised ground, and there was nowhere to crawl. I got the feeling that there were many bullets hitting the snow behind me. I wanted to disappear into the ground, but you couldn't even have made a hole big enough for your head with your bare fingers in that. The machine gun was hacking at the snow so relentlessly that it was blowing into my eyes. These few moments seemed to me like a lifetime: my nerves couldn't wait for the end.

In truth I was cornered, but there was no other way out than to wait for the firing to stop. Finally it did, so I jumped up and ran the 100 metres [into cover] in one go, neither hearing nor seeing anything clearly. When I fell to the ground again, I felt safe. Though red and green flashes were appearing before my eyes and the sound of jackhammers was in my ears, my feeling was still good: that again another 'occasion' was behind me. I opened up my tunic down to my bare chest, because I was gasping for air. After that, I carried on. I think that was also the last place we were fired on, because no-one bothered us after that.[8]

Halfway up the road to Landeck and sitting at the junction for the turn west to Ratzebuhr, Podgaje-Flederborn was a supply point for the German and Latvian forces along a defence line known as the *Blücherstellung*, where food and ammunition could be distributed.[9]

---

8   Ķīlītis, *I Go To War*, pp.173–175.
9   The Blücher Line, named after the famous Prussian-German General Gebhardt Leberecht von Blücher, who, with Wellington, defeated Napoleon at Waterloo.

A defensive perimeter had been thrown around the village by the 48th SS and snipers from the German 59th Infantry were posted as look-outs. They repelled an initial Polish advance from the east at Grudna on 30 January but Soviet tanks and armoured cars hit directly at Podgaje-Flederborn when the Germans failed to blow up the bridges across the Gwda river [see pages 169 and 170]. A group of 40 German officer cadets in Podgaje-Flederborn stopped the attack, killing many Soviet soldiers and destroying a tank. That evening Russian tanks tried again to attack the village from the south-west sparking rumours – which were wrong – that the Russians had taken the town.

The next day, 31 January, the 1st Polish Infantry was sent across the river to attack Jastrow, but its commander Colonel Aleksander Archipowicz became disoriented and attacked Flederborn instead.[10] German snipers posted as look-outs spotted a column of Soviet armoured cars and trucks coming out of the forest near Grudna and began to fire Panzerfausts at them. The Polish scouts reached Flederborn and pushed the Germans defenders out, then spread out across the village, 'plundering the houses.' Control of Podgaje-Flederborn then changed hands again, as German troops arrived from Ratzebuhr with armoured cars, and pushed the Polish back out towards Grudna.

As the Latvians leaving Jastrow for Flederborn came under fire, they got off the road and into cover. Some continued towards Flederborn along the drainage ditches by the road; others, including the group that doctor Pauls Dzintars was with, moved towards the forest.

> The Russians held the road, [so] our route was over an open field. After about an hour, we got caught up in a bog where the horses got stuck and we lost five carts. It was no easier further on in the forest, which became dense. We were way behind those on foot. Going in single file, they left behind them a path in the snow which we followed kilometre after kilometre, over fields and forest fire-breaks, over ditches and marshes, but we couldn't catch them up. Motorcyclists were designated as liaison but in the thick snow their machines were incapable of getting through. It was already dark. The forest was dense, so dense that we couldn't go on any further. We didn't know where to go as the path had disappeared. The foot soldiers had spread out into a chain.
>
> Heavy fighting broke out in front of us. It seemed as if it was coming closer and closer and surrounded us on three sides. Grenades began to fall and two men were injured. We were all nervous. A driver ran up to me. 'Lieutenant, sir, shall we cut the horses free now or wait for a bit?' I felt honoured as I wasn't a lieutenant but amongst the drivers I was top-dog. I shouted that they mustn't do that but in a few minutes a black mass surged towards us: panicked, gasping-for-breath drivers made into fighting men. It was impossible to get any sense out of them about the situation. 'Russians all around, the officers have left us, we are lost!'

---

10 H. Kochanski, *The Eagle Unbowed – Poland and the Poles in the Second World War* (London: Penguin; 6th edition, 2013), p.517.

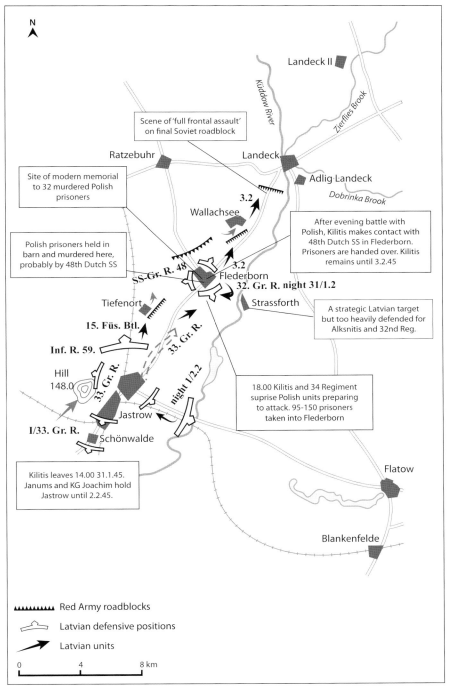

N

Landeck II

Küddow River

Zietflies Brook

Scene of 'full frontal assault'
on final Soviet roadblock

Ratzebuhr

Landeck

Adlig Landeck

Site of modern memorial
to 32 murdered Polish
prisoners

Dobrinka Brook

3.2

Wallachsee

After evening battle with
Polish, Kilitis makes contact with
48th Dutch SS in Flederborn.
Prisoners are handed over. Kilitis
remains until 3.2.45

Polish prisoners held in
barn and murdered here,
probably by 48th Dutch SS

SS-Gr. R. 48

3.2

Flederborn

32. Gr. R. night 31/1.2

Tiefenort

Strassforth

A strategic Latvian target
but too heavily defended for
Alksnitis and 32nd Reg.

15. Füs. Btl.

Inf. R. 59.

33. Gr. R.

Hill
148.0

33. Gr. R.

night 1/2.2

18.00 Kilitis and 34 Regiment
suprise Polish units preparing
to attack. 95-150 prisoners
taken into Flederborn

Jastrow

I/33. Gr. R.

Schönwalde

Flatow

Kilitis leaves 14.00 31.1.45.
Janums and KG Joachim hold
Jastrow until 2.2.45.

Blankenfelde

Red Army roadblocks

Latvian defensive positions

Latvian units

0   4   8 km

Major Ķilītis approaches Podgaje-Flederborn, with modern landmarks.

I'm ashamed to say my feet itched to run with them. Ameriks kept the coolest head. 'Doctor, it's not worth it.' No power on this earth could have stopped this mass. With them fled all our soldier cart drivers with the horses.[11]

Extracts from the autobiography of Jūlijs Ķīlītis translated for this book describe the lack of trained men at critical moments, and how the attitude of a Polish prisoner changed when he realised his captors were Latvian:

We neared thickets and the forest. When we got there we were protected from the dangers we had experienced up to that point. However, we didn't know what awaited us in the thick, unfamiliar forest. I was satisfied with what we had achieved so far. As far as I could tell, we hadn't lost more than three or four men. That was a relatively cheap price compared to what could have been predicted and expected. Reaching the forest, I stopped the head of the column so the tail could catch up. I tried to keep everyone together as much as possible. The evening was drawing in and it became much darker. One had to be prepared for it to be fully dark in about an hour.

Our estimate of getting into Flederborn in daylight was gone: the detour around the enemy blockage and the need to move across snowy fields meant that it had taken all day. I still couldn't fully imagine how I was to actually get into the village with my men and how that might be welcomed by the current defenders [the 48th SS]. At night, one had to expect surprises. After a short break, when I saw that most of the men had arrived, I re-started the movement forward. The snow in the forest was deeper than in the fields, sometimes up to one's knees, and there were soft drifts on the edges of clearings. That alone slowed down the speed of our march. The darker it got, the lighter the area seemed where Flederborn was, with the light from the burning houses reflected in the low clouds. I fixed a direction straight towards it.

After a good while, it seemed we were almost there. There was a depressing silence everywhere. We came to the edge of the forest, behind which there was some kind of space. Suddenly, a few metres in front of me, I saw the dark silhouette of a tank, around which a number of unknown people were busying themselves. They probably noticed us at exactly the same moment, because they stopped working and looked in our direction. There was no point hiding anymore, so I called out some words to them in German just to avoid any misunderstandings. I received a foul-mouthed tirade in Russian or Polish in response: the tank fired angrily in our direction with its machine gun and cannon. It was clear this was the enemy!

---

11 Pauls Dzintars, in *Daugavas Vanagu Mēnešraksts*, Nr. 5 (01 September 1999) online at <periodika.lv>. Dzintars makes the next comment in brackets: '(Alberts Eglitis in the magazine *Kara Invalids* No. 43, p.60 writes that "after the Flederborn battle on 03 February 45 in the Landeck forest, in two days the Russians shot 400 unarmed, captured Latvian youths.")'

We took cover amongst the trees in the thick snow and fired back with rifles. The deep snow and the less-than-ideal position meant we didn't have much success. Nevertheless, we had to blow up the tank. I shouted out a number of times: 'Men with Panzerfausts – to me!' No-one rushed up, and I had to repeat the order a number of times with pretty strong language attached. Then, at last, a man arrived alongside. I showed him the target and where I reckoned he should be firing from. The tank-destroyer crept to the desired spot and after a short delay, the 'Faust's characteristic hiss and bang was heard, but no luck: the shell had hit the tree opposite the tank, rather than the tank itself.

The tank was now trying to start its motor while firing back angrily, but the engine wouldn't kick in. It was perfect for blowing the tank up, but the soldiers I needed didn't turn up fast enough. When the next man finally arrived, he also blasted his rocket into the tree. Then the tank's engine fired and it turned round quickly and roared off, waddling along the forest track. For a long time we could hear it rolling, happily escaped from its death.

One man had rolled off as the tank turned: we had caught him. There were two anti-tank cannons right next to where the tank had been standing. There was no sign of the unit responsible for them: they had either run off into the forest or escaped on the back of the tank.

After this short and unexpected clash, which involved a lot of noise and firing, silence returned. We went from the edge of the forest into the clearing. Most of our people were in the dark parts of the forest and didn't fancy coming out. I tried to pull our forces together again, because what we needed now was tight [firm] leadership. It seemed to me there weren't very many of us, and probably half of them were still hiding in the forest, affected by the explosions and the bullets hissing everywhere.

When I was studying [at the Latvian War School] and later when I was teaching others, we always said leadership is difficult in a forest, because the ability to have oversight is constrained. Now I was experiencing that in practice. With a full set of cadres, it wouldn't be so bad, but I had hardly anyone to give orders to.

Our prisoner had listened to us talking and realised we weren't German; he probably saw the Latvian shields on our uniforms. He asked for me – he said he had something important to say. The prisoner already knew that I was a major by rank and addressed me as *'pan major.'* He was Polish, conscripted in Warsaw. He told me how, half an hour previously, two battalions had gone into battle order. They were quietly pressing forward so as to launch a surprise attack on Flederborn. Our big fuss with the tank will have fouled that up because Flederborn's defenders [the Dutch 48th SS] would now know something was up. I admonished the Pole as a member of a friendly nation for fighting against us. He became completely 'soft' and clung to me like a drowning man clinging to a straw. He probably realised that I wouldn't do anything bad to him and that he would be safe with me.

The situation became interesting and intriguing. The tank we had chased away had been securing the rear of the battalion. Taking on a certain degree of risk, it might be possible to achieve notable success. I decided to grasp the opportunity. But, if we were to fail, I would turn around that same night and make a break for Landeck on my own initiative. If that were to happen, there would be no chance of the Division then making it through as a single unit, because its fighting capabilities would have been severely reduced.

I readied my battalion and told Major B. my decision, exchanging shouts. I told him to take his forces to the right and attack Flederborn simultaneously with me. Our internal flanks were to be aligned in the direction of the burning house as a dividing and coordination line. I decided to destroy these two enemy battalions by squeezing them between us and the defenders in Flederborn village.

A snow-filled valley lay in front of us, rising steeply on the other side. In the darkness I could see thickets to the side. Having called out again to Major B. to check he was ready, we started to move forwards. It was silent in front of us. When we reached the other side of the clearing, where it started to rise, a firefight started on the left flank. There was machine gun fire from both sides: I could hear our rapid firing and the enemy's slow *knock-knock* clearly.

Everyone threw themselves to the ground and started to shoot, clearly just on the off-chance, because you couldn't see anything. I shouted to keep moving forward because this kind of fire at an unseen enemy is just a waste of ammunition. My words had no effect and everyone carried on lying in the snow and firing. My new Company commanders were also unable to pick people up and get them moving forward.

There was nothing left for me to do but to go forwards myself and take direct charge, otherwise something nasty might happen here. On the other hand, there was a risk that collegiate leadership might fall apart, but the most urgent thing was to take the initiative. I reached the forward line in a few minutes and with a sharp command I got the men lying down back on their feet. Walking ahead of them by myself and encouraging them, I 'pulled' people along with me.

We moved quickly forward again and at least the first line followed me. When we got to the other side of the valley and started to climb up it, I saw long black lines lying in the snow not far ahead. I realised immediately they were enemy 'chains' – in fighting formation, ready to attack. 'Fire!' I shouted, and across the front a vicious firefight began. Joining the rifle and machine-gun fire was a four-barrelled anti-aircraft gun, as well as a heavier calibre gun. This vicious exchange lasted about 20 minutes and then, like with a wave of a magician's wand, it stopped. A long line of soldiers came towards us with their hands up and without their weapons which, presumably, had been left in the snow. We let them through the first line and the men behind surrounded them and took them away. Many who no longer moved were left in the snow.

We moved forward again at the command. On the right flank I could hear Major B. shouting 'Forward!' Looking at our lines of attack, I noticed that our centre was going forward well but that the wings were falling behind. We needed the exact opposite. The left wing should be pushing ahead to cover us from any threats from the flanks by reaching the dark bushes first.

When we reached the other ridge, where the enemy forward lines had been lying in the snow waiting to attack Flederborn, I saw what an unfortunate and hopeless position they were in when we rushed them. They couldn't use their weapons effectively against us because they had to lie down with their heads down the slope and their legs in the air. Clearly there had been a panic and after a short period exchanging fire, they surrendered. The rest were dead, or gone. Some fell, some surrendered, but the majority managed to escape to the side, to the open flanks.[12]

In his later journal Ķīlītis revised the number of prisoners taken to 95–96, with 15th Division staff officer and historian Arturs Silgailis estimating that 150 POWs were taken. Then, as the Latvian troops moved toward Podgaje-Flederborn, the Dutch 48th SS defending the village fired on them with flak and smaller calibre weapons, not knowing they were a friendly force sent to relieve them. Several Latvians in Ķīlītis' battalion and in the other two battalions were killed or wounded before the misunderstanding was cleared up. Ķīlītis described the incident in his book *I Go To War*:

Our left wing was increasingly lagging behind. It was a big risk to ourselves. Then, just here in the chain I heard a familiar voice. It was my old veteran, Sergeant Reskājs. Straight away I asked him to go to the left flank and re-orientate it in the direction that I wanted, which he did without delay. When the front straightened out we moved forward a bit, as the division of the landscape demanded, but as soon as we did, we received a devilish blast from the Flederborn defenders, using all the weapons at their disposal.

Explosions in many colours lit up the sky like a firework display with flashes of blue, green, yellow and red. In between, you could clearly hear the quick-firing Bonesaw [MG-42 machine gun]. It was clear these were Germans and the Polish-Russian mixture was no longer in the middle. Having surveyed the scene a couple of times, I thought about how to stop the firing and communicate with those on the other side. It's hard to judge distances at night, but I estimated based on the noises that it would be about 200–300 metres. I was amazed that those on the other side hadn't guessed what might be happening, and hadn't realised that we were firing with the same weapons as they were.

I decided to stop our fire so that the defenders would do the same, and then try to shout across. I had to assume that it wasn't clear to the defenders who we were and they probably weren't expecting us. The Division had promised to inform them using radio-telegraphy. But no sooner had I stopped the firing in one sector than it started again in another and, like a virus, it then spread across both sides. I struggled through this four times until finally there was silence across the front. The defenders must also have heard my shouting and now had some idea of what was going on.

12 Ķīlītis, *I Go To War,* pp.176–180.

I gathered a group of about 20 men and we shouted in German: 'Don't shoot, this is a Latvian unit!' (in the original, it sounded quite different to that). We repeated these shouts multiple times, until at last some chap from the other side came forward and asked for someone to come forward for talks. I called my adjutant, Lieutenant I., and the ordnance officer R., a German national, and ordered both to go over. Both my men got up from the chain, smartened themselves up and went across No-Man's Land to their side. The rest of us, squatting in the snow with our noses over the ridge, watched as the men went over and waited to see what would happen. After a long couple of minutes, my adjutant came back some ten steps and said: 'They're ours and they are asking for you, Major sir, to join them.'

I got up from the chain and went across the front to the other side. The whole of my front now got up and watched me go. When I got there, towards me came Captain T., whom I knew personally from the earlier battles at Flatow. We greeted each other, both happy this incident had been sorted out well. Straight away the German asked if they had caused us any casualties. The fight with the tank and the Poles resulted in a couple of injured men, but there was no further news yet about the rest. In a few words I described our battle experiences and how I had used the circumstances to squeeze and wipe out a couple of Polish battalions. We then discussed the order in which our forces would come in and where to base them temporarily, until the swap-out had happened.

'Captain T' was Helmut Träger, commander of the 2nd Battalion of the 48th Dutch SS Panzer Grenadiers, the main unit of the Flederborn garrison at that time. Ķīlītis continued:

Captain T. told me that Flederborn was encircled on three sides and that we have to expect a new attack or artillery barrage at any minute. We agreed to bring our men in one column at a time to identify them from others and potential infiltrators in the dark. I gave detailed orders to our adjutants about entering the village, which they then quickly delivered for implementation. I stayed on the high ground to watch the columns form and see how the entry began. We have broken into, as it were, such a hell!

As we moved in, sad news came: among the few men fallen in this action was my brave scouting expert Sergeant Reskājs; an 88mm cannon shell had torn him apart. I regretted the loss of such a good man, but that is a soldier's fate – today it's you, tomorrow it could be me...[13]

After the initial barrage that caused the rookie recruits with him to panic and flee, doctor Pauls Dzintars was sheltering in the forest.

---

13 Ķīlītis, *I Go To War*, pp.180–182.

There were three of us left in the forest. We crawled into a thicket of fir trees and considered our position. We heard the sound of battle all around us, continuously. Machine guns barked, grenades exploded. The worst were the exploding bullets: they hit the trees with a sound like a gun discharging. The feeling was that any minute the Russian chain will appear in front of us. I thought about shooting myself but immediately cancelled that thought.

Listening to the sound of battle, we heard in one spot the German MG-34 answer the machine guns. I looked at my compass: it was to the west – so that was the direction we took. We saw a fire in that direction; a house on top of a hill was burning and we could hear the discharge sounds from there. All the retreating mass veered to the east.

Suddenly a machine gun began to fire so close to our hideout that we ran hell for leather. It was difficult to run in the deep snow. In my left hand I carried my doctor's bag, in my right a pistol with the safety catch off. I had never fired at anyone before and probably wouldn't do so now either, but somehow a weapon in my hand gave me a sense of security. A thaw had set in and we were sweating. Every now and then a shadow would glide past us. We threw ourselves to the ground as it might have been a Russian, but it was more likely to be one of ours, just as scared of us as we were of him.

The shooting suddenly stopped. The silence was eerie. Following the compass we moved slowly westwards and finally reached our regiments, with my old commander Major Alksnītis. It turned out that we, together with the Germans, had taken the burning village – Flederborn – and now we [the 15th] were marching there. In the light of the fire the snow looked bloodied and in places it really was. The traces of the battle were everywhere: overturned, broken carts and weapons, even a burning tank. In one spot there were two American-made trucks, while round and about lay 20 or so corpses, mainly Germans.

Before we entered Flederborn we had another task, to take the forest village of Strassforth, which was about three kilometres away. Alksnītis sent a messenger on a horse to Flederborn to ask for artillery support. After a while Alksnītis came back with a Polish prisoner, taken on a forest path. The Pole was slightly faster at putting his hands up. Alksnītis questioned him. It turned out that Poles mobilised by the Russians were opposite us, and the village was defended by two battalions.

We didn't send a second messenger. We didn't have any artillery support and the moment of surprise had passed because the Poles had started shooting at us.[14]

Alksnītis decided to abandon the attack and moved into Flederborn on the night of 31 January–1 February. Zigurds Kārkliņš was a Divisional messenger – possibly the man Alksnītis sent back to the *štābs* [HQ] in Jastrow with a request for artillery

---

14 Dzintars, in *Laiks*, Nr.24 (14 June 2008) and Nr.25 (21 June 2008) online at <periodika.lv>.

support. In later memories he described the column of wounded men on wagons stretching back along the road for a kilometre as being 'exposed on a stage.'

> Because of the heavy guns we can only make slow progress. Some horses die from exhaustion or are hit by bullets. Russian snipers and artillery begin to throw terrific fire on the front of the column from the nearby wood. Some soldiers pull a heavy gun to the side of the road and fire back. That obviously works, as the firing stops. We are surrounded on all sides, and the heavy battery is at the tail end of the column. At some points we have to cross a few 100-metre gaps on a completely open road.
>
> I stand out on this empty part of the road on my horse. People are dashing across one by one in order to draw the least attention to themselves. I try to get my horse up to a good run [before reaching the gap]. I gallop across the open space lying flat with only one thought in my mind: 'If only I can get to the edge of the forest in one piece.' A shell whizzes past in front of my horse – he is ready to bolt. Suddenly he shoots forward like an arrow and very soon we're in the shelter of the forest. Fear makes for quick feet! I feel proud the Russians donated an anti-tank shell just for me.
>
> Having delivered my message, I make my way back. Not on a horse this time but on a sledge, holding the reins in my hand, across the gap again. The February day is short and dusk falls. We haven't covered more than 20 kilometres in the day. As darkness falls the enemy becomes bolder, and more forces are thrown against the road. They pay for this bravery. The four-barrelled anti-aircraft cannon we have ploughs almost all of them down as they cross the field.
>
> In the nearby forest a larger battle takes place at dusk. Our units have surrounded a Polish group and those captured are brought onto the road. They are dressed in Russian uniforms with Polish caps. One Polish officer has an old cavalry sword taken from him, and our boys show off with it for a long time.
>
> In the dark we reach Flederborn village. We are meant to overnight here, so we make ourselves comfortable in a haybarn. The horses eat contentedly: I haven't eaten all day. Divisional HQ is on the opposite side of the yard, and I know the cook well from training. In the attic of the house I meet a group of guys I know who offer me some food then fall asleep. I decide to have a nap.[15]

Regimental doctor Pauls Dzintars had made it into Flederborn too.

15 Zigurds Kārkliņš, 'Izvilkums no manas Grāmatas [Excerpt from my book]' in *Daugavas Vanagi Mēnešraksts* Nr 3 (01 July 2010) online at <http://periodika.lv/periodika2-viewer/?lang=fr#panel:pa%7Cissue:217835%7Carticle:DIVL259%7Cquery:Flederbornas>. An estimated 150–210 Polish prisoners are believed by researchers Juergen Fritz and Edvard Anders to have been taken here, most likely by the Dutch 48th SS. These are not the 32 men massacred and remembered on the memorial at Podgaje-Flederborn, the subject of the next chapter, who were captured earlier in the day.

There we found an empty house with the body of a German lying in a big pool of blood in the porch. It was probably the owner of the house. Our prisoner pulled the corpse outside, made up a fire, carried in straw and we squashed closely together one against another in a warm room and slept deeply. The house was on the edge of the village. Exploding bullets hit the walls but we didn't take any notice of that. I carried my doctor's bag but all ammunition, medicines and bandages had been lost. They would have been useful in the next two days!

Flederborn was the 15th Division's Golgotha. We were completely surrounded. Actually, the siege had two pockets. Connections had been broken with Jastrow where Janums was with Divisional Command HQ. In Flederborn there was an 88mm anti-aircraft battery and the 48th Dutch SS Regiment. Alksnītis had been told a German attacking force was coming towards us and our job was to hold Flederborn at any cost. The enemy would then be caught in a pincer movement. Our enemy was mainly Poles mobilised into the Red Army and used as cannon fodder, just like they did with the mobilised Latvians in Latvia.

I set up a medical point. Apart from me there were three Battalion doctors, Vēriņš, Prīmanis and Beldavs, but only I had a doctor's bag. We carried straw into the room, I put my bag on the table and we waited for the wounded. They turned up very quickly. Some hadn't received any help since yesterday. The enemy disturbed us with occasional shelling. We were thankful for well-built German houses. The smaller shells didn't do much damage. One shell exploded outside the window, sending shrapnel pieces whistling over our heads, hitting the opposite wall. That went on the whole of the day on 1 February.

There was a fairly serious enemy attack but this was quickly deflected as ammunition was still available for the flak gun and we had automatic weapons. Our lines were only pushed back a little. More and more wounded came in and enemy fire continued. When the first house was full of wounded, we moved on to the next house, which up to now had been the headquarters of the 34th Regiment. I left a 34th Regiment medic to look after the first house. The evening and night of 1 February was calm and we could rest a bit.[16]

Ķīlītis described in his memoirs the atmosphere that evening inside besieged Flederborn:

Each hour brought more victims and the roads and courtyards filled up with corpses that no-one wanted to collect. There wasn't anywhere to bury them anyway. The ground was frozen and you couldn't walk around because that created more victims. Low clouds, a light mist and the warm, windless weather made the air stink sweetly of spilled blood. Sometimes a horrible feeling came over you, so that shivers crept down your spine.[17]

---

16 Pauls Dzintars, article in *Daugavas Vanagu Mēnešraksts,* Nr. 5 (01 September 1999) online at <periodika.lv>. Latvians translate 'cannon fodder' as 'cannon meat.'
17 Ķīlītis, *I Go To War,* p.182.

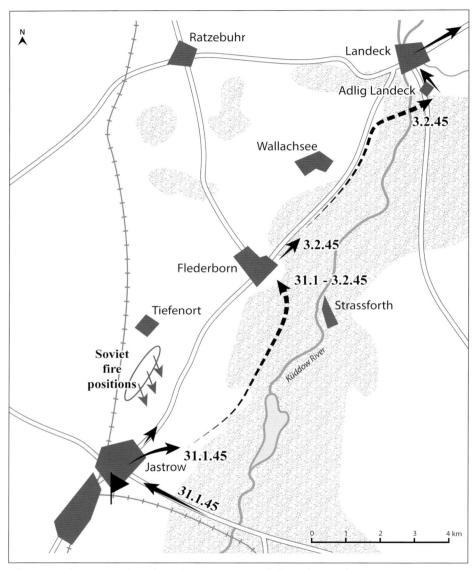

Operations by Major Ķīlītis along the Jastrow to Landeck road. From his memoir *I Go To War*.

10

Podgaje-Flederborn: The Memorial

Road 22 leads north out of Jastrowie today, with the river Gwda [Küddow] and forest on my right. Flat fields and the occasional farmhouse rise on the left up to woods on the higher ground, like a ridge of hills, just like on Ķīlītis' map – but now the road is a fast and busy dual carriageway. The turn I need at Podgaje is quite complicated; across oncoming traffic at a farm equipment showroom just after a large fuel and service station and before a crossroads.

I am here to see a memorial: to 32 Polish soldiers murdered here during the German withdrawal along this road in February 1945. This is tucked away down the side road I am turning into. The memorial lies past the tractors and giant agricultural machinery on the forecourt of the farm showroom, and there is a cluster of large bungalow-type homes opposite.[1] I trundle a short distance past them, trying to get a feel for the place as it might have been in the war. I turn the car around, park and walk to the memorial. In the first days of February 1945 – and, I discover later, for some time afterwards – Flederborn was a scene from hell.

Because death rates were so high among frontline units in Pomerania at the time, very few Latvians survived to tell their stories of what happened here. The murder of the 32 Polish prisoners at Flederborn is still not fully explained, but the Latvians have been considered among possible suspects.

One Latvian officer who was here and survived was the commander of the 34th Regiment, Jūlijs Ķīlītis, who moved to the UK after the war, wrote and published his memoirs in 1956 and died in Coventry in 1961. Doubts have been cast on his account on the grounds that he might have been trying to avoid admitting to war crimes, but his testimony of the time is extremely detailed and personal and gives a very human insight into how he saw events. Lengthy excerpts from his book *Es Karā Aiziedams: Mani Raksturīgākie Piedzīvojumi Otrā Pasaules Karā [I Go To War: My Most Characteristic Adventures in WWII]* have been translated for this book for that reason.

---

1   The monument is at 4 Pamięci Narodowej, Podgaje.

His testimony of actual events, and the scale of the slaughter here revealed by Ķīlītis and others, including Colonel Janums, doctors and priests, serves to question whether the existing monument at Podgaje-Flederborn is an adequate and accurate memorial to the actual and vast loss of life here, not just of soldiers but wounded men and fleeing refugees, including women and children. These translated accounts suggest that perhaps only selected passages of the story of the road to Landeck have been told so far.

The allegation against the Latvians at Podgaje-Flederborn is that, led by Ķīlītis, they surprised a Polish unit attacking the town, overcame it and took the survivors as prisoners to the village. There they were held in a barn, questioned and then murdered. Who murdered them is at the centre of the controversy. Ķīlītis says he handed the prisoners over to the Germans after the battle and that was the end of Latvian involvement with them.

It's possible that what actually happened involves the murder of five times as many Polish prisoners, but in less cruel circumstances than the gruesome deaths of the 32 Polish men described in 'official' accounts from Soviet and post-war Polish Communist sources. There is also a suggestion arising from research for this book that 400 young Latvian recruits drafted into battle on 3 February – possibly their first day in action – panicked under fire and ran. A Soviet tank unit came across them on the edge of the forest, and they surrendered. They were held prisoner – again in barns – before allegedly being executed in groups of 50–100 in the forest, where their bodies were left.

A senior Latvian officer, Vilis Hāzners, made reference to this incident 30 years afterwards in the 11-volume Latvian Legion official history, known as the 'Green Books', which also contains a second reference in another account. The context of this unconfirmed and previously unreported alleged Red Army massacre of Latvian prisoners – no more than terrified teenage conscripts, if truth be told – is explored and researched further in subsequent chapters.

The Latvian version of events is that they came across two Polish battalions preparing to attack as they advanced towards Flederborn led by Vīksne and Ķīlītis.[2] Surprised from behind, the Polish forces were routed. Legion historian and second-in-command Arturs Silgailis describes what happened next, including the friendly fire incident which killed Sergeant Reskājs.

At twilight, the battle group stumbled into enemy forces that were attacking Flederborn. The battle group immediately attacked from the rear and scattered them. The enemy lost 150 prisoners and three anti-tank guns. The prisoners were Poles from the Sikorski and Kostushko divisions. As the battle group moved towards Flederborn they were greeted with fire from the 48th SS-Grenadier

---

2   Having been alerted to their presence by the Polish soldier taken prisoner after being thrown off the tank.

Regiment, which had mistakenly assumed them to be Russians. The battle group did suffer some casualties.[3]

The Polish historical researcher Arnold Koslowski has researched the battle at Podgaje-Flederborn in detail, and adds the story from the other side.

> The prisoners were men of the 1st *Tadeusz Kostushko* Infantry Division, a unit of the Polish Army in the East, politically subordinate to the PKWN, the Polish Committee of National Liberation: an organization of Polish communists subordinate to Stalin. The commander of the 1st Infantry Division from November 1943–September 1945 was General Wojciech Bewziuk, a Russian of Polish origin. Bewziuk was an artillery officer throughout his career and, until he became commander of the 1st Infantry Division, had only commanded artillery units.[4]

Podgaje-Flederborn is controversial to this day because of Soviet and now Russian claims that the Latvians murdered the 32 Polish prisoners from the 4th Company, first tying them up with barbed wire, dousing them in petrol and then burning them alive. From a Polish perspective, the evidence includes testimony from men in the area at the time and from a soldier who escaped the killing. The discovery of charred bodies is among the detail confirmed by Polish research. The following account was published by the government-affiliated historical research body, the IPN [*Institute Polish Narodny*], which set out to re-examine periods of the Second World War and Communist-era history to get to the truth of what the Nazi and Soviet regimes did in Poland.

> In the afternoon of 31 January 1945, the 4th Company (about 70–80 soldiers) led by Second Lieutenant Alfred Sofka was sent to scout German defences on the western bank of the Gwda river and to establish the strength of the enemy defending themselves in Podgaje. The company was part of the 2nd Battalion led by Captain Wacława Zalewski from the 3rd Infantry Regiment of the 1st Infantry Division of the LWP [Polish People's Army].
>
> The reconnaissance company was surrounded and cut off from the rest of the battalion and, despite fierce resistance, was destroyed. The company was without radio or wire communication and runners sent back did not reach the rest of the battalion. Only two soldiers escaped from the encirclement: Stanisław Życzyński and Antoni Tytanik, who in the early morning of 1 February arrived back at the Polish positions. About 50 Polish soldiers were taken prisoner and the badly-wounded prisoners were executed. This was witnessed by Private Władysław Gąsiorowski, whom German soldiers left on the battlefield thinking he was dead, and by Second Lieutenant Zbigniew Furgała who was taken

---

3   Silgailis, *Latvian Legion,* p.167.
4   Arnold Koslowski, correspondence with author, August 2021.

The original burial site of the 32 Polish soldiers murdered at Podgaje-Flederborn in February 1945, marked with a birch tree cross. They were from the 4th Company of the 3rd Infantry Regiment. (Picture courtesy of the Military Historical Office, Warsaw. Ref: 1560.3)

prisoner but escaped. According to Edward Rohatyński, a soldier who got to the site of the battle a few hours later, the dead Polish soldiers could only be identified by their Army identity books.

The rest of the 2nd Battalion was stopped by the 48th Motorised SS Regiment *General Seyffardt*. This unit consisted of Dutch volunteers and mobilised *Volksdeutsche* units from Romania and Hungary, commanded by the Latvian Panzergrenadiers from the 15th Division SS.[5] They were not able to break through.

The surprise appearance from Jastrowie [Jastrow] of the 34th Latvian Regiment on the outskirts of Podgaje at exactly the same time as the Polish soldiers was their undoing. Podgaje was eventually captured after several more heavy battles on 3 February 1945. Extra artillery was brought in to break the resistance of those defending a small farming village on a crossroads, but the price of victory was high: 800 men killed, wounded or missing.

Then, in a burning barn, a macabre discovery was made: the remains of 32 prisoners from the 4th Company. They had died horribly. An investigation reported they were bound with barbed wire and chains and – from the blisters on their bodies and the lingering smell of gasoline – had been burned alive. Some prisoners appeared to have put up resistance: several had gunshot wounds to the skull. The fate of these Polish soldiers while prisoners of the Germans became known thanks to Second Lieutenant Zbigniew Furgała, who managed to escape in a breakout with Corporal Bernard Bondziurecki.[6] The company commander Second Lieutenant Sofka and a dozen or so other soldiers who also escaped were killed, and the remaining prisoners murdered.

Second Lieutenant Furgała said they decided to try and escape because the Germans were mistreating soldiers during interrogation:

> …Our colleagues, including Ensign Zdisław Piława were brought back. They had been badly beaten up, and some had broken arms and legs. Some were carried in. Knowing that the same thing was waiting for us, we decided to organise an escape. There was no choice. We wanted to give a chance to those who could still save their lives.[7]

Polish historians have considered the possibility that the executions were carried out by Latvian troops and concluded that the subsequent deaths of many of the unit

5   Command rested with Adolph Ax, not the Latvian officers. As the example of Colonel Janums and the German 51st Infantry at Jastrow shows, German units did not like to be given orders by non-Germans.
6   In some documents, Bolesław Bondzielewski. He died at the front in May 1945.
7   M. Maciejowski, *Zbrodnie Niemieckie na Pomorzu Zachodnim I Ziemi Lubuskiej Popelnione w Latach 1939–1945 w Swietle Sledztw Prowadzonych Przez Oddzialowa Komisje Scigania Zbrodni Przeciwko Narodowi Polskiemu w Szczecinie* (Warsaw: Instytut Pamięci Narodowej [Institute of National Remembrance – Commission for the Prosecution of Crimes against the Polish Nation], 2013), p. 103.

officers makes establishing the truth problematic. Polish historical researcher Arnold Koslowski adds the following thoughts to the Polish military move that led to the tragedy of the massacre at Podgaje-Flederborn.

> Most studies on Podgaje (Flederborn) say that Lieutenant Sofka's company was sent for reconnaissance, in order to recognize the enemy. It is not a precise term. The 4th Company of the 3rd Infantry Regiment of the 1st Infantry Division was part of the unit that was to attack Podgaje (Flederborn) as part of the 'reconnaissance by fight' tactic. [That meant] a unit of soldiers is sent with an order to attack, without any preparation, so that the enemy will reveal his forces and positions in combat. This is evidenced by documents from the Central Military Archives. The 4th Company was in the lead of the attacking battalion.
>
> There is an unusual overlapping of several factors here. The errors in the command of Polish units; the efficiency and determination of Latvian and German troops. It is interesting that the information about fierce resistance is provided only by the Polish side. Ķīlītis describes that the fight lasted about 20 minutes. Information about the hours of defence comes from the only survivor who survived the war, Zbigniew Furgała, who gave different versions over the years. Amateur field studies also do not confirm fierce fighting. It was probably a short, dynamic clash, ended by the withdrawal of most of the Polish battalion and the captivity of the soldiers of Lieutenant Sofka.
>
> Information about the barbed wire [used to tie up the prisoners] appears in the medical report from … February 15. In a report written by, among others, a female military doctor, there is information about the 'wire.' A man who was a member of a group burying the fallen speaks of a 'telephone cord.' Barbed wire and gasoline appear in the feature film 'Elegia' ['Elegy']. This is all contained in the article by [researchers] Fritz and Anders. However, they make one basic mistake. The film 'Elegy' is not a documentary and the story told in it, [although] inspired by real events, is however a screen adaptation of the novel, the action of which takes place in a completely different place, but at the same time.[8]

The Latvian divisional commander during the battles for Podgaje-Flederborn was Oberführer Adolf Ax, ethnically a Walloon from Belgium but a member of the Nazi Party from 1930. He was an early SS volunteer, who fought his way up the ranks to Hauptsturmführer [Captain] by 1936 and had won the Iron Cross First and Second Class by July 1940.[9]

Ax was despised by the Latvian officers, who believed he sacrificed their men to save German lives. Colonel Janums and others described him as 'an elderly, untalented and hapless officer.' Ax was 39, but looked much older. Latvian military history is disparaging about him, and one officer, Captain Tūte from the 15th Artillery, wrote:

---

8   Correspondence with author, August 2021.
9   Felgrau.net forum pages online at: <https://www.feldgrau.net/forum/viewtopic.php?t=1590>, accessed 11 May 2021.

After [the previous divisional commander] Obwurzer was taken prisoner by the Russians on 26 January, our division's and the artillery's 'black days' began, because the new divisional commander Ax was not capable of leading the fighting. One of his most not-thought-through orders was to change positions during the retreat in five to six kilometre bounds, ignoring any opportunities arising from the lay of the land. New positions continually had to be taken up under enemy fire or even by attack, because the enemy was in front of us.

This situation was best described by Major Balodis: 'After leaving Nakel, I had to carry out three types of activity – retreat, attack and defence – and, on top of that, I had to carry them all out at the same time.'[10]

With the battle still raging, the column of wounded men on horse-drawn wagons set out from Jastrow towards Podgaje-Flederborn. Artilleryman Zigurds Kārkliņš described the scenes as they left, with the road clearly not secured.

Slowly, column after column leaves the town. Artillery, baggage, army transport and refugee carts, in multi-coloured file. Infantrymen on each side. All round are the sounds of fighting. That means that until we reach the next inhabited place we'll have to free up the route step-by-step again. At the edge of the town, we found the first of the fallen. They're Latvian and German soldiers who were sent in the black of the night to find out where the Russians were. At the edge of the road is a lorry, badly shot-up, and all around are our comrades who were ambushed in the dark.

The road alternates between forest and open fields. On the right, 300 metres from the road, is a wood, from which there are flashes of fire in our direction and the shells from grenade launchers. On the other side, at a similar range, is a valley, from which we can be seen as clear as day. Still, there's no other way. And so, in full view of the enemy and powerless in our anger and desperation, we move forwards.[11]

Ax reached Podgaje-Flederborn on the night of 2 February. He was there only briefly to assess the situation and come up with a break-out plan. He considered his move all night – 'dithering', the Latvians called it – and gave the order for the column to move out at dawn on 3 February. This left his men sitting ducks in the morning light. The German officers considered this order 'insane', according to Fritz and Anders.[12]

The result was that almost the entire command structure of the Latvian 15th Waffen-SS Division was wiped out in desperate fighting through the roadblocks at

10 Latvian 'Green Books', vol. 6, p.218.
11 Kārkliņš, in *Daugavas Vanagu Mēnešraksts*, Nr. 3 (01 July 2010) online at <periodika.lv>. Trans. Daina Vītola.
12 J. Fritz, and E. Anders, 'Murder of Polish POWs at Podgaje (Flederborn), February 1945' in *The Second World War and Latvia: Events and Consequences 1940s–1960s*, Research of the Commission of the Historians of Latvia, 2011, and reports of conference 'Extermination of the Latvian Army, 1940–41'. (Rīga: Zinatne, 2011), pp.130–131.

Wallachsee and later in a full-frontal assault to silence the last machine gun position blocking the road into Landeck. The highest-ranking survivor of those 48 hours was Ķilītis, who took charge of the 34th Regiment when regimental commander Alberts Vīksne was wounded. Extracts from his book relating to the handover of his Polish prisoners and his subsequent inquiries about them – as well as his detailed descriptions of the scenes in the town – are among the few eyewitness accounts of this period.

Born in 1902 in Sloka, Ķilītis had joined the Latvian Army in 1927, graduating from military school as a captain in 1939. In 1943 he joined the Legion and was rapidly promoted, becoming commander of the 1st Battalion of the 34th Regiment and then Major in June 1944. In his 1956 memoir, Ķilītis wrote that his battalion captured the Polish soldiers and handed them over to the Germans, and it was the Germans who murdered them at some point on the night of 31 January–1 February. He discovered their fate the next day.

> During my visit to the German Command, I asked about the fate of the Polish prisoners, whom we passed on to them after our arrival in Podgaje. The Germans exchanged meaningful looks, grunting, and then one of them said I should not worry because they don't need anything anymore. Such a response surprised me and was extremely embarrassing, which showed on my face. Before I could say anything, one of the officers added that they did not have food or quarters themselves, and only a few troops guarding the prisoners, so they had no choice.
>
> Although the war has little to do with human feelings, I take it as a necessary and inevitable evil. But there is a huge difference between face-to-face and ordinary murder. In general, it is a matter of human conscience, and I did not want to lose mine.

Ķilītis described the same event a little more descriptively in a later journal:

> Podgaje itself left rather disgusting impressions. Several houses were burning, filling the village with smoke. The colour of the fog was milky-pink. There were dead cattle and many human bodies on the streets, among them Polish prisoners shot dead by the Germans. The German units were rather cruel to them. It makes me feel ashamed, because they are people just like us, fighting for their reasons, and you cannot blame them for it. The smell of burning was rising in the air and – making you feel sick – the sweet smell of bodies. The thaw made muddy puddles of dirt and blood.[13]

Certainly there were prisoner executions. At 13:00 on 31 January, Czesław Krystman and other soldiers of the Polish 3rd Regiment [most likely 3 Battalion]

---

13 Extract from Ķilītis, *I Go to War*, p.104, and extract from the diary of Major Ķilītis, trans. M. Wiklacz in *Polish People's Army Records in Communist times* at <www.dws-xip.pl/LWP/ podgaje2.html>.

witnessed the killing of Polish prisoners about three kilometres north of Podgaje-Flederborn:

> On the other side of the river we saw our scouts shot in the back of their heads and put on the ground close to each other.[14]

In his wartime diary for 2 February 1945, a Latvian serving in the Red Army Guards, Captain Jānis Grīnvalds, described the short shrift given to Latvian prisoners. As he travelled from Flatow to Jastrow that day, he came across nine Legion prisoners being held in a barn.

> The Latvians told me that they had been conscripted and that they had carried an injured Red Army captain out from the forest. They were from the 15th SS Division. They also asked me – will they be shot? I think I said they wouldn't because in those days I thought that our people didn't shoot [prisoners]. I didn't see them again. Later I was told they had been shot.
>
> The Poles are suffering great losses, nevertheless all Latvian prisoners were killed. On the roadsides I saw the corpses of Latvian Legionnaires. They hadn't fallen.[15]

Establishing the truth of what happened in Podgaje-Flederborn prompted further investigation by American-Latvian historical researcher Edvard Anders – a Jew who escaped the Holocaust in the western port city of Liepāja in 1941 – and UK-based German historian Juergen Fritz. They considered whether responsibility for the prisoner killings lay with the 48th Dutch SS *General Seyffardt* Panzergrenadiers. This was a unit of Dutch Nazi volunteers that had been almost wiped out at Narva in Estonia a few months before which had been shipped back to Germany to rebuild with Romanian and Hungarian *Volkssturm* men under German command.

Russian sources consider a battlegroup named after an officer called Elster as a potential suspect for the murders: Ax's orders for 31 January 1945 contained in the war diary of the 15th Division in the Latvian National Archives in Rīga (reproduced right) include a reference to a battle group commanded by 'Elster' used in the defence of Jastrow.

During the battles for Flederborn between 31 January and 2 February, the commander of the 48th SS, Obersturmführer Paul Massel, was killed. His subordinates were Hauptsturmführers Wolfgang Vieweger and Friedrich Träger. In Ķīlītis' view, the Polish prisoners were murdered by the 48th SS. According to his account, on 31 January and 1 February, the main German unit defending Flederborn, independent of Latvian formations, was the 2nd Battalion of the 48th Regiment commanded by Friedrich Träger (Ķīlītis calls him Helmut Träger). Ķīlītis doesn't

---

14 Fritz and Anders, *Murder of Polish POWS,* p.132.
15 Grīnvalds, *As I Saw Those Things,* trans. Aivars Sinka, p.280.

KTB

89

15.Waffen-Gren.Div.der SS
(lett.Nr.1)
Ia

Div.Gef.St., den 31.1.45
12.20 Uhr

An

Kampfgruppe
V i k s n e

Kampfgruppe Viksne (Gren.Rgt.34 mit unterstellten Teilen Rgt.32) setzt den Marsch nach Norden auf Flederborn fort, löst in Flederborn die Kräfte des verst. Gren.Rgt. 48 ab um sie für den weiteren Angriff auf Landeck und Ratzebuhr frei zu machen. Des Regiment sperrt den Übergang über den Kuddow - Abschnitt westl Straßforth und sichert gegen NW und W.

i.V.

SS-Oberführer

Aktenvermerk

Div.Befehl mündlich persönlich am 31.1.45, 12.1o Uhr:

Feind in Blietnitz wird wahrscheinlich weiter nach Norden vorstoßen. In Flederborn ist der Russe erneut eingedrungen und hat die Pi.-Kp. geworfen.

A.K. hat von Norden her eine Kampfgruppe von Hamme restein aus auf Landeck und von Nordosten eine Div. über Preuß.Friedland nach Landeck angesetzt, mit der sich die 15.Div. vereinigen soll.

1.) Rgt.48 hat den Auftrag, Landeck und Ratzebur zu nehmen. Dazu tritt das Rgt. in Flederborn an.

2.) Kampfgruppe Viksne setzt den Marsch nach Norden fort und löst das Rgt. 48 ab, um dieses für den Angriff auf Landeck freizumachen. Das Rgt. sperrt den Übergang über den Kuddow-Abschnitt nördl. Straßforth und sichert nach Westen und Norden.

3.) Kdr. Rgt.33 wird mit der Verteidigung des Abschnittes Jastrow, Grenze rechts:Jagdhaus (16 km SW. Jastrow) - Bethkenhammer - Tarnowke (Orte einschl.); linke Grenze: Südrand Pinnow - Nordrand Neuhof (5 km SW Flatow)

Dem Rgt. werden dazu, die in diesem Abschnitt eingesetzten Kräfte unterstellt. I./J.R.59 mit einer Kp. zur Sicherung von Tarnowke, einer nach Südwesten in Gegend Försterei Büschken (1 km SW-Rand Jastrow). Masse des Btl. in Betkenhammer. Verst.II./59, verst.durch 1 Kp. schw.Gr.W. zur Sperrung des Überganges über den Kuddow-Abschnitt bei Kuddowbrück. Verst. Füs.Btl. verst.durch eine Kp. Gr.W. im Raum Gursen in der Aufnahmestellung der Div. Fest.Gr.W.Btl.Elster eingesetzt ohne 2 Kpn zur Ortsverteidigung von Jastrow. Aufklärung gegen Gursen, Pinnow, Briesenitz, Zainborst; Plietnitz, Sakolnow, Petzin. Das Rgt. ist mit Masse in Jastrow und mit Teilen zur Sicherung im Westen eingesetzt.

Orders signed by Oberführer Adolph Ax giving a situation report at 1220 hours on 31 January, 1945. KG *Viksne* (made up of the 34th and 32nd Regiments) will relieve the 48th SS in Flederborn so it can attack Landeck and Ratzebuhr. The Elster group has been defending Jastrow. (From 15th Division war diary, Latvian National Archives, Riga. LV_LVVA_F296_US1_GV)

blame Träger personally for directing the execution, but does say the 48th 'shot them all.'

Fritz and Anders say the men killed in the barn were from a group of 37 prisoners captured by the 48th Dutch SS before the Latvians arrived. Then Ķīlītis brought a second group of between 95 and 150 prisoners, taken in the fight with the Polish they surprised on the outskirts of Flederborn. These men were handed over to the 48th according to standard procedure, they wrote:

> Alas, the 48th shot them that same evening. The 37 prisoners had remained silent during interrogation soon after their capture. All managed to escape, but three were killed, 32 were re-captured, and only two got away. The 32 were then bound with telephone wire, not barbed wire, and almost certainly were not burnt alive but were shot that same evening. The fire that burnt the bodies started two and a half days later, when a devastating artillery bombardment by Soviet and Polish forces caused 90 percent of the village to burn down. The burn blisters that the medical commission cited as evidence for burning alive are not a reliable criterion, according to modern forensic pathology sources.
>
> However, the total number of POWs shot by the Nazis in Podgaje was 160–210 rather than 32, so the crime, though less savage, was much greater in scope. Most likely, the murders were committed by Dutch SS men of the 48th Regiment with any attached German SS battle groups. The Latvian troops apparently were not involved.[16]

In an article for the Latvian Commission of Historians Fritz and Anders conclude that two separate battles at Flederborn – one in daylight and one at night – have been regarded as one. They wrote:

> The first battle, in which 37 prisoners of 4 Company were taken, began *in daylight* between 14:00 and 15:00 and involved Dutch troops of 2 Bn 48 Regt and perhaps attached German SS troops. *There were no Latvians yet in or near Podgaje during this firefight.* The second battle, in which between 95 and 150 prisoners were taken, began *in darkness* after 18:00 on 31 January. It involved two Latvian and two Polish battalions.[17]

Another possible perpetrator suggested is Sturmbannführer Siegfried Scheibe who led a small fighting group in the area with a strength of less than a battalion; Kampfgruppe [Battle Group] Scheibe.[18]

---

16 Fritz and Anders, *Murder of Polish POWs,* from English summary pp.185–186 in Europa Orientalis 3 *Studies in the history of Eastern Europe and the Baltic States* (2012) online at: <http://dx.doi.org/10.12775/EO.2012.009>.

17 Fritz and Anders, *Murder of Polish POWs,* p.129.

18 Scheibe was killed at Halbe on 26 April 1945 in an attempt to break out from the encirclement there.

The barn at Podgaje-Flederborn where the 32 Polish soldiers were killed. (Picture from 1945 courtesy of the Military Historical Office, Warsaw. Ref: A.16666)

The Polish IPN historian Maciej Maciejowski has investigated the massacre at Podgaje. During a visit to Szczezin researching this book, I asked him who he thought had carried out the killings:

> MM: Who was responsible for this war crime? Latvian soldiers, German soldiers or Dutch soldiers serving in the German Army? Many historians in Poland say responsibility for this crime is Latvian, but in the memoirs of the Latvian officer Jūlijs Ķīlītis, he says that it was not possible. He says Helmut Träger, a captain from the 48th SS Netherlands Regiment – Dutch soldiers – was responsible for this crime. Maybe. It's one of the possibilities.
>
> VH: The Latvians have said to me about the Polish: 'We didn't want to fight the Polish. We considered them to be on the same side as us, fighting the Soviets.'
>
> MM: Julius Ķīlītis said in his memoir that he wasn't fighting against the Polish soldiers, but the Soviets. It's a problem. The Polish are victims; Latvians too. German historian Helmut Lindenblatt said that Polish prisoners killed Russian artillerymen in Podgaje: that's the German version. Latvians say they are innocent in this battle. Ķīlītis said: 'Captivity, yes – but not murder.'
>
> VH: And he spoke to the Germans and they looked very shifty. Why would he lie? Perhaps to avoid a war crimes tribunal?

MM: Yes.
VH: Do you ever have conversations with Latvian historians in Rīga?
MM. No.

Maciej Maciejowski believes the tragedy at Podgaje should be seen 'in the broad context of war crimes committed on both sides on the Eastern Front' and be freed from the 'self-serving perspectives of political propaganda.'

> MM: We have more information about the struggle of *Festung* Posen [Poznan]. After the battle of Posen we know that Russians killed many wounded German and Hungarian soldiers. It is a horrible crime: they burned 100 wounded German and Hungarian soldiers on 23 February 1945, after they had surrendered. It's horrible, but the Eastern Front is generally horrible.
>
> The Eastern Front was not fighting between nations, German and Russian, but a struggle of two horrible totalitarian systems. Podgaje, Lędyczek [Landeck, another set of horrors which unfolded in the next two days] and the crimes in *Festung* Posen were just one side of this horrible conflict. I think that many soldiers in the First Polish Army were fighting in Pomerania for freedom for Poland. For many Polish soldiers it is revenge against the Germans for defeating them in 1939, for the Warsaw Uprising and so on. For many Polish people the Germans are the first enemy in this war. The Russians are the second.
>
> VH: That's what the Latvians say, but the other way around.
>
> MM: In Poland the German occupation was horrible. In Latvia, the Russian occupation was horrible. There are parallels between Latvia and Poland. Middle Eastern Europe is a tragic place. Today Polish and German people live in one structure: Europe. That's a good thing. Young people have modern thinking. It is a time of freedom, but particularly of conflict of memory.
>
> The Germans have created many films about 1945, but they show themselves as the victims. Their perspective at the end of the war is that of victims. They don't focus on the attack of Poland in 1939 and other [things]. Today Polish society is free, but for many decades we lived under the Communist regime … Because it was provincial, many people in Poland didn't know about Podgaje. I want history to be re-examined through clear eyes, not with a political lens applied to it: not Communist, not national-ist – through clear eyes.[19]

Political propaganda has added grotesque details to versions of the Podgaje-Flederborn 'myth.' The Polish historian Piotr Zychowicz wrote that vivid, gory details of the

---

19 Interview with author, IPN offices in Szczecin, 20 August 2018. For a Latvian perspective on Podgaje-Flederborn, see the Museum of the Occupation of Latvia website at: <http://okupacijasmuzejs.lv/en/history/independent-latvia/fake-news-latvian-legionnaires-burnt-polish-pows-alive>.

incident were circulated by Red Army political officers shortly afterwards, and the tying of the prisoners' hands with barbed wire contradicts the testimony of one of the soldiers assigned to bury them, who specified the use of telephone cable. He wrote:

> There is no excuse for the murderers of Podgaje. In the name of historical truth, it should be noted that the crime was not as cruel as the Communists portrayed it.[20]

In an article titled *Fake News: Latvian Legionnaires Burnt Polish POWs Alive* the Latvian historical journalist Viesturs Sprūde noted that Russian accounts of Podgaje added macabre claims, such as that while burning the bodies of the Polish soldiers:

> …the troops of the Latvian Legion 'were singing songs and dancing around the shed' [barn]…[21]

Sprude dismisses this as Russian propaganda, adding:

> …only Russian language media are currently attributing the Podgaje massacre to Latvians, although it would be logical to assume that the Polish would have much more grounds to do that.[22]

Fritz and Anders considered whether revenge might have been a motive for the massacre.

> Several posts on Polish websites suggest that the Latvians may have sought revenge for the Red Army's murders of unarmed 17-year-old Latvians in RAD *(Reichsarbeitsdienst)* camps. Hundreds of bodies were found on 23 January 1945 during a counter-attack at Immenheim near Bydgoszcz. At Ogardy [then Wugarten, 150 kilometres west of Landeck] US POWs witnessed the gang rape of all girls in the Latvian RAD camp and [the murder of all the males]. The boys were executed by the standard NKVD method; shots in the back of the neck.
>
> Some 600 boys were executed the same way in the RAD camp Landeck-Lędyczek, only 9 kilometres from Podgaje. Those Latvian units that found out about these atrocities surely turned more vengeful. But there is no mention of this in Ķīlītis' diary, so presumably the Latvians in Podgaje did not know. The fog of war was very dense at that time and place: Lieutenant Sofka [who led the

20 P. Zychowicz, 'Tajemnica mordu w Podgajach. Jedna z największych polskich zagadek II wojny światowej' ['The Mystery of the murders in Podgaje. One of the greatest Polish riddles of WWII'], *Do Rzeczy*, (19 April 2019) <https://dorzeczy.pl/historia/100018/Tajemnica-mordu-w-Podgajach-Jedna-z-najwiekszych-polskich-zagadek-II-wojny-swiatowej.html>.   Trans. Janusz Korona, accessed 26 July 2020.

21 V. Sprūde, *Fake News: Latvian Legionnaires Burnt Polish POWs Alive* at <http://okupacijas-muzejs.lv/en/history/independent-latvia/fake-news-latvian-legionnaires-burnt-polish-pows-alive>. Undated, accessed 26 July 2020.

22 Sprūde, *Fake News*.

attacking 4th Polish Company] did not know on 31 January whether Germans, Russians, or nobody held Podgaje, and neither did Ķīlītis later that day.[23]

Fritz and Anders examined Ķīlītis' accounts of events at Podgaje, both in his original diaries, written at the time (referred to here as K1) and later in the Zedelghem camp in Belgium where he was held after the war (K2). His 1956 autobiography was also used as a third source in their analysis (K3). Ķīlītis was then commander of 1 Battalion of the 34th Grenadier Regiment, the unit that fought the night battle with two Polish battalions on 31 January.

> The Latvian troops moved toward Podgaje but the Dutch (and German?) troops holding the village fired on them with flak and smaller calibre weapons, not knowing that this was a friendly force sent to relieve them. Several Latvians in Ķīlītis' battalion and in the other two battalions were killed or wounded before the misunderstanding was cleared up. Still outside the village, Ķīlītis met with Helmut Träger, commander of 2 Bn of 48 SS PzGren Regt, the main unit of the Podgaje garrison. [K1]

> 'I handed over the prisoners to the 48th Regt, which later shot them all.' [K1]

> 'The German SS 48th Regt shot all prisoners after searching them, including those captured by us.' [K2][24]

The Latvian military historian Valdis Kuzmins is considered one of the experts on the 15th Division, and has views on events at Podgaje-Flederborn.

> I believe that what Ķīlītis says is true, even though he has several attempts at explaining himself in his diary. I think the Polish prisoners were killed by the Germans, who were the last ones left there. By that time the 15th had already moved on to Landeck, trying to break out of there.[25] At one point some of the Poles had already tried to escape, and two were caught, so I think that explains why the other prisoners were all killed on the spot like that.
>
> In those battles from late January to March there was a lot of heavy fighting. In those two months there were plenty of cases when the Latvians captured

23 Fritz and Anders, *Murder of Polish POWs*, p.142. Latvians, of all people, would know the difference between NKVD units and Polish conscripts. Every veteran the author met said resisting a repeat of the Soviet horror of 1940–41 was why they were fighting. It was considered a national duty, and they had no argument with the Polish. Veteran Laimonis Ceriņš told the author that Ķīlītis instructed surviving Polish soldiers after the battle at Flederborn: 'Go back to your unit. Tell them we are Latvians. We don't want to fight Polish.'
24 Fritz and Anders, *Murder of Polish POWs*.
25 Ķīlītis was the last commander in Flederborn, and the rearguard pulled out at 10:30 on 3 February 1945.

prisoners in the fighting. In the next hour or the next day they faced the situation of having to break out of encirclements, and there's no way they say: 'We take the two or three or fifteen – or fifty – prisoners with us.' There's always the dilemma of what to do with prisoners. I've never read an account that says: 'Yes, we shot the prisoners.' No-one will write this in their memoirs, but all sides faced the same situation. You can't take the prisoners with you, so what do you do?

The Poles, the Russians, the Germans and the Latvians all faced the same dilemma. [The Soviet Latvian captain] Jānis Grīnvalds writes in his war diary about finding Latvians shot by the roadside on several occasions. The way the bodies were lying in ditches showed they had been captured, stripped of belongings and then executed. Those two months in Pomerania were very messy. I wouldn't be surprised if someone made the decision, 'I'm not going to leave these bastards alive' … on all sides.[26]

The remains of the 32 murdered Polish soldiers were buried in a mass grave. Later, they were transferred to a cemetery in Wałcz dedicated to the men killed in the battles to breach the Pomeranian Wall. In 1974 the investigation into who was responsible was suspended. Five years later, director Paweł Komorowski reconstructed events in Podgaje based on the story of Second Lieutenant Furgała for his film 'Elegia' ['Elegy']. Because of the difficulty of filming at night, some events were transposed to daylight.[27]

When the former Mayor of Podgaje returned to the village on 19 February 1945, he found the unburied bodies of 400 soldiers: 'mostly Latvians.'[28] Of the scenes greeting him, Fritz and Anders wrote:

Russians and Poles had evidently been buried in the preceding two weeks, but the predominance of Latvians among the dead suggests that the heaviest losses occurred in the final hours, after the Dutch and Germans had left. Ķīlītis' battalion (1/34) had previously been ordered to cover the retreat of the Division staff from Wandsburg-Więcbork to Jastrowie on 29–31 January, nicely illustrating a high Nazi official's argument for the formation of non-Germanic Legions: 'For every Ukrainian [or Latvian] who gets killed there will be one less German mother in tears.'[29]

They conclude:

Our main conclusion is that the 32 POWs from Lt. Sofka's 4th Company were not burned alive but were murdered by shooting during the night 31 Jan–1 Feb

---

26 Interview with author, Rīga, 27 November 2019.

27 The film, in Polish, can be found on You Tube at: <https://www.youtube.com/watch?v =HtEyd0v0gXQ>.

28 Given the scale of the slaughter here this number may include the bodies of Latvians killed when the transport column was shot up and also those killed in the defence of Flederborn village, which was shelled heavily, and in the final rearguard action.

29 The phrase was used by SS general and recruitment chief Gottlob Berger.

The original Podgaje-Flederborn burial site, 1945. (Picture courtesy of the Military Historical Office, Warsaw. Ref: A.8996)

The memorial which stands today at Podgaje-Flederborn to the 32 Polish soldiers killed there in February 1945. (Picture: author)

1945. That same evening between 95–150 POWs captured in the evening battle were also shot. There no longer seems to be a reason to single out the first 32 victims. Most of the 258 Polish soldiers buried at Podgaje did not fall in battle but were murdered – by shooting, not by burning alive. All should be equally honoured and acknowledged on the memorial as defenceless victims of a cruel and brutal enemy.[30]

The memorial at Podgaje-Flederborn seems to symbolise the trauma and pain of what happened here. Two jagged stone columns mark this tragedy, hollowed out like teeth, or two split halves of a husk of wheat – as though something has been ruptured or fractured. The names of those who died within metres of here have been carved inside: Piotr Lewsza, born 1925; Jozef Lozowski, born 1915; Feliks Bujewicz, born 1897 ... the list goes on, 32 names in all, remembered with red and white flowers both inside and out. Stone plinths in front of the memorial bear their names too. I have an old map showing the barns that once stood here, now replaced by five or six good-sized houses following the curve of what was probably a track leading to the barns. It's a strange feeling. The Polish historical film-maker Arnold Koslowski says of the memorial at Podgaje-Flederborn:

> The present monument was created in 1969. The monument is to symbolize the flames of fire or a cracked rifle bullet. Previously, built in the 1950s, there was another monument [erected] after the exhumation of the remains. That had an eagle and a list of fallen soldiers. Earlier, the place of the war grave was marked out only by a birch cross erected in 1945, where the remains [of the men] found in the ruins of the barn were buried. The bodies of other Polish soldiers were buried in the Grudna cemetery...
>
> Local historians have told me that the bodies of German, Latvian, and other Axis soldiers killed in the battles in the Flederborn-Landeck region could still be found months after the war. In the summer of 1945 new inhabitants of these areas wrote to the Soviet war commander in Szczecinek about the problem of 'piles of corpses' in the area of the villages of Flederborn and Landeck. There are also reports that these remains were also found two years after the war. There was simply no-one to bury them. The German inhabitants fled, were killed or expelled.[31]

Despite my now-detailed knowledge of the gruesome events here, the memorial at Podgaje-Flederborn is quite a peaceful haven, and I stand looking at the memorial to the 32 men who died so horribly – however it happened. Around me swallows chase flies in the summer sunset and traffic flashes by on the road from Flederborn to Landeck at 100 kilometres per hour.

---

30 Fritz and Anders, *Murder of Polish POWs*, p.144.
31 Correspondence with author, August 2021 and March 2022.

The names of the 32 Polish soldiers who died at Podgaje-Flederborn in February 1945 are remembered at the memorial. (Picture: author)

There is no dispute that Poles were killed by Latvians at Podgaje-Flederborn, but not the 32 unfortunate men commemorated. A tragic irony is that the soldiers of Lieutenant Sofka's 4th Company who died at Latvian hands on the battlefield there were betrayed by a fellow Pole, a Red Army conscript from Warsaw. He was possibly a member of a gun crew positioned near there at the time. The killing by the Latvians of Major Ostrowski, a popular commander, also appears to have been a turning point in this savagery.

What I will subsequently discover is that this road witnessed scenes of indescribable death and unforgettable horror on a scale far beyond the murder of those tragically unlucky 32 soldiers. The IPN has said 800 Polish soldiers were killed or wounded in the taking of Podgaje-Flederborn and a conservative toll from Latvian accounts of the slaughter here by the Red Army reaches towards 5,000 dead even with very limited data, and possibly higher. (See Table 1, p.275-278).

This was an annihilation. Piecing together eyewitness accounts translated for this book from people who were there – senior officers, commanders, doctors, veterinary surgeons, a Catholic priest later made a Prelate by Pope John Paul II – it reads like an atrocity. Who were the refugees who strayed into this slaughter, recounted in harrowing detail over the pages to come? No-one seems to know. The 32 unlucky Polish soldiers are remembered, but possibly hundreds of refugees are not.

11

The Road of Slaughter 2: Flederborn, Wallachsee and Landeck

The column breaking out from Jastrow towards Flederborn ran straight into fierce fire from Soviet positions on the high ground to the north, centred on Tiefenort. Attempts by the German 59th Infantry to drive the Russians back had not been successful, so at 12:00 the Recce Battalion was ordered to attack. The 'Green Books' describe the assault.

> To support the attack, two artillery batteries with a total of ten shells were assigned. In addition, one German infantry company and one German mortar company were subordinated to the battalion, although they were not directly involved in the battle.
>
> The attack began at 14:00. The battalion attacked on both sides of the Jastrow-Flederborn railway. In fierce combat, the soldiers of the battalion exhibited the utmost heroism and self-sacrifice. The plateau was defended by a Russian regiment. Their side also had a considerable superiority in material: several anti-aircraft and anti-tank cannons, and powerful mortar and artillery support as well. The enemy exhibited a complete disdain of death; every little knoll had to be captured in close combat. By 18:00, the assignment had been accomplished.
>
> These battles had demanded very heavy sacrifices; the battalion had shrunk to about 70 men. Many soldiers of the battalion were later given awards for heroism. An Iron Cross First Class was awarded to First Lieutenant Krūka; Lieutenant Lejiņš received the Iron Cross First and Second Class. Only two officers of the battalion had not been wounded. Russian losses in this battle were about 100 men dead, one Colonel and one Major among them. Captured were two 7.5cm cannons, seven 4.5cm anti-tank cannons and one 4.5cm long-barrelled anti-tank gun.[1]

Catholic chaplain KazimirsRučs reached Flederborn village on the night of 1 February.

---

1   Freivalds p.189., trans. Arturs Grava, sent to author 20 July 2022.

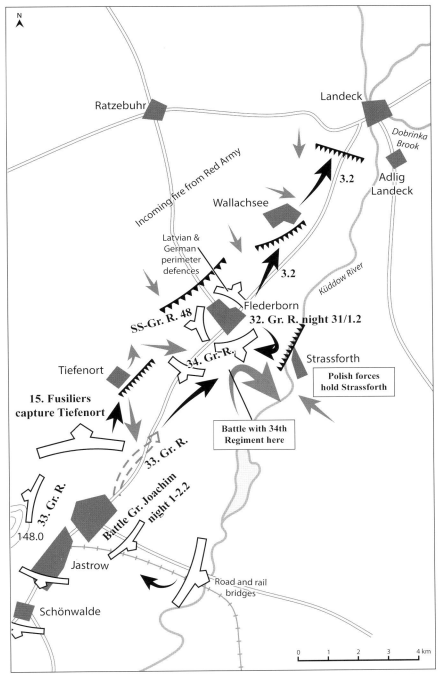

N

Ratzebuhr

Landeck

Dobrinka
Brook

Incoming fire from Red Army

3.2

Adlig
Landeck

Wallachsee

Latvian &
German
perimeter
defences

3.2

Küddow River

SS-Gr. R. 48

Flederborn

32. Gr. R. night 31/1.2

34. Gr. R.

Strassforth

Tiefenort

**Polish forces
hold Strassforth**

**15. Fusiliers
capture Tiefenort**

**Battle with 34th
Regiment here**

33. Gr. R.

**Battle Gr. Joachim
night 1-2.2**

33. Gr. R.

148.0

Jastrow

Road and rail
bridges

Schönwalde

0   1   2   3   4 km

Flederborn detail. Flederborn was heavily shelled during the Latvian advance, and infantry
attacks supported by tanks were repulsed in a desperate 48-hour defence of the village.

We are in Flederborn. A miserable darkness covers the village, which is lit up by the flames from burning houses. Dirty water poured through the ditches: water mixed up with the blood of cattle and humans. All around there were broken wagons, dead people and horses thrown hither and thither. The shelling had smashed everything: parts of bodies were thrown into trees and bushes.

There is no order what to do next. We move around on the spot. In those times Flederborn village, about 10 kilometres from Landeck, was defended by the 34th Regiment 1st Battalion under Major Jūlijs Ķīlītis. He warns us that we must expect an attack, and he's not mistaken because the Russian tanks are here, helped by artillery fire. The column of wounded suffers the most … On 2 February 1945 – Candlemas Day – many Catholics received their last Holy Communion because straight away the great break-out battle started, which many did not survive.[2]

A series of original orders, some typed up on pages ripped from notebooks, can be found in the 15th Division's war diary archive, bought by the Latvian National Archive for a reported 55,000 euros in 2006 having been missing since the war. The orders offer a startling insight into the drama unfolding. At 09:30 that morning Adolph Ax issued his orders, signed by Lieutenant Pape.

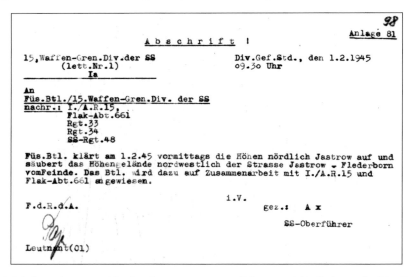

Adolph Ax orders, signed by Ltn Pape at 09:30 on 1 February 1945. Order reads: 'Fus. Btl. explored the heights north of Jastrow in the late morning on 1.2.45 and cleans the high terrain north-west of the road Jastrow–Flederborn of the enemy. The battalion is therefore ordered to collaborate with I./A.R.15 and Flak-Abt.661'. (Scan of 15th Division war diary, Latvian National Archive, Rīga)

---

2   Ručs, *Dzīve ar Dievu*. Ručs adds, which I have included here as a footnote: '*Later Ķīlītis in his book 'How I Went to War' tells about the horrific night of attacks by Stalin organs and Red Army assaults.*'

The 15th's divisional commander Erich Wulff followed with an update on the morning of 1 February, again signed by Pape, at 10:10.

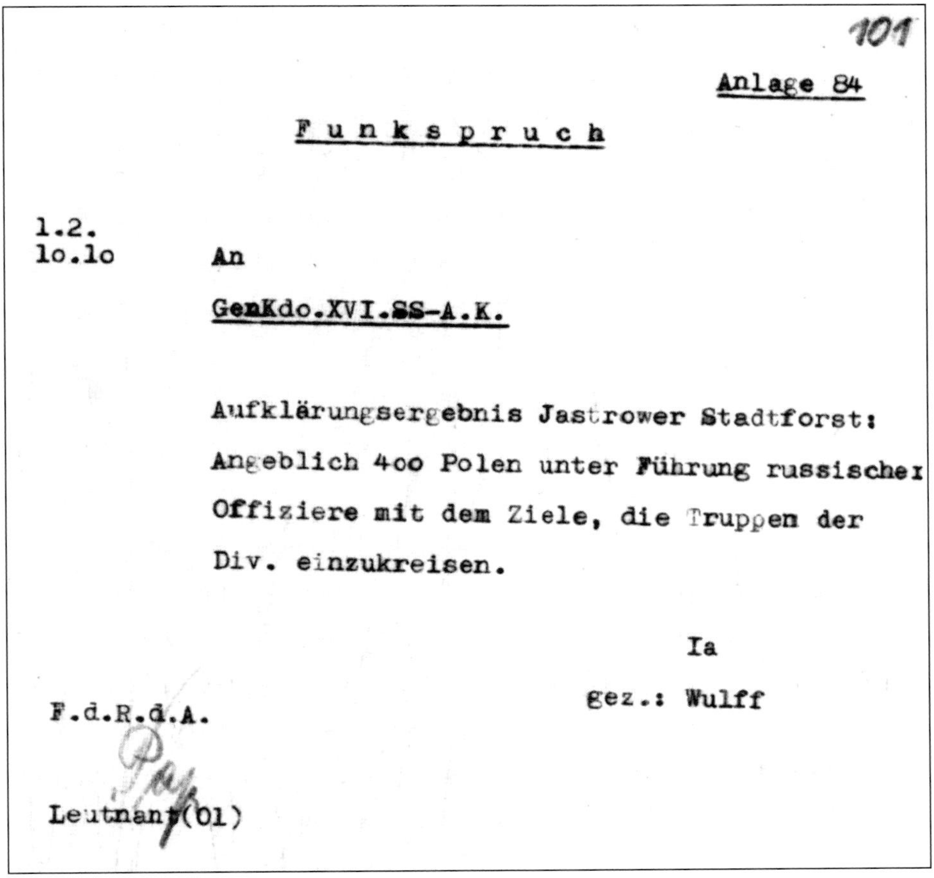

```
                                                          101

                                            Anlage 84

               F u n k s p r u c h


1.2.
lo.lo        An

             GenKdo.XVI.SS-A.K.


             Aufklärungsergebnis Jastrower Stadtforst:

             Angeblich 400 Polen unter Führung russischer

             Offiziere mit dem Ziele, die Truppen der

             Div. einzukreisen.


                                                  Ia

                                      gez.: Wulff

F.d.R.d.A.


Leutnant (01)
```

Message reads: '*Result of the exploration of the Jastrow city forest: Allegedly 400 Polish under leadership of Russian officers with the goal to surround the troops of the division.*' (Scan of 15th Division war diary, Latvian National Archive, Rīga)

At 10:30 he sent a message warning that *'Division has serious ammunition concerns.'*

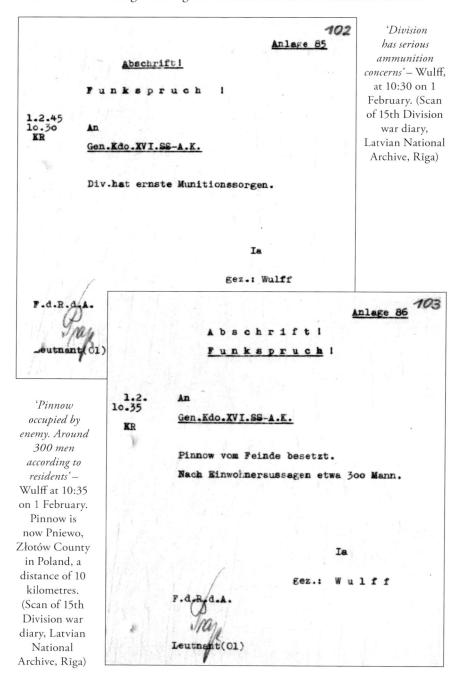

'Division has serious ammunition concerns' – Wulff, at 10:30 on 1 February. (Scan of 15th Division war diary, Latvian National Archive, Rīga)

'Pinnow occupied by enemy. Around 300 men according to residents' – Wulff at 10:35 on 1 February. Pinnow is now Pniewo, Złotów County in Poland, a distance of 10 kilometres. (Scan of 15th Division war diary, Latvian National Archive, Rīga)

In another message five minutes later he warns of a strong Soviet presence in Pinnow, to the west, with an estimated 300 men there.

By 13:00 he is very concerned about running out of ammunition.

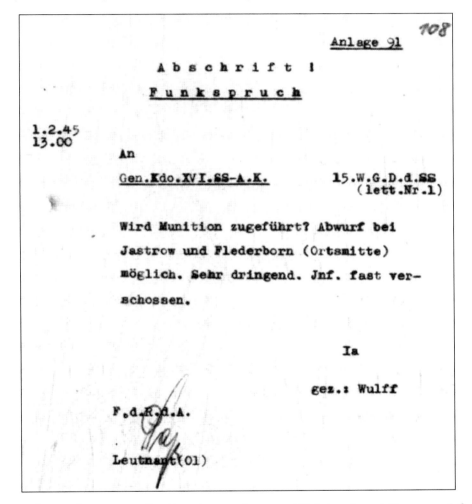

'Did you send ammunition? Possible to drop near Jastrow and Flederborn (centre). Very urgent. Jnf (infantry ammunition) almost all fired out' – Wulff at 13:00. (Scan of 15th Division war diary, Latvian National Archive, Rīga)

At 14:20 an update is issued on what appear to be pages from a notebook. Scouts have been sent to check the road to Freudenfier to the south-west of Jastrow, which suggests the consideration of a completely different plan, given that the Latvians had just come from there.

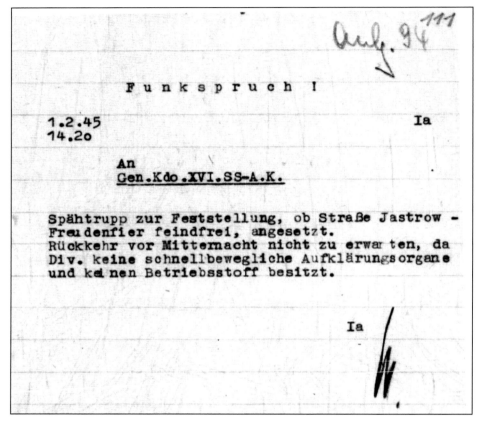

Message at 14:20 reads: '*Scout platoons sent to assess whether road Jastrow-Freudenfier clear of enemies. Return before midnight not expected since division does not have [transport] and fuel.* (Scan of 15th Division war diary, Latvian National Archive, Rīga)

By early afternoon, the Ia [chief of operations] Lieutenant Pape sent an assessment of ammunition remaining, along with a plea for an airdrop of more weapons.

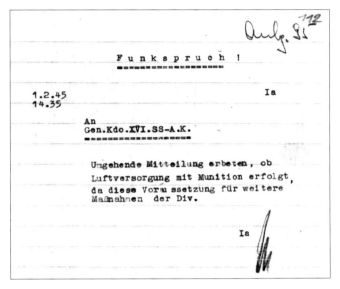

'Requested immediate information whether ammunition will be provided by air, since this [is the] condition for further actions of the division.' (Scan of 15th Division war diary, Latvian National Archive, Rīga: LV_LVVA_F296_US1_GV12_0114)

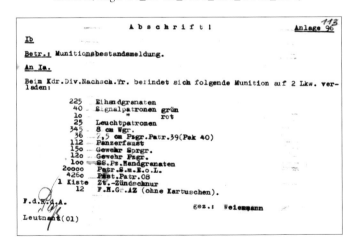

Ammunition supply levels at 14:35 on 1 February. (Latvian 15th Division war diary: LV_LVVA_F296_US1_GV12_0115).

On a second page, a tally of the remaining stocks of ammunition and signal flares shows how desperate the situation had become.

> The following ammunition is loaded on 2 trucks with the Kdr.Div.Nachsch.Tr.3
> 225 egg hand grenades
> 40 signal cartridges green
> 10 signal cartridges red
> 25 Very light
> 345 8cm thrown grenades
> 36 7.5cm armour defence cannon bullets 39 (PAK 40)
> 112 rocket-propelled grenades
> 150 high-explosive rifle grenades
> 120 shaped charge rifle grenades
> 100 SS anti-tank grenades
> 20,000 bullets S.m.E.o.L.
> 4,260 Rolled homogeneous armour bullet 08
> 1 box time fuse
> 12 F.M.Gr.AZ (without cartridges)

At 18:00 Pape issued a grim update of the numbers of wounded.

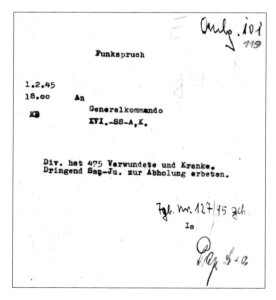

'Division has 475 wounded and sick. San-Ju [Sanitaets, or a medical unit] urgently requested' – Pape. (From 15th Division war diary, Latvian National Archive: LV_LVVA_F296_US1_GV12_0121).##

3 *Kader-Division-Nachschub-Truppe* – cadre division supplies troop.

At 01:15 on 2 February 1945, Ax is trying to make sense of the chaos around him, and does not appear to know that 48th SS commander Paul Massell has been killed. Massell's death had a big impact on the morale of the 48th Regiment, and their grieving was immediate. His body was laid out on a stretcher at the *štābs* in Flederborn with two soldiers serving as an honour guard.[4]

In orders drafted at this time, Ax tasks Massell with the leadership of all forces in Flederborn (see point 4). In those orders, he writes:

1. Enemy broke through around 00:00 near Küddowbrueck.
    Kdr.II./J.R.59, Captain Selle, bearer of the Knight's Cross of the Iron Cross, fallen.
    Division uses all reserves available in Jastrow to stop the enemy break-in and for the counter-strike.

2. To this hour since noon the division is without any message about the course of events in Flederborn.
    Reports of Regiment 48 are missing about:
    —the attack on NW planned for 14:00,
    —the results of the exploration against Landeck and Ratzebuhr,
    —the arrival of the regiment staff in Flederborn.
    Of Regiment 34:
    Details about the battle that led to the destruction of two PAK and to the bringing-in of prisoners. The report that an armoured train was destroyed is incomprehensible, explanation was ordered.

3. Verst.Fues.Btl. [Fusilier Battalion] has cleaned the high terrain north of Jastrow through Kol.Tiefenort to Tiefenort of the enemy against tough resistance at 16:15. Gen.Kdo.XVI.SS-A.K. reports that Gruppe Scheibe should line up for the attack on Landeck at 20:00 and received the order to connect with Flederborn. The division was ordered to seek the creation of this connection with a storm troop. Order was given to the Regiment 48 via radio communication. In case this has not happened yet, Regiment 48 must immediately assemble a storm troop and set it marching in the direction of Landeck, to create a connection with Gruppe Scheibe during the night under any circumstances, and thus to open the only supply replenishment route for the vital artillery and infantry ammunition.
    This order, which is already of significant importance for the general situation of the division, **has become a question of life for the division** through the enemy's breakthrough near Küddowbrueck.[5] The storm troop must therefore be put under the command of the most vigorous leader that

4   Ķīlītis, *I Go To War,* p.188.
5   Author's emphasis.

15.Waffen-Gren.Div.der SS   Div.Gef.Std., den 2.2.45
        (lett.Nr.1)   01.15 Uhr
            Ia
    Tgb. Nr. 129/45 gl.

An

Waffen-Gren.Rgt.der SS 34 (lett.Nr.5),
SS-Rgt.48

1.) Feind gegen oo.oo Uhr bei Kuddowbrücke durchgebrochen.
    Kdr.II./J.R.59, Hauptmann Belle, Träger des Ritterkreuzes zum
    Eisernen Kreuz, gefallen.
    Div. setzt sämtliche in Jastrow verfügbaren Reserven zur Abriegelung
    des feindlichen Einbruches und zum Gegenstoß ein.

2.) Bis zur Stunde ist die Div.seit den Mittagsstunden des 1.2. ohne
    jede Nachricht über den Verlauf der Ereignisse in Flederborn.

    Es fehlen die Meldungen vom Rgt.48 über:
    den für 14.oo Uhr angesetzten Angriff gegen NW.,
    die Aufklärungsergebnisse gegen Landeck und Ratzebur,
    das Eintreffen des Rgt.Stabes in Flederborn.

    vom Rgt.34:
    Einzelheiten über das Gefecht, das zur Vernichtung zweier Pak
    und zum Einbringen von Gefangenen führte.
    Die Meldung, dass ein Panzerzug vernichtet sei, ist der Div. un-
    verständlich, Erläuterung war befohlen.

3.) Verst.Füs.Btl. hat um 16.15 Uhr das Höhengeländenördlich Jastrow
    über Kol.Tiefenort bis Tiefenort einschl. gegen harten Widerstand
    vom Feind gesäubert.
    Gen.Kdo.XVI.SS-A.K. teilt mit, dass Gruppe Scheibe um 20.00 Uhr
    zum Angriff auf Landeck antreten sollte und Befehl erhalten habe,
    Verbindung nach Flederborn aufzunehmen.
    Der Div. ist dazu befohlen worden, durch einen Stoßtrupp die Her-
    stellung dieser Verbindung zu suchen. Auftrag dazu ist dem Rgt.48
    durch Funk erteilt worden.
    Falls noch nicht geschehen, hat Rgt.48 unverzüglich einen Stoßtrupp
    zusammenzustellen und in Richtung auf Landeck in Marsch zu setzen,
    um unter allen Umständen noch im Laufe der Nacht die Verbindung mit
    der Gruppe Scheibe herzustellen und damit der Div. die einzige
    Nachschubstraße für die Heranführung der lebenswichtigen Art.-und
    Jnf.-Munition zu öffnen.
    Dieser Auftrag, der an sich schon von entscheidender Bedeutung
    für die Gesamtlage der Div. ist, ist durch den Einbruch des Feindes
    bei Kuddowbrück geradezu zu einer Lebensfrage für die Div. geworden.
    Der Stoßtrupp ist daher dem tatkräftigsten Führer, über den das Rgt.
    verfügt, zu unterstellen und so stark zu machen, auszurüsten und
    zu bewaffnen, als es die Lage im Raum um Flederborn irgend zulässt.

4.) In Anbetracht der bisher nicht hergestellten Nachrichtenverbindung
    wird zum Zwecke einheitlicher Kampfführung SS-Ostubaf. Massell mit
    der Führung der Gesamtkräfte im Raum Flederborn, der Verteidigung
    dieses Raumes, alle Angriffe des Feindes beauftragt.

5.) Dem Überbringer dieses Befehls ist eine kurzgefasste Schilderung
    der Entwicklung der Lage im Raume Flederborn seit 14.00 Uhr mitzugeben
    Er ist alsbald beschleunigt zur Div. zurückzusenden.
    Herstellung der Verbindung mit Kampfgruppe Scheibe ist der Div.
    auf dem schnellsten Wege zu melden.

                                           i.V.

                                                 SS-Oberführer

Ax at 01:15 on 2 February 1945: Now 'a question of life for the division'. (From 15th Division war diary, Latvian National Archive: LV_LVVA_F296_US1_GV12_0121).##

the regiment has, and it must be armed as much as the situation in the area around Flederborn allows in any way.

4. Considering the so-far not-established messaging connection, for the purpose of unified warfare SS Obersturmfuehrer Massell is tasked with the leadership of all forces in the Flederborn area [and] the defence of this area against all attacks of the enemy.

5. The bringer of this order must be given a short description of the development of the situation in the Flederborn area since 14:00. He must be sent back to the division at utmost speed. Establishment of a connection with Gruppe Scheibe must be reported to the division as fast as possible.

As 2 February dawned over the village of Flederborn, the scale of the slaughter and the desperate situation the Latvians were in became apparent. Doctor Pauls Dzintars wrote:

The morning of 2 February started badly. The enemy had reinforced overnight with heavier weapons and ammunition, and this began to rain down on our heads. There were now anti-tank guns too. The intensity of incoming fire stepped up. Even the good sturdy German houses couldn't cope with this.

A series of Katyusha rockets hit the roof of the house. We were lucky it wasn't something worse. The upper floor of the house collapsed. The haybarn next door set alight but no-one was injured. We had to move the wounded to another house and only found a place on the other side of the village with some difficulty. It was not nice transporting wounded men under fire but everything turned out well. We left the flames and the bloody clothes behind, as well as eight corpses, including a young boy with the name Priežbogs, who had got a bullet in his liver. I remember him because of his unusual name, and also because he looked so young.

In the new house we had an unexpected visit. Two doctors, Vieže and Balul, arrived from Jastrow with some men from the medical corps. They had come in two motorised *sankas* [ambulances]. One – which Lakševics was travelling in – had taken a hit from an anti-tank gun which killed the driver and smashed it into pieces. The windows had been blown out, there were dents and holes in the bodywork but fortunately they'd got through. I remember that in Russia Lakševics' *sanka* was shot to pieces by Russian aeroplanes and set on fire, but he'd survived.

I gave him a pistol as they weren't in short supply. We took all the ammunition from the wounded, as that was needed. We only had 100 bullets for each automatic rifle, so we could only fire when there was serious direct contact with the enemy. As throughout the retreat across Pomerania, food wasn't brought to us and the wounded had to be fed too. We killed a pig, ate our share and fed them too. The boys on the frontline didn't have it so easy. We heard that some wounded men had been lying in the snow 36 hours already without food or drink, and also that a few left the lines and made their way to the houses in Flederborn, so our frontline was becoming very sparse.

Dzintars' description of a Red Army attack on Flederborn conveys the desperation of the time.

> After a hellish barrage from artillery, anti-tank guns, mortars and machine guns from the forest nearby, a brown mass of people began to move across the snow-covered fields towards the village. They didn't have white sheets to help camouflage themselves in the snow like our boys, and I don't know if they even had rifles. Our ammunition reserves were very low, so every bullet had to find a target. It was impossible to stop this huge human wave: it just came nearer and nearer. I stood on the hill next to the flak gun and watched, as though it was a performance. Still our men didn't fire. Had they run out of ammunition? Were they all wounded?
>
> I thought my life would end there and then, and then the shooting began. Many men were shot and fell. It was sad to see what a dreadful weapon the 88mm flak gun was, firing shells that exploded in the air. With each shell fired, at least 50 corpses lay on the ground. The guns worked quickly and the tidal wave stopped. Those remaining alive hesitated and raced back into the forest. The entire snow-covered field was strewn with badly-wounded men and the bodies of the fallen. [And] we didn't get through lightly.
>
> The streets in the village [Flederborn] were unrecognisable. Everywhere you could see broken wires, dead horses and people, smashed wagons and carts, burned-out vehicles. There was hardly a house that hadn't been damaged. Floods of wounded came to my medical point. We did what we could, tore up sheets for bandages, used chair legs as splints and when one house was full we moved on to the next. In this way in a few days we had amassed a few hundred wounded, but there was no chance of any transport.[6]

Adolf Ax and the Divisional command now moved out from Jastrow along the road to Flederborn, leaving Colonel Janums and his rearguard of the 33rd Regiment and two German units to hold Jastrow as long as possible. Defensive lines were strengthened along the river Gwda, while two motorised guns were sent from Jastrow to help the defenders of Flederborn. The remaining artillery was hooked up to horses, and medical staff loaded the wounded onto wagons.

The division moved up to positions at Tiefenort under heavy Russian artillery, rocket and small arms fire, especially from the high ground to the west. As the experienced Russian gunners corrected the range, Latvian casualties began to mount. The motorised artillery units reached Flederborn as darkness fell, but got caught up with trucks and carts lined up in three columns which then came under a hail of

6   Pauls Dzintars, *Daugavas Vanagi Mēnešraksts Nr. 5*, (1999) online at <Periodika.lv>.

machine gun fire from both sides of the road. The artillery batteries were ordered to get off the road, but the congestion was so bad and the Soviets so close – less than a kilometre away and closer in some places – that the guns could only fire over open sights. German units were sent ahead to Wallachsee [Chwalimie] to clear Red Army positions there and open the road to Landeck but when two Russian tanks suddenly appeared they panicked and fled, leaving the column's flanks exposed. The tanks began shelling and machine gunning the unprotected column with little opposition.

Major Jūlijs Ķīlītis was commanding the 34th Regiment inside Flederborn, under fire from all sides.

> The foreigner battalion's attempt to broaden the field of operations in the direction of Ratzebuhr [the 48th Dutch SS] was unsuccessful and the next evening they all came back into Flederborn. The loss of their commander [Paul Massell] was probably a factor in this, because the spirit had clearly gone out of them. Now we were just watching and waiting, desperately, for when our Division would finally break through and our torture would end.
>
> At last the news came that the break-out would be the next evening [3 February 1945]. The critical moment was approaching: to be or not to be. A long day of waiting – and the next night also seemed the longest. The enemy stopped attacking but tried to just bomb us out. By now it was only the odd house that hadn't been hit or partly destroyed. Among those rare examples was my house, which hadn't received a direct hit, though the courtyard and the street opposite were pockmarked with small craters. The Division was still holding Jastrow, where the bulk of the fighting was falling on our Colonel Janums and some German units reporting to him.
>
> At last they started to come. Together with the first units, the Divisional Commander, Colonel Ax, also appeared. They drove in noisily with all the carts and all sorts of stuff. To sum it up, there were a lot of back-line units and very few fighting men. For us, this noise made our hair stand on end. We had waited here as quietly as mice, and were very annoyed.
>
> I warned the Divisional leadership to expect a major artillery attack at any time after all this fuss. The only question was a matter of when – how quickly they would be re-supplied with ammunition. I suggested to the Divisional Commander that he should pull his forces through the village and stay outside somewhere, in the forest. Nothing could be worse than if a whirlwind artillery barrage were to surprise the columns of wagons, lorries and masses of people in the narrow streets. A column like that, after such a barrage, would no longer be able to move forwards or backwards. There would be high casualties, because there would be no cover for people.
>
> Colonel Ax agreed and left me pretty quickly. With that, some of the transports left and the roads became emptier. Nevertheless, the shouting and the flashing of torches continued. The biggest shouters were the *Fritzes* themselves, and especially the *Verwaltung* [administration]. If only they would get out faster

and free up the streets before it all starts! All this commotion sounded to my ears like blasphemous pleas for death.

Then, finally, the firing started. I don't really remember how long it lasted, but it seethed like it hadn't done for a long time. The air was so full that you couldn't stick your nose out. This time my little house also took a few shells, but my end of it came through unscathed. There was another load of injured, and nobody was taking any notice of the dead any more. Among the injured was my German ordnance officer Lieutenant R., and Jung, the German liaison officer for the Division, who had to have a leg amputated at the hip.[7]

Colonel Janums and the men of the 33rd Regiment left Jastrow as night fell on 2 February. When he reached Flederborn to report to Ax, Janums was dismayed to find the road to Landeck still blocked by Soviet guns at Wallachsee. Ax had not yet launched an operation to clear it. With Janums present, Ax ordered a transport column to clear the road then told Janums to go back to Jastrow and hold it for longer.

Janums refused: the last covering units had left and the town could not be re-taken. Ax agreed instead that Janums should form a delaying defensive line a few kilometres south of Flederborn. Janums took up the new positions at around midnight just as the Red Army launched a concentrated barrage of fire at the Latvians from both the east and west of the town. From a kilometre away artillery shells, mortars, tank fire and machine guns slammed into the tightly-packed columns. Legion chief of staff and historian Arturs Silgailis gave this account.

> The enemy suddenly opened an intensive artillery barrage from both sides of the road onto the troops and refugees who were jammed together. The barrage, which lasted only ten minutes, had caused severe casualties and great damage. The road was littered with dead men and horses. The already heavily-depleted divisional artillery lost three light and two heavy guns. The barrage also set several buildings alight, which illuminated the area and aided the observed fire for automatic infantry weapons.[8]

Regimental doctor Pauls Dzintars described the scenes:

> On the evening of 2 February, the transport columns began to come through Flederborn from Jastrow. Rumours spread that the road ahead was free. In fact it wasn't. We wanted the Divisional wagons to take our wounded, but they had so many of their own, they wouldn't. They said they would take theirs and come back. We knew that would never happen. We didn't have any more ammunition to defend Flederborn and the anti-aircraft gun had been knocked out.
>
> Now it was my turn to think. As a doctor, I have to stay with the wounded. The medical company I first served with had come in. They were all wearing

---

7   Ķīlītis, *I Go To War*, pp.188–189.
8   Silgailis, *Latvian Legion*, p.168.

white sheets [makeshift snow camouflage] round their coats, whilst mine hadn't been white for a long time. I was told that the medical company had been sent into defensive positions to fight near Vandsburg. They were now in Flederborn. [One medic] Birzlejs had even taken out a tank.

We were all talking and having a smoke when suddenly a hail of shells and fire began. Basically, Armageddon broke out. I ran into a house with two Germans. I was on the stairs when a shell exploded behind us. The force of the explosion blew me into a corridor along with a door. My neighbours began to scream and moan because both were injured. I crawled into a room which turned out to be German HQ. The people in HQ were on the floor, wouldn't let us in and wouldn't even let their own wounded in.

I fought for a place at the window but then a shell exploded and the window shattered, showering me with glass. A second shell hit the floor above and made all the plaster fall from the ceiling. For a while the whole village boiled as if in a hellish cauldron but the tornado of fire stopped as suddenly as it had started. I shook myself and discovered there were a few holes in my coat but not a mark on me. Luck. I went upstairs to [a room on] the floor above where six Dutch SS men had been sitting. They'd all been killed by the pressure of the explosion. They'd all died where they sat. It was a dreadful sight.

I went back to the medical point. There had to be so many wounded in the village but nobody came to us: they couldn't find us in the dark. In any case, we didn't have anything that would help them. My doctor's bag was empty.[9]

Legionnaire Jānis Čevers was part of a team evacuating hundreds of wounded men from the *lazarett* [field hospital] in Jastrow on wagons heading for Flederborn.

There were no lorries so they sent horses and carts, with four soldiers. The column went back about a mile. I was with one German officer and one tank. We were travelling from the hospital through the forest and suddenly there was an attack. The shells were landing accurately in the road because they'd been firing on that position before.

All the horses panicked and ran, and the soldiers, hundreds of them, all badly wounded, were seeking shelter in the ditches by the side of the road. The German officer said: 'Quickly – get under the tank.' All those badly-wounded soldiers in the ditches, and we survived because we were under the tank. In the morning we went past all the soldiers screaming – still alive, but screaming – and we survived, me and the German officer. I was only a corporal. Why did they select me for that kind of job?[10]

Zigurds Kārkliņš was woken from a nap by this new blitz of shelling.

9   Dzintars, in *Daugavas Vanagi Mēnešraksts Nr. 5*, online at <Periodika.lv>, trans. Daina Vītola.
10 Interview with author, Derby, UK.

I've barely fallen asleep when I hear the first shell explosions in the village. The explosions come nearer and get more frequent. Some of the guys make their way down from the attic. I'm so tired, so I remain sleeping. Sometimes the shelling is so near that bits of plaster start falling from the roof. The light of the candle flickers.

Suddenly a shell falls into the house, the candle is extinguished and I race downstairs. As I run through a room there's a bright light, then an explosion which makes my head spin. An HQ officer still collecting papers over by the window collapses. There's soil, sparks, wood – all flying through the air as a result of the explosion. Quickly I run out into the yard.

Everything is on fire. Sparks are flying through the air with clumps of earth and bits of wood, because of the exploding shells. There's a tremendous heat: it's impossible to breathe in this heat and smoke. Bent double, I make my way out of the yard. Behind me, in flames and with more shells exploding, the barn collapses where I had tied up our horses. All around are smashed-up wagons, vehicles, people, horses. Everyone who can move is trying to get away from this witches' cauldron.

Luckily I managed to jump onto the back of a truck and get out of the burning village. Day is beginning to dawn when we finally stop at the edge of a wood. Here some officers try to organise a completely disorganised bunch. They manage to get some men together. I've lost my unit and I'm grabbed by a gendarmerie officer, who gives me an automatic rifle and tells me to lie on the gendarmerie bus roof and, in the event of an attack, to repel it.[11]

Scenes from hell ensued around those caught on the road when the blitz began. Corporal Irbe described the horrors of the close-range slaughter:

A couple of kilometres from the town everything stopped. The carts formed three stationary columns. In between the wagons with the injured were refugee families with their carts. At around midnight the columns suddenly started to move. On reaching the small town of Flederborn, suddenly there was the sound of explosions. Shells fell everywhere and some of the houses started to burn.

The enemy fired from the edge of the forest with tracer bullets and the columns of horses on the road were illuminated by the fires like it was daylight. Amidst this were screams, neighing and the sounds of explosions, while body parts and the remains of carts were blown into the air. The remaining transport columns charged forward in complete disorder. The injured and the dead lay in the shallow roadside ditch or on the road itself; no-one had the time to help or even be aware of them. People tried to save their own lives. The lightly-injured tried to drag themselves to safety as best they could, even though the road was under ceaseless enemy bombardment.

---

11 Kārkliņš, in Latvian 'Green Books', vol. 6, trans. Daina Vītola.

The mad dash suddenly stopped in a wood just outside the small town. Many were injured; many injured for the second time. There was a shortage of carts and drivers and part of the company was missing. Maybe they had scattered, maybe [they were] killed or injured. From time to time the wood was fired on by Katyushas, which pulled out the teeth of the people packed together. In some places the enemy shot up the road with small arms fire and again there were casualties.[12]

Among those casualties was artilleryman Laimonis Ceriņš, who remembered that time in conversation with the author seventy-five years later.

LC: We were number eight battery. On the left was a village, Flederborn. And of course we couldn't move out. So we had Russians – probably quite far away – 400 yards [365 metres] or so. There was a forest, and there was a farmhouse as far as I remember, and there were Poles. That's what we were told. We exchanged fire. I noticed from the left, Russians, probably 150 yards [137 metres] away.

VH: And what's your position? Are you in the open?

LC: No, on the roadside. Trees. And there were a lot of supply units and even quite a few German refugees. The Russians had cut the road and we couldn't move. There was the village and then forest on the side. We waited for an order what to do. And then we had the Poles coming in on us. There was an exchange of fire but that was it. Then an explosion on the road, nearer. There was a call for ten men or more to go into the forest – stormtroopers – because there was a sniper. So get ready, load your rifles. I was on one knee, waiting for the order 'Go.' Then there was a big blast, fire all around, and I was lifted up about so high [indicates chest high] and I landed back down. Stars. Blue skies. Funny, there's something wrong. There was a hole in my leg, probably about two fingers … and I felt wet. Now then, ah. There is a piece of metal in it. I could walk. I was yelling for a *sanitar* [medic] but I couldn't find him.

It's OK. It wasn't bleeding so far – only a little bit. Then we wait until next morning. There was quiet afterwards.

Major Jūlijs Ķīlītis met Colonel Janums that night at his command post in Flederborn after the shelling.

Near midnight, when the big blow was over and again there was a pause, Colonel Janums and his adjutant came in to see me. We greeted each other. He had been looking for me because he wanted to have a chat and to get warm. It got colder again outside. Having sat down next to me on a stool next to the

12 Irbe, in *Daugavas Vanagu Mēnešraksts,* Nr.1 (01 January 1982) online at <periodika.lv>. The pressure of the explosion pulled teeth out of human heads.

German anti-tank gun [PAK] in snow, as used by the 15th Division. This same image, reproduced in volume 6 of the Legion official history, locates this at Hammerstein in February 1945. (Picture courtesy Laimonis Ceriņš, from his private collection, common among Legionnaires)

stove, he aimed his comments at the Germans: 'Look, those animals completely destroyed my regiment!'

Having said those words, his head slid to one side and at that very moment he exhaled heavily and was fast asleep. I sat without moving and let the tired colonel sleep on my broad shoulder. The adjutant's head also slipped lower and lower. After about 15 minutes the colonel again exhaled heavily, lifted his head and said: 'Right. I think I've told you everything now and I have to join my men. Thanks for the warmth and I hope it goes well for you. Adjutant – let's carry on!'[13]

Colonel Janums thought that he had been talking to me all the time he was there. I smiled and said nothing and, having wished him the best, I accompanied him out. And so they both went. It was a few days later before I saw them again, after we had been through all the horror. The colonel, in his disenchantment at the actions of the Germans, broke through independently with one of his battalions at Peterswalde.

Later, the German Major Pomrehn came in who, all evening, had hammered his way through along the back of Long Hill and covered the left flank of the Division. He was leading our Fusilier battalion. He was full of praise for our

13 Ķīlītis, *I Go To War*, p.189.

boys and genuinely sorry for the enormous losses. There were only 50 people left in the ranks.[14]

In Flederborn, the regimental doctors were taking matters into their own hands, Pauls Dzintars wrote.

> Dr Viežе had been speaking to the higher-ranking officers and they had decided, against all orders, to load our wounded onto their wagons. The trucks had already been through Flederborn but horses and carts were still coming into the village. The drivers, very afraid, wanted to get through Flederborn as quickly as possible. We argued with them forcefully.
>
> With Dr Vēriņš we stood at the crossroads with pistols in hands, and, in the name of our commander, ordered that the wagons divert and collect our wounded. The wagons turned out to be full of stolen property – that was thrown off to make room for the wounded. This all took place with a tremendous amount of swearing in the pitch blackness.
>
> It was amazing that only occasionally someone let out a moan, because to transfer wounded without stretchers in the dark can't be done without pain. They were basically thrown onto the carts. We hadn't had morphine in ages but at least the lads had the chance to get away. So in these two houses only bloody rags and corpses were left behind.
>
> For a short time I was 'unemployed.' With difficulty I found Alksnītis' HQ in a haybarn and joined them. Our orders were to defend Flederborn until the following evening to the last man. A 105mm howitzer had been sent to help us defend the village, but it only had six shells. We send the wounded away during the night [of 2–3 Feb]. Two doctors, Bākulis and Tillers died, and Dr Eggerts was injured.[15]

Regimental vet Lieutenant Augusts Ķikāns left Flederborn with the column as night fell on 2 February.

> At dusk, the whole column moved. We stood in three rows. The whole road was lit up for the enemy by the flames from the burning village [of Flederborn]. The wagons couldn't move forward so we changed direction and went for Landeck. Again we had to stop because the Russians had taken the road by Wallachsee. Our attacks were badly organised. Everything happened randomly, without previous planning.

14 Ķīlītis, *I Go To War,* pp.189–190. Pomrehn was decorated with the German Cross in Gold for his bravery with the Latvians in Pomerania. 'Long Hill' is possibly a reference to the hills to the west of Flederborn.
15 Dzintars, *Daugavas Vanagi Mēnešraksts,* Nr. 5 (01 September 1999) online at <periodika.lv>, trans. Daina Vītola.

The column consisted of about 600 wounded soldiers so we stood here for the third day. All the wounded were blue with cold. In many carts the dead lay next to the wounded. This wounded tragedy became apparent later when the Russians shot the whole column to bits. Here we also experienced panic – unseen up to now – which was caused by Russian firing. People fled as they could. The columns got mixed up, the horses and carts went in all directions. The carts were smashed, horses fell … at last somehow we moved on.

At Landeck again the enemy was in front of us, once again blocking our way. Next to the column very well-equipped German groups marched past that could easily have broken the enemy assault, but there wasn't anyone to command them. From the point of the division leadership, there was no attempt to do anything.[16]

In their report on events at Podgaje-Flederborn, historical researchers Fritz and Anders assessed the situation inside the village on 2 February:

The village is surrounded on all sides and remains under mortar and sniper fire, which keeps getting heavier. On 2 February the Latvians count [incoming] mortar rounds but give up after the total passes 2,000. The streets are very unsafe in daytime; many defenders are killed or wounded. Most houses still standing have all windows broken. A few Russian attacks are repulsed, and a couple of counter-attacks are launched to clear several houses in which Russians had entrenched themselves.

The new division commander SS-Oberführer Adolf Ax arrives from Jastrowie in the evening of 2 February with his staff, the weapons troops and several troop units. They know that they will have to break out of Flederborn, and Ķīlītis urges them to do so that very night, but Ax is indecisive. Strong mortar fire begins around midnight. Finally, at 05:00 on 3 February Ax's order arrives for 34th Regt to relieve 48th Regiment, which is to break out and fight its way to Lędyczek-Landeck. It is too late to withdraw under the cover of darkness, and the German officers at first resist this 'insane' order – but then agree.

The 48th Regiment leaves hastily, and so do part of the Latvians, despite the orders to stay. A major attack by Russian and Polish forces begins, with a devastating barrage by heavy artillery and mortars. Several German and Latvian officers are wounded, some mortally.

All houses are literally smashed one after another, and after 10:30 [the Latvian rearguard] is at the edge of the village … two Russian tanks enter Podgaje, as well as infantry moving along the houses. The rearguard marches toward Landeck-Lędyczek, but at Wallachsee Ķīlītis discovers that 'apart from a few messengers, there was no man at my command.'[17]

---

16 Ķikāns, in Latvian 'Green Books' vol. 6, pp.140–142.
17 Fritz and Anders, *Murder of Polish POWs,* pp.130–131.

At his home in Derby seven decades later artilleryman Laimonis Ceriņš recounted a strange event... the appearance of a wounded German general.

>   LC: About 10:00 or something … we started to move with all sorts of horses and everything. Slowly. Stop again. There was a river, then a village, Landeck. And from time to time one shell came, then another. I remember there were three or four chaps sitting in that wagon, and I was here, standing. Then a shell landed straight on the wagon, blew up and there were only bits and pieces left of one of the chaps there.
>
>   VH: In the wagon?
>
>   LC: Yes. Nothing happened to the horses and the other men. Just one man dead. Then moving slowly again … a large open field, on both sides. That's dangerous because Russians from the left are shooting all the time. Even tanks were seen, one or two. I couldn't move much, just a little bit. I was sitting. Nice sunshiney day, snow all over the place. I moved to the side of the road, by the trees. Everything was quiet.
>
>   Then I noticed from where we'd come, somebody coming. In a grey uniform. It's the famous Colonel Janums, with his men. Of course he couldn't go on the road – he moved through the forest. From time to time a shell exploded, then another. I was sitting down, and then suddenly some men with rifles are coming in a line. I noticed the first one was an officer. I said: 'I'm wounded. I can't move.' The officer says: 'Yes, OK.' He moved on and didn't stop. A short while later he took out a dagger and as high he could reach, he stuck his dagger in and hung his binoculars up. Then he went to the left, towards the Russians. When they'd gone I was thinking: 'A pair of binoculars is a very good thing, if you have some.'
>
>   I stagger to the tree, pull them down. It's a fine pair of binoculars. I started to move towards where we should go, and I met one [soldier], then another … probably another 20 or 30 from different units, all the time thinking, thinking: 'What can I do?' Then the Russians start shooting with Katyushas, from time to time. And then, somehow, a German Army general appears, in uniform, with his arm in a sling, about as far away from me as here to the door.[18]

We look. It's about four metres.

>   LC: My binoculars are round my neck. He didn't say a word. That made me suspicious. Then somehow, a split second, there's no general any more. And then after a few minutes, bloody hell, another Katyusha coming. I had to run 15 yards at least, then flat down on the floor. I'm thinking, 'what are the rest doing?' but I don't know. Then I notice the general is there again.

---

18   See Chapters 2 and 8 for similar claims of Russian deceptions.

> He moved towards me and said something in German, but funny German:
> 'Give me your binoculars.' And I said: 'I want them myself.'
>
> That's it, he went away. He wasn't a German, he was a bloody Russian
> observer. Of course, he disappeared.[19]

Corporal Irbe remembered the retreat through Flederborn as a violent and morale-sapping experience.

> On the afternoon of the next day the column of injured started to move again.
> There was a headlong flight from wooded copse to copse but where there was
> no cover there were further casualties, with no-one to care for them. Some
> units tried to fight a way through for the retreat, but it was unsuccessful. The
> soldiers were downcast, even apathetic. There was no belief in the German high
> command of the Division.[20]

In his memoirs, Jūlijs Ķīlītis describes how he was left in Flederborn with the job of covering the division's retreat.

> The Division moved forward slowly. The loads were still standing, unmoving,
> on the edge of the forest. When they got to enemy strongpoints, they hung
> around for a long time and got past with difficulty. The logistics regiment, with
> Major B. at its head, fought at the vanguard at Wallachsee. The resistance was
> pretty tough there and with his non-frontline troops, he couldn't get forwards,
> i.e., they moved very slowly.
>
> In the middle of the night, a motorcycle courier came with an order from
> the Divisional Commander, saying that I should take over all the defence of
> Flederborn with the 34th Regiment and that everyone else, including Massell's
> battalion [the 48th Dutch SS], should move forward under his command to
> Wallachsee.
>
> Together with the regimental commander Vīksne we went to the German
> *štābs* to give them the new order and to coordinate activities. At first the
> Germans were unhappy with the new order but slowly, having thought things
> through, they came to the conclusion that it would be better to go forwards
> than to stay on the spot and bleed. In any case, it was an order and they were
> under the command of the Divisional Commander.
>
> After a short consideration, we realised that the pull-out would have to take
> place in daylight, but there was nothing to be done about that. The Germans
> decided that one heavy 88mm anti-aircraft cannon and a machine gun unit would
> be left under my control, because we couldn't get them out of their positions.
> When they left, they would have to blow up their weapons and leave them behind.

19 Interview with author, Derby, UK.
20 Irbe, in *Daugavas Vanagu Mēnešraksts* Nr.1 (1982).

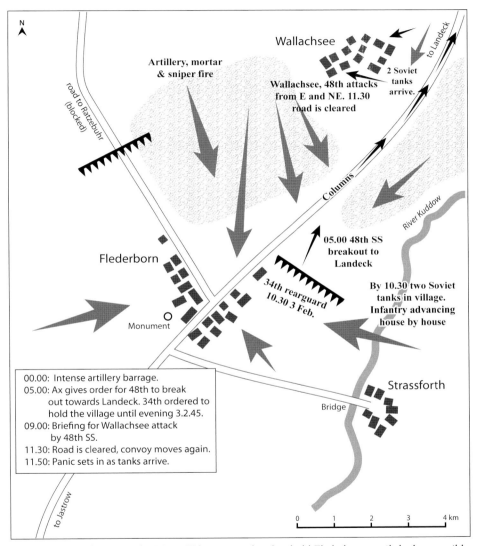

N

Wallachsee

Artillery, mortar
& sniper fire

road to Ratzebuhr
(blocked)

to Landeck

2 Soviet
tanks
arrive.

Wallachsee, 48th attacks
from E and NE. 11.30
road is cleared

Columns

River Kuddow

05.00 48th SS
breakout to
Landeck

Flederborn

34th rearguard
10.30 3 Feb.

By 10.30 two Soviet
tanks in village.
Infantry advancing
house by house

Monument

Strassforth

00.00: Intense artillery barrage.
05.00: Ax gives order for 48th to break
        out towards Landeck. 34th ordered to
        hold the village until evening 3.2.45.
09.00: Briefing for Wallachsee attack
        by 48th SS.
11.30: Road is cleared, convoy moves again.
11.50: Panic sets in as tanks arrive.

Bridge

to Jastrow

0   1   2   3   4 km

Flederborn, 3 February 1945. Major Ķilītis was ordered to hold Flederborn until the last possible
moment.

I was again greatly concerned that if the pull-out happened in daylight, a lot of my men would pull out with them. It wasn't now possible to get the order through that everyone should stay in their places, because it takes time to walk round all of the positions. Everyone sensed that the critical moment was approaching and that Flederborn wasn't a place where we would be able to hang around. I still had a couple of artillery pieces which functioned effectively under the redoubtable Captain B. The leader of the Division's artillery, the empathetic Captain F., had fallen this very morning. The ammunition was running out.

As it was time for fast action, the Regimental Commander then authorised me to act on my own initiative, and if needed, in his name, because we had to speak German (which he didn't) to pass orders and exchange information with the units under our orders and with the German HQ. Having organised the swap-out with the German HQ, the regimental commander, Major Pomrehn, his adjutant and I went back to my command point, hiding behind fences and the corners of houses all the way, so that we could pass the orders to our three battalions. I had previously announced that we would be having a meeting where the commanders or their replacements would need to attend.

The circumstances now demanded sharp and definitive action, because the critical moment was about to arrive. We had to find the right words and the right balance between the following of orders without regard, and civilised behaviour. I think that I found that balance better than I ever had. For the many, to whom I gave the order to stay until the last moment and the last bullet, I winked to show that they had to each find the right moment to do what they had to do. Eyes open, a cool head and decisive action – those were the only factors that could prevent us from destruction.

Having given my orders, I put forward the idea that we should move the command point closer to the exit towards the forest, because our current cross-roads was being shelled heavily by the enemy's artillery, which got in the way of communications with the units as well as our own movement. At this point Major Pomrehn again started to talk enthusiastically about our boys and how bravely they fought in clearing the enemy from Long Hill. We sat by the table on which my landscape map was laid out while two younger lieutenants were getting ready to leave the room.

At that moment, the talk was interrupted by a numbing explosion. The lights went out and we all fell over in groups by the table. An enemy shell had hit the ledge outside my window and exploded, showering the room with some of its shrapnel. When we had recovered from the explosion and had got the lights back on, we saw that Lieutenant Ulrich lay on the floor and his breath was rattling in an awful way: his head had been shattered. Lieutenant K. stood holding his elbow; regimental commander Vīksne was holding his head and blood was seeping from between his fingers. The other two and I weren't affected, except for the ringing in our ears.

The sanitary personnel [medics] that were called out immediately administered first aid. They couldn't do anything for Lieutenant Ulrich, and he died shortly afterwards. The regimental commander [Vīksne] had skin wounds above his temples – quite deep, through to the bone. My limbs were in working order and my shoulders had been protected by the thick and well-padded cloth of my coat. At this point the regimental commander ordered me to take over the regiment and all the other forces under our command, and he and his adjutant walked over to the first aid point.

A crisp, clear dawn broke. The day promised to be sunny with a spring-like warmth. We quickly went out with the objective of finding a new command point. I decided at first to place myself in the command point of one of the battalions that were assigned to me.

Ķīlītis gave orders for the Dutch 48th SS to set out towards Wallachsee and Landeck and prepared to leave himself.

At this point, the German/foreigner battalion began its withdrawal and, as I had already thought to myself, some of my people 'hopped' along. We stopped the ones we could reach but nevertheless, about a quarter left with them.

The enemy, having noticed the withdrawal, now pushed onto us and tried to attack again. Their machine gun and mortar fire got more intense. The cross-roads that I needed to get across was under such strong fire that there was no question of trying to at present. I hid in a shot-up little house behind a stone wall and waited, in case the fire should pause for a moment or so. The bursts of fire followed one after another so incessantly that I began to get tired of it and I lost the patience to wait for a break.

Even so, it was difficult to choose a moment to set off through it because each time, just as I decided to go, a new burst would ruin the moment. At this point, Captain Brīvkalns, who led the infantry battery, ran over to me. He asked for permission to pull his battery out of the village because his men were taking heavy casualties.

Captain Brīvkalns wanted to take up a position on the edge of the forest from which they would be more effective. I let him make this change of position. And then, finally, I made the choice to run across – and fortunately I got over. A couple of minutes later, my hiding place was destroyed by a direct artillery hit.

It deserved incredible respect seeing how Captain Brīvkalns's men, with their commander at the fore, under heavy artillery and infantry fire, selflessly pulled out their guns and dragged them to the edge of the forest. Brave boys, that you can really call heroes!

When I got to Major R. and Major A.'s command point, it was empty. The house had been shot up and the commanders themselves had already gone somewhere towards the edge of the forest. We took cover in some kind of shed next door so that we could get a hold of the situation. Suddenly it [the shed] was hit in the roof by a mortar. It caught fire. We put a guard outside, who was to watch the roof burning and warn us if it was likely to cave in. After about a quarter of an hour, that moment arrived. We moved on to the next building. After two more hours, there was nowhere left for us to crawl to.

You could say that we were swept out of the village by a 'broom of fire.' It was the middle of the day, but the tail of the Division's column hadn't started to move. When I reached it, I saw that it never would. The road was so crammed full of wagons that had been driven so closely together they could go neither forward nor back. They were all destined for destruction. No-one considered them and there was nothing that could be done about them.

Some enemy tanks appeared individually in Flederborn, making several careful sorties. Later, there was a real Sodom and Gomorrah [moment], when the tanks, emboldened, started to shoot up the transport column.[21]

---

21 Ķilītis, *I Go To War,* pp.190–193. The question of why the rear of the column was left unprotected amid such slaughter is puzzling.

12

The Road of Slaughter 3: Wallachsee To Landeck

By the night of 2 February 1945, under intense artillery bombardment, the situation for the Latvians in and around Flederborn was desperate. The column on the road was horribly exposed, and snipers and machine guns were able to fire on it from the southern edge of Wallachsee. Twice in the night attack groups sent by divisional commander Adolph Ax to silence them were thrown back.

At 05:30, Ax sent the 48th Dutch SS Regiment out from Flederborn to break the Soviet encirclement centred on Landeck and get the column of wounded through. In their place, the Latvian 34th Regiment was to hold Flederborn as long as possible with stragglers from other units and men from the reserves. In this extract from Latvian military archives in the USA describing the battle to hold Flederborn, the courage of Lieutenant Bonoparts is again highlighted.

> 3 February 1945: Exhaustion was overwhelming; despite the heavy and continuous fire the company slept until morning. Colonel Janums had already moved ahead. When the enemy penetrated Flederborn, Colonel Vīksne did not allow the company to follow the departing regiment, and ordered it to prevent the enemy from deeper penetration. Again Lieutenant Bonoparts led his 23 men in a counter-attack through the burning village: crawling on the main road, he destroyed enemy automatic weapons himself. The attacking lines were stopped and thrown back. The enemy had sustained heavy damage, and did not launch additional attacks in this direction. Because of this, the pullback following an order was successful.[1]

Dr Pauls Dzintars was in a group of men leaving Flederborn early on 3 February:

> In the morning we gathered in the northern part of the village. The nearest wood was 200 metres away across an open field. The enemy knew that very well

---

1   Writer unknown, Latvian Military Archives, USA. Trans. Arturs Grava, sent to author 20 July 2022.

and had the range. Hoping I stood a better chance of getting across on my own than in a group, I ran over with Jevelevs [his assistant] behind me. A few badly-aimed bullets whistled past my ears but we weren't really an important target.

We reached the safety of the wood, sat down by the edge of it and looked back at the village. We couldn't see very well, but we could hear shelling, mortar fire and automatic weapons. The group around us was getting larger but the 200-metre dash was getting more dangerous and a good number were left lying in the field. The shelling was getting nearer so we went deeper into the forest.

After a few kilometres we came across the wagons which should have been away by this time but weren't. They were just standing on the road. Luckily the weather wasn't too cold or the injured on the carts would have frozen. Already many looked like walking corpses: pale, bled out, not having eaten or drunk in days, in pain.[2]

Jūlijs Ķīlītis had taken over as commander of the 34th Regiment when Alberts Vīksne was injured by shellfire, and gave the order to pull out from Flederborn.

We began marching alongside the road in the direction of Landeck. On the way we got to see the destruction and detritus that was left of our transport units. Destroyed wagons, dead people and horses, discarded to the left and to the right. The heavy artillery had smashed up all sorts of things. Remnants of human flesh were hanging in the trees and in the branches of bushes. A man had been thrown into a thicket by an explosion and his skin had been torn off so that you could see all his tendons and bones, like in an anatomical museum.

All sorts of goods were lying around. I found a helmet for myself by the ditch, as mortars were hacking the tops of the trees. As well as shrapnel, bits of wood were also flying about. From someone who had passed into eternal rest I borrowed a rifle and ammunition, because I didn't possess any weapons apart from a pistol in my belt. Then, together with the adjutant and two messengers we went through the forest towards Landeck.[3]

Zigurds Kārkliņš had been ordered by a gendarme to take a machine gun and set it up on top of a police bus on the road to give covering fire.

We drive like this with the whole long column for a few kilometres when suddenly a fierce battle begins. The bus I'm on is covered by a wood on one side but on the left is an open field. Next to me a bus full of refugees pulls up. From

2   Dzintars, in *Daugavas Vanagi Mēnešraksts,* Nr.5 (01 September 1999) online at <periodika.lv>, trans. Daina Vītola.
3   Ķīlītis, *I Go To War,* p.194. Ķīlītis led his men through the forest on the eastern side of the road towards Landeck and crossed the Küddow before the final roadblock, thus avoiding the artillery barrage hitting the road.

the left-hand side, mortars begin to fall on us, and after each explosion there are cries of 'Medic!'

The wood is full of wounded men. The deeper dips are full of injured soldiers who have been collected there. A couple of medics try to deal with their wounds. The air is full of sniper bullets, which burst in tree branches with loud explosions.

For a time I lie on the truck and don't know what to do. I'm too good a target. Sniper bullets have already lodged in several places around me. Finally a shell hits the refugee truck next to me, killing some women and children. The rest run to the wood and the cries of the children and the women mix into the noise of the battle with a dreadful effect. Lying on the vehicle isn't good, so I climb down and make my way into the wood with my automatic rifle. A wounded Latvian officer with a pistol in his hand has collected a group of soldiers and put them in a chain to defend us.

We dig holes in the snow, lie down and wait. All around us shells are exploding in the trees and bullets are whizzing through the air. On the right and left of me about five paces distant lie two German comrades. We're lying by the trunk of a plane tree. Suddenly a shell explodes above my head and cries for a medic sound on both sides. By the time they run to us both German soldiers are dead. Behind us, deeper in the wood, a Latvian Legion doctor is trying to help the more seriously wounded. The explosion of a shell leaves a mass of body parts in that place.

We lie in that position for about a couple of hours. Finally the column begins to move again and we move forward slowly, accompanied by Russian mortar fire. On the flanks separate groups are advancing that are trying to push the Russians further back from the road. One group comes across a Russian machine gun position. It's not possible to get near them and there's nothing left for the lads to do but to retreat over the open field. Only a couple of them escape. The rest fall, one after another, like black spots on a snowy background. Slowly the encircled army moves forward, paying a bloody price for each step of the way.[4]

Ax ordered the 48th Dutch SS to attack and take Wallachsee by circling round to the north-west of the village and launching a surprise attack from there. This account of the battle comes from the records of the 15th Sapper Battalion in the Latvian Legion's official history, the 'Green Books.'

On 3 February on the road to Landeck the battle for Wallachsee began. Special mention has to be made here of a small group of Latvian sappers. About 22:00

4   Kārkliņš, *Daugavas Vanagu Mēnešraksts* Nr. 3, trans. Daina Vītola. Born in Daugavpils in 1927, Zigurds Kārkliņš survived the war and emigrated to the United States in 1951 where he enlisted in the US Army and served with the Tropical Lightning Battalion in Korea, later working as a tool designer until he retired. A member of the Latvian Lutheran Church, the Latvian welfare association Daugavas Vanagi and the Latvian Community Centre, he died aged 87 in Indianapolis. Obituary at: <https://www.legacy.com/us/obituaries/indystar/name/zigurds-Kārkliņš-obituary?pid=175375972>.

Wallachsee was taken street-by-street and house-by-house, but the Russians wouldn't give in and launched a counter-attack, which completely mixed up our supply wagons with the refugee column on the road. Unimaginable panic broke out and everyone tried to get to Landeck.[5]

Ķīlītis wrote in his memoirs:

This was a pretty heavy day. The losses had to be huge. In front of us was the sound of fighting but behind and to one side was the sound of tanks. I had the impression that fighting was going on all around. After about an hour we got to Wallachsee. Here there was still an atmosphere of battle: there was the odd shot exploding here and there and on the left in the hillocks the chains of the foreigner battalion men were running around. The blockage that was preventing forward movement had supposedly just been freed up and in an attack on a group of houses on the roadside the Recce leader fell, Major D.

We started to march on further, because quite close behind you could hear the roar of the tanks and the clanking of their caterpillar tracks. That sped up our movement forward. The men felt the critical moment was approaching and they became unsettled, just like forest animals whose future depended on instincts and senses, whereas it seemed one's mind had little left to do. Everyone was just trying to find a way forward, where there was hope of freedom away from this throttling noose.

You couldn't stand on the road for long because from time to time, from somewhere or other, there would be mortar or machine gun fire. Horrifying and hopeless was the fate of those people lying injured in carts who couldn't move by themselves. Many were injured for a second or third time; a good proportion died and the rest were taken prisoner.[6]

Chaplain Kazimirs Ručs and fellow minister Jūlijs Straume were moving towards Landeck with hell breaking out around them.

In a column we made our way to Landeck … where a pitiless battle was already underway. Chaplain Straume was given a rifle. I put grenades on my belt, in my boots and in my pockets. My messenger was in the break-out spearhead. Straume's messenger Andrejs Briedis, an ex-Jaunjelgava school inspector, came along with us. The medical company Lieutenant sighed heavily. 'The battle will be fierce and bloody,' he said. 'God only knows how many will survive.'

Chaplain Straume and I find ourselves in the part of the column that has already left Flederborn. We were shot at by the artillery but luckily the shells explode some way from the road. To save themselves the column ran into the

---

5   Extract from the diary of the 15th Sapper Battalion in Latvian 'Green Books', vol. 6, p.259.
6   Ķīlītis, *I Go To War,* p.194. Ķīlītis refers to the Dutch 48th SS as men 'from a volunteer unit of a Western nation related to the Germans, with German officers.'

forest but it wasn't safe even there. Snipers in the trees shot at them. Bullets whizzed past heads like bees but luckily nobody was hit.

The reality of the battlefield is dreadful. There are fields full of fallen men. All around I can hear moans of agony. The field is trampled flat: the earth soaked in human blood. It wasn't possible to bury our fallen because of the Red Army attacks. For the dead and the wounded, the battle was over. Those who remained alive had to continue the fight. The battlefield chaplains had to fight alongside their men, giving succour where possible, holding services even when the battle is raging all around.

I experienced a tragic event on the battlefield. A Latvian boy, drafted from Latgale I think, fell into my arms and cried. 'I wanted an education,' he said. 'I wanted to make something of my life. But now I'm on a battlefield and I might not live much longer.' If I recommended that he deserted, the gendarmerie would catch him and hang him. If I recommended he go over to the Red Army, he wouldn't have a better future. And would any of these recommendations be honest with regards to those left behind? Therefore the young Legionnaire had to be calmed down and made brave in another way.[7]

Colonel Janums had been ordered to cover the right flank of the push forward. He was so disgusted at the loss of life that he interpreted his orders to the maximum range and set off through the forest to cross the Dobrinka river north-east of Landeck. Alksnītis, with the men remaining from the 32nd Regiment, headed for Peterswalde.

The battle for Landeck was a brutal struggle. The town itself was not entirely under the control of the Germans. Kampfgruppe Scheibe held the north of the town, but crucially Russian units supported by tanks controlled the southern half. There, the bridge into the town from Flederborn and Jastrow was a critical strategic point.

The fight for control of Landeck to break the Soviet encirclement of the Latvians on the road from Jastrow had begun several days earlier, with a German attack on the night of 1–2 February, when Kampfgruppe Hämel and Kampfgruppe von Bargen established a bridgehead across the river Küddow but then could not expand it despite several attempts the next day.

On 3 February the Red Army tried repeatedly to regain control of the bridge, but these attacks were thrown back. One account of this battle says Russian soldiers, possibly with tanks, were pushed out of Landeck and regrouped in the forest just south of the bridge. Several Latvian accounts mention the surrender of 400 teenage Latvian RAD drivers to a Russian tank unit and their subsequent massacre in the forest on 3 February.[8]

---

7   Ručs adds here, which I have included as a footnote: 'Amongst other things it was said that a Legionnaire had gone over to the Red Army and fought against the Germans. After the war he was locked up in a Soviet war camp. He protested that this wasn't fair, as he had fought against the Germans. But now he was sentenced and in a camp. And the Communists had answered: "But you're a deserter! You could also desert from us."'

8   It is possible – if the story is true – that the 400 Latvian drivers were massacred at this point. With military priorities responding to a rapidly-changing situation and, needing to launch

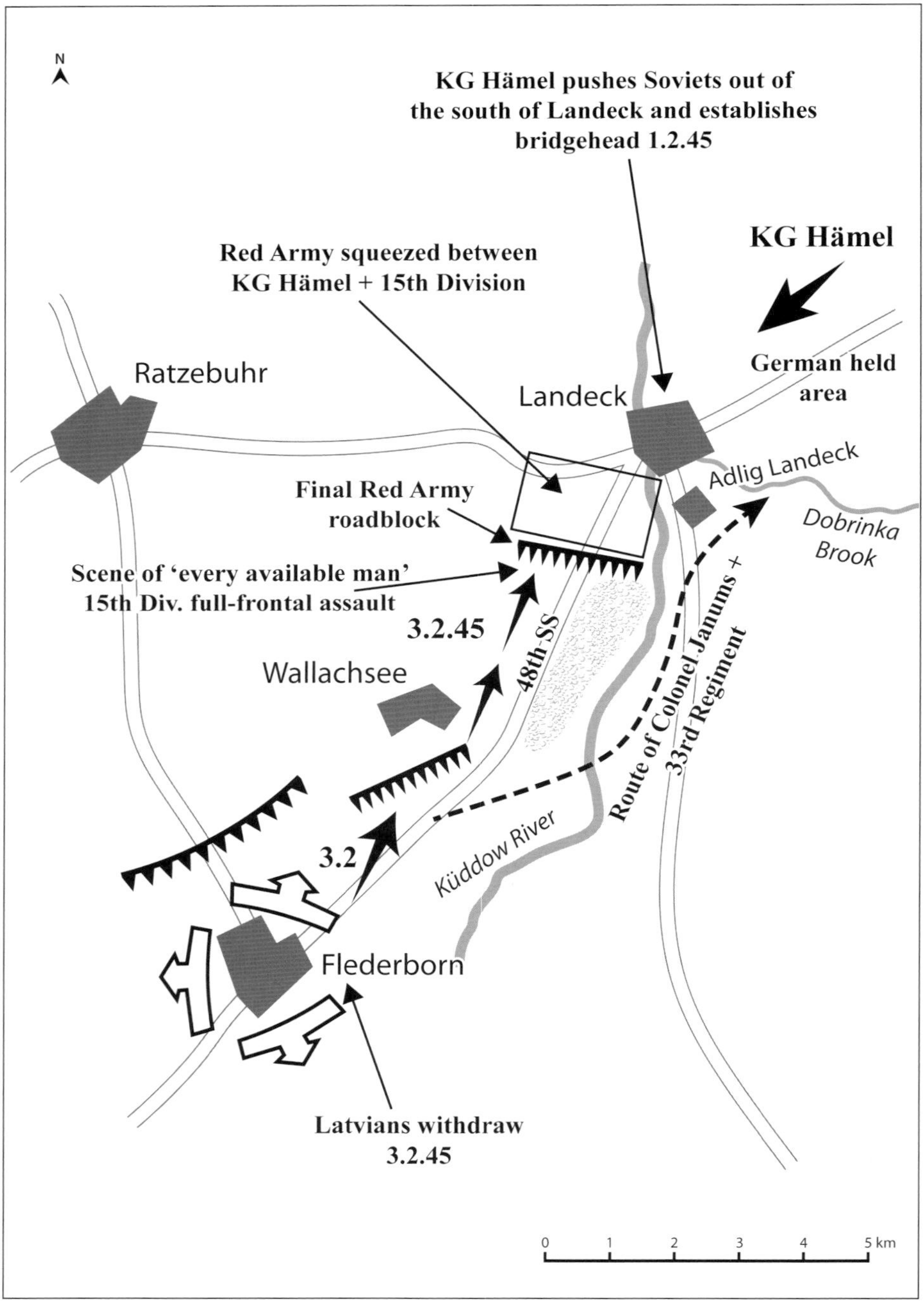

N

KG Hämel pushes Soviets out of
the south of Landeck and establishes
bridgehead 1.2.45

KG Hämel

Red Army squeezed between
KG Hämel + 15th Division

Ratzebuhr

German held
area

Landeck

Adlig Landeck

Final Red Army
roadblock

Dobrinka
Brook

Scene of 'every available man'
15th Div. full-frontal assault

3.2.45

48th-SS

Wallachsee

Route of Colonel Janums +
33rd Regiment

3.2

Küddow River

Flederborn

Latvians withdraw
3.2.45

0   1   2   3   4   5 km

Assault on Landeck. The final stages of the breaking of the encirclement on the road to Landeck. After clearing Red Army positions at Wallachsee, Adolph Ax gathered 'every available man' for a full-frontal assault on the last remaining machine gun positions blocking the road into the town.

The footnotes from a fact-based novel covering these events look at the role of Battle Group Hämel, attacking from seven kilometres west opposite Hill 106, to help clear the road. This same account mentions the number of 400 dead, but says it is 'hard to confirm that in the Landeck forest alone, the Russians and Poles over two days shot some 400 Latvian POWs.'[9]

At this point artilleryman Zigurds Kārkliņš was witnessing terrible sights as the slaughter on the Flederborn side of the roadblock continued on 3 February.

The afternoon has arrived and we are now only about one kilometre from Landeck town. The Russian fire is unrelenting and that's joined by the famous Stalin Organ [Katyusha rocket launcher] which, with its firing, levels field after field, area after area.

Nearing the town we meet freedom! A German battle group has been ordered to break the encirclement and is coming towards us. We are separated from the town by a small river with banks overgrown with fir trees, but the Russians have dug in there. We can't get near them with just rifles, and Russian infantry are coming closer and closer to our area. In some places there's already hand-to-hand combat.

A sniper has crawled up a tree in the nearest wood and can see our positions very clearly. He has begun to fire upon us, and with tremendous anger uncountable rifle barrels turn towards him. Finally a German four-barrelled flak gun comes to help us, and only then a Russian, well-wrapped in warm clothes, falls from the top of the tree. He's full of holes, leaking like a sieve.

All the wagons and the vehicles still remaining are full of wounded. Many men are killed in the ceaseless shellfire, many horses die and the motor vehicles are wrecked. Nobody cares about the wounded. Man has turned into an animal.

Everyone tries to save their own lives. A wounded man jumped out of the cart and ran along the road in his underpants, screaming in a dreadful voice, until an explosion from a shell ends his misery. Calls from the wounded sound from all sides: 'Take us with you. Don't leave us.' These calls are useless.

At this point, our Divisional commander Egons Eglite is killed. He didn't want to bow down to enemy fire and an explosion from a shell tears open his stomach. That's the second Division commander we have lost in the last couple of months.[10]

---

counter-attacks, perhaps the Russians felt they could not risk leaving so many of the enemy alive unguarded.

9   The original account, by a soldier called Alberts Eglitis, is filed in an as-yet unidentified archive. Major Hämel was not popular with the Latvians either, perhaps because they felt he 'lost all his men' – i.e., he didn't give orders that ensured their survival.

10 Kārkliņš, in the Latvian 'Green Books', vol. 4, p.276. Egons Eglite (25 July 1915–3 February 1945) was previously an adjutant with the 15th Artillery Regiment until 29 January 1945, when he was promoted to commanding officer. The holder of both the Iron Cross First and Second Class, he was killed five days later. From: Axis History Forum online at <https://forum.axishistory.com/viewtopic.php?t=134999>.

Catholic chaplain Kazimirs Ručs ran for his life into the Landeck forest.

> The last and bloodiest battles lay ahead of us. Our spearhead force went forward but was met with deadly fire. The Red Army shot at us individually and deliberately. Among those killed here was Lutheran Minister Jūlijs Straume and his messenger Andrejs Briedis. No-one can get near to them because heaven and earth are spinning and our only hope of safety is the Landeck forest.
>
> In order to get there, you had to run across a field a kilometre wide. My messenger is still fighting in the attacking force. There are snipers in the trees hunting and killing individual soldiers but the sound that is the background to everything is that of the Stalin Organ.
>
> Ammunition of all kinds is raining down all around. Trees are brought down, falling on us, flying through the air like pieces of firewood. Afterwards everything is covered in black soot. I couldn't help Straume and Briedis even though they fell only 300 metres away from me. There were bullets, mortars, shells: you couldn't lift your head.
>
> I reached the Landeck forest on the other side of the field alone. The Red Army blasted the forest with Stalin Organs: fiery shells fell around us. Sparks flew in front of you and your ears were blasted by the sound of the explosions. It seemed as though the whole forest was on fire and full of smoke.[11]

The 15th Division War Diary describes the position on the road at this time:

> In the meantime, about 500 men of all Div. units have gathered at the head of the column. The situation before Landeck is the following. The enemy blocks the Flederborn to Landeck road with a PAK [anti-tank gun: *Panzerabwehrkanone*], several a. [artillery pieces) and le.MG [Light Machine Gun], from Height 118. Moreover he is pushing strongly from the direction of Wallachsee and from the heights north of Wallachsee supported by artillery and salvo gunfire. The fire is presumed to be directed by aerial observation. Units of our own troops have been detected in Landeck.[12]

Legion artillery commander Lieutenant E. Ģērmanis described the scenes on the road into Landeck:

> There were a lot of dead and wounded soldiers left on the road, shot horses, destroyed vehicles and other war material. The remainder of the column pressed into the forest for the next section of the road, for 1.5 kilometres from Wallachsee into Landeck. Well-targeted enemy artillery, tanks and small arms positions were all along the road from Flederborn to Landeck.

---

11 Ručs, *Dzīve ar Dievu* in *Daugavas Vanagi Mēnešraksts* Nr. 3, p.63.
12 15th Division war diary, Latvian National Archive, Rīga. Author's visit, November 2019. Trans. Patrick Howse.

The final section of the road between Wallachsee and Landeck was only taken [by the infantry] after blasting enemy positions with salvos of cannon fire … with every man in the division pressed into the final assault into Landeck which had previously been held by some German units (Kampfgruppe Scheibe).[13]

Regimental doctor Pauls Dzintars could only watch the scenes of carnage around him.

The 32nd Regiment wagons were the last, and we came across those first. I saw my black *sanka* with my bicycle on its roof. I wanted to take my camera but it wasn't possible. There were six wounded men lying on my doctor's bag. Even those who weren't wounded didn't have it easy. It was chaos.

We went to the north on the right side of the road. Mortars and shells hit the road and the forest, sometimes very close to us. Officers, even squadron leaders [senior officers], wandered around the forest without escorts, without their units. It was every man for himself.

Even after the battle to take Wallachsee, the road was still blocked near Landeck. Colonel Janums writes that the road was only cleared in a full-frontal assault with heavy losses. Among those killed were Divisional HQ leader Sturmbannführer Wulff, 32nd Regiment commander Major Rubenis and a large number of officers and soldiers. Their heroism opened the road to Landeck and to freedom for the rest of us. This road was no Sunday stroll for us.

Out of the blue I came across Dr Upītis, Major Alksnītis and a small group of men. They'd got through mostly unharmed, but Corporal Lindbergs had been wounded. Alksnītis had shrapnel in his coat but otherwise hadn't been touched. There were only about ten men left from the original group: his adjutant and a small number of soldiers.

Alksnītis organised the fleeing mass to get in a chain and protect our right flank, but these chains could unravel very quickly. We didn't know that we already had a good guard on our right flank in Janums. When we reached the area around Wallachsee there was a battle raging. Shells aimed at the column of wagons flew over our heads. We saw phone wires so we cut them, and when we did the guns fell silent, so somewhere they had a spotter.

When Wallachsee was taken, the column moved forward but at Landeck the road was blocked again, and the fighting became heavier. The column got it worst of all. Many vehicles and horses and carts were smashed up. Some drivers had abandoned their wagons and run off into the forest. There were explosions, moans, shouts, curses – everything was chaos.[14]

13 Lieutenant E. Germanis, translated from Latvian 'Green Books', vol. 8, pp.99–100.
14 Dzintars, in *Daugavas Vanagi Mēnešraksts*, Nr.5 (01 September 1999) online at <periodika. lv>, trans. Daina Vītola. The War Diary notes that during the attacks on Landeck, the General Staff officer SS-Stubaf Wulff, the Io SS-Ostuf. Dr. Neimer and SS-Ustuf. Adrian (Nachr.Abt.) all fell. Wounded: SS-Stuf. Martin (03), W.-Ostuf. Martinsons, SS Stubaf.

It took nearly four hours for the Latvians and Germans to break the resistance of the Red Army defences north-west of the Landeck road at Height 118, but just before 16:00, after what the War Diary calls 'a short hard fight', the enemy positions were silenced. Most of the men who had gathered at the head of the marching column joined in, the diary noted:

> ...so that the Russians were thrown from Height 118 and ran away, leaving behind all their weapons, wounded and dead.[15]

The 'short hard fight' was in effect a full-frontal death-or-glory assault by whoever could carry a rifle: the commanding officers, the men of the transport column, the wounded and slightly injured – now numbering nearly 1,000 men – and a Special Assignments penal battalion. An account for the Legion official history by the sappers' battalion describes what happened:

> About one or two kilometres from Landeck the whole panic-driven column stopped because the Russians had blocked the road. The Russians had dug in very firmly in the hillocks by the river and on the bridge and had very good machine gun nests and gun positions. Here again the sapper group fought with good results and together with the other Latvian units defeated the Russians and opened the road to Landeck. There was very fierce hand-to-hand combat where all the men showed not just bravery but also ability to fight in this way.
>
> Whilst the battle for the road to Landeck took place, the jumbled Division and refugee columns were fired on by the Russian Stalin Organs, killing many and causing absolute chaos. Here again were more indescribable scenes and sounds, punctuated by the occasional single shot as people committed suicide.[16]

Closer to Landeck, Ručs' group came under shellfire again.

> There just on the other side of a little river is Landeck. There are Germans here but the bridge across the river has been blown up. A shell explodes next to me. A soldier and a refugee who was running away get blown to pieces. I fly through the air and fall into a puddle of mud.
>
> Slightly concussed, my head is ringing but I'm whole. I wasn't even injured. Really you have to say that one of the Psalms has come to pass: *Even though thousands fall to the left of you and ten thousand to the right, you will not be harmed.* The Holy Mother of Aglona has saved me. How can you not believe in miracles?

Dr Berndt (IVb), SS Stuf. Berndt (IVa), SS-Stuf. Meyer (V), SS-Stuf. Gürtler (VI), Oblt. Coulurier (Ia/P1.)

15 15th Division War Diary, Latvian National Archive, Rīga.
16 Extract from the diary of the 15th Sapper Battalion in Latvian 'Green Books', vol. 6, p.259.

Whilst the battle continued for the road to Landeck, the Red Army Stalin Organs laid flat the 15th Division and the refugee columns, killing many and causing unimaginable chaos. There were scenes that cannot be described. The wounded screaming, terrified refugee women and children. A few, in despair, shot themselves.[17]

The group Pauls Dzintars was with took cover deep in the forest to escape enemy fire when they reached the roadblock outside Landeck:

When our group came close to the roadblock we got a volley of artillery fire as a 'hello'. We were covered in pine needles, snow and clumps of earth. We fled deeper into the forest but the next series of shells seemed to explode even closer. I became separated from my group, lost them and was alone.

After another series of explosions I came across three doctors: Vēriņš, Prīmanis and Beldavs who, to my mind, were going in the wrong direction. I couldn't convince them, and so we parted. Using my previous experience of being in situations like this, I tried to go where the fighting was heaviest, which led me to the Dobrinka river. From there I could see Landeck.

We gathered a large group. We didn't know if Landeck was held by the Germans, but from that direction we were greeted by fire from German MG-34 machine guns. The braver ones crossed the river and took cover in dips on the other side of the bank. When I got ready to join them, Baluls appeared leading a white mare. It was still wearing the remains of a saddle and a bridle, so I got on it. Baluls was about to climb up behind me when there was another volley of fire. Baluls disappeared but the mare didn't react, so just like 'Skobolevs on a white horse' I rode across the Dobrinka, then sent the horse back.[18]

Major Ķīlītis and the 34th Regiment had made cautious but steady progress through the forest towards Landeck.

Looping back on ourselves and moving around places that looked dodgy, we finally came out onto a bend in the road, from which we should soon have seen the Landeck bridge. Lots of people were walking around, obviously without

---

17 Ručs, *Dzīve ar Dievu*, p.63. The quote is: *Jebšu tūkstoši krīt tev blakus un desmit tūkstoši tev pa labo roku, tačū tevi tas neskars.* Ručs gives the reference of Psalm 90, verse 7. The Roman Catholic Basilica of the Assumption of the Blessed Virgin Mary in Aglona is one of the most important Catholic centres in Latvia. Many Catholics make pilgrimages there, some carrying crucifixion crosses.

18 'Skobolevs on a white horse' is a reference to the famous Russian general Mikhail Skobolevs, who conquered Central Asia and was noted for his bravery in the Russo-Turkish War of 1877–88. Always dressed in a white uniform and riding his white horse, he had a reputation for leading his men in the thick of the action but also for being a ruthless commander, ordering the massacre of 14,500 Turkmen soldiers and civilians after the Siege of Geok-Tepe in 1881. This incident is now commemorated in Turkmenistan with a national day of mourning.

any leadership, but not far from there on the side of the road was the Divisional leader's car, where the commander himself was sitting with the whole of his team. They were all waiting for something. I don't know if they were waiting for better times, the Dutch [SS] or for God's forgiveness? They could still hope for the Dutch, but there was no chance of getting God's forgiveness.

Among the crowd of people there was a good proportion of officers – both ours and Germans. I didn't even try to get involved, so that we wouldn't be chosen again as tongs to pull hot coals from a fire. I decided not to wait, but on my own initiative to find a way of getting over the river and thus behind the enemy line. I thought if we couldn't achieve that during the day, then at least we could cross at night.

On the way, I also found a strong horse that had been left behind by someone. I wanted to use that further down the road to protect my already worn-out feet. There were about 30 guys around me, and when they found out that I would be trying to get across the river, the numbers swelled visibly. At the same time, I heard a specific and familiar noise: *runk, runk, runk…*

'Stalin Organ!' I cried and at the same moment I ordered: 'Hide in the potholes!' The old stagers knew this sound from the Russian fields, but amongst us was a large majority hearing it for the first time. About 30 seconds later, fiery bombs were falling onto us like beans. There were gold, red and black flashes in front of our eyes and the noise of the explosions drummed into our ears. Nevertheless, it so happened we were pretty spread out and no-one received a direct hit. Instinctively, after that I threw myself a couple of hundred metres further into the wood because I thought that the next salvo would hit the road or the roadside.

This time my instinct was completely wrong and the next salvo centred on just where we had run to. Again we threw ourselves into the deepest hiding places we could find. It seemed like the whole forest had caught fire from the flames and was full of smoke. Some bombs exploded just a couple of steps from me. How badly hit we were I just didn't know. My second messenger was injured in two places. He had shielded me with his body, because he was pressed right up against me in the hole into which I threw myself. I bandaged him myself with my individual bandage packs and, having sat him on my horse, sent him to our dressing station once the firing died down.[19]

…Straight after the barrage I went to the river to find somewhere we could get across. In a small bend on the river, where there wasn't any direct enemy fire, some of our men used poles to bash the ice and measure the depth of the water. The river wasn't any wider than 20 metres. The water by each bank was frozen with a covering of ice but the middle was free-flowing, dark water. The ice had already melted there. We quickly found a shallower spot where the water didn't come up over our belts. Some of the more hot-headed men were soon over

---

19 He continues: 'For a long time I didn't know what happened to him. Only a couple of years after the war I found out he was alive and well in some German camp.'

and already wringing out their wet trousers. Even though it was a sunny and warm day, it was still February and evening was approaching. The water seemed warmish – see what dire need does for you!

We quickly crossed and gathered in the shelter of the side of the river valley. Having crawled out to the edge of the forest with my binoculars, I started to investigate the edge of the forest on the other side and the nearest houses. One, it turned out, was the small Adlig Landeck manor house. At first it seemed like no-one was there, but when I looked hard enough, I could see that enemy soldiers were gazing out, bent around fences and the corners of houses.

At one corner there was some kind of device that looked like a big kitchen pot, around which about a dozen men busied themselves. The distance was a bit more than a kilometre. I put approximately 50–60 men in a line along the gorge. The first objective that I chose was the corner of the forest with a small hillock and road cutting behind where it might be possible to take cover. I thought I would then decide whether to attack the manor house across the open field or go further along the road into the wood.

To get some reaction from the enemy and to find out what we had in front of us, we decided to cover the first 100 metres in one go, loudly shouting 'Urrāh!'. One man had a quick-firing machine gun with him. I thanked him effusively for his bravery and diligence for carrying that heavy thing all this way. That was going to be so useful to us now! I kept this man next to me and, once everything seemed in order, I ordered: 'Forwards! Running march!'

At the same time, together with the soldier with the machine gun, we threw ourselves over the ridge and ran without stopping for 150 metres. The next ridge was further away than I had thought. When I got to the new position, after a couple of calming gulps of air, I looked through my binoculars again to see what effect we had made with our running and shouts of 'Urrāh!' It seems that our sudden appearance on the enemy's flank has given them quite a surprise. There is a lot of running about and activity around that funny thing (i.e., the kitchen pot). Soon there was a flash from it and a shell landed just in front of our noses. The funny kitchen pot was nothing other than an infantry cannon.[20]

[It was] fortunate that the distance was too close and there was a slight slope. All the shells ricocheted and exploded somewhere behind and over our heads. The soldier with the machine gun and I both took aim at this target and fired quite a few rounds. However, there was something not quite right with the sights, because the bullets didn't fly as they should have done towards the target. But whatever; after firing a few shells, the cannon crept away.

I asked Lieutenant X from Janums' regiment, who was right beside me, to take a small fighting unit and go into the small wood and see if there were any enemy forces to the right of the small manor house. After a while I decided to follow him, because there was no point in going across an open field.

20 He calls it a *lielgabals*.

Morale was good, because it looked like we were going to get through here somehow. Everybody who had a firearm shot towards the boundary of the manor house and the enemy men who were buzzing around. After we had fought like that for about 20 minutes, I reasoned that we should also follow Lieutenant X's small unit into the wood. The unit hadn't come back and there were no sounds coming from the forest.[21]

Desperate measures were needed to break through the Red Army lines on the road, as Zigurds Kārkliņš describes:

We can't kill the Russians along the side of the river and the situation becomes more serious. A shell exploding in a tree covers me in soot, and the people standing around me are forced to laugh. At last the order comes: 'Everyone take a Panzerfaust and advance. Try to destroy this last roadblock with them.'

We arrive too late because three Latvian lads have already managed to pull an anti-tank gun into the middle of the road and, defying death, destroyed this nest of death. In doing so they lost their own lives, but the road is now open. When we pass this place, the bodies of our three fallen heroes lie next to the cannon.

On the other side of the bridge we are greeted by the oncoming German units. At the end of the road, next to his machine gun, lies a bearded Russian. The last shells are still falling in the town but that doesn't bother us anymore. We have freed ourselves from the encirclement.[22]

The slaughter all around left 30-year-old chaplain Kazimir Ručs with tragic and vivid memories:

Thousands of Latvian Legionnaires fell in the break-out from the Landeck encirclement. Dusk fell on the battleground and the fallen, and, looking at that, one had to sigh. These boys … the scythe of war has cut you down in your prime like early wheat.

Many Latvian men were wounded, some dreadfully disfigured. Comrades dragged back a torso. Their friend had had both arms and legs blown off. Someone gave him a bullet.

On the break-out road, about 200 paces away from the Red Army machine gun nests which had been shot to pieces and the bodies of the two Red Army soldiers who had been killed [resisting], was an anti-tank gun on which a Latvian Legionnaire lay dead. A badly-wounded soldier lay nearby.

The Latvians had destroyed the hidden Red Army machine gun position and cleared the way out of the encirclement, but died in the process.

---

21 Ķīlītis, *I Go To War*, pp.195–197.
22 Kārkliņš, in the Latvian 'Green Books', vol. 4, p.276.

At the side of the road into Landeck Ručs found the body of German commander Erich Wulff. As a chaplain, he remembered that Wulff had stopped the Latvian Christians celebrating Christmas a few months before. He wrote:

> We have to pray to God for his mercy, and also for him. Give him everlasting peace. But those who remained alive had to fight on. I had to find even more courage to hold services for the Legionnaires without showing my fear and to deliver sermons even though all around the Red Army artillery and Stalin Organs boomed and machine guns rattled.[23]

There are few accounts of the assault on the bridge at Landeck, but it's very likely that the 32nd Regiment led the attack, commanded by Major Fricis Rubenis. He was killed in the attack, leading his men. In post-war correspondence in the Kripens archive at the Latvian War Museum, Major Alksnītis said of this time:

> All the units are mixed up all over the place. It's very hard to keep hold of them. All are rushing northwards. When we reached Landeck it turned out that the German Scheibe group was there but that the Russians were in the southern part of the town. We can't get into the town. We are located between the Flederborn-Landeck road and the Küddow river. The enemy fires with mortars and machine guns and tanks are also active. With gruelling effort ['ar lielām mokām'] the men were got forward for the attack on the Landeck bridge. We took the bridge. Our forces entered Landeck.[24]

In his account of the battle, Major Ķīlītis describes the moment the Latvians broke through:

> Suddenly someone shouted out loud: 'The bridge is free. Our lot are driving in!' It was true: when I looked at one end of the bridge, our columns were going into Landeck. The enemy had fallen back and freed up the road to the small town – we had broken the encirclement! That was now a sign. All those who had joined us just to get over the river ran to the banks and ran to the bridge in the shelter of the bank. All the rest of us could do was watch.
>
> My adjutant said: 'Now what do we do? We'll probably have to go there as well. There doesn't seem any point in buzzing around an unfamiliar forest when the road is clear.'
>
> 'That's how it is,' I said. 'All our great warriors have scarpered – let's do the same!'
>
> We started to go back to the river bank at a light trot. Lieutenant I., who was younger, quickly got to the head of the group. He was dressed in a short pilot's

---

23 Ručs, *Dzīve ar Dievu*, p.63, trans. Daina Vītola.
24 Major Augusts Alksnītis, correspondence with Arvīds Krīpēns, in the Krīpēns Archive, Latvian War Museum, Rīga. Trans. Aivars Sinka.

jacket with warm boots and armed with a machine gun. The rest of us were in coats, wearing helmets and armed with rifles.

As we were running, I noticed that my adjutant Lieutenant I. was jumping about in a funny way. He shouted: 'Bloody hell, that Ivan is aiming at me!' It was true. Someone was firing bullet after bullet at head-height towards my adjutant, who was making hare-like jumps and loops. A few minutes later we fell, breathless, in the cover of the ridge in a hollow. There, we felt safe.

Everyone was pleased that we got through without any casualties and we all laughed about Lieutenant I.'s problems. I laughed: 'That's what happens if you dress up in someone else's fur!' If he had kept his soldier's coat and cap, the Ivans wouldn't have focused on him first. They probably decided he was the only officer, and therefore he would be the main target, at whatever cost. Lieutenant I., lying on his back, breathed out heavily and said: 'My back is wet from running and my forehead is wet from fear!'

After taking a breather, we got up and quickly went along the shore in the direction of the bridge. When I considered it afterwards, you have to think that the enemy, impressed by our flanking manoeuvre and probably thinking that their flank was under attack, decided that it would be wiser to pull back and free our route into Landeck. The foreigners [the Dutch SS] were also attacking frontally and showed that they could use their weapons well.

When we got to Landeck, we still had to go over the bridge, because the river splits up there. There were a lot of people crammed into Landeck and the gallant gendarmes [German military police] with their phosphorescent metal tags on their chests were directing the traffic and collecting people into assembly points and registering them all. The enemy threw over the odd shell, but that was no longer able to affect anyone.

At one crossroads, a gendarme was berating a soldier. Now they were at the height of their grandeur again, but where had they crept so we didn't see them in Flederborn? I could have done with them on the last night in Flederborn. Now, looking at them, I involuntarily felt anger towards them: they annoyed me with their actions that were full of bravura and haughty sense of importance.

Looking around for some transport, I spotted my black 'Wanderer' with my driver Corporal J. at the wheel! He'd been wounded in the left arm, just below the shoulder, but was still capable of driving.

We sat in the car with the adjutant and the messenger and I said: 'Drive.' When the driver asked: 'Where to?' I said: 'Keep going until we find a house where we can wash, shave, eat and sleep!'[25]

The previously-unpublished 15th Division war diary in the Rīga archives adds new details as to how the Flederborn road into Landeck was cleared. The Kampfgruppe Hämel was sent to attack the Russians from the Landeck side of the bridge, force them into the forest and resist any counter-attacks. The combination of pressure from

25 Ķīlītis, *I Go To War*, pp.198–199, trans. Aivars Sinka.

both sides – from the remnants of the 15th Division on the forest side of the bridge and the KG Hämel on the Landeck side – led to the encirclement being broken.

Hämel's after-action report of that period, written several weeks later during a rest period, notes:

> The Gefechtsgruppe receives orders from the Corps to take Landeck and push on through Wallachsee and Flederborn in order to link up with the 15.W-Gren. Div (Lettisch Nr. 1) which is encircled at Flederborn. Reconnaissance shows that Landeck is heavily occupied by the enemy.
>
> After an attempt to take Landeck with a reinforced company fails, Kampfgruppe Hämel, along with the subordinated Kampfgruppe v. Bargen sent from Barkenfelde following mopping-up operations there, receives orders to take Landeck and establish a strong bridgehead on the western bank of the Küddow.
>
> Landeck is taken in a night attack on the night of 1–2 February and, in the face of heavy enemy resistance, a small bridgehead is established on the western bank of the Küddow. An operation to expand the bridgehead on 2 February fails.
>
> On 3 February the enemy attacks the Landeck bridgehead and the southern part of Landeck several times with strong forces. Attacks are mopped up with the exception of a small incursion into the southern part of Landeck. At 15:00 the first elements of the 15. W.-Gr. Div. D. SS (Lettisch Nr. 1) reach own [our] lines having broken through from Flederborn. This development is exploited to expand the bridgehead.[26]

Casualties were high. Countless numbers of soldiers were killed; many were wounded, missing or lost. Hundreds of horses lay dead and 80 percent of the vehicles had been destroyed. One account from the 15th Fusiliers 'Recce Battalion' tells of heavy losses when they were sent to clear the enemy from higher ground between the railway line and Flederborn village. By the time they had done this, there were only 'tens of men' left alive from a unit that started out 650-strong.[27]

Men from a penal battalion from Rīga were used in the final assault too, according to chaplain Kazimirs Ručs.

> An officer from the Special Assignments Battalion, Ltn Prūsis, led the final breakthrough to Landeck and about 16:00 on 4 February an even more depleted battalion made its way through Landeck to Krummensee where the men were billeted in Breitenfelde Manor.[28]

---

26 Regiment Hämel after-action report 27 March 1945. Reproduced with permission of the Latvian National Archive, trans. Tom Fane. Reproduced in full in Appendix IV.

27 The Latvian 'Green Books', vol. 6, p.171.

28 Ručs, *Dzīve ar Dievu*. The penal battalion – or 'Special Assignments Battalion' – was made up of prisoners and deserters drafted in Latvia in summer 1944 and sent to Germany that October.

At 16:20 on 4 February, the 15th Division War Diary records, Division HQ was set up in Landeck at the positions of the Kampfgruppe Scheibe. Ax ordered Alksnītis to collect all the Latvian parts of the division and go to Peterswalde. A collection commando stayed in Landeck to gather scattered troops and follow Alksnītis. The supply vehicles were driven to the area north of Breitenfelde towards Hammerstein. SS-Stubaf. Scheibe was left to defend Landeck with the 48th Regiment and the surviving troops of the various units that had been on the road. Division HQ was moved to Krummensee.[29]

Artilleryman Laimonis Ceriņš, who had been wounded on the road, was among the Legionnaires who crossed into Landeck.

> It was about 22:00 when we crossed the bridge into Landeck village. It was dark and difficult to walk. I'd given my rifle to someone else so I didn't have that to lean on. I was holding onto the carts. There was a big German refugee cart, a really big wagon. I was holding onto the side of it. There was a German on top of the wagon telling me to clear off. It was two days before I got to a first aid post: that was in Landeck, at a school.
>
> He [the doctor] wanted to load me into a medical car on the railway but I refused. I said: 'No. I'm not going.' The Russians had cut the line and we'd be stranded. I wanted to move with the units. He gave me some sort of injection and told me to see my doctor in my unit. I kept quiet and did nothing. It was another three weeks before I could walk. I was wounded on 2 February. Two days to get treatment: 4 February, back to unit [at Hammerstein] on 5 February.[30]

The battle to clear the road into Landeck had taken 11 hours. The final full-frontal Latvian assault on the Red Army roadblock into Landeck from Flederborn took a terrible toll in lives, but, combined with the actions of the Hämel and von Bargen battle groups to break the encirclement on the Landeck side, at least some men survived to tell the tale of Latvia's Golgotha.

---

29 The order reads: (Remaining parts I. and II/J.R.59, Kampfgruppe Joachim, Kp.Veit, Festungs. Gr.W.Btl.22. The gen.Flak-abt.661 [anti-aircraft section] is attached with the Kgr.Scheibe. I./A.R.15 along with 5 le.FH. subordinated to the Kgr.Scheibe). Breitenfelde and Hammerstein are Sierpowo and Czarne in modern Poland.
30 Interview with author.

13

Colonel Janums at Flederborn and Landeck

As one of Latvia's military heroes, the after-action memories of Colonel Janums in his self-published autobiography *Mana Pulka Kauju Gaitas [My Regiment's Battle Journey]* shed light on the chaos all around the 15th SS Division as the soldiers prepared to fight their way out of Jastrow towards Landeck. By this time relations between the Latvian commanders and German officers had become fractious, heavy weapons were scarce and ammunition was running low.

On the orders of Adolph Ax, Janums was to hold Jastrow and protect the rear of the column as it moved to Flederborn.

13:00, 31 Jan: The divisional commander [Ax] informs squadron commanders about the present situation and delegates orders. The enemy has gone through Deutsche Krone with great force and continues to attack in the direction of Polzin, with Pr. Friedland already taken.

The German 51st Infantry is defending Jastrow. Their 1st Battalion is defending positions on the west bank of the Küddow river on both sides of the road from Jastrow to Schneidemühl. The 59th German infantry have taken the high ground (hillocks) one kilometre north of Jastrow to safeguard the town from the north. Flederborn is defended by the German 48th SS, although reports are that the enemy has them completely surrounded.

The divisional commander orders my regiment to take over and organise the defence of Jastrow, giving us in addition the German 51st Infantry I and II Battalions but command of this unit will remain under Divisional Command (artificially done so the 51st Infantry wouldn't be under my command). Direct support is to be provided by a German 88mm anti-aircraft battery, which has taken up a position one kilometre south-east of Jastrow station.

The 34th Regiment commanded by Lieutenant Colonel Vīksne has to go to Flederborn and replace the German 48th Regiment. Both regiments have to jointly establish communications with German forces in Hammerstein, in Neustettin district. The 34th Regiment is supplemented by the remains of the 32nd Regiment led by Major Alksnītis.

Cover of Colonel Vilis Janums' self-published war memoir *Mana Pulka Kauju Gaitas [My Regiment's Battle Journey]*. (Picture: author)

As divisional reserve, the 15th Recce Battalion will remain in Jastrow, with the KG Joachim fighting group and a German mortar unit. There is not much enemy activity in the Jastrow area. My regiment has been in non-stop action the previous week, so I want to keep them in reserve in Jastrow. I divide the men into two companies.

About 15:00 the 34th Regiment begins moving towards Flederborn. The leading units are greeted with heavy cannon fire. The enemy has already taken the rises, which stretch parallel along the road at a distance of a kilometre, and the road is continually under fire from tank shells. The 34th Regiment wagons turn back to Jastrow.

This is bad news for me as it means the road to the north is not free for our retreat. We only got into Jastrow this morning and already the enemy is not far behind us: we are still surrounded. Conditions were good in Jastrow though: there were lots of empty houses so the soldiers could spread out in comfort and get some rest.

The 1st Company went back the next day, 1 February. The enemy had blocked the road with three tanks east of Jastrow at Dorotheenhof. Lieutenant Bonoparts destroyed one and the other two disappeared. There is great uncertainty as to what lies west of Jastrow so at 07:00 I sent out reconnaissance patrols under Sergeant Siliņš to clarify if there were enemy forces in the direction of Brizenitz. At 10:00 the commander of the 51st German infantry battalion reported that about 1,000 enemy soldiers coming from the south-west had crossed the Jastrow-Betkenhammer [Ptusza] road at the railway crossing and entered the forest south of Jastrow. Shortly after that, the 1st Battalion commander reported that small enemy groups had bypassed his defence positions.

I sent out patrols to check this and they came back saying they could find no enemy in the forest and there were no signs in the snow of 1,000 men going into the forest. At 13:00 Sergeant Siliņš returned to say that the forest four kilometres north-west of Jastrow had been taken by large enemy forces. As a result I gave orders to strengthen the defences to the west of the town. At the same time reports came in from the 51st Regiment II Battalion commander that a strong enemy force with vast superiority had attacked Betkenhammer at 12:00 forcing the II Battalion to withdraw towards Schonwalde.

At 15:00 I ordered Major Lazduzieds to attack in the direction of Betkenhammer with two companies and for the German 51st Regiment to support him by blocking the road 2.5 kilometres south-west of Schonwalde and keeping in constant touch with my attacking II Battalion.

Major Lazduzieds reaches the railway viaduct north of Schonwalde to find the German II Battalion withdrawing towards Jastrow. Major L. clarified the order to support him, but the German avoids carrying out the order. I notify the divisional commander and postpone the attack. At my request the divisional commander dismisses the German battalion commander from his post. A German anti-aircraft battery takes up positions to the right and left of the road by the railway viaduct.

At 21:00 the enemy attacks Schonwalde but is repulsed. We set up a command post and billet the 4th Company reserves in a house west of Jastrow station. The German 59th Infantry was north of Jastrow at this time, where the enemy had taken the high ground one kilometre west of the Jastrow to Flederborn road and blocked the road with fire from there.

At 09:00 on 1 February the divisional commander orders the 15th Division Reconnaissance Battalion to attack and expand the defence area, throwing the enemy back northwards. I send a German infantry company and a mortar unit, but these men are completely untrained and without aiming devices. The artillery battery can help, but there are only six shells left.

I send the 59th Infantry to gather as reserves on the north side of Jastrow after our Recce Battalion commander Pomrehn has gone through. Pomrehn decides to clear both sides of the road and reach Tiefenort, which he does by 19:00. After taking the railway crossing west of this village he sets up defences and gathers weapons and ammunition from the enemy.

At 03:00 on 2 February the 59th Infantry relieve the position and the Recce Battalion heads back to Jastrow for some rest, but they have to go back and save the situation at 08:00. In an attack an hour before, the enemy has re-taken Tiefenort and the 59th is retreating chaotically.

The Recce Battalion attacks at 09:00, pushes the enemy out and takes the high ground north-west of the village and makes contact with the 34th Regiment units which are defending Flederborn. The high ground is held until 22:00 when my regiment takes over.

At 02:00 on 2 February reports come in that the German 51st infantry I Battalion are retreating chaotically under fire to the east of Jastrow and that the battalion commander has been killed. There is no leadership and the soldiers are just fleeing pell-mell. It's chaos.[1]

---

1   Janums, *Mana Pulka Kauju Gaitas,* pp.169–174.

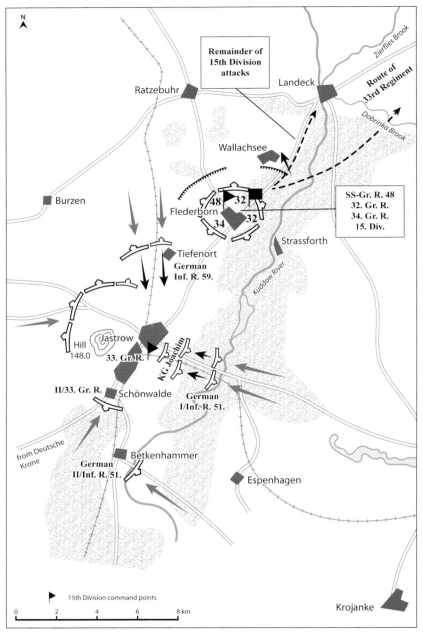

N

Zierflies Brook

Route of 33rd Regiment

Remainder of 15th Division attacks

Ratzebuhr

Landeck

Dobrinka Brook

Wallachsee

SS-Gr. R. 48
32. Gr. R.
34. Gr. R.
15. Div.

Burzen

48 32

Flederborn

34 32

Strassforth

Tiefenort
German Inf. R. 59.

Küddow River

Hill 148.0

Jastrow

33. Gr. R.

KG Joachim

II/33. Gr. R.

Schönwalde

German I/Inf. R. 51.

from Deutsche Krone

German II/Inf. R. 51.

Betkenhammer

Espenhagen

15th Division command points

0   2   4   6   8 km

Krojanke

Adaptation of a hand-drawn map by Colonel Janums showing blocking positions first at Jastrow with Kampfgruppe Joachim and the 51st and 59th German Infantry, then his progress to Landeck. He moves off the road into the forest before Wallachsee and heads for the north-east of Landeck, thus avoiding the final and very bloody Latvian assault on the Soviet roadblock into the town. (From Janums' autobiography *Mana Pulka Kauju Gaitas*)

Janums continues:

> I'm given an under-strength unit of Kampfgruppe Joachim men so I send them to attack in the general direction of the Jastrow to Flatow road and reclaim the earlier 51st Infantry positions. Bonoparts takes the eastern side of Jastrow to secure the town against a sudden attack, and also to stop German soldiers fleeing to the rear.
>
> At 05:00 I go to the command point at the Joachim positions to check on progress. On the way I come across our I Company positions. Bonoparts, acting independently, has taken 15 men and gone to recce in the direction of the Küddow river. By the time I get to the Joachim positions, the time set for the attack has passed, and nothing has happened.
>
> There are a number of SS officers at the post, who one after another disappear into the night. It's an awkward position. Joachim explains that he has postponed the attack as he was waiting for Bonoparts to come back. It seems to me that he was looking for an excuse not to start the attack. I go back to my car and observe preparations for the attack to start.
>
> I've been standing there for about 20 minutes when a burst of machine gun fire comes from the Küddow bridge. After that there are a few more bursts. It's so sudden I can't tell if they are German or Russian guns, but most of my 1st Company have Russian guns anyway. I'm straining to hear and then I get an instinctive feeling that someone or something is approaching from the north. Is it my men or the enemy? It's my men … and I am very happy to see them.
>
> Lieutenant Bonoparts reports that he came across an enemy patrol not far from the river Küddow. He called to them in Russian, then fired a few rounds. Four Russians were killed: the rest ran away. Bonoparts took their documents and weapons. This bravery has an effect on Joachim's men. At about 07:00 in a chain they begin to move to the Küddow bridge, but coming across the enemy they take up positions on the east side of Jastrow. The enemy doesn't attack and Joachim's men stay here until the retreat begins.[2]

Colonel Janums was a very experienced and skilful soldier, having fought in the First World War first as an artilleryman then as a machine gunner with the Latvian Riflemen. He was called up to the Red Army in the period of Soviet control of parts of Latvia in 1919 but deserted, instead joining the Latvian Army and fighting in the battles for independence. He joined the General Staff in the interwar years, then built a reputation on the Russian Front in the Second World War for some miraculous escapes from Red Army encirclements. In his autobiography he describes the way the battle for Jastrow developed:

02 February: Battle on the south side of Jastrow involving II Battalion, 33rd Regiment

2   This is the bridge on the road out of Jastrow bearing the plaque.

About 06:00 my 4 Company relieves 8 Company and takes up new positions on both sides of the railway line by the viaduct, together with a German anti-aircraft battery. About 08:00 the enemy opens fire on the old 8 Company positions. 4 Company repel the attack. There's a second attack at 09:15, this time under cover of smoke from smoke grenades. This attack is repelled again, strongly supported by the AA battery.

At 10:30 the battery changes position to the south side of Jastrow. As they are moving the enemy attacks again, and without the support of heavy weapons the company is forced to withdraw. The enemy takes the viaduct. Major Lazduzieds orders 8 Company to take positions SW of Jastrow and for 4 Company to hold Jastrow station.

The end of the battle for Jastrow

At 10:00 on 2 February the 15th Division HQ leaves Jastrow to move to Flederborn to organise a breakthrough to Landeck. The head of HQ, Sturmbannführer Wulff, tells us that large enemy forces are moving through Deutsche Krone to the north. The road to Landeck has been cut at Wallachsee, the 32nd Regiment have been unable to take Strassforth and the operation to take Ratzebuhr has been a failure.

The 32nd Regiment attacked from the north and by the evening of 1 February has reached the Landeck-Dobrinka river line at Preußische-Friedland [now Debrzno]. HQ will now transfer to Flederborn together with the 34th and 32nd Regiments to organise the breakthrough to Landeck. My regiment is to stay in Jastrow and hold it as long as possible, before withdrawing to Flederborn.

I tell the divisional commander that it's impossible to get away from Jastrow in daylight without heavy losses and that I want to try and hold on till nightfall. He wishes us good luck with this task, and leaves.

At the same time as the Divisional HQ left, so did the German 51st Infantry – without their battalion commander notifying me. I've now lost two battalions that were under my operational command.

At 12:00 the situation in Jastrow is this:

- Jastrow east side positions: Kampfgruppe Joachim
- Jastrow station to Height 148: II Battalion, 33rd Regiment
- Height 148 to Vucke river: Regiment HQ and 13 Company
- Tiefenort and heights to the west of this village: 15th Div Recce Battalion. The regiment is still supported by the German AA battery.

At 13:00 the enemy renews its attack and takes Height 148. Shortly before dark the enemy reaches Jastrow station. I send in my last reserve, 1 Company.

At 17:00 I give the order that we will pull out of Jastrow at 18:30. I Company is to hold the viaduct at the south-west end of the town until 19:00. 13 Company is to hold the woods at the south-west edge of Jastrow one kilometre north-east of the town until 21:00. HQ Company is to hold Tiefenort. Then we will join the regiment in Flederborn. Our main strength is the German AA battery and my 4 and 8 Companies.

Under cover of darkness the retreat goes well, and the last units leave Jastrow at 22:00.[3]

Janums includes a dramatic description of those last few hours by Private First Class [Dižkareivis] H. Magrics.

A strong south-west wind, carrying a huge lapful of rain clouds, falls across the hills of Jastrow, trying to penetrate as deeply as possible into the snowy, white peace. The darkness, thick and heavy, lies over the restless wind, hiding our positions and machine gun nests, which have been primitively built due to the lack of suitable tools.

'These are cursed times!' The tall guy swears, looking for his dinner portion in his bread bag. 'Stop complaining, you'll have to bear it anyway,' lectures a hefty Vidzeme guy fiddling with his pipe. 'Won't you ever stop lighting up?' someone else complains, noticing the pipe in the Vidzeme guy's hands. 'Let Ivan come,' the smoker retorts self-assuredly and crawls into a snow-hut that had been swiftly dug out to give some shelter from the wind and rain, which has made the hillside black and sticky.

The quiet is oppressive across this sector of the front, which winds its way threateningly all around the mountains and forests of Jastrow. Both nearby and in the distance, the enemy has crept up to our position, trying with its murderous hands to overcome the tenacity of men tired from the previous days of battle. In vain!

In spite of everything these men still hold on, even though they are over-cold and over-tired from these past days. And even in this stormy evening there is only one thought: to hold off the enemy with its enormous superiority of numbers, to allow the other units of the division to clear and recover the route of the retreat, which has been cut off by enemy units.

So far, it has succeeded. Two days and nights have been passed in these hills. We still have to endure this last Jastrow night and the following day, then the units will start to retreat. Time passes slowly in the rain, cold and dark. Someone is raving in his sleep, shouting out broken commands, then jumps to his feet and hurries to the machine gun. Someone else is hopping from one foot to the other to get warm, because the cold soaks through wet clothes. The morning is approaching ever so slowly.

Then a rocket blossoms up. One, two, three. Slow seconds slip by. It bangs, the air moans, then the ground trembles and wobbles. Nature's restlessness is compounded by man-made unrest. And in this unrest, cold and fatigue are suddenly forgotten. The men are back at their machine guns, whose barrels

---

3 Janums, *Mana Pulka Kauju Gaitas*, pp.176–179.

are menacingly facing the enemy. 'Come on! We'll cope!' grunts the guy from Vidzeme, grabbing the handle of the machine gun.

And they come … In the morning half-light, it's hard to get a proper view over the chains of men. But anyway, we know there's a lot of them. Our machine guns bark brightly and sharply. The first enemy chains fall onto the soggy ground, but others follow.

'To the last cartridge, boys!' orders the company commander. And the men understand these words. To hang on until the road will be free! But they come and come.

And then, clenching their teeth, the boys rise up and go forward against these chains of the enemy. It helps. There are hundreds left lying on the field, but the rest run away.

With the advent of the new day, their attack was eliminated. The wind breaks up the clouds. The greyness of Jastrow's nights sinks behind the hills. The front is silent again for a moment. But the men know they will still try to come today.

'We'll cope!' the guy from Vidzeme says and stuffs his pipe, because you need a thorough smoke after a fight like that.[4]

Arriving in Flederborn, Janums was not impressed to find all escape routes still blocked, a situation he blamed on the 'indecisiveness' of Ax, the divisional commander. As a seasoned soldier and always a man to seize the moment – successful till now – Janums put a plan forward:

Due to the unwillingness or inability of Division HQ to organise a breakthrough I take it upon myself to take action. I send my adjutant out from Flederborn with a recce squad and wait in the forest 1.5 kilometres south of Wallachsee. Regiment HQ [company] takes up position at Tiefenort, and the II Battalion also returns there. The situation is very uncertain and I am worried the enemy will surround my men.[5]

Together with Special Assignments officer Esis we go back to Tiefenort. The car has disappeared so we can't go by road. Instead we head over fields through deep slush. The artillery fire hasn't reached Tiefenort and HQ Company have held their positions. Also there is 13 Company, waiting for the enemy fire to stop.

We gather all the men together and go back across the field to Flederborn. When we get there we find Div. HQ has already left. We find the 34th Regiment commander and tell him I have withdrawn my troops from Tiefenort and will break through towards Landeck.

4 Dižkareivis H. Magrics, *Jastrovas Naktis* in Janums, pp.179–180, trans. Aivars Sinka. Janums added the pen name 'Eriks Sala' as this was possibly used in a previous publication where he found the passage.

5 Janums describes the position as an *'uztverošo poziciju'* – a blocking position.

3 February:
By 07:00 we are approaching Wallachsee. About 1.5 kilometres south of the village we find Div. HQ in the forest by the road. It turns out that when the bombardment of Flederborn began, Div. HQ together with all the wagons and transport vehicles that were on the road raced forward, but hadn't got further than this corner of forest, as the enemy was blocking the road with machine gun fire.

An enemy anti-tank gun had taken up a position in the bend of the road and had shot up several vehicles. On the road here and in the forest there were people from Div. HQ, soldiers from various companies, horses, carts and in among them the divisional commander and HQ leader [Ax and Wulff].

Even though they had been there since midnight, they had still not organised a breakthrough. As there had obviously been no action from HQ, I presented myself to the divisional commander and requested permission to organise a breakthrough.

I gave orders for Lieutenant Freimanis and 13 Company to circle round Wallachsee and attack from the west while Major Lazduzieds gathered all the other soldiers with HQ Company to attack the road from the forest.

Around 10:00 when my men have begun to move, Div. HQ changes the task, ordering the 48th SS to free the road and instead for my men to secure our right flank east of the road to a distance of between 1.5–2 kilometres. An hour passes before I can gather all the men together. We have to wait for the 48th SS as they are still not ready.

I move HQ Company to the side of the clearing in order to take up our positions. I can see the area quite well. Not far from us, probably on the road, there is an enemy mortar team and an anti-tank gun, which doesn't touch us. We wait for the 48th SS. The forest is very big, and probably the enemy hasn't had time to set up more comprehensive defences. I'm trying to think of possibilities, and the men are tired.

It's 12:00 when our units finally start to move. My orders are for 13 Company to move along the east side of the road and for HQ Company to go through the forest between 1.5–2 kilometres east of the road. Both companies move into the forest, move parallel to the road and then cross the Küddow on the ice about two kilometres from Wallachsee. My men find Dr Eggert badly wounded in the forest. We sit him on my orderly's horse and I tell them to move him carefully. About an hour later the orderly says the doctor can't manage to sit on the horse any more. We lift him down and lay him on some pine needles.

By now I think we should be near the frontline, so I send out a patrol. They come back in 20 minutes with news: the Dobrinka river is about half a kilometre away on the other side of a field in which ponies are grazing. I go to check. The southern side of the river is hidden in a thicket of fir trees, so I conceal myself there and survey the opposite bank. The ice has melted but the water doesn't look too deep. There is another field about 200 metres wide and, on the other side of the small gorge the river is in, there is more forest. I notice that the ponies in this field are small Siberian horses, which is proof that the enemy is nearby.

I use my binoculars to scan the forest but there's no sign of movement. I send an order for the battalion to move carefully towards the river bank but to stay in the forest and cover a patrol crossing over the river and the open field, aiming for the forest on the other side. The patrol scares the horses, and they gallop off towards Landeck. We don't see or have any contact with the enemy. When we all reach the forest, we rest. The mood of the men has improved: we found a hole in the front!

We continue marching towards Wusters, reach the road crossing three kilometres south-west of Peterswalde and by late evening we reach Krummensee. For the core of the Division which moved along the Flederborn to Landeck road the breakthrough was much harder. The 48th SS had taken Wallachsee in a surprise attack. The road remained blocked at Landeck but the Div. chief of staff [Wulff] used all the remaining soldiers in a head-on attack. It worked, but there were heavy casualties.

Among them were Chief of Staff Wulff, 32nd Regiment commander Rubenis, Division communications chief Sturmbannführer Dostmann and a large number of soldiers. All the medical wagons got through but the vast majority of horses and carts didn't. Units which broke through surrounding areas made it to Krummensee, where they rested. Many soldiers have frostbite on their hands and feet; many are ill. They were taken to field hospitals. There are only 650 men left in the regiment.[6]

6   Janums, *Mana Pulka Kauju Gaitas*, pp.181–184.

14

Landeck:
the 15th Division's Golgotha

Even now almost eighty years later there is still uncertainty about what actually happened in the slaughter and carnage of Flederborn, Wallachsee and Landeck. Reports of the possible execution of 400 young Latvian conscripts in the Landeck forest on 3 February 1945 warrant further research. Dr Dzintars references an article in the veterans' journal *Kaŗa Invalīds* [*War Invalids*] by Alberts Eglītis that describes the mass killing of the 400.[1]

Eglītis subsequently wrote about the incident:

> It makes you shiver what happened in the Landeck forest after the battle at Flederborn, where, on the 3rd February 1945, 400 unarmed, tired, hungry young Latvian conscripts surrendered to a Red tank unit. Over the next two days, they were split up by those who took them prisoner and all shot and just left under the fir trees.[2]

Those who escaped the road of slaughter were not allowed to rest long. At 07:00 on 4 February, Soviet troops crossed the Dobrinka river three kilometres south of Landeck, threatening the road to Peterswalde [Pietrzwałd]. Battle Group commander Sigmund Scheibe ordered a company to clear the forest on the northern banks of the river to make the way safe to Krummensee. Latvian reinforcements arrived before lunchtime but by mid-afternoon it became clear they had little training and no machine guns. With a battle group of survivors from his regiment, Colonel Janums was sent to stop Russians troops bridging the Dobrinka two kilometres to the east of Landeck 'at all costs.'[3]

Augusts Kikāns, a veterinarian with the 15th Division, was part of the move to Krummensee.

---

1   *Kaŗa Invalīds*, issue 43, page 60.
2   *Daugavas Vanagu Mēnešraksts* No. 3, 01 July 2005.
3   Extract from the KTB [war operations diary] for the period from 01–12 March 1945 compiled by 1st Leutnant Pape, Latvian National Archives, Rīga.

At last the Russians in Landeck were pushed out by the German Hämel unit. The Russians had left the village and moved into the surrounding forests, from where excellent work was done by their snipers. After the break-out the squadron marched on to Krummensee. Here we began to pull together the squadron carts.

On 4 February until about 02:00 I collected together about 16 horses and carts and about 60 men. That was all that was left over. We reached Krummensee at 04:00 on 4 February. First I found the dressings point, because the carts were full of wounded. When I asked the dressings point doctor where I should put the wounded he said: 'Have a look. Wherever there's a free place.' I found another two houses which were full of wounded too. The less badly-wounded carried out their dead comrades. Then I went to look for the Division HQ, but I couldn't find it.

At last I found a room with a light on. At the door I met Captain Maiers. He was looking for the Division Commander too, so we went in together. At a table sat a small bald-headed old man in a jumper with a boyish Lieutenant [Pape]. Captain Maiers introduced himself and announced that he'd just arrived with his battalion. Then the little man stood up, breathed out and said: 'Ax' and shook hands with the captain. Then he sat down, cleared his throat and seemed surprised: 'So. Battalion? Where have you come from?' The Captain told him.

Ax turned to the Lieutenant:

'So, what should we do with him? Shall we send him to Landeck II?'

The Captain said his men had already found quarters in a barn and added: 'So we could stay here.'

Ax looked at the Lieutenant questioningly, who nodded his head.

'OK, then stay here. You will receive orders tomorrow.'

The Captain said goodbye and in turn I introduced myself and asked where my squadron headquarters was. The Divisional commander looked at the Lieutenant questioningly again. He looked at him. They had no idea where the 34th Regiment HQ was.

At last I found squadron HQ and I asked the Adjutant where I should put people and horses. He told me to find anywhere that it was free. It was the middle of the night, and it was dark. On 5 February the wagon column had to make its way to Hammerstein. Lieutenant Kummermanis led the way.

In Hammerstein there was a Latvian gathering point, led by our Captain Maeders, who was now an SS Sturmbannführer. They put us in blocks and said that we're now under his orders, as the 15th Division and the 34th Grenadier Regiment didn't exist anymore.[4]

At the conclusion of his account of this period of battle, 34th Regiment commander Jūlijs Ķīlītis reflected on the losses.

---

4   Ķikāns, the Latvian 'Green Books', vol. 6, pp.140–142. Maeders was one of the German officers who had commanded the regiment in October 1944.

The break-out from the encirclement near Landeck was successful for all the units; however, with heavy losses. About half were lost, including killed, injured and missing in action. After we counted the people in the 34th Infantry, it amounted to just one full battalion.[5]

Adding Polish historical sources to Latvian, an incomplete but very different picture of events in and around Podgaje-Flederborn emerges to that commemorated there officially. A conservative estimate of the possible numbers of Latvians killed between Jastrow and Landeck [Jastrowie and Lędyczek today] is in the region of 5,000 dead or missing, with 832 Polish casualties. This figure does not include civilians, German or Red Army casualties. The very general figures compiled in Table 1 (below) could be considerably higher.

Who were the civilians, and what happened to them? They may have been fleeing from towns and villages north of Deutsche Krone [Wałcz] and south of Jastrow ahead of the Soviet and Polish push west targeting Freudenfier, Rederitz and Stabitz as the weak spots in the Pomeranian Wall.[6] They may have been Baltic Germans, re-located under the terms of the Molotov-Ribbentrop Pact, and thus not considered 'Polish', rendering investigation into this incident beyond the remit of modern Polish investigators.

Then there are the prisoner killings by all sides and the alleged Red Army execution of the 400 Latvian teenage soldiers who had surrendered in the forest at Landeck, as yet unverified but akin to a massacre of innocents if true, plus the 'NKVD-style' murder of 600 more unfortunate Latvian RAD conscripts at the barracks in the village.

A grim and very bloody picture is building up.

Table 1. Estimated Death Toll Jastrow-Podgaje-Flederborn to Landeck 31.01–4.2.45

15th Division units on the road between Jastrow and Landeck	
32nd Regiment: Lieutenant-Colonel Celle, Major Rubenis, Major Alksnītis, Major Siliņš 1,763 were in training camp on 22nd January. After removing the *tross* (wagon train that went to Stettin – assumed 160), Siliņš and his *stabs,* possibly between 20 and 50 men who reached Neubrandenburg and the 456 who stayed in Sophienwalde, there is an assumed strength of 1,127 men who might have retreated with the 15th Division to Landeck. *GB6 (Latvian Legion official history 'Green Books' p.76) says that when Alksnītis went to Peterswald on 4 February, he had gathered together approximately 160 men left from the 32nd Regiment.* Based on that, assume 967 dead or missing in the period Nakel-Jastrow-Landeck (eleven days from 24.1–4.2.45) **Casualty figure at Immenheim, Nakel to Jastrow then 617.** Assumption that by 31 January there are 350 soldiers left of the 32nd regiment in Jastrow: 240 with Alksnītis (GB6 p.75) and the rest with Rubenis or mixed up with other units. If 160 were left after Landeck, this means the loss of 190 on the road between Jastrow and Landeck.	**Estimate 190 dead or missing**

5   Ķīlītis, *I Go To War,* p.200.
6   Świecja, Nadarzyce and Zdbice in modern Poland.

33rd Regiment, Colonel Janums One incomplete battalion was left at the Sophienwalde training camp. *GB6 (p.319) says 1,600 left camp, received 900 reinforcements after Landeck and on 23 February had a strength of 1,410.* So 1,090 were either killed, missing or wounded in combat at Nakel, Jastrow, Flederborn and after Landeck. The 33rd was the rearguard at Jastrow, so would have borne the brunt of attacks from 31.01–2.2.45. Janums said to Ķīlītis when he reached Flederborn of the German command: "Those animals completely destroyed my regiment." Assume split in 1,090 casualties between Nakel (300) and Jastrow to Landeck (500), and 290 in actions to 23 February including Kamin (totalling 1,090).	**1,090 dead, missing or wounded from Nakel and Jastrow-Flederborn-Landeck and Kamin. Estimate 500 killed Jastrow to Landeck.**
34th Regiment, Major Ķīlītis Reported 'one full battalion left, about half killed, wounded or missing in action' Estimate 50 percent casualty rate = 700 men Estimate 35 percent casualty rate = 490 men *p.132 GB6 says the regiment had 2,800 at the beginning – "the full complement" but only about 1,400 went into battle on 22 January.* *p.139 GB6 says that they had the following casualties since Nakel: 135 fallen, 335 missing and 245 injured. 13 officers and 386 others got out of the encirclement.* That leaves 500 men unaccounted for. Assume a 50 percent CR = 250	**1,400 went into action 470 dead or missing and 245 injured Possibly 720 dead or missing?**
15th Fusiliers 'Recce' Battalion commanded at that time by Major Pomrehn *GB6 (p.175–176) gives the numbers setting off as 595. There were only 'about 50' left after Tiefenort. (p.190 says "a few tens of men")*	**Significant casualties. Estimate 550 dead or missing**
15th Division Transport column Supply/logistics regiment (organised like a regular regiment) *p.287 in GB6. They had two squadrons of drivers plus a repair company and a supply company. They reported to I.b. in the HQ.* *p.290 GB6 describes how, right at the beginning on 27.1.45, they were ordered by Wulff to create a reconnaissance fighting unit at Zempelburg. They were shot up by two tanks, losing 39 men out of 42. The text describes Wulff's order as "not thought through".* *p.290 describes how the initial order was to hold Jastrow to the last. Also, that there were 800 injured in Jastrow.* *Numbers of soldiers isn't given when they start out. However, when the Division is reinforced at Neustrelitz after Kolberg, the strength is given as 2,000 in the regiment. The text also says that they suffered less than the fighting units – that the first squadron of the regiment suffered most.*	**Not known, but may include the 400 drivers who panicked south of Flederborn.**
15th Artillery Regiment, Wallachsee-Landeck *One "Divizion" of four batteries was sent towards Nakel, about half the complement.* *p.220 GB6.*	**200 casualties, lost 300 horses, 80 per cent of their transport and their guns**

Other 15th Division units Communications – *no overall figures given. But must be multiple hundreds, because the radio company alone had 100 conscripts attached to them. At Jastrow, 60–70 communications soldiers were formed into a battle group.* Sappers – *possibly a full battalion. No overall figures given, but the December reinforcements to the training camp alone were 475 men. It suffered grievously in the days prior to Jastrow. GB6 p.258 says that on 28 January they only had 53 left. A whole company disappeared at Nakel. They were formed into a battle group and participated in the fighting at Wallachsee and Landeck seconded to a battle group, (Kampfgruppe Scheer).* Anti-tank unit (plus one anti-aircraft company) – *2,000 were added to a group of existing officers and NCOs, presumably after the fighting in Russia. This group left for Danzig in August 1944 and later received further reinforcements. No accurate figures of casualties, but the GB6 p. 274 says that there were "a few hundreds" of fallen left on the battlefield.* Feld Ersatz Depot – *some of these soldiers were assigned to Divisional units prior to Jastrow, but most weren't involved. Assume 200.* 15th Division's 'battle school' – *200 men under Captain Wally. They participated in Flederborn/Landeck* Special Assignment battalion (Prūsis' penal battalion) – *no mention except at the Landeck battle* Other units: veterinary, sanitary, etc *GB6 gives establishment figures from 23.2.45 for 33rd (Janums) of 39 officers, 200 NCOs and 1,171 men, and 34th (Ķīlītis) of 39 officers, 194 officers and 836 men. Figures for other units are in an appendix that is not reproduced.*	**Casualties not known Assume 200.** **Estimate 400 minimum** **Estimate 300 fallen + 200** **+35 percent CR = 75** **+ penal battalion, vets, sanitary etc**
Reports of 400 RAD recruits used as drivers from Ax's HQ Group executed in the forest by a Red Army tank unit on 3.2.45	**400**
600 Latvian RAD/Legion soldiers executed 'NKVD-style' at Landeck barracks 4.2.45	**600**
800–1,000 Latvian wounded on wagons (500 at the lazarett in Jastrow Jānis Čevers cleared, 300 at the school in Jastrow and wounded from Flederborn that were caught up in the encirclement crossfire outside Wallachsee) – Estimate 50 percent fatality – Estimate 75 percent	 **450** **750**
Estimate of dead and missing in action **Executions in forest and at Landeck barracks** **Total estimate of possible Latvian dead or missing Jastrow to Landeck**	**3,785–4,085** **1,000** **4,785–5,085**
800 Polish LWP killed or wounded in action at Flederborn (IPN figures)	**800**
32 Polish 4th Company men executed at Flederborn	**32**
Polish dead	**832**
German units The **Dutch 48th SS Regiment**, commanded at Podgaje-Flederborn by Friedrich Träger and used to attack and clear Wallachsee: *As a fighting unit, estimate casualties as similar to the 33rd.* The **German 51st Infantry**, which slipped out of Jastrow ignoring Janums' orders to stay and defend it. The **German 59th infantry**, posted as snipers in Flederborn on 30.1.45. Facing tanks and armoured cars, they would certainly have been outgunned. Sent to capture Tiefenort and forced out. **Kampfgruppe Hämel**, which broke the encirclement from the other side of the bridge at Landeck, supported by **KG von Bargen** and **KG Scheibe**	**Not known** **Not known** **Not known** **Not known**

Soviet non-Polish forces	Not known
Estimated death toll of Latvians and Polish, not including Red Army, German Army, SS and refugees	5,617–5,917

Table compiled by author and Aivars Sinka from the Latvian Legion 'Green Books': Freivalds, Caunītis, Bērziņš, Kociņš and Hāzners (eds). *Latviešu Karavīrs Otra Pasaules Kaŗa Laikā [The Latvian Soldier During World War Two]*, vols 1–11 (Västerås, Sweden: Ziemeļblāzma, 1979)

The Latvian National Archive in Rīga, where the 15th Division war diary is held. (Picture: author)

I am reading microfiched pages from the 15th Division's War Diary at the State Archives in Rīga. The boss has given me permission to photograph the files to translate later. The War Diary was lost for six decades and surfaced in Belgium in 2006. Presumably it was sold or swapped by a former soldier at the camp at Zedelghem where many thousands of Latvians were sent in the immediate post-war period. It was offered to the archive, which recognised its value and bought it. Written in German, it has never been published in English.

I load up a microfiche. The heading reads **KRIEGSRANGLISTE** (War Ranking). This record is dated 12 April 1945 when the unit stopped to rest after making it across the Oder. They are taking stock of numbers. Some men have been missing since Landeck and Flederborn. These are casualty/unit strength figures for the Artillery Regiment.

Mannschaft [unit strength]: auf 20.1.45 = 108 (on 20.1)
auf: 3.2.45 = 56
auf: 7.2.45 = 145
auf: 12.3.45 = 122

Among the following pages, one has the heading: **VERLUSTLISTE** (List of the Fallen). This page is dated 18 April 1945 and lists the dead from the Artillery Regiment from 22 January until 12 March, taking in action at Landeck, Wallachsee, Flederborn, Kolberg, Klein Küdde and Ost-Dievenow. I look through the pages, taking photographs as I go.[7]

It's quite sad, seeing a list of names of men and the place of their death: Landeck, Landeck, Wallachsee, Landeck, Landeck … There are the names of 37 men on one page alone. The next page is the 1st Battery of the Artillery Regiment. I count 85 dead.

71.	1.	Battr.	W-Kan.	Zaksis Ernests	8.12.23.	3.2.45.	Landeck
72.	1.	"	-"-	Zorge-Zorgevics Otto	2. 1.11.	-"-	-"-
73.	1.	"	-"-	Zuze Gunārs	19. 4.26.	-"-	-"-
74.	1.	"	-"-	Rostoks Arturs	26.12.14.	-"-	-"-
75.	3.	"	-"-	Baginskis Verners	1o. 4.25.	-"-	-"-
76.	3.	"	-"-	Butka Jānis	11. 9.26.	-"-	-"-
77.	3.	"	-"-	Aizpuris Meinhards	22. 6.12.	-"-	-"-
78.	3.	"	-"-	Bieberis Arnolds	2.11.14.	-"-	-"-
79.	3.	"	-"-	Boneparts Arvids	8.12.26.	-"-	-"-
80.	3.	"	-"-	Buls Staņislavs	14. 1.1o.	-"-	-"-
81.	3.	"	-"-	Eiduks Antons	12. 5.21.	-"-	-"-
82.	3.	"	-"-	Galītis Arnolds	6. 6.23.	-"-	-"-
83.	3.	"	-"-	Graudiņš Raimonds	3o. 5.23.	-"-	-"-
84.	3.	"	-"-	Gulbis Alfreds	5. 3.11.	-"-	-"-
85.	3.	"	-"-	Kapteinis Roberts	1o. 3.25.	-"-	-"-
86.	3.	"	-"-	Kimerāls Kārlis	4. 3.12.	-"-	-"-
87.	3.	"	-"-	Kozelis Aleksejs	1o. 2.13.	-"-	-"-
88.	3.	"	-"-	Landrats Verners	9.6.21.	-"-	-"-
89.	3.	"	-"-	Lūsis Andréjs	13. 6.12.	-"-	-"-
90.	3.	"	-"-	Kadars Alfreds	16. 3.12.	-"-	-"-
91.	3.	"	-"-	Ošās-Osis Gunars	24.12.25.	-"-	-"-
92.	3.	"	-"-	Ozoliņš Elmārs	7. 3.11.	-"-	-"-
93.	3.	"	-"-	Ozols Voldemars	23.11.25.	-"-	-"-
94.	3.	"	-"-	Pauns Jānis	23.1o.24.	-"-	-"-
95.	3.	"	-"-	Poikāns Jānis	-	-"-	-"-
96.	3.	"	-"-	Priedītis Jānis	3.4.13.	-"-	-"-
97.	3.	"	-"-	Pulksis Jēkabs	9.2. 2o.	-"-	-"-
98.	3.	"	-"-	Pupa Kārlis	4. 6.13.	-"-	-"-
99.	3.	"	-"-	Pudāns Jāzeps	2o. 3.2o.	-"-	-"-
1oo.	3.	"	-"-	Putniņš Imants	15. 9.25.	-"-	-"-
1o1.	3.	"	-"-	Putrs Jēkabs	5.1o.19.	-"-	-"-
1o2.	3.	"	-"-	Ragowskis Staņislavs	11.1.26.	-"-	-"-
1o3.	3.	"	-"-	Ruiga Kārlis	8. 8.26.	-"-	-"-
1o4.	3.	"	-"-	Samlajs Oskars	23.1o.26.	-"-	-"-
1o5.	3.	"	-"-	Silenieks Jānis	24. 8.24.	-"-	-"-
1o6.	3.	"	-"-	Slavietis Arnolds	19. 8.13.	-"-	-"-
1o7.	3.	"	-"-	Strādnieks Alberts	16. 8.2o.	-"-	-"-

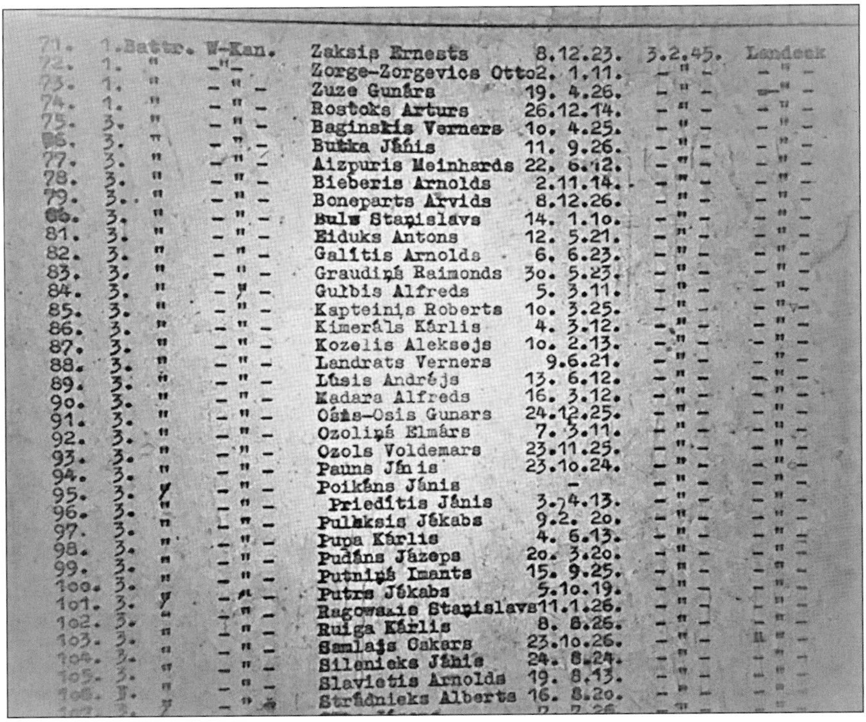

A list of Landeck dead from the 15th Division war diary. Photograph of microfiche archives, 15th Division War Diary, Latvian National Archives, Rīga. (Picture: author)

7 File reference: A1588/55–56 [file nr. 296-1-34]. Ost-Dievenow was the final rearguard action on the Baltic coast to enable the Latvians to cross the Oder.

I insert another microfiche and slide it along until I come to words I recognise. Flederborn. Landeck. Wallachsee, Plocsic [Ploetzig]. The names of the places and the family names of the casualties are double-spaced between each letter – presumably for clarity amid confusion – which is a style also found in the diaries of Žano Mūsiņš.

A list of soldiers who were 'proven' at Landeck. Photograph of microfiche archives, 15th Division War Diary, Latvian National Archives, Rīga. (Picture: author).

These are typewritten lists of men of the 3rd Battery of the 15th Artillery Regiment (1 Latvian Artillery Regiment) who 'proved themselves' during this mission.

V e r z e i c h n i s [Directory]
Über soldaten, welche sich während des Einzatzes besonders bewahrt haben
[about soldiers who have proven themselves during the mission]

2.2.45. F l e d e r b o r n

Name	Date of birth
W-Ustuf Bebris, Arvids	14.1.14
W-Hscha Saulitis, Jānis	5.10.14
W-Hscha Birks, Manfreds	3.3.10 (listed elsewhere as killed 3.2.45 at Wallachsee)
W-Kan Bērziņš, Alfreds	20.04.15
W-Kan Lapins, Arturs	11.12.20

3.2.45. L a n d e c k

W-Ustuf Bisenieks, Žanis	9.12.11
W-Hscha Bakis, Eduards	24.1.15
W-Hscha Dzintarnieks, Gustavs	18.12.02
W-Hscha Zalcmanis, Peteris	9.6.04
W-Kan Tutans, Alfons	8.7.26
W-Strmm Kaulins, Imants	22.12.24
W-Strmm Alekss, Jazeps	18.9.21 (also listed killed on 11.3.45 at Putschow)
W-Strmm Baumanis, Imants	17.11.21

3.2.45. W a l l a c h s e e

W-Ustuf Gulbinskis, Jānis	8.1.17 (fell 3.2.45 at Wallachsee)
W-Hscha Bakis, Eduards	24.1.15 – (also listed at Landeck)
W-Strmm Neijs, Eriks	23.6.20
W-Kan Osmanis, Peteris	9.7.12
W-Strmm Spuntelis, Valfrids	25.12.22
W-Kan Vanags, Jazeps	30.12.11

12.2.45. P l o c s i c

W-Hscha Reagalis, Leonids	26.2.13
W-Hscha Bembers, Voldemars	25.7.17
W-Uscha Ilens, Aleksandrs	21.10.13
W-Uscha Vanags, Arturs	11.8.24

I keep scrolling through the microfiche. In a list compiled on 18 April 1945, the regiment appears to be coming to terms with the scale and intensity of the past three months.

> V e r l u s t l i s t e [List of losses]
> 22.1.45 bis 12.3.45 – 1. Gefallen [The fallen between 22.1.45 and 12.3.45]

There are many names from Landeck, Wallachsee and Flederborn of men who died in that catastrophic 24-hour period between 2–3 February, and several from before that at Dorotheenhof on 29 January and Karnowko three days earlier. One man is

Landeck – now Lędyczek – is a small village with the church of St Peter as a focal point. There are reports of 600 teenage Latvian reserves being executed 'NKVD-style' at a barracks in the town. (Picture: author)

listed as fallen at Kolberg, a siege the Latvians managed to avoid or escape from. The names of the dead go on for pages at a time. Most of the men named as 'having proved themselves' appear to have died fairly soon after this recognition. The diary curators have even microfiched sketch maps and hastily-written orders dashed off in pencil on scraps of paper. Even though the dead were left behind, the officers got their men out – and this is how.[8]

Landeck, known today as Lędyczek, looks to my untrained eye like an old country village nestling around a good-sized red brick church on the main road about 10 kilometres from Podgaje. Outside the church is a small grassed area with a stone memorial topped by a cross. The surrounding houses are squat, solid single-storey buildings with lofts, some with paint peeling from weather-beaten facades, others topped with red roofs. Some have not had much recent attention. The roads between them are wide and open. The Dobrinka river – more of a brook – flows nearby. It seems not much has happened here for a long time. The church has been repaired

8   Heavy casualties are also recorded on 13 February at Wordel, 27 February at Sparsee and Klein Küdde, then again on 11 March at Pustchow in the battle to get to Dievenow and across the Oder. Author's research visit to the State Archives, Rīga, 22 November 2019. Files A-1589/2 [296-1-36].

using European money, with brick patches evident in the tower. Around it are wide streets with solid-looking buildings: it's the kind of place that looks like it might need a concerted effort to take. There are no monuments that I can see to events here in early February 1945.

Žano Mūsiņš was at Landeck and told me about it at his home in Coventry. His diary of combat experience reveals how intense the fighting was.

> Our units tried to force the Landeck river, but received terrific fire from mortars, heavy machine guns and anti-tank fire. We are forced to dig in and spend eight hours under fire without getting anywhere. We manage to withdraw in the night.

Prompted by his diaries, we talk through his memories. I ask him how he spent eight hours under fire.

> ZM: Quite simply, you put your head down and wait. That's all you can do.
> VH: So you find a foxhole and crawl into it?
> ZM: You were lucky to get a foxhole. This is February and the ground is frozen. It's too hard to dig a fox hole. We were lying on flat ground and you were lucky to have a hump in front of you. If it's a ploughed field you have little humps and you can hide behind them.
> In war not everything they shoot at you hits the target. There's stuff flying all over the place. If you lift your head up one of them will get you, so you don't! You don't have a choice. While the hell is going on around you, you just stay put. When it eases off you might get up and have a look around and see what you can do but otherwise you don't.
> VH: How about making a run for it?
> ZM: After eight hours you don't get up and run. Your limbs are so stiff and frozen that you have to start moving [slowly] otherwise you could do yourself harm.

I read from his diary.

> We receive [an] order to attack Landeck village with all available force. The Russian line gives way because from the other side they were attacked by the German tank division *Deutschland*. So for the first time we can breathe again but only because the German HQ wanted to save their own division which were also with us.

He continues with the story.

> ZM: The Russian lines were attacked by the *Deutschland*. They were a hell of a force: very little could resist them. They pushed the Russians towards us and the Russians didn't stand a chance. They were simply milled down

between the two forces. That was [us] out of the Big One: Landeck. That one the whole division was in. The rest of it in Pomerania was just [us] running from the Russians all over the place.

We were saved because they wanted to save their own division. That was the breakthrough that got us out. The Germans didn't owe us much. They only sent the *Deutschland* in to break the encirclement because there was another German division in there with us. I can't remember the name of it now.[9]

He continues:

There were all sorts of units in there. We tried to keep our units intact but most of them were scattered everywhere. There was the Army Group *Wisla* [Vistula] – they were directly under Himmler – a couple of regiments, the size of a corpus. Because of them they broke the encirclement so we had an opening to get out, otherwise we would have had our chips. We lost a hell of a lot there. After all the Landeck battles there were only about 17 of our company left alive. Some of them could have been scattered and joined other units but the core of the company [which survived] was only about 17 from 120. I'd say at least 35 to 40 percent were killed in the forest between Jastrow and Landeck.

That's the worst place you could ever have a war in. The shells are exploding above you so you can't lie down; the shrapnel is coming down like rain so you have to stand up. You can't stand up because then you're a target for the machine guns. We got really milled down in that forest. That's why we had such big losses there, because it was a really deadly situation.

When people say: 'Do you believe in God' I say: 'I do.' Because God is the only one who could make me survive all that hell without a scratch. It makes me wonder why others got hit and injured and I never had a scratch, anywhere.

VH: People say the ones who weren't in the thick of the action are the ones who survived, but you WERE in the thick of the action.

ZM: It just happened. There's no way you can describe it. Landeck was what they call the soft belly of that particular time where we could get out. Otherwise with the encircling we'd all have been finished there. It could have been all of us wiped out. That was the first time I met Colonel Janums. Our unit was with Colonel Janums' regiment. They were the solid ones. They were the only ones who had 88mm guns. I joined them later. Any time you needed tanks moving from somewhere Janums sent his lads in. The 88mm gun took a tank out with the first shot.

---

9   Possibly the 48th Dutch SS General Seyffardt, volunteers who became the 23rd Nederland Division, later sent to defend the Oder then annihilated at Halbe. Led by Major Rubenis, who was killed in the action, the 32nd Regiment bore the brunt of the fighting at Landeck bridge. Post-war correspondence with unit veterans reveals they believed they did not get enough credit for what they did.

He [Janums] was the only one whose regiment was always ready for battle. How he could organise them so well I don't know. They had losses like everybody else, but they had minimal losses. He just had this ability.

He was always close to the frontline: I don't know how the hell he didn't get killed. It was hell on earth. Mostly we tried to move at night because the Russians didn't fight much at night. The main fighting was usually during the day. One of us had a Panzerfaust and if the tanks came too close, without being too careful, it was their fault. Once you're within about 50 metres the Panzerfausts were deadly – you're out. The infantry would dig in, hide, stay under cover and if the tank got too close and didn't spot the danger in time they'd stand up and fire off the Panzerfaust. It was a rocket-propelled thing and you just pressed the trigger and that was it.

You know the tower on the tank? If you got it right it usually knocked the tower right off it. It had a hell of a power. I don't know what was in it, but once you got hit by that you didn't stand a chance. They were T-34s we took out.[10]

Latvian military historian Valdis Kuzmins has studied what happened in Landeck and is critical of the decision-making that sent many men to their deaths there.

By the end of January the Latvians understand they are encircled and have to break out: the 15th Division has a couple of German units attached as well, including one Waffen-SS unit. In Landeck there was the 32nd German Infantry Division waiting for them to give them a helping hand. That division had been moved a couple of days before from Courland. They had been fighting in Courland for a long time and in the middle of January they were shipped to Pomerania. So were the 4th Panzer Division – another Courland division.

So in a way the story that Hitler wouldn't allow troops to be evacuated from Courland is false. The 15th Division is actually a beneficiary of that. Hitler allowed it. If not, the 15th Division would have been gone. All of them.

From October 1944 to roughly the last days of the war there were about 15 divisions transferred from Courland to mainland Germany: some went to Königsberg, some to Berlin, like the 11th Nordland SS. They unloaded at Gotenhafen and got on trains. The Germans surprised themselves at how quickly these troops could be moved about.

In the early days of February 1945 we have the Polish Army and the Russian 2nd Guards Cavalry Corps north and south of the Germans and Latvians, east and west. Each wants to go in different directions, everyone feels encircled and in trouble. The Poles want to connect with the Russians: the 15th want to connect with the 32nd. It's like three-dimensional chess – and then add winter, night, shelling, bad communication … there was not going to be an easy way through. The big problem was the wounded who couldn't walk and the difficulty of moving vehicles along those roads. There are accounts of hundreds

10 Interview with author, Coventry.

The main street at Landeck-Lędyczek. (Picture: author)

of vehicles being stuck on that road: trucks, horse-drawn wagons, everything. There was no way they could move through the woods.

Who was responsible for clearing the roads so the vehicles could move through? The person who drew up the plan was the chief of staff of the 15th Division, Wulff, but he died in an attack on Landeck. The commander of the [15th Division's] 32nd Regiment Fridrichs Rubenis was killed as well. Janums, the commander of the 33rd Regiment got through the woods, as did the commander of the 34th Regiment, Ķīlītis. I've read some accounts that aren't published that those guys who escaped were actually supposed to be leading that attack. But Janums wrote that he wasn't responsible for that: Rubenis was. There's no way we'll know the truth about what the plan was.

But what we do know is that hundreds of wounded men ended up on this road being shot to pieces. That was the tragedy.

Having taken Landeck and halted the Soviet offensive across Pomerania, the Latvians prepared and reinforced defensive positions. This had been a disastrous week of shattering blows for the Legion, with vast numbers of dead and wounded. In Krummensee they re-grouped and recovered from their injuries. Many men were treated for frostbite. The 32nd Grenadiers lost the equivalent of one battalion before Jastrow and the rest on the road: the 160 survivors were merged into the 33rd and 34th Regiments. There were now only two artillery batteries, not four: the 1st battery had three guns and the 3rd had two. Reinforcements were sent in from the reserves in Toruń. What was left of the division was sent to defend the banks of the Dobrinka brook between Landeck and Prutzenwalde [Prusinowo].[11]

The official details about what happened in Landeck are vague in English language versions of history, even today. Valdis Kuzmins has his own thoughts as to why there is no definitive account of that battle:

> I've never read a good account of what happened in Landeck itself. Wulff was killed, Rubenis was killed and none of the men who were there wrote accounts. My feeling is that those guys didn't want to write anything because they'd have to ask the question: 'Where's everybody else?' And that's why they decided: 'Leave me out of this!'

There appears to be no definitive figure of how many men died in the fighting and chaos at Jastrow, Flederborn, Wallachsee and Landeck, whatever their nationality. Valdis Kuzmins believes there was a consensus among Latvian officers involved in recording what happened:

> The way the Germans and Latvians counted their dead was later, when the combat was over. Then the questions are: 'When did you last see X?' and it becomes a puzzle. Who is wounded, who is missing in action, who is in hospital, who escaped? One battalion commander was court-martialled by the Germans.[12] The Latvian officers after the war did not want to talk about it. I've read some of the letters and there are definitely some things that were not talked about, and those being private letters they are no more than rumours, really. You can't use it as a source. The War Diary is a poor example and there is information missing.
>
> After the war when the Latvian officers wanted to write an after-action account, they left things out that didn't look very good. I believe they said: 'We must now stick together and not blame our fellow Latvians, even though there is a case. The war is over – let it go.'[13]

Three officers were recommended for Knight's Crosses for their courage at Landeck. The regimental commander of the Dutch SS Panzergrenadiers, Siegfried Scheibe was one, as was 15th Division commander Adolph Ax. One award was posthumous: for SS-Sturmbannführer Erich Wulff.[14] Whether these decorations are valid is an issue, as they are dated 09 May 1945 – the day after the German capitulation.

Ax was no stranger to frontline soldiering, having won the Iron Cross First and Second Class in the German military campaigns of 1940, and then taking part in the invasion of Russia in 1941 before steady promotion to be chief of staff for General

---

11 Pencz, *For the Homeland,* p.235 and Silgailis, *Latvian Legion,* p.169.
12 Sturmbannführer [Major] Mārtiņš Siliņš has the distinction of being the only Latvian commander court-martialled. See Appendix III for further details.
13 Interview with author, Rīga, 27 November 2019.
14 Pencz, *For the Homeland,* p.235.

View of Landeck, now Lędyczek, approaching from Flederborn, now Podgaje. (Picture: author)

Carl-Maria Demelhuber, commander of the Waffen SS *Niederland*. Demelhuber became head of the Command Staff in Mecklenburg, and repeatedly promoted Ax, eventually to command the Latvian 15th SS.[15] Then came Nakel, Vandsburg, Flatow and finally the disaster of the 15th Division's 'Golgotha' – Jastrow, Flederborn and Landeck.

The citation for Ax's Knight's Cross reads:

> On the 25.01.1945 SS-Oberführer Ax, chief of staff for the XIV SS-Armee-Korps was assigned command of the 15. Waffen-Grenadier-Division der SS (lett. Nr. 1) following the loss of its previous divisional commander. SS-Oberführer Ax went on to achieve the following in the course of the Division's many subsequent offensive and defensive actions:
>
> 1. Breaking through the encirclement ring around his Division near Flederborn on 03.02.1945. The Division had been encircled here due to its own steadfastness, but by holding its ground in this way it tied down strong elements of two tank-reinforced Soviet divisions and prevented the enemy from continuing their swift breakthrough towards the north-west.

---

15 Compiled from Feldgrau.net, Traces of War and Axis History Forum (https://www.axishistory.com/).

2. Directing this breakthrough in the face of strong Soviet forces whilst serving with the rest of the divisional staff in the foremost line.

3. Dispersing and destroying the bulk of a Soviet division before the bridge-head and cornerstone at Landeck during the process of this breakthrough.[16]

Although Ax as commander got them through, the Latvian historian Visvaldis Mangulis noted that the entire chapter is notable for the harsh treatment meted out to the men from the Baltic and their comrades-in-arms as the Red Army moved across Pomerania.

> The Soviet advance was marked by extreme brutality toward both soldiers and civilians. For example, in Wugarten the American prisoners of war witnessed the rape of women of all ages and the murder of sixteen. The Fusilier Battalion also discovered the bodies of several Latvian soldiers and of civilians captured and then gunned down by the Reds. Dozens of Latvians in the construction regiments at Thorn [Toruń] were murdered by the Russians when captured. However, such treatment was not confined to Latvians; for example, all Russians from the Vlasov divisions were shot as soon as captured.[17]

There were big gaps in the ranks and command structure of the 34th Regiment after Landeck which needed to be filled urgently. On 4 February men were drafted in from a punishment battalion led by Captain Meijers which had been in Germany since October digging trenches and building defences. That would be I Battalion, made up of 13 officers, 73 NCOs and 369 soldiers and billeted in Gut Amalienruh Manor. The next day Major Mežgrāvis took command of the former Rīga Police Regiment which had just arrived, which would be designated as II Battalion, with 13 officers, 104 NCOs and 413 soldiers, billeted at Krummensee. Soldiers in the reserve who had combat experience were used to strengthen the Reconnaissance battalion.[18]

Another month's hard fighting lay ahead for the Latvians, but this was far from the end of the catastrophe for Flederborn, lying as it did on roads west to the Oder, Stettin, Küstrin and, if possible for those travelling west along them, beyond. German

---

16 Traces of War website, Adolf Ax pages online at <www.tracesofwar.com /persons/28147/ Ax-Adolf.htm>, accessed 09 March 2021.

17 V. Mangulis, *Latvia in the Wars of the 20th Century* (Princeton Junction: Cognition Books online at <http://old.historia.lv/publikacijas/gramat/mangulis/09.nod.htm345>, 1983), pp.294–298. The Vlasov divisions were Russians, mostly former POWs and White Russian exiles, who fought against Stalin under the command of former Red Army general Andrey Andreyevich Vlasov, who had been captured at Leningrad in 1942. He turned Nazi collaborator and formed the Russian Liberation Army in 1944.

18 The 'Green Books', vol. 6, pp.141–2. The men of the 'Recce' Battalion would find themselves in the centre of Berlin at the death of the Third Reich defending key locations like Gestapo Headquarters to the end. After the war Jānis Meijers (1901–1989) went to live in Adelaide, Australia, where he died.

accounts from the 1970s and 1980s referenced in the Latvian press suggest that the fighting in Flederborn did not end with the capture of the town by the Red Army.

A week after the Latvians left, according to these accounts, 320 trainees from a German cadet officer school fought almost to the last man against the 1st Polish Cavalry brigade, with the deaths of 2,400 Polish soldiers. When the town finally fell, the Poles (or Russians according to one of the two accounts) murdered every male in the town from babies to old men, including all the wounded Germans. The writer also cites details from combat of Russians tying German women onto tanks so they weren't attacked with Panzerfausts.[19] In nearby Preussisch Friedland, the Red Army attack was repulsed on 29 January 1945 but the town fell in a second attack on 20 February. Around 70 percent of the town was destroyed in the fighting.[20]

Contemporary historical researchers looking again at the region's Second World War history are uncovering a story quite different from the official accounts. With translator Jacek Cielecki, Arnold Koslowski is making the memoirs of Latvian commanders Vilis Janums and Jūlijs Ķīlītis available in Polish to bring what he hopes will be 'a new perspective' to the way these events are understood in Poland.

> I was born and raised in Wałcz (Deutsch Krone). The battle for the Pomeranian Wall – Wał Pomorski – was fought in this area. It is 30 kilometres to Jastrow, 45 kilometres to Złotów (Flatow) and 40 kilometres to Podgaje (Flederborn). I've known the stories about the battles of the soldiers of the 1st Polish Army (1 AWP) since I was a child. Every summer I went to a scout camp in Podgaje.
>
> For several years, I have been presenting the battle of Wał Pomorski as a clash of two sides rather than a 'liberation' – which is how it is still thought of. I want to change it. Lots of people want to change that and get to know the real story. Although I admit that not everyone is ready.

Arnold says that in Flatow and Jastrow, the Latvians fought with soldiers of the 4th Infantry Division; conscripts, with the highest average age in the entire 1st Polish Army. The senior commanders were Russian: many of the men could have served in the Polish resistance movement.

> The Russians did not entrust them with important tasks: it was primarily an army for propaganda purposes. Many soldiers did not have much experience in combat. The junior officers had only recently graduated from officers' school. Many mistakes were made in the fighting. Morale wasn't high. There were large losses, with many killed and wounded, which are attributed to the fierce fighting

---

19 Article Treji Vārti, Nr. 76 online at <periodika.lv> dated 01 May 1980 citing Erich Murowski: *Die Eroberung Pommerns durch die Rote Armee* and Hans-Edgar Jahn: *Pommerz Passion*.

20 In the summer of 1945, the town was given back to Poland under the Potsdam Agreement and renamed Debrzno. The German population was expelled, with Poles re-settled in their place.

and a strong opponent. The whole 'art of war' of the Red Army assumed that a soldier was the least important because he could always be replaced by another.

Of course, in the course of the fighting, the soldiers acquired skills and experience. The 4th Infantry Division commander General Kieniewicz, was strong, did not have high losses and was successful – he captured Wał Pomorski (the Pomeranian Wall), and Kołobrzeg (Kolberg).

The massacre of the 32 prisoners among so many dead at Podgaje-Flederborn was picked up by the NKVD's political officers as the Red Army and the 1st Polish Army began to cross into Germany for the final assault on Berlin. It became politically useful, Arnold says:

Finding the burnt bodies in the barn ruins at Podgaje was an opportunity that was used very well. The Poles, as a nation, were tired and exhausted from five years of war. But they wanted to defeat the Germans and liberate their homeland.

But war in enemy territory is something else. The soldiers received information from across Poland about the activities of the new communist authorities and about the activities of the NKVD. No-one knew if it would be possible to return home after the war – a lot of soldiers came from the area occupied by the USSR in September 1939, east of the Curzon Line. The soldiers were not well trained, the young ones did not have much experience, the old ones were tired of the war. In direct combat, they encountered a trained and good opponent, who, however, defended his home. You defend the area you occupy differently and you defend your own home differently. Even when you are a Nazi.

The Polish divisions were exhausted from their strenuous march from the Vistula line, day and night, on foot, in severe weather conditions with strong wind, snow, frost. Fuel supplies to vehicles were interrupted. The infantry regiments went to the front with only a few heavy weapons in support.

A number of mistakes were made at each level of command, from the staff planning the 'March-Manoeuvre' operation to tactical errors at the level of company commanders. The inexperienced army suffered heavy losses, which added to the lowering of fighting spirit. This could lead to a deep crisis, and the 1st Infantry Division had fought very hard since its first action at the Battle of Lenino a year earlier, in 1943. The division never regained full combat capability.

Maybe you don't want to fight in a foreign land, with a strong opponent, maybe you want to go home, maybe you want to finish the fight because you are already tired … but if the war becomes your personal revenge because your mates were killed, then you will fight mercilessly until the very end.

The massacre at Flederborn was used to build a strong narrative to motivate the military for a long and brutal fight, even though Polish troops had not been involved in this part of the fight to a great extent.

Time was important here. The next report from Podgaje is dated 15 February and it clearly states that the prisoners were tied with barbed wire and burned alive. But it does not indicate Latvian soldiers as the perpetrators. The writer talks about 'German soldiers.'

This report is signed by senior political officers. It was created after the end of the hard phase of the fighting, breaking the Pomeranian Wall. Then it was time to use this for propaganda agitation.

Arnold has also gathered estimates of the scale of the combat here, and tales of what happened next in Flederborn when the fighting eventually stopped.

> In the Flatow-Jastrow-Flederborn area, the losses of the 1st Polish Army are about 1,400 soldiers killed, missing and wounded. In the Flederborn area alone, the losses of the 1st Infantry Division are 811 soldiers – 233 killed, 58 missing, 520 wounded.
>
> The wounded were evacuated to field hospitals. The dead were buried in the war graves in the area of the fighting – the burnt remains of 32 soldiers were buried in Flederborn, they were not fit for transport. Over 300 bodies were buried in the war grave in the village of Grudna [Strassforth] east of Flederborn, near to the Evangelical Church. In the mid-1960s the remains were exhumed and buried at the Flatow War Cemetery. Those buried in Flederborn were exhumed and buried at the War Cemetery in Drawsko Pomorskie [Dramburg] in 1953. In the fighting area of the 1st Polish Army we are discussing, there are also the War Cemeteries in Szczecinek [Neustettin] and Wałcz [Deutsch Krone], the latter being the largest military cemetery of Polish soldiers. There are plaques and monuments in the places where the fighting happened.
>
> Local historians have told me that most of the bodies of the German, Latvian and other Axis soldiers killed in the battles in the Flederborn-Landeck region were practically unburied until 1947. There was simply no-one to bury them. The townspeople fled or were killed. There were not enough survivors to handle the numbers of dead. New settlers [from the east] buried bodies and human remains in random places and most often … threw them into the Gwda River.[21]

At Krummensee there was little escape from the realities of war for the Latvians. Ruthless discipline was meted out by German officers to set examples to the men under their command. One 97-year-old veteran, Legionnaire Arturs Grava, then a teenage RAD conscript, shared his memories of German justice at this time by e-mail seventy-seven years later.

> On 11 February 1945 near the town of Schlochau in West Prussia, two Latvian Legionnaires were ordered to be shot in front of 500 fellow soldiers, in order to maintain discipline. I witnessed this shooting. I was too far away to hear the accusation being read: according to another witness, they had stolen two cans of tinned food from an abandoned German house.

---

21 Arnold Koslowski, correspondence with author, August 2021.

This was at a time when there was virtually no supply, and units of German soldiers wandered through abandoned houses and shops in search of food. I remember that all I had eaten that day was half-cooked beans, the cooking of which was interrupted by an order to go to the place of execution. We were sent to Hammerstein on the same day.

In the same e-mail, Mr Grava makes clear his dim opinion of Adolph Ax, who first said he understood the Latvians were fighting for a free Latvia, then later that they volunteered to fight for Hitler. He concluded his account of the executions with the words: 'I am writing this so this event will not disappear from the history of the Legion. Please forward it to the historian Dr [Karlis] Kangeris or another researcher of the Legion's history.'[22]

One final insight into the events on the road to Landeck comes from Arvīds Arājs, who served as the communications leader in Colonel Janums' 33rd Regiment. After the war, when he was being held with 11,000 Latvian as 'disarmed enemy forces' in Zedelghem in Belgium, he wrote of his friend Fridrichs 'Fricis' Rubenis, who was appointed commander of the 32nd Regiment two days into the campaign, following Lieutenant Colonel Pauls Celle's nervous breakdown.

On 25 January we started fighting the Russians – me as the leader of communications in Janums' regiment, Fricis at the head of the 32nd Regiment. After the first heroic and bloody battles we met again on 27 January. These three days had passed quickly, but we had already experienced many moments of terror in that time. We discussed them sitting down in some Polish village. Fortune, so far, was with us.

The horror journey of the 15th continues. The first encirclement on 30 January by Dorotheenhof, then Flatow, then Jastrow. The whole division is surrounded. Fricis sets off with his regiment to make the break out towards freedom in the Flederborn-Landeck direction. Janums' regiment as the covering unit stays in Jastrow. We stay there until the evening of 2 February, then leave for Flederborn and then a bit further towards Landeck. Russians are both in front of and behind us. We have to spend the night in the forest so that we can start the break-out in the morning.

The dawn of 3 February breaks. We start working. At 09:00 – 'see you Fricis … See you.' Each has their task to do. Today we have to get through Landeck. The attack starts. By the evening, we are out of the siege. The soldiers of the 15th gather together again.

The preceding days were bloody. The furnace at Jastrow, Flederborn and Landeck has claimed many Latvian boys as sacrificial victims. They sacrificed themselves, so that the others could escape the claws of the Russians. We gathered together, but Fricis, too, isn't with us. He led his regiment against Landeck

---

22 Arturs Grava, correspondence with Daugavas Vanagi, forwarded to author and used with permission 19 January 2022.

bridge, and there, it seems that Lady Fortune had too many people to look after. For a brief moment she had turned her back on him and the bullets of our most deadly enemies erased the life of the heroic leader of the regiment – Major Fridrichs Rubenis. He had only one week at the front.

But what's left of that 15th Division that left Sophienwalde on 22 January? Maybe half, maybe not. But the battle-march through Pomerania has yet to be completed. In front of us were still Kamin, Petersvill, Sparsee, Hammerstein, Grunvald, the Horst seaside, Hoff and Dievenow.

Latvian boys and men in these places gave what was most dear to them – their lives – while cutting great gashes into the flesh of the 'Red monster.' Their eyes shone with great heroism. But what was the heroism for? For freedom? Not yet. It was for revenge, for payback.

Payback for the sacrificial victims that the Red devil took in 1941. Payback for the blood of our brothers in Courland. Was this heroism worth the lives of the heroes that were left in the fields of Pomerania? Let's not ask that now. The wheel of history has turned and pulled our fates with it. And, just like the heroes of Courland, the heroes of Pomerania – Latvians – did their job with just one slogan – FOR LATVIA.

We'll remember that sometime, as we think about our friends and country-men who fell on these sacrificial altars. Let's be proud. They died so others could live.[23]

23 Arvīds Arājs, memoirs 1945, from Museum of the Occupation of Latvia archive, trans. Aivars Sinka.

Part Three

The Road to the Sea

15

Schneidemühl, Deutsche Krone and the Pomeranian Wall

Dusk quickly becomes night as I drive south to Schneidemühl, now known as Piła. In 1945 the city was a cornerstone of Hitler's Pomeranian Wall defences and a key target for Polish forces in the Red Army offensive. Piła was literally obliterated in that battle, and, as it is the nearest big city to Flederborn, offers me the chance to pause and reflect on how the Second World War changed this region. To my right the setting sun floods the forest pines with a reddish glow, while the lakes and golden fields to my left still bask in the late afternoon summer sunshine, at least for now. My bed for the next two nights is on the seventh floor of a 12-storey tower block on a roundabout on the ring road. It's topped with masts, aerials and a neon sign advertising itself: Hotel Gromada.

The roads around the Gromada are lined with vast districts of flats in all directions. They are all different shapes and sizes. Some rise vertically, some are built around a courtyard, some are long and low – all have their numbers painted prominently on the outside. While the living areas are quite intense and dense, there are large parks lined with trees along big wide boulevards. My room has full-length windows looking out across the town, and the sunset behind the flats in front of me is magnificent. I look out in admiration at what Communist town planning can achieve: a strictly-proportioned and choreographed system of urban flats in deck access blocks with ground floor-level shops with restaurants and parks. I feel like this is a very Soviet sunset, and of course it is a moment for reflection. Schneidemühl didn't become Piła by accident.

Piła's origins date back to the 13th century, but it became Schneidemühl and part of Prussia in the First Partition of Poland in 1772. Both names reflect its importance as a woodcutting town: Piła means Saw, Schneidemühl means Sawmill. Prussian defeat to Napoleon at the battle of Jena in 1806 meant the town had to be handed over, but it was returned by the Congress of Vienna nine years after the French Emperor's downfall.[1] The Prussians connected Schneidemühl to Berlin and Bromberg by rail

---

1   Website of the Polish Genealogical Society of America at <https://pgsa.org/polish-history/translated-descriptions-of-polish-villages-and-provinces/poznan/> (accessed 26 July 2020).

Hotel Gromada, Piła. (Picture: author)

Sunset in Piła. (Picture: author)

The Pomeranian Wall from the Baltic coast south.

and it became an important European interchange, then in the First World War, a production centre for the Albatross fighter. Then the Nazis extinguished 300 years of Jewish life and traditions in the district as 544 Jews from the town were sent first to the Lublin ghetto and then on to concentration and labour camps.[2] Schneidemühl

2   P. Longerich, *Holocaust: The Nazi Persecution and Murder of the Jews,* (Oxford: Oxford University Press, 2010), p.157.

was then reinforced as a strongpoint at the southern end of *Die Pommernstellung* [the Pomeranian Wall, or *Wał Pomorski*].[3]

In January 1945 Schneidemühl was home to 45,000 people, with two military airfields and the *Albatros Werke* factory now making parts for the new German jet fighter, the ME 262.[4] The city was strategically important and lay directly in the path of the Soviet drive towards Berlin, and Colonel Heinrich Remlinger, a highly-decorated and proven commander, was sent in by Himmler to take charge of the 12,000 strong garrison and defend the city at all costs.[5] His operations officer was Major Karl-Gunther von Hase, whose uncle Paul, the commandant of Berlin, had been executed for his part in the July 1944 bomb plot against Hitler. Major Von Hase was cleared of any involvement, but was posted to defend Schneidemühl.

Remlinger and von Hase set deep defensive lines at the vast railway marshalling yards, with an armoured train and some self-propelled assault guns backing up the seasoned Wehrmacht troops, 6,000 *Volksturm* men and teenage cadets from an NCO school.[6] Civilians were pressed into digging anti-tank ditches and rationing was introduced.[7] Any soldiers who tried to retreat were hanged as deserters, with placards round their neck saying: 'This is what happens to all cowards.' Himmler sent messages of congratulations for such ruthlessness: urged on by Hitler, the Wehrmacht executed 15,000 of its own men for desertion.[8]

There were still large numbers of civilians in Schneidemühl when the Red Army began shelling it in late January. A continuous barrage of mortar fire and Katyusha rockets slammed into the city as the 2nd Guards Army and 5th Shock Army closed in to cut off escape routes. Control of areas outside the city centre tipped one way and then another in heavy fighting with the Soviet 47th Army. There were dramatic encounters in the fighting around the marshalling yards. The German armoured train managed to rescue a whole trainload of ammunition and supplies while fighting went on around it. In another incident, Germans and Russians were plundering either end of the same train simultaneously. The 14 and 15-year-old NCO cadets put themselves in the firing line time and again to help win back ground lost to the Soviets. Von Hase said:

> It was terrible. They tried so hard to be brave. We had to get back lost ground ... so we used them.[9]

On 30 January Soviet tanks closed the gaps in the Red Army ring around the city. Schneidemühl's fate was handed to a special 'liquidation group' so the frontline

---

3   Many of the bunkers in the eastern suburbs are still there.
4   From the article 'Festung Schneidemühl' in *Weapons and War*fare, online at <https://weapon-sandwarfare.com/2015/12/10/festung-Schneidemühl/>, accessed 19 June 2019.
5   From Traces of War website at <https://www.tracesofwar.com/persons/16516/Remlinger-Heinrich.htm>, accessed 26 July 2020.
6   From the article 'Festung Schneidemühl' in *Weapons and Warfare*.
7   M. Hastings, *Armageddon: The Battle for Germany 1944–45* (London: Pan Books, 2015), p.516.
8   R. Bessel, *Life in the Third Reich,* (Oxford: Oxford University Press, 2001), p.63.
9   Hastings, *Armageddon,* p.ccivi.

combat units could press on towards Berlin.[10] Within three days German ammunition was running short.[11] Fresh weapons and food were brought in by Ju-52s flying from Köslin and Stolp, and 1,026 wounded soldiers and 215 civilians were flown out. Trains were sent from Deutsche Krone to evacuate civilians but not enough for the numbers wanting to leave, so people began to walk, despite 50 centimetres of snow on the ground [20 inches: nearly two feet deep] and temperatures of minus 25 Celsius.[12] Hitler's 'no retreat' order meant there was no question of the Germans giving the city up and shortening their frontlines, but one commander did – and lived to tell the tale. Erich von dem Bach-Zelewsky was a high-ranking Nazi and commander of the X SS Corps based in Deutsche Krone, reporting to Himmler, who was then commanding Army Group Vistula. Bach-Zelewsky's unit were forced out of Schneidemühl by the Red Army, then, between 8 and 9 February, routed in attacks by the 1st Polish Army. The frontline had to be restored by combat teams from Army units, and when Himmler demanded he explain why he retreated, Bach-Zelewsky blamed his men.[13]

As the Red Army's siege tightened, endless streams of Katyusha rockets hit the city. Loudspeakers broadcast appeals for the defenders to give themselves up. Remlinger gave orders that 'cowards' be shot as an example to others. At this point, Polish historians wrote:

> …the fights in Piła resembled those from Stalingrad, with fights for individual buildings, basements, floors and even apartments and rooms.[14]

Two hundred Red Army soldiers died in the fighting for the railway station alone. In five days between 9 and 14 February, Polish pilots from the 4th Mixed Aviation Division flew 166 missions against Piła in Ilyushin Il-2 ground attack planes, destroying defensive positions, weapons and equipment.[15] By 10 February the Red Army controlled all but the city centre and relief flights in stopped on 12 February

---

10 Historical accounts online from <www.konflikty.pl> quoting Miniewicz, and Perzyk. (1997) *Wał Pomorski* on Piła history forum at <http://www.forum.dawna.Piła.pl/viewtopic. php?f=12&t=521&start=25>, accessed 26 July 2020.

11 Thread at Festung Schneidemühl forum online at <https://forum.balsi.de/index. php?topic=2189.0>.

12 From the article 'Festung Schneidemühl' in *Weapons and Warfare*.

13 Philip Blood, *Hitler's Bandit Hunters: The SS and the Nazi Occupation of Europe*, (Lincoln, NE: Potomac Books, University of Nebraska Press, 2007), p.277. Bach-Zelewsky was captured by the Americans after going into hiding at the war's end. Despite having overseen the mass murder of thousands of Jews in Rīga and Minsk and 'bandits' in Belarus, the creation of Auschwitz and the brutal suppression of the Warsaw Uprising, he was never charged with war crimes, having made a deal to give evidence against Nazi leaders at Nuremberg.

14 From an article compiled by Pawel Czyzykowski titled *Schneidemühl Fortress 1 – warfare* on the historical forum <www.dawna.Piła.pl> at <https://www.dawna.Piła.pl/czytelnia/ twierdza_Piła_01.php>, accessed 26 July 2020.

15 Historical accounts from <www.konflikty.pl> quoted on Piła history forum at <http://www. forum.dawna.Piła.pl/viewtopic.php?f=12&t=521&start=25>, accessed 26 July 2020.

when the airfield was captured. Von Hase was awarded the Knight's Cross that day for repeatedly leading the counter-attacks in Schneidemühl.[16]

With ammunition running out, Commander Remlinger drew up a breakout plan for the following day. He lined up the remaining artillery, assault guns and armoured train to blast a hole through the Russian lines, then his men split into three groups and shot their way through the Soviet encirclement in the hope of making it to their frontlines 48 kilometres [30 miles] away. Most were killed or captured by Soviet search teams in the following days. Only 1,000 men reached safety.[17] Those not killed on the outskirts of town within the first two weeks went into the forests where they sometimes met survivors of the *Festung* operation at Posen [Poznan] which had fallen on 23 February.

Remlinger and von Hase were captured. The former commander told Soviet interrogators he estimated 4,000 Germans were killed, wounded or captured in the defence of Schneidemühl.[18] The civilian population of between 15,000–18,000 people – even at this moment – was abandoned to its fate. The Red Army entered the shattered city on 14 February triggering, according to historians, a wave of rape and looting.[19] Three-quarters of Schneidemühl was destroyed, with the city centre more or less obliterated. Piła lost its German past when the rubble of 1945 was cleared away, but the destruction gave the architects an almost blank canvas to work with.[20]

The question of whether Piła was 'liberated' or 'returned to Poland' continues to this day on online forums, along with questions about the German heritage that was eradicated: the statues of Emperors Friedrich and Wilhelm around the town, the bust of Bismarck and so on. And while physical reminders can be destroyed, memories cannot. Some historians may argue that oral history is unreliable, but memories are passed on this way when other methods are suppressed or not available. These two messages were posted on the Piła historical forum <www.dawna.Piła.pl> from a contributor in Germany:

> As a German city, Piła was not spared by the Soviets, and in retaliation for the damage done by the Germans in the Soviet Union, everything German was destroyed. Everything that was of any value was taken away, from bicycles to entire factories. German women and girls were exposed to particular cruelty,

16 Hastings, *Armageddon: The Battle for Germany 1944–45*, p.ccivii.
17 Duffy, *Red Storm over the Reich*, p.106. Some of these men may have passed through Flederborn on their way to Landeck around two weeks after the Latvian 15th Division.
18 Remlinger interrogation details from article posted on historical forum <dawna.Piła. pl> quoting interview with Piła district museum historian Marek Fijalkowski at <http:// www.forum.dawna.Piła.pl/viewtopic.php?f=12&t=521&start=25>, accessed 26 July 2020. Remlinger died in a Soviet prison camp in 1951.
19 From the article 'Festung Schneidemühl' in *Weapons and Warfare*.
20 Under the 1945 Potsdam Agreement, the German population was expelled and replaced by settlers from the east, and over the next decades the population rose steadily to the present level of 75,000. From the 2012 population report of the Polish Central Statistical Office at <https:// stat.gov.pl/cps/rde/xbcr/gus/p_population_in_poland_size_and_structure_30062012.pdf>.

and drunk Soviet soldiers repeatedly raped them. One woman in her memoirs put it this way: 'Young girls were made into women, and adult women were made corpses.' Drunken soldiers raped 12-year-old children. Houses and farms were burned so the Germans would have no place to live, although they were forced to stay in these places for over a year.

A second post by the same contributor relates an episode from the liberation of the village of Dzikowo [then Sickau], 150 kilometres to the east, near Toruń:

> Soviet soldiers stormed into the Wolfshof forester's lodge near the village of Dzikowo behaving inhumanly. The family of forester Benno Benzel saved themselves by escaping. The mother-in-law of the forester, jumping from the attic window, breaks her collarbone and is caught up by one of the soldiers. The woodsman shoots him, killing him. The roar of the shot reveals their place and in an act of despair and fearing the cruel revenge of the Soviets, the forester shoots his entire family of six: his wife, daughter, son, sister, mother-in-law and himself. After identification, the bodies were buried in the forest by the Germans.[21]

Accounts like this, relaying personal or family stories or a town's collective memory, are at least once removed from eyewitness testimony and difficult to verify but they convey the desperation to protect loved ones from capture by Red Army soldiers. That sentiment is echoed in multiple accounts from across the region at that time, triggered by reports of atrocities at Nemmersdorf and fuelled by Nazi and Soviet propaganda, particularly by Soviet writer and propagandist Ilya Ehrenburg, who urged Red Army soldiers to kill Germans in revenge for crimes against them by Nazis.

> If you haven't killed a German in the course of the day, your day has been wasted ... If you have killed a German, kill another. Nothing gives us so much joy as German corpses.[22]

The British politician and historical author Alan Clark writes in *Barbarossa* about the Russians 'blazing their trail' across Silesia and Pomerania:

> The Russians soon discovered that the inhabitants were hiding their womenfolk in the cellars of their houses and adopted the practice of setting fire to the buildings they suspected were being used for this purpose. An incendiary shell from a T-34 proved the quickest way to assemble the occupants for scrutiny.[23]

21 Message boards at Piła historical forum www.dawna.Piła.pl at <http://www.forum.dawna. Piła.pl/viewtopic.php?f=12&t=521>, accessed 26 July 2020.
22 S. Merritt Miner, *Stalin's Holy War: Religion, Nationalism, and Alliance Politics, 1941–1945* (Chapel Hill, NC: University of North Carolina Press, 2003), p.67.
23 Clark, *Barbarossa* (London: Cassel, 2000), p.417.

The story of what happened in the town of Wugarten [now Ogardy], a town 110 kilometres west of Deutsche Krone and Schneidemühl, is told in detail in John Toland's *The Last 100 Days*. US Army Colonel Hurley Fuller had been captured at the Battle of the Bulge commanding a regiment of the 28th Division. He was taken to Schokken, where he was held with other Allied prisoners until they were moved west in late January 1945. Their group included 79 Americans and 200 Italians, including 30 elderly generals. Fuller had wanted to be liberated by the Russians so was slowing the group's march to the Oder when they reached Wugarten, 32 kilometres west of the German border. When all but one of their German guards fled, Fuller dressed him in an American lieutenant's uniform to use as a translator, with the promise of getting him through American lines. Fuller also took command of 185 Polish soldiers who had 'offered to help' and 17 French prisoners, one of whom spoke Russian.

> He set up a German command post for his growing army in the Mayor's house and ordered all weapons in town turned over. Once armed, he prepared to defend Wugarten from all comers – German or Russians.

By that evening Fuller had 26 rifles and two entrenched machine guns defending Wugarten, with rifles, shotguns, pistols and even swords to hand. The Russians came into the village and demanded to know who they were. When they got over their disbelief that Americans were on the Eastern Front they embraced them and promised them whatever they wanted. Fuller asked for weapons and ammunition and to hand over his prisoners. The Russians agreed, imposed an immediate curfew, then shot the Burgermeister – standard practice for victorious Red Army commanders, in this case Captain Mayarchuk – and then a badly-wounded prisoner being transported in a wheelbarrow. Shocked, Fuller complained this was against the Articles of War:

> 'Tell the colonel that we won't shoot any more Nazis in town,' he [Mayarchuk] said. 'From now on we'll take them out in the country and do it.'

Then the Russians began drinking vodka. There were no rapes in Wugarten that night, possibly because of Fuller's objections, although the Russians did shoot all ten members of a family which had decorations up for the twelfth anniversary of Hitler's rise to power the following day. The next day – 30 January – a Russian liaison officer called Lieutenant Colonel Theodocius Irshko arrived with fresh supplies of food and wine, and made Fuller commander of the town. As he left, he collected all the weapons from Fuller's group. That evening groups of Russian soldiers, drunk on vodka, came into Wugarten and went on a rampage, raping and murdering women. Females 'of all sorts' were raped and 16 were murdered, according to Toland's sources. Without weapons, the Americans were powerless to stop them.[24]

---

24 Col. Hurley Fuller, in Toland, *The Last 100 Days* (London: Arthur Barker, 1965), pp.21–25, 36.

Two hundred men on the Soviet side alone died in the fighting at Schneidemühl [now Piła Główna] station. Young German cadets were thrust into the firing line, with terrible casualties. (Picture: author)

A stroll through Piła is like walking through a town planner's fantasy, with everything divided into areas: a living district, a central district; wide boulevards and parks where families can relax, play games and have picnics. I walk down to the station to see where so many lives were lost past a beach party in a park alongside the river. It's serving beer, cocktails, ice cream and coffee. I have a coffee, then continue.

The four-storey station building sits in the middle of four or five tracks in each direction linking Piła with Sczecin and Bydgoszsz, but there is precious little cover for a ground attack. A tunnel under the station building links entrances from both sides to the platforms, and as I walk through I get a sense of how horribly exposed soldiers would be fighting in this confined situation. No wonder the Red Army lost two hundred men here. Even from the road bridge where I take my pictures my heart runs a little cold imagining the scenes in the frantic battle for control of the station below.

The next day I visit the cemetery where the Soviet and Polish soldiers who fell at Piła are buried. It's not easy for a stranger to find as it lies a considerable distance from the centre of the city in the district of Leszków. There are separate graveyards for the fallen of the First and Second World Wars on either side of the road. The Second World War cemetery is a very large and sombre place, carved out of the surrounding forest and in some places, being reclaimed by it.

The Soviet cemetery at Piła-Leskow, the last resting place of those who died at Schneidemühl. (Picture: author)

A stone staircase rises into the trees, lined with mass graves to left and right, highest ranks first. I count 130 steps up to the lonely white needle at the top of the cemetery, stopping for a rest halfway up. There are a lot of steps, and graves everywhere. Each level of the terraced cemetery is a repository for the remains of the young men who died fighting for control of this town. I walk along a row. The dates of death read 14 February 1945, 10 February, 6 February – matching the Soviet assault on the town. Whitewashed some time ago, but not recently, the stone needle is marked with a solitary five-pointed red star at its base, with '1945' painted underneath. There are candles and small lamps at the base.

The scale of this cemetery is staggering. There are Lieutenants, Majors, Captains; all laid out in rows, but only the occasional bunch of flowers here and there. The level of casualties when laid out on a human level like this takes some believing. From the top of the cemetery a whole avenue of stairs curves around and down the left side, lined with graves. Some are for individuals, some are mass graves. One plot, with 50 names chiselled into the plaque, is overgrown, unloved and unvisited. Standing at the top of this hill makes me wonder what the scenes were like here when it was constructed: lorries laden with bodies exhumed from their battlefield graves, men sweating as they dig out a final resting place for them.

Death on this scale may have been simply a matter of a necessary process to be completed as respectfully as possible – the satisfaction of a job done and then onto the next. The Soviet star tops the lists of names in each plot. The majority of the dead are from the years 1921, 1922, 1923, 1925. Occasionally there's a 1910, 1912, 1915, 1917, but this is a young man's war. The stone plaques have faded over time: almost everybody who survived Piła would be dead by now.

Along the top level of the cemetery there are sombre stone blocks to both left and right. The headstones are leaning back, almost offering their names up to passers-by, wanting to be remembered. Here's the grave of Kapitan Zoldybaj Nurlybajew from Kazakhstan, who died on 30 January 1945, aged 22. He would have been 23 at the end of the war, had he lived. There's a picture of him in his uniform, with medals on his chest. He shares his grave with four other men, two of whom died in March 1945. The graveyard is becoming in need of a tidy-up. It's not neglected, but not quite spruce either. Here, overgrown with ferns, is the grave of Major Aleksiej Kubiakow, who died in January 1945. He was 41.

The rows of graves are quite close together. From the individual and small group blocks they become mass graves with one headstone crowded with names, quite densely packed, getting overgrown with grass and bushes. I walk down the path at the edge of the cemetery, down about 11 levels, where a stern stone figure carved from a monolith guards the entrance to this cemetery.

A sign nearby explains that this cemetery – Piła-Leszków – is the last resting place of 1,372 Soviet soldiers killed in the taking of Piła and surrounding areas. Their bodies were transferred here to the edge of town when the cemetery was built in the 1950s. There are also four Polish soldiers buried here who died of their wounds in September 1939 in Piła hospital, and civilians – including children – who were tortured in Nazi labour camps in Piła. There are 2,638 dead from the First World War here, when the south-eastern outskirts of Piła housed a prisoner of war camp,

. 1,372 Soviet soldiers who fell in the battle for Schneidemühl in 1945 are buried at Piła-Leszków cemetery. (Picture: author)

mainly for captured German soldiers, but also Russians, British and French, as well as Tatars, Jews and Latvians.[25]

It's tidy and respectful but old, quite silent and sombre. Time has claimed those who loved them too, and these dead men have become statistics. I walk back to my car and set out west towards the Pomeranian Wall, the next challenge to be faced by those who survived the battles of *Festung* Schneidemühl.

The Pomeranian Wall was built by the Germans in the years 1932–39 as a defence line against the threat of a Polish attack west. It's a 300-kilometre-long line of fortifications stretching from Gorzow on the Warta river in West Pomerania to the Baltic Sea west of the medieval coastal town of Darłowo, known by its German name of Rugenwalde between 1871 and 1945.

The Cegielnia fortifications, part of the defensive line running in an arc around Deutsche Krone, were supposed to withstand anything, but the 1st Polish Army broke

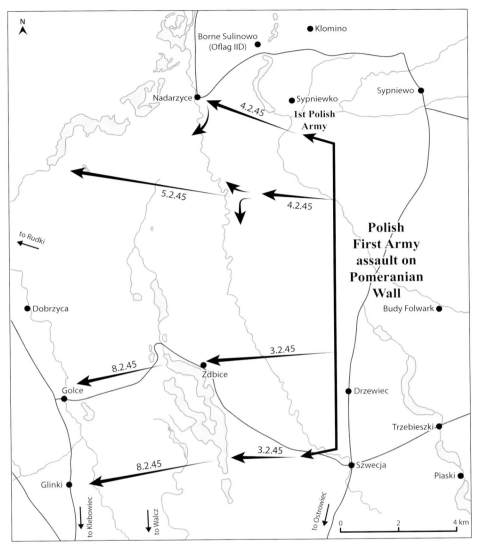

The Pomeranian Wall: close-up of Wałcz, Szwecja, Zdbice and Nadarzyce, 3–4 February 1945. Points of breakthrough.

through quickly in early February 1945. The remains of the bunkers were named 'the Pomeranian Wall' to mark the fierce fights here.[26]

The breakthrough came on 4 February in a gap between the towns of Rederitz and Stabitz [now Nadarzyce and Zdbice]. The 1st Polish spearhead fanned out left and

26 Information boards, Muzeum Ziemi Waleckiej, Cegielnia-West, Wałcz. Author's visit 19 August 2018, online at <www.MuzeumWałcz.pl>.

right and pressed on west to the village of Haugsdorf [Ilowiec] the next day. Other sections of the Wall – south of the breakthrough at Zdbice, and further south of there at Freudenfier [Swecja] – took another five days to break down.

The town of Deutsche Krone [Wałcz] was a garrison at a crucial section of the fortified defences, split into five sections. There were two infantry regiments based there with a unit of fortification engineers. One key target to defend was the railway line, curving in a lazy S around the lakes on the outskirts of the town. At various intervals along the track the Germans had infantry barracks and artillery, machine gun and anti-tank cannon capability in the bunker defences. The barracks complexes were well-equipped modern buildings, with kitchens and mess rooms, stables, coach-houses and garages for equipment and weapons. There was a blacksmith's forge, and an assembly area lit by floodlights. The camps bristled with firepower. There were three machine guns covering the gate, stables and garages, with shelters and a 22-metre high observation tower to direct fire against any approaching forces. A heavily-fortified defensive base at Mariansee [now Marianowo] kept guard against approach from the south-east. Artillery spotters could direct fire from armoured cupolas and an isolated combat area with a double armour-plated door and a trap hole meant the men assigned to defend this place could keep fighting until the very end. As at Cegielnia, Mariansee had its own infantry squad to tackle any Soviet troops able to penetrate this field of defensive fire.

What's left of one of the strongest points in the German fortified Wall, the Brickyard [Cegielnia], survives today. It's a complex of bunkers and strongpoints built on the edge of a series of cliffs with concrete firing positions and strengthened command posts. Outside, set back from the bunkers, is a shelter for an anti-tank gun. There is a small museum with Soviet uniforms and equipment on display: a mannequin with a PPsh machine gun slung across his chest, a Maxim machine gun on wheels with the bullet guard to protect the gunner, a Degtyaryov DP-27 machine gun with its disc-shaped magazine on top and two small legs at the front of the barrel. There are radios, artillery rangefinders, signal pistols and shell cases. In the German display case there's the fearsome MG-42, an MP-40 machine pistol, a Luger, a long-barrelled sniper's rifle and a mannequin wearing a snow smock and gloves with a belt stuffed with stick grenades.[27]

There were two wings of this defensive fortification in the Wall: Cegielnia West and Cegielnia East. The West defences stretch across 50 metres, in two parts, with a forward battle bunker connected by an 85-metre long underground tunnel. There were four heavy machine guns at the forward bunker in armoured cupolas, with another armoured cupola for artillery observers to direct fire. Around 50 officers and soldiers were based here, with an infantry troop able to fight from the trenches around the fortification. A walk around the site shows how German engineers built low-profile bunkers into the existing landscape and the phenomenal thickness of concrete used in the construction of these defences. At the end of the war, the bunkers at Cegielnia were blown up and stripped of their armour, which went for scrap.

27 Information boards, Muzeum Ziemi Waleckiej, Cegielnia-West, Wałcz.

The remains of the Pomeranian Wall bunkers at Cegielnia, Wałcz; formerly Deutsche Krone.
(Picture: author)

But it's when a visitor leaves the information boards and military equipment behind and goes to look at what's left of the frontline fortifications at Cegielnia East that a sense of what this once was is apparent. There are the battle bunkers linked to the command post by tunnel, manned by a crew of 30 with two heavy machine guns. An infantry squad for close combat had another two to four machine guns. One of the concrete bunkers has slipped down the slope, its foundations washed away following sand mining at the site. It once overlooked this ridge, connected to the main bunker by a tunnel and a vertical shaft and protected against enemy fire from below by a thick concrete shield. It now rests on one of its corners, facing into the ground it was supposed to protect, upended, a mess of concrete angles and steel reinforcing struts. The path along the ridge is punctuated by the ruins of other strongpoints, one still perched on the crest of the ridge, partially obscured by trees now.

I walk back to my car past what appears to be a 'last stand' fighting trench behind the museum, to cover any survivors in the event of defenders being driven out of these positions. The trench is a shadow of what it once would have been: a full-height trench with a firing step, protected by camouflage. Now it is a shallow scar lined with logs on the way to the car park, and – compared to the obstacles just overcome by the

The cemetery at Wałcz. (Picture: author)

attackers – a rather ineffective barrier. It strikes me that whoever was still alive at this point would be better off making a run for it.[28]

My next stop is on the road out of Wałcz towards Szczecin, at the cemetery for the Soviet soldiers who died conquering the Pomeranian Wall. It is also the last resting place of the men who were murdered at Podgaje-Flederborn. A large car park has been cleared out of the forest and the entrance is dominated by a statue of a Polish soldier leading an attack in full flight. The cemetery at Wałcz is a place of remembrance on a vast scale, split into Soviet and Polish zones and laid out in semi-circles of the fallen, almost like theatre seating.

The graveyard is spotless, dignified and respectful. At its centre is a set of memorials and flagpoles. Each row of graves has been tended and maintained, and in the woods where the car park is there are tracks for walking and for children to run in the woods. How many might be the great-grandchildren of the men who died here? There doesn't seem to be any special mention of the men who died so horribly at Podgaje-Flederborn. Everyone here, Polish, Russian and from the Soviet republics, is equal in death.

28 Information boards, Muzeum Ziemi Wałeckiej, Cegielnia-West, Wałcz.

16

The Road to the Sea

The commander of 15th Division's 33rd Regiment, Colonel Vilis Janums, was no stranger to tight situations like Landeck and the Flederborn road. He was an officer who cared about his men and, through his years of frontline service, had built a reputation as a Houdini-esque figure who could get out of any type of mess.

Janums had a long and dramatic active service career long before Pomerania. Latvia had been caught up in war and revolution for most of the first half of the 20th century, and Janums was there for much of it. Born in Courland in 1894, he was drafted into the Russian Army at the start of the First World War, aged 18. He served in artillery regiments until 1916 then transferred to the Latvian Riflemen reserve as a junior officer. He joined a machine gun unit in February 1917 and fought in the Battle of Jugla from 1–3 September, defending Rīga against German attack.[1]

Backing the Bolshevik revolution against the Tsar, the Latvian Riflemen were sent to crush White forces in the Russian Civil War of 1918–20. Demobilised, Janums returned home but was then drafted into a Soviet Riflemen regiment when the Latvian Communist leader Pēteris Stučka set up a Bolshevik republic in 1919. Janums deserted and joined the Latvian Army to fight for independence at another critical moment: the June 1919 Battle of Cēsis where Latvian and Estonian divisions broke pro-German forces and restored the ousted government of Kārlis Ulmanis. In the January 1920 Battle of Rēzekne he fought in the liberation of Latgale from the Communists then joined the general staff.

After the Red Army occupied Latvia in June 1940 he left for Germany. That in itself was an achievement for a man with his record: he was extracted from Latvia in the 1941 repatriation of Baltic Germans on the grounds that his family was 'German.' The evidence for this was that Janums' wife had been christened in a congregation in Liepāja that also held services in German – 'proof' of German roots.[2]

---

1 The vast number of Latvians killed at the Battle of Jugla fighting for a foreign power inspired the famous book *Blizzard of Souls* by Alexandrs Grins, made into the 2019 film *Dvēseļu Putenis*.
2 Candidates for repatriation had to persuade not just the German officials but also Russian ones. On the day of the interview, Janums had a very bad cold. The German official who knew that Janums could barely speak German, said: 'You can see that man has such a bad cold, he can barely speak. Let's not make him suffer.' He spoke German to Janums' children, who were all bilingual.

Janums returned to Latvia after Operation Barbarossa forced the Red Army out and in June 1943 was made a regimental commander in the 15th Waffen SS. He was sent to the Russian Front in November 1943 where he distinguished himself, being awarded the Iron Cross Second Class in February 1944 and then First Class in August 1944.[3]

In the aftermath of Landeck, Janums' 33rd Regiment was reinforced by 1,000 men from the Toruń camp with combat experience in Russia. The 33rd and 34th regiments were then sent by Adolph Ax on 10 February to replace a German unit defending Kamin, an important strategic town in plans to delay Soviet progress across Pomerania. But almost as soon as they arrived the Red Army launched a powerful attack, and tanks broke through at Ploetzig.[4]

Janums fell back to the centre of Kamin and ordered the 15th Fusiliers to re-take the area west of the railway. Without artillery support, and with German units along-side retreating without telling them, they took heavy casualties.[5] In his book *Mana Pulka Kauju Gaitas*, Janums describes an encounter at 15:00 on 11 February with 18th Mountain Corps commander General Friedrich Hochbaum.

> I pointed out the impossible position the regiment was in, because of the complete absence of artillery support. At first, the corps commander wouldn't hear of the possibility that Red Army columns might be openly in daylight moving across our front, and tried to persuade me that they were retreating units of the 4th Tank Corps. But when a cavalry squadron riding small Siberian horses appeared, the corps commander is forced to admit that they are, after all, the Red Army.[6]

The next day, fresh attacks forced the 34th Regiment back to Grunau, opening a gap in the defensive line which almost led to Janums' battle group being surrounded. Once again the situation was desperate. The road north from Kamin to Wordel was still open, and the only real option. But the divisional commander – Ax – ordered Janums to hold the town 'at any price' to buy time for tanks to counter-attack. A battalion from the 32nd Infantry was sent to help.[7]

3   Latvian Legion webpages, Traces of War website at <https://www.tracesofwar.com/persons/28846/Janums-Vilis.htm> and de-classified CIA files at <https://www.cia.gov/library/readingroom/docs/JANUMS%2C%20VILIS_0018.pdf>, accessed 26 July 2020. For the series of successful defensive battles in Pomerania recounted in this book, Colonel Janums was awarded the German Cross in Gold on 01 March 1945.
4   Kamin is now Kamień Krajeński; Ploetzig [Plocsic], 38 kilometres south of Słupsk, is now Plocko.
5   Silgailis, *Latvian Legion*, p.169 and Janums, *Mana Pulka Kauju Gaitas*, p.109. Their left flank was endangered by the retreat of the German 4th Tank Corps and the 79th armoured sappers which fell back three times in the course of this battle – once before Janums arrived and twice while he was there but without telling him – and then disappeared completely.
6   Janums, *Mana Pulka Kauju Gaitas*, p.110.
7   Silgailis, *Latvian Legion*, pp.170–171.

Brunis Rubess had been attached to Janums' command and now saw first-hand how he made decisions.

> I arrived at the regiment's *štābs* [HQ] in Kamin. The regiment is soon surrounded. In the *štābs* room, Colonel Janums listens to a number of reports and marks them up on an unfolded map. Once in a while he goes out in the company of his adjutant or a German communications officer. The special assignment officer always stays close to the Colonel.
>
> Officers come and go. Around the room, propped against the wall, messengers snooze. People like me. With an order for the 1st Company of the 1st Battalion I am sent to Lieutenant Bonoparts (by the way he really did, compared to others, resemble a reincarnation of Napoleon: he lived with his company, ate with them, slept with them), who died a few days later. On the snowy hillock I'm a good target for a Russian anti-tank weapon, which teaches me to move like never before. Until I'm behind the hill. After I've passed on my message, I find another route back to the regimental *štābs*, which in the meantime had been under shell fire. There are two casualties.
>
> Then the last night in Kamin arrives. Everyone in the half-darkness has fallen asleep. The last people in discussions with the Colonel are the adjutant and the special assignment officer. Then they also fall asleep, sitting in their chairs. At the table, inspecting the map, the Colonel is left by himself. I observe how he is looking for a way out for his sons. I am with Janums![8]

Shelling the next morning set fire to many of the houses left standing in Kamin, and the 1st and 4th companies of the 33rd fell back from Lake Mochel into the woods north of Wordel. Janums radioed the divisional HQ to say Kamin was surrounded and they were running out of ammunition, but the reply came back: 'Kamin must be held.'[9]

By midday Wordel had fallen and Kamin was attacked again. Again Janums asked to withdraw and, according to the account by Legion historian Arturs Silgailis, his request was refused again. The Legion's official history, the 'Green Books', say permission *was* finally given, but never reached Janums. A detailed, day-by-day recollection of that period in the accounts of the Fusilier 'Recce' Battalion notes at one point: 'Chaos again.'

On the night of 13 February the weakened battalion was ordered to attack and throw back enemy groups which had infiltrated between the two regiments, but there would be no supporting artillery fire. The battalion commander went to Divisional

---

8   Rubess, *Brīnumainā Kārta*, p.78. Janums' son, Lieutenant Linards Janums, was among the 4,000 Latvians killed defending Danzig in 1945, according to his biographer, Leitītis. Linards had couriered documents from Janums to Upelnieks in the nationalist LCP under the noses of the Germans.
9   Silgailis, *Latvian Legion*, p.171.

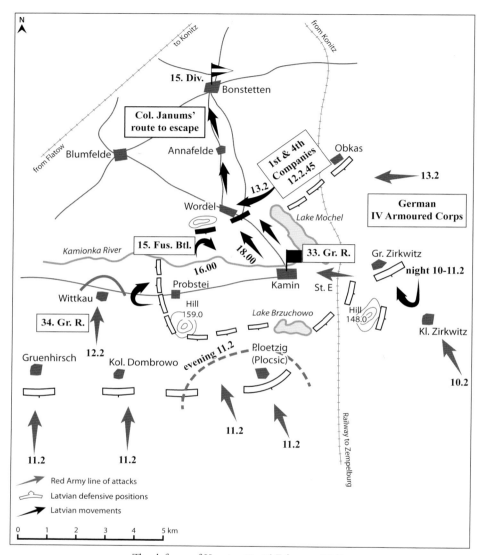

The defence of Kamin, 10–14 February 1945.

command and refused to carry out the order. The account says: 'It has to be admitted that there was a clear lack of rational leadership in the Divisional *štābs* [HQ].'[10]

Janums decided to ignore further orders and take matters into his own hands. As night fell his men moved along both sides of the road from Kamin to Wordel and launched a surprise attack on the Soviet forces new in the area. Outgunned, the Red

10 Latvian 'Green Books', vol. 6, p.35.

The diary of Cadet Officer Jūlijs Bebris is held at the Latvian War Museum in Rīga. (Picture: author)

Army men withdrew, leaving a clear road to Bonstetten [Zamarte] nine kilometres away and from there to Klausfelde, where the Latvians arrived in the early hours of 14 February.

The Latvian War Museum holds the personal diary of Cadet Officer Jūlijs Bebris, who won the Iron Cross First Class for his courage in Pomerania. Here he tells how the breakout plan was carried out.

a) Major Alksnītis' battle group should take up its exit position by 16:45 in the small wood which is 1 kilometre South-East of the northern edge of WORDEL, starting the attack at 17:00 along the KAMIN-WORDEL road, occupy WORDEL village and after that to secure the regiment's travel through from the east, with no less than one company, taking up positions at the northern end of Lake Mochel. From the west with one company – at the western end of WORDEL village; but with one company the hillocks about 700 metres south of WORDEL. The guard companies should join the regiment once the 8th Company has gone through WORDEL.

b) Captain Noltes's battalion should hold current positions until 17:30, after which they should withdraw from the enemy and gather for the march at the road from KAMIN-BONSTETTEN with the head of the column by the lone house 0.5 kilometre north of the bridge of the KAMIONKA river.

March to be commenced upon receiving the order. Leave a covering unit of two platoons' strength in the current position.

c) The covering positions of the 8th Company and Captain Noltes's battalion to stay until 18:00, after that pull back and join the main force.

d) After passing through WORDEL, Captain Noltes's battalion should continue the breakout but Major Alksnītis's battle group should follow at a 0.5 kilometre distance

e) I will follow the vanguard along the road KAMIN–BLUMENFELDE.

The enemy's attack on Kamin from the south-east and south-west continues. At about 13:30, the regimental commander orders a radiogram to be sent to the Division:

The enemy has taken the railway station. He has reached the southern end of KAMIN, where he has been stopped. The companies have used up all their munitions.

Shortly before 16:00, Major Pomrehn arrives at the regimental command point and announces that the Recce Battalion has tried to break through in the direction of Blumenfelde but, as the enemy has taken the hillocks about 1.5 kilometres from Wordel with a large force, the battalion has suffered heavy losses, fallen back to Kamin and put itself at the disposal of the 33rd Regiment. Taking into account this report, and since all three battalion commanders are still in the regimental command point, the regimental commander changes the order for the breakout as follows:

- The regiment, instead of breaking out towards BLUMENFELDE, should go north, along the KAMIN–KONITZ road.
- The two companies of the Recce battalion are added to Major Alksnītis' battle group.
- The breakout time is set for 18:00.

At 16:00 there is finally a radiogram from the division: Kamin is to be defended. There is no order from the higher leadership to leave the town. Despite this order, the regimental commander nevertheless sticks to his intention to break out on his responsibility, because one must be wary that the enemy will further strengthen his forces overnight.

Major Alksnītis sets out his battle group as follows:

- First line, the 3rd Company and the 1st Company of the Recce Battalion attacks on the right of the KAMIN–BONSTETTEN road; the 2nd and 13th company attacks on the left of the road opposite WORDEL village. The left flank is secured by the 6th/7th Company and the 2nd Company of the Recce Battalion.

At 16:40 a new radiogram is sent to the Division:

We are fully surrounded. We have run out of ammunition.

This radiogram is transmitted blind, as the Division is no longer answering. It is no longer possible to re-establish radio contact. As it later became apparent, the Division had left its Bonstetten command point just before 17:00 and the radio station went with it, without informing the Regiment about changing its position. The distance to the new Divisional command point was too far to establish communications with the Regiment's small (Gustav 5) radio station.

The whole of the western side of Kamin is burning. The night is dark but the reflection of burning Kamin and the snow-covered fields provide some 200 metres of visibility.

The regimental *štābs* leaves its command point and Kamin at 18:15 with covering units. The Kamin telephone exchange and the bridge over the Kamionka river is destroyed. The attacking units start moving at 18:00 in a thick chain along both sides of the Kamin–Bonstetten road. The enemy in Wordel village notices the attacking units only when they have reached the first houses in the village.

The enemy tries to organise resistance in vain. Using hand grenades, a number of automatic weapons are destroyed, a number of prisoners are taken, also the kitchen and horses. The defenders of the village flee westwards. The personnel from some battery and the *štābs* is discovered. Talking to the prisoners later it seems the battery itself was in position 200 metres to the north-west of the village but the attacking units hadn't noticed it in the dark and went past it.

After the main force of the regiment had passed Wordel village, the covering units, with the exception of the 13th Company, joined the marching column. The latter, according to orders, under the command of Dumpis took up positions by the fork in the road on the western edge of the village. As the Company commander hadn't been informed of the change of direction of the breakout, they waited in vain in their positions for the regiment to pass through.

At approximately 19:00, the Russian counter-attack from the west began. The company was pushed back. Later, it also took incoming fire from a house on the east of the village. It then turns northwards and hides in a barn, where it stays the whole of the next day and only returns to the regiment on 15 February 1945.

Protected by the vanguard, the regiment continues its way on the Kamin–Bonstetten road and, not meeting any resistance, reaches Bonstetten at about 22:00, where the Division's sapper battalion was in position. The Regimental commander comes across the Division's Special Assignment officer, who informs him that at 19:00 an order had been made to leave Kamin. The Regiment continued its march through Gr. Jenznick-Schlochau to the assembly point Klausfelde, which it reached on 14 February 1945 at about 03:00.[11]

11 Extract from the diary of Lieutenant Bebris (pp.10–11), used with permission of the Latvian War Museum, trans. Aivars Sinka.

Janums' escape from Kamin was the latest example of what some observers have described as his 'independent thinking.' Others might judge this in military terms as disobeying orders. Legion chief of staff and historian Arturs Silgailis criticised the divisional commander Adolf Ax for being 'too inexperienced' – a charge he also levelled at the Ia (Chief of Staff) of the division, Lieutenant Pape, who was 'young and inexperienced.' Pape had replaced Wulff, killed at Landeck the week before. Ax had been in charge of the division for just under three weeks, in which time the Division experienced the slaughter of Flederborn and Landeck followed by an encirclement and near-wipeout at Kamin. On 15 February, Ax was removed and SS-Oberführer Karl Burk took over.[12]

Janums' reluctance to sacrifice his men – and himself – inspired loyalty among those he led which lasted the rest of their lives. However, the Latvian military historian Valdis Kuzmins believes that in a rapidly-fluctuating situation, with both Russian and Polish units disconnected and Latvian and German defenders split up and often encircled in the chaos of combat, Kamin was not a high priority military objective – so the Russians let Janums escape. As we talk in a café in Rīga Old Town, Valdis sketches out a map of the battlefield in my notebook.

> The reason they managed to break out was that the Russians didn't care about Kamin. That was never one of the Red Army's objectives. It was just one of the obstacles in their way in a long line of obstacles as they tried to cover 50 kilometres a day. They simply didn't care about Kamin – if it was occupied by Latvians, Germans or someone else. When there was a fight in Kamin itself they would outmanoeuvre, go around, carry on, leave it for later. For the Russians, objective Number One was Schlochau [Człuchów].
>
> The battles in Kamin started about 10 February and lasted until 13 February. By then the 15th Division was down to two regiments, the 33rd and the 34th. The 34th was made up of the remnants of four battalions that were mixed, sent from other places – Meijers' construction battalions and some others; it was a mess. There were units assigned to the 15th who didn't know each other, had no officers, no training. The reason Janums got encircled was because the 34th Regiment got beaten back over the railway line here—

He marks a cross in the map he's drawing in my notebook

> —at Grunau. They were in a very tough position, being attacked by the 2nd Guards Cavalry Corps and by two Rifle divisions. They had limited artillery

---

12 Silgailis, *Latvian Legion,* p.171–172. Despite his medals being clear evidence of his courage, Adolph Ax is not well-remembered in Latvian military history. Latvians say his poor leadership made him responsible for the disasters at Flederborn, Landeck and Wallachsee, which led to much loss of life. Then he tried to blame his Latvian officers immediately afterwards. When Burk took over from Ax, his orders illustrate how he had been briefed by Ax: a number of Latvian units were disarmed and there was an attempt to replace the Latvian officers with German ones. This was resisted at the highest levels before being resolved by General Bangerskis.

support and were scattered all over very difficult terrain, so they retreated. That's why Janums got encircled. The Germans were quite concerned about Janums and wanted him to get out. That fight was a mess. The 15th didn't have the necessary resources needed for command and control. No wireless, no phone, undisciplined messengers and runners; fighting in the middle of nowhere, for no obvious reason.

The Russian Cavalry Corps used horses to move the heavy machine guns into position, then attacked. The cavalry dismounted two kilometres from the front-line, got their equipment into place, put the horses somewhere safe, then went into battle. Horses were used very efficiently until the last days of the Second World War.

Kamin was a well-led battle from Janums' perspective, but Janums had a mission and he mentions several times that his main concern was for his own men. He feels like he owns his regiment and he says: 'My regiment should be safe and out of trouble – what happens outside that is no big deal to me, even if those other men are fellow Latvians.' He did this several times. Kamin was one example, and [it also happened] several times up north.[13]

He marks a cross on the map where Schlochau should be, lets the pen drop and looks at me.

If the Russians had wanted to destroy Kamin, they would have done that easily. They left small units behind as a covering force – they didn't care about it. They would deal with it later. Janums used this opportunity to sneak out. That's it. That's the story.[14]

In his biography, Colonel Janums describes interrogating Soviet prisoners at Kamin on 11 February 1945 and concluding that the sending of the Latvians to the town was deliberate, and planned in advance by German commanders. He writes:

I found out that the regiment was being attacked by the 162nd Guards Division, with 18–20 artillery batteries, 10 salvo cannons [Katyushas] and 10–35 tanks. After I received this news, it became very clear to me that the hurry with which our division was moved to the Kamin area this time wasn't just a matter of circumstance, but that this swap out was arranged after the German HQs had already received news that the enemy was preparing a major attack.

---

13 Another interpretation is that Janums valiantly held his positions while the Germans aban-doned theirs, and he decided not to sacrifice the lives of his men for a lost [German] cause. The Latvians appear to have been the 'fall guys' at Kamin: sent in with no artillery support to prop up collapsing and retreating German units, which see their arrival as the opportunity to get out. In the aftermath, and having saved themselves, the Latvians are accused of looking after their own men.

14 Interview with author, Rīga, 27 November 2019.

Taking advantage of the situation where the General Inspector [Bangerskis] had no operational control over how his units were deployed, the SS leadership, with cynical lack of guile, pulled German units out of an at-risk sector just before the attack began so that they could be replaced with the 15th Latvian Division. I am highly embittered about such behaviour.[15]

After the breakout at Landeck, Ax was replaced by a new German commander, Karl Burk. Born in Bavaria in 1898, Burk had served in the First World War and stayed in the military during the inter-war period. He joined the Nazi Party in 1933 then the SS, working his way up to the rank of SS-Oberführer. In summer 1944 he was appointed chief of staff of the 2,000-strong French-speaking collaborationist Walloon Legion founded by politician and commander Leon Degrelle, which served on the Eastern Front at Cherkassy and the Tannenburg Line, losing many men. When Burk took charge of the 15th SS, Degrelle commanded Belgian, French and Spanish volunteers in a re-formed Walloon Legion until the end of the war.[16]

Jūlijs Ķīlītis, commander of the 34th Regiment, later wrote of Burk:

SS-Oberführer Karl Burk, who replaced Adolph Ax as divisional commander in February 1945. (Picture: Latvian Legion 'Green Books')

After moving to the new positions, there were larger changes in the leadership. As Divisional Commander, instead of old, incapable Ax, came the German Colonel Burk, who was an energetic and pitiless officer. He wanted to gradually swap out all the senior Latvian officers, because he thought that they protected their people too much. Information about this was sent to Gustrow to the General Inspector [Bangerskis]. After about a month, Burk was forced to reinstate all the commanders he had replaced.[17]

15 Janums, *Mana Pulka Kauju Gaitas*, pp.110–11.
16 J. Trigg, *Hitler's Gauls: The History of the 33rd Waffen-SS Division Charlemagne* (Hitler's Legions Book 1) (Stroud, Gloucestershire: The History Press, 2009), p.50; T. Borowski, *Last Blood on Pomerania – Leon Degrelle and the Walloon Waffen SS Volunteers, February – May 1945.* (Warwick: Helion, 2016), pp.52–87 and S. Mitcham, *German Order of Battle: Panzer, Panzer Grenadier, and Waffen SS Divisions in WWII* (London: Stackpole Books, 2006), p.76.
17 Ķīlītis, *I Go To War*, p.202.

In his farewell address as he handed over to Karl Burk, Ax said:

> I really can't congratulate you on your new responsibilities. It's most likely that with this task you could easily lose your good name and reputation and discover that, one fine day, you will be pushed aside with shame and dishonour.[18]

Colonel Janums watched Ax handing over to Burk in that meeting in Divisional HQ:

> In his farewell address, Oberführer Ax said that the Division had failed to live up to expectations … Nothing much surprised me from this sleepy individual, but I didn't expect this level of impudence. He was now trying to make up for his hopelessness and inability to command the Division by heaping the blame on Latvian soldiers…
>
> This assessment of the earlier battles sparked dark and angry feelings. As one of the most senior Latvian officers I was extremely offended: this was very rude. I told Divisional Commander Burk that I had a different point of view with regard to the leadership of the division and the conduct of the fighting and I requested permission to speak. Probably realising that my reply might be not pleasant for old Ax, Burk said the meeting was finished but he would like to hear my point of view, so he invited me into his office.
>
> Once we went in, I sharply reminded Oberführer Ax that my regiment had been encircled three times, not because the regiment was at fault, but because it fulfilled its orders and held its position, while its neighbours – German units to the left and right – kept on deserting us, leaving our regiment behind. I reminded him of the 51st German Infantry Regiment's retreat at Jastrow, and the 4th Tank Corps' falling back at Kamin. Oberführer Ax tried to cover his tracks clumsily, saying I misunderstood him and in the end started to praise my conduct and personal bravery.[19]

Legion chaplain Kazimirs Ručs met Burk early into his appointment, and recorded his thoughts:

> He told me that battlefield clergy were known for fleeing from the front, taking others with them. But having found out that I didn't flee and was in the Landeck encirclement with the Lutheran chaplain [Jūlijs Straume, who was killed] he became polite and helpful.[20]

However, Ķīlītis saw another side to Burk as the battered 15th Division regrouped in Krummensee. Burk took charge and the Latvian officers were replaced by Germans. Ķīlītis was put in charge of a back-line unit attached to the *štābs*. The Legion's official history recounts Burk's first meeting with his Latvian commanders.

18 The 'Green Books', vol. 6, p.38.
19 Janums, *Mana Pulka Kauju Gaitas*, p.213.
20 Ručs, *Dzīve ar Dievu*.

The new divisional commander SS-Oberführer Burk took over the leadership of the Division. He heroically promised to improve the discipline and fighting capability of the Division. The meeting ended with the words: 'Any officer who won't order his soldiers to fight to the last, or whose unit abandons its weapons, will be shot.'

The officers dispersed quietly. He couldn't intimidate us with these words, because we had neither fled nor abandoned our weapons. It was the remains of the German Army and the disparate units that had been gathered together which had often fled and left us by ourselves, until we were surrounded.[21]

In his autobiography published 11 years afterwards, Ķīlītis suggests Burk may have ordered the execution of Latvian soldiers at Krummensee to 'stiffen morale' and punish those whose nerve had faltered under fire. Ķīlītis writes:

At night I thought over all our joint experiences, his earlier brutal behaviour, needless acts of violence and shootings in the Krummensee region, and finally came to the conclusion that I couldn't trust him.[22]

He also reflected on Burk's later decision in the final days of the war in the forests of Mecklenburg to allow the Latvians to head west to surrender to the Allies.

That act was the only really civilised one by him. With that, he couldn't atone for his roughness and pitilessness in the field and for Krummensee.[23]

Military historian Aivars Petersons, a Latvian ex-Red Army officer who interviewed Legionnaires for his 2003 book *Mums jāpārnāk [We Have to Get Home]* describes in some detail SS methods at Landeck and afterwards: an SS 'penalty' group of six officers and 40 SS men, led by a Knight's Cross holder, Oberst Schulz, was positioned by Burk behind the forward lines at Landeck. What really happened in Krummensee needs more research, but there is a further remark in the official history of the Legion that references dark events during Burk's first days in charge. Burk, on taking over from Adolph Ax:

...started his endeavours with tried and trusted SS methods: death sentences.[24]

Four days after their escape, Janums and his men were moved back to their previous positions along the Dobrinka river around Landeck to rest and reorganise. As the 34th Regiment rebuilt again alongside them, an officer was assigned to the unit who was complicit in one of the greatest crimes of the Holocaust: the murder on

---

21 Latvian Legion 'Green Books', vol. 6, p.195.
22 Ķīlītis, *I Go To War,* p.221.
23 Ķīlītis, *I Go To War,* p.231. The full story is told in the author's forthcoming accounts of the 15th Division in Germany.
24 Latvian 'Green Books', vol. 8, p.288.

30 November and 8 December 1941 of 25,000 Jews in the Rumbula forest.

The Latvian Arājs Kommando was a group of collaborationist 'irregulars', initially between 300–500 men at its creation which grew to 1,500 strong at its height. Under Brigadeführer Walter Stahlecker it proved its worth to the Nazis assisting and enabling the murder of thousands of Jews in July–August 1941 at Biķernieki and in the 'Blue Bus' actions: the Kommando roamed across Latvia rounding up and killing Jews, Roma and mental patients and guarding prisoner camps.[25]

On 30 November and 8 December 1941 at Rumbula, 24,000 Jews from the Rīga ghetto and 1,000 Jews from Germany were murdered in SS boss Friedrich Jeckeln's 'sardine packing' operation. The victims were ordered to

Viktors Arājs, leader of the notorious Arājs Kommando, pictured in 1937.
(Picture: public domain)

lie down in killing pits in the forest, then shot in the back of the head with Russian weapons. Viktors Arājs led the unit of Latvian volunteers which marched them to their place of their death and funnelled them to the killing pits. Jeckeln had developed his method for mass killing at Babi Yar in Ukraine two months previously, where 33,371 Jews from Kiev were murdered.

The Arājs Kommando men were then given military training and sent to Belarus, where they cleared ghettos, fought partisans and carried out reprisals against the local population. The unit was disbanded in 1944 as the war turned against the Nazis and every man was needed at the front. Richard Plavnieks, who researched Arājs' life and the history of the Kommando extensively, wrote:

> They could then better serve Hitler as soldiers than police paramilitaries, so the Arājs Kommando's personnel were absorbed into front-line combat units of the Latvian Legion along the rapidly-approaching Eastern Front.

At this point in the war the Germans were replacing Latvian commanders with German ones, and Arājs – now a Major – was attached to the 34th Regiment on the orders of the new German commander, Pomrehn. Arājs had been wounded in

---

25 R. Bettina Birn, and V. Riess, *Revising the Holocaust* (Cambridge: Cambridge University Press, 1997), p.207.

combat in 1943 and by late February 1945 had graduated from officer school in Berlin. He was also wearing an Iron Cross.[26]

Arājs was put in charge of the 1st Battalion, with Major Fricis Mežgrāvis commanding the 2nd Battalion. When Pomrehn was wounded he was replaced by an SS captain from headquarters. Mežgrāvis was told that evening by Divisional Commander Karl Burk to form two battalions from the men remaining and lead them 'to the ultimate victory.' In the same order Arājs was removed from his command of the 1st Battalion and Captain Osvalds Meija reinstated. Mežgrāvis remembered his time with Arājs in this article in the Latvian diaspora press:

> My regiment was taken over by Major Pomrehn on 21 February. An officer turned up in my 2nd Battalion in Visengrund and introduced himself as Arājs. He handed me an envelope, which contained an order as follows:
>
> > *'After completing his officer training Major Arājs has been seconded to the 34th Infantry Regiment. From today I attach Major Arājs to the 2nd Battalion for an unspecified time for practical training in commanding a battalion. I ask that you give him all possible assistance.'* Signed, Major Pomrehn.
>
> Major Arājs had only been with me a few days when he was made commander of the 1st Battalion in place of Major Ķīlītis. Those were difficult days whilst Arājs commanded the battalion. Rarely was it possible to establish communications with him and if anything was decided as a joint venture, it was impossible to rely on things being done. When Arājs got on the back of a horse, he was impossible to find. Co-operation between the two battalions suffered greatly. He was an individualist.
>
> One time he had been given a divisional order which was secret and to be given to me, so I could retreat with my battalion. Arājs, having read it, made off with *his* battalion, leaving the order on the table in his company and omitting to tell me about it. It was only through a lucky accident that I managed to retreat on my own initiative.
>
> This order was later found by the division communications officer in Arājs' company, left on the table. He was due to face a court martial but that never happened. Now, however, being squadron commander, I was in a position to remove Arājs from his post and send him to the division reservist units.[27]

Arājs's Legion career had lasted about eight days, before he was kicked out by the Legionnaires themselves.

26 R. Plavnieks, *Nazi Collaborators On Trial During The Cold War: Viktors Arājs And The Latvian Auxiliary Security Police*, (London: Palgrave Macmillan, 2018), p.121. This detail came from Kommando member Ričards Ligotnis, who was captured and interrogated by the Soviets towards the end of the war.
27 Mežgrāvis in A. Ruņģis, article in 'Uz Tām Prūšu Robežām' from *Latvija Amerikā* Nr. 27 dated 07 July 2001, accessed 30 November 2020, trans. Aivars Sinka.

Former Legionnaire Jānis Urpens, interviewed at his home in Fenstanton, Cambridgeshire, UK.
(Picture: author)

Among the men who joined the 15th at this time were Legionnaires Jānis Urpens and his friend Alberts Balodis. Both were wounded in the final stages of the war, made it to the west, surrendered to the British and came to the UK to work afterwards. Alberts is now dead, but his daughter Astrid has put me in touch with Jānis and his wife Aina, who live in the village of Fenstanton, ten miles [16 kilometres] north-west of Cambridge. I go to see them, and we talk over a seemingly-endless pot of tea.

Mr Urpens grew up with a brother and sister in Vaivari, a neighbourhood of Jurmala, a popular town along the coast west of Rīga. His older brother Laimonis joined the Legion but was killed aged 27 in Jelgava during the Russian attacks in July and August 1944. Jānis was sent to Germany for ten months for his RAD labour service and then 'voluntarily mobilised' into the 15th Division after returning to the division HQ at Schlochau.

> They'd taken very heavy casualties at Kamin. I believe one regiment, the 32nd, was more or less destroyed. I joined the 34th and Janums' regiment – the 33rd – were the main fighters there. They were very good. We marched from Schlochau and had a week in positions 20 kilometres from there – I don't know in which direction – in a wooded area. A week later we started to retreat, which was quite

heavy. The march went to Neustettin, but that took probably a couple of days. After that, really, we were running. 'Go, go, go!' from Neustettin west.

I joined the Army on 8 February 1945, so I had only three months running from the Russians. It was mostly running![28]

The rolling punches from all directions and the intense combat needed to break out of encirclements caused mental as well as physical casualties. The stress of battle and constant movement combined with blizzard conditions and lack of food meant morale was low and men became desperate to escape the fighting, as Russian Front veteran Jānis Čevers remembers:

Everybody was so fed up on the Polish front. There were a lot shooting themselves. It was very risky and difficult. It's too close to shoot yourself – it had to be from a certain distance. If the Germans found out they would shoot you themselves.

One thing soldiers did was get behind a big tree and put their hand out, and then their mate or someone else would shoot them through the hand. That way they'd get to hospital and not have to fight any more. There was a lot of drinking because of course the soldiers expected to die any minute. You never think you're going to survive, so soldiers do certain things – get drunk, go crazy.

Behind the lines was worse than being in the lines sometimes, because there were bastards everywhere. In these forested countries like Poland, they hide anywhere; you can't get them out. The Germans tried but without success. The Communist partisans were ruling some parts of the country. They were Polish, Russian. They were well organised. Russian soldiers had headquarters in the deep forest. The same as in Yugoslavia, with Tito. The partisans were big trouble for the Germans, more trouble than at the front, because they could blow up the lorry, disrupt your supply behind the lines: that sort of thing.

Mr Čevers' stories illustrate just how thin the line between life and death could be.

One time we were in a little forest and there was a two-man machine gun crew, must have been Wehrmacht, and us to the right. The Russians were in the forest shooting at us and we were shooting at them. One Russian shot into them – *boof!* – and the two Germans and their machine gun were blown sky-high. One of the Russians came out of the forest so I aimed at him and he fell. The Russians pulled him back into cover. Maybe I wounded him or killed him? You can't say. No-one knows. But that's the nearest I can say that I probably did [kill someone].[29]

28 Interview with author, March 2019.
29 Interview with author, November 2018. As mentioned previously, Mr Čevers was a machine gunner and suffered intense nightsweats for twenty years after the war. The author only discovered much later that he was bedbound, and got out of his bed on two occasions to be interviewed.

Vivid soldiers' stories from this time on the Russian Front are still emerging in Latvia. One shared on Facebook concerns the names soldiers gave their bunkers. One, inhabited by a group of hard drinkers, was called 'Drink it to the last drop.' One night the men in the bunker had the night off and drank their schnapps ration. Once drunk, one soldier pulled the pin from a grenade and put it to his ear saying: 'Hear how it hisses!' The least drunk soldier in the group grabbed the grenade and threw it beneath the bunk beds, where it exploded, injuring all six men in the bunker, but not seriously.[30]

The war had become fluid and unpredictable and little mercy was shown on the battlefield. Legionnaire Žano Mūsiņš noted in his diary for February 1945:

> I have been attached to a special unit to quell any local problems. That was more like a special squad of stormtroopers. A unit of 20–25 men, sent in whenever there were Russians breaking in. Something locally, they sent us in and said: 'Mop it up.' More or less, like the British SAS. We had a couple of small skirmishes and the Russians did the same. Everyone was feeling their way.[31]

On 15 February, 200 kilometres to the west towards Szczecin [Stettin], the German six-day counter-offensive Operation Solstice [*Sonnenwende*] aimed to stop the rapid progress of Zhukov's 1st Belorussian Front. Centred on Stargard, the plan was to rescue the garrison surrounded at Arnswalde then turn against Soviet forces at Küstrin, a strategically-important railway hub on the Oder now known as Kostrzyn nad Odrą.

The Germans wanted to stretch the gaps developing between the two armies advancing towards them; Zhukov driving west and Rokossovsky in the north, whose offensive had slowed. Russian armour was proving easy prey for the Panzerfaust 'tank killer' teams, and this would be a major problem for Red Army generals. Of 580 Soviet tanks destroyed in action between 22 February–9 March 1945, 380 were by individual infantrymen using Panzerfausts.[32]

To the horror of his generals, Hitler had appointed Heinrich Himmler to command Army Group Vistula, a re-organised 450,000-strong force in Pomerania. Himmler had no previous military leadership and defending this region against the combat-hardened fast-moving Red Army, which switched attacks to stagger the blows and strain defensive lines, would be a tall order for even the most experienced commander.

In a briefing with Hitler, Army chief of staff Heinz Guderian suggested that his deputy, the 'Boy General' Walther Wenck might be a better choice for an operation as critical as *Sonnenwende*. At this, Hitler exploded into a two-hour rant.[33] Once he

---

30 <Lacplesis.org>webpages,onlineat<http://lacplesis.org/WWII/Latviesu_Karaviri_Volchovas_Fronte/Latviesu_Karaviri_Volchovas_Frontes_Sektora.pdf>.

31 Interview with author, Coventry, UK.

32 S. Newton, *Panzer Operations: The Eastern Front Memoir of Generaloberst Erhard Raus*, (Cambridge, Mass., Da Capo, 2003), p.340.

33 A moment from the film *Downfall* made famous on social media.

calmed down, Hitler agreed to this but changed the operation from a pincer attack on Soviet spearhead units to a mass attack by 300 tanks. Although this began well, Wenck and his driver Hermann Dorn had to make 320-kilometre (200-mile) round trips every day to Hitler's briefings in Berlin.

After three nights without sleep he and Dorn were exhausted, and, having fallen asleep at the wheel, Wenck drove into the parapet of a railway bridge on the Berlin-Stettin highway at 100kph [60mph] on the way back to the front.[34] Dorn and a Major asleep in the back were thrown clear down the railway embankment, but Wenck, unconscious, was trapped behind the wheel as the car burst into flames hanging over the parapet. Dorn, roused by the sound of ammunition exploding in the heat, scrambled back up to the car and smashed a window to drag Wenck clear, then rolled him in the snow to put out his blazing clothes.[35]

Wenck regained consciousness in hospital with a fractured skull and five broken ribs and was out of action for several weeks. General Hans Krebs took over the operation but the initiative had been lost and it was abandoned.[36] Hitler relieved Himmler of his command shortly afterwards and the SS boss retreated to his sanatorium at Hohenlychen, replaced by Colonel General Gotthard Heinrici. Bombed and shelled into near-obliteration, Küstrin fell on 31 March.[37]

Having snuffed out Operation *Sonnenwende,* Soviet commanders moved to split and destroy German forces in East Pomerania with a rapid two-pronged thrust north between Kolberg and Köslin [Kołobrzeg and Koszalin]. The 2nd Belorussian Front turned east to cut off Danzig and Gotenhafen through Stolp and Lauenburg [Słupsk and Lębork] while the three armies of Zhukov's 1st Belorussian Front moved to split and destroy the Third Panzer Army and cut off the port cities of Stettin and Swinemünde.[38]

Launched on 24 February 1945, the East Pomeranian offensive made rapid progress. The defences of the Pomeranian Wall were breached at Baldenburg by Rokossovsky's III Guards Tank Army on 26 February; Neustettin, considered a well-defended target, fell with little resistance the following day. Again civilians were innocent victims, with 300 killed in a pincer attack by the III Guards Cavalry Corps. Then the aftermath: women raped and murdered, and a wave of suicides.[39]

The 2nd Guards Tank Army and 3rd Shock Army drove north-east to Kolberg, along the way crushing the French 33rd SS Charlemagne Division at Belgard, the Korps Gruppe [Corps Group] Tettau at Schivelbein and surrounding then wiping out the X SS Corps at Dramburg.[40] The 4,500-strong Charlemagne Division volunteers

34 Guderian, *Panzer Leader,* p.415; Toland, *The Last 100 Days,* p.154.
35 Toland, *The Last 100 Days,* p.154.
36 Duffy, *Red Storm on the Reich,* pp.181–185.
37 Duffy, *Red Storm on the Reich,* pp.241–242, 248.
38 Now Szczecin and Swinoujscie.
39 Buttar, *Battleground Prussia – the Assault on Germany's Eastern Front 1944–45* (Oxford and Long Island, NY: Osprey Publishing, 2010), p.285. Neustettin is Szczecinek today; Baldenburg is Biały Bór.
40 Duffy, *Red Storm on the Reich,* pp.186–188. Now Białogard, Świdwin and Drawsko Pomorskie.

took heavy casualties in a series of frenzied battles against overwhelming numbers from 24 January onward in the area around Bärenwalde, Elsenau and Hammerstein.[41]

Without heavy weapons initially, the Charlemagne fought with Panzerfausts and machine guns, inflicting serious losses on tanks and men alike, often at close range and in hand-to-hand fighting.[42] Hammerstein fell on 26 February as the Frenchmen fell back alongside the Latvians to Neustettin. Realising the town could not be held, a rearguard covered an 80 kilometre forced march in the snow first north to Belgard and then to reinforce Körlin an der Persante [Karlino], a town on the road towards both Kolberg and Stettin, which they held against overwhelming odds for most of 4 March.

A planned withdrawal to Belgard under cover of darkness started late and turned into disaster. As dawn broke and the morning fog lifted, the French were caught in open fields only 100 metres from columns of Soviet tanks and infantry, which then set about slaughtering them. In less than an hour 500 men were killed or captured. One battalion led by Henri Fenet had left earlier, avoided the carnage and made it to the muster point at Meseritz; another group of around 100–150 French and German survivors headed north to the coast.[43]

To the south of Belgard, the Corps Group Tettau led by Lieutenant-General Hans von Tettau was a force of between 10,000–15,000 troops with up to 40,000 civilians in tow. Surrounded, and having lost radio contact with headquarters, von Tettau broke through the encirclement and headed north for the coast, reaching Hoff and Horst on 9 March. There he established a bridgehead, hoping to be evacuated by sea. Stragglers from Nazi units smashed by the Soviet operation were directed here until the force was strong enough to force its way down the Baltic shore to Dievenow, where the Kriegsmarine ferried men across the Oder to Wolin.[44]

The X SS at Dramburg was surrounded and wiped out when the First Polish Army sealed its escape routes to the south-east and east. Its badly-wounded commander Lieutenant-General Gunther Krappe and 8,000 of his men were taken prisoner on 7 March.[45] Small groups of survivors hid in the woods by day and moved under cover of darkness towards the Oder. The 1st Guards Tank Army moved on to Kolberg to join the siege of the city and close escape routes from there west. The Second Army was now cut off.[46]

One of the few accounts of life on the frontline for Latvian battlefield engineers comes from Imants Jansons, a 'sapper', who surrendered to the Allies at the end of the war and later emigrated to Australia. His memoir *Manu Dienu Grāmata* [*The Book of My Days*] was published by his daughter Zaiga Jansone in 2017. The diary he kept is the first published account of the experiences of the 15th Sapper Battalion from

---

41 Now Binze, Olszanowo and Czarne.
42 Trigg, *Hitler's Gauls,* pp.112–115.
43 Trigg, *Hitler's Gauls,* pp.118–123 and Forbes, *For Europe: The French Volunteers of the Waffen-SS* (Mechanicsburg, Pennsylvania: Stackpole Military Series, 2010), p.330.
44 Duffy, *Red Storm on the Reich,* p.197.
45 Le Tissier, *Zhukov at the Oder,* p.102 and Duffy, pp.195–196.
46 Duffy, *Red Storm on the Reich,* p.196,189.

15th Division Sapper Imants Jansons with friends. (Picture courtesy Jānis Jansons)

this time and is considered 'a high-value resource' by Latvian War Museum historian Jānis Tomaševskis. It's important, he writes in the foreword, because Jansons 'documents the role of an ordinary man in a global military conflict.' It makes for vivid and painful reading.

Mobilised into the 15th SS on 11 December 1944, Jansons trained in Pomerania as a heavy truck driver. His brother Tālivaldis was mortally wounded on the first day the unit saw action. Many men around him lost their lives at Flederborn and Jastrow and he was sent to help dig ditches and build barriers near the village of Klausfelde [Jaromierz]. On 25 February, Jansons was sent to the front: the men in the platoon did not have enough weapons to go round. A fierce Soviet attack forced them back through Hammerstein where they set up camp in a forest. As night fell they realised they had been surrounded, so the sappers provided cover for Janums' 33rd Regiment to escape.

The Russians pursued them throughout the next day. As they emerged from the forest into bright sunshine they saw Soviet tanks attacking Neustettin. Suddenly shells started to fall among them.

> At the front of the column dirt and mud is flying in the air and some human silhouettes begin to tumble and moan. While running for cover we disperse in all directions. The explosions cease and we hurry to the injured. The tank's fire had severed both feet of our platoon messenger Baumanis.
>
> Brants, Brakmanis and Feldbaums are slightly wounded. We bandage the injured and wonder what to do. The situation is absurd. We don't know the

positions of the Russians or our own units. There are only 12 of us left. Lieutenant Sirons, the platoon's sergeant, four injured and us: six intact soldiers.[47]

With night falling they loaded the badly-injured Baumanis onto a stretcher and carried him 10 kilometres to the nearest town with medical orderlies.

Another Legionnaire, Gunārs Rozens, was a radio telegraphist in a group of 100 men sent east from Neubrandenburg to resist the Russian offensive. Rozens served with the 33rd Regiment between February–April 1945. This is an extract from his memoirs, written after the war and held in the War Museum archive.[48]

A 100+ soldier transport group was sent on 25 February from Neubrandenburg to the 15th Division. We were from various division units, coming from hospitals or different training camps, therefore I know only a few names. The leadership consisted of a lieutenant, whose name I don't remember, but everything was led by an energetic sergeant called Mangulis. There was also Oberjunker Kugrens and Sergeant Zilgme.

We travelled by train from Neubrandenburg to Stettin but were unable to go further as the line ahead has been bombed. We are diverted to Stargard. The Russians are mounting a big offensive there. In Stargard the local commandant wants to involve us in the defence of the town. We have no weapons and are sent from place to place. We spend three days there.[49]

A fresh Soviet offensive on 25 February broke through the Landeck to Schlochau road at Heinrichswalde, forcing the Latvians back across the Zierflies Brook to positions just east of Krummensee, now the Division's HQ. The full-frontal attack was stopped but the Russians then attacked the left flank, capturing Domslaff and Neubergen. Janums' 33rd Regiment fought back by pushing the Soviets off the hills at Neubergen.[50]

At Domslaff, a Latvian officer considered one of the most promising in the Legion was fatally wounded: Lieutenant Eižens Bonoparts (22 May 1917–25 February 1945). In constant action with the 33rd since the first Latvian contact with the Red Army near Bromberg in late January, Bonoparts was ordered to scout the roads up to Domslaff and clear them. His men took up positions at 10:00 in the hills one kilometre east of Domslaff and fended off a Soviet attack, but big holes in the frontline meant that Soviet units worked round the Latvian left flank as night fell and cut off

47 I. Jansons, *Manu Dienu Grāmata* [*The Book of my Days*] (Australia, self-published by Zaiga Jansone, 2017), pp.149–150.
48 Courtesy of the Latvian War Museum and published for the first time in English. Trans. Daina Vītola.
49 Memoirs of Gunārs Rozens, written in Scotland in 1946, sent to the Latvian War Museum. Courtesy of Jānis Tomaševskis at the Latvian War Museum, Rīga, September 2019.
50 Silgailis, *Latvian Legion,* pp.173–174. Krummensee is now Krzemieniewo, Heinrichswalde is Uniechów, Domslaff is Domisław and Neubergen is not featured on modern maps.

the retreat from Domslaff Heights. Bonoparts was badly wounded in fierce fighting at 18:00 and died on the way to the field hospital.

Deputy Officer Alfons Banders, who took command when Bonoparts was wounded, paid this tribute in the 'Green Books', the history of the Latvian Legion. In a chapter titled *Ltn Bonoparts' last battle,* he wrote:

> On 25 February, at 18:00, 1st Company had just returned from carrying out the order to protect the flank and settled in the forest not far from the Schonwerder

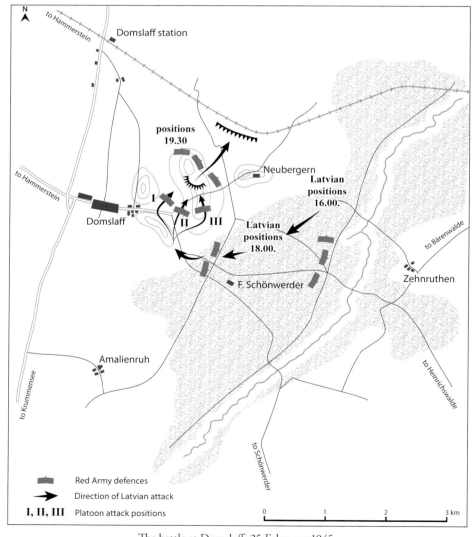

The battle at Domslaff, 25 February 1945.

forest. It turned out that the squadron had been surrounded again. Except for the hillock, situated 120 metres east of the Schonwerder-Domslaff road, the enemy with its mortars and automatic weapon fire had completely blocked this road. The squadron leader gave our company the order to free the road.

After taking the hillock, we had to hold it until all the squadron units had passed. It was raining, mixed with snow. As the company left to carry out the order, it was getting dark. We gone about one kilometre when we met 2nd Battalion HQ soldiers. Lieutenant Ždanovskis told us that the enemy had been on the hillock for several hours already and is blocking the road in both directions with automatic fire. The road is also being hit by fire from mortars [from a] position at the side of the forest past the hillock. The squadron HQ company had been lying at the side of the road about half a kilometre from the bend.

Taking into account that the enemy had taken the hillock several hours previously, it was obvious that they had already dug in and set up their firing weapons. Every hesitation would have made the situation more difficult, therefore having called his company commanders to the front, Lieutenant Bonoparts ordered:

- 'First section (platoon) led by Deputy Officer Banders to make their way to the bend in the road and then to take up exit position for the assault at the foot of the hillock.
- Second section (platoon) led by Deputy Officer Bebris to make their way along the hollow on the SE hillside.[51]
- Third section (platoon) led by Deputy Officer Kažoks. The company commander will go with this section to move along the edge of the elevation and attack the enemy from the SE.
- The attack must come simultaneously from all the sections. The start is when 3rd section reaches a solitary tree, which is possible to approach hidden. After that, to take up positions on the N and NE hillsides. To defend these positions. The order to leave will follow'.

Silently the sections disperse. The hillock, occupied by the enemy, looked menacing. To begin with, as their weapons were silent, it looked like the enemy had not noticed our approach. We had almost reached the bend in the road when suddenly four enemy automatic rifles began firing. Because of the dark, they were unsuccessful.

In order to get the enemy's attention and make easier the other section's taking of exit positions, we began firing from two automatic rifles. The HQ company began firing from Domslaff. Enemy fire increased by the minute. In the end, the whole hillock crackled with automatic rifle and machine gun fire, interspersed with grenades and rifle grenades. We gave back as good as we got.

---

51 Bebris was awarded the Iron Cross First Class for his courage in Pomerania, notably at Domslaff and earlier at Kamin.

The hill at Domslaff where Lieutenant Eižens Bonoparts was killed on 25 February 1945.
(Picture: Aivars Sinka)

At last 2nd and 3rd section had reached the solitary tree and we rose and went on the attack. Although it was only a mere 60 metres to the peak, which was covered by bushes, our feet sank in the muddy terrain and we felt that we would never cover this distance. Some soldiers fell behind but we had no chance to wait for them. When we had begun to clear enemy trenches with grenades, the tardy soldiers began to throw grenades into our cleared trench positions. I was forced to run back in order to clarify the situation with them.

After the taking of the enemy trenches, with my section I took up position with the front to the north, but the remaining sections more to the NW. After a short while, the enemy overran the company's right wing. Amongst the enemy soldiers was also a Latvian, who shouted at us not to fire on our own, whilst others shouted in Russian that they surrender. The company beat off this enemy assault.

With that the escape route for the squadron was free. Sleet was falling. We tried to somehow dig in on the muddy hillside. We counted 31 enemy killed, as well as eight captured Red Army soldiers. Amongst them was one Latvian who had been conscripted into the Red Army from Latgale at the end of 1944.

For us too, it was a costly victory. Among the injured were Lieutenant Bonoparts, Deputy Officer Kažoks, Corporal Luste and two additional soldiers.

Men of the 15th Artillery Regiment pass through a village in Pomerania, February 1945. (Picture: Latvian 'Green Books' [*Latviesu Karavirs Otra Pasaules Kara Laika*] vol. 6.)

It was already 23:00. The soldiers were soaked in the rain and freezing. It seemed that all the squadron sections had already gone but we were still waiting for 5th Company, who were the rearguard.

Finally, and soaked to the skin the same as us, they marched past. We waited another half an hour, then destroyed the four enemy machine guns we had captured and got ready to move on. There was non-stop rain mixed with snow. We were covered in mud and so were our weapons. Our firing power, however, had improved with the 15 [PPSh] machine guns taken from the enemy. We re-joined our battalion after midnight in Hammerstein.[52]

Brunis Rubess remembered those times with a mixture of excitement and relief:

Having got out of the Kamin encirclement, where the Germans thought we would perish, we had about a week and a half's rest in a small town not far away called Peterswalde [Cierznie]. In the meantime I got even closer to Colonel Janums. I have been accepted into the regiment's *štābs* [HQ] and report to Captain Vilis Akermanis. Akermanis, starting from Peterswalde, fills the role

52 Deputy Officer Alfons Banders, in *Ltn Bonoparts' Last Battle*, the Latvian 'Green Books', vol. 6. Banders was promoted to Lieutenant, awarded the Iron Cross Second Class and survived the war. He came to Britain in 1947, living near Derby and working for the National Agriculture Advisory Service, part of the Ministry of Agriculture. He died in 1996.

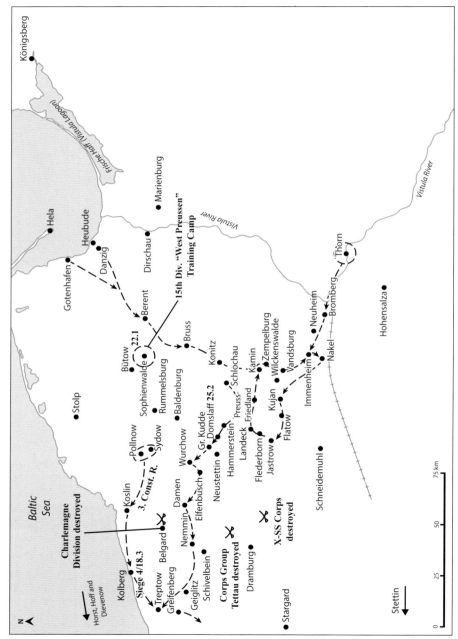

The road to the sea. Hammerstein to Horst, 31 January–11 March 1945.

of local commandant. That usually means arguing with the Germans for facilities, and my language capabilities come in handy. The pause in Peterswalde in February 1945 ends suddenly, when the Russians break into the next town – Preussisch-Friedland – and the big retreat begins.

The proximity of the end of the war was obvious to all. Will Colonel Janums be able to get his 'sons' out from the Red Army's siege in Pomerania? From listening to BBC and other radio stations in secret at the *štābs* it was clear to the Colonel that the Oder had to be crossed. If not the Elbe. A two-month movement began — mostly with the whole German armed forces — in a westerly direction. The first weeks involved going from manor house to manor house. And what houses they were! There were soldiers who, going through the wealth of Pomerania, took silver candelabra with them, and there were others who got drunk in the many distilleries, often drinking to unconsciousness and then capture. Here and there in the distilleries the spirits spilled onto the floor and a puddle formed as deep as a finger. You would see guys, just like puppies, lapping up the moonshine straight from the floor.

The regiment's *štābs* was usually in the local manor house, while the soldiers were in the surrounding houses. Pomeranian manor houses are built in a horseshoe shape — manor house in the middle and servants' quarters around it, [then] stables and sheds for the animals. In one manor house Janums quickly found out that the cellars contained an enormous collection of wines. Janums needed drunk HQ soldiers like a hole in the head. Knowing that I didn't drink, he ordered me to guard the cellar. I didn't care about those bottles, I was just waiting for those two hours to pass and for the guard to be changed so that I would be free to sleep in the library, where there were enormous leather chairs. The shelves were full of leather-bound books, and further on in other rooms were two grand pianos and three *pianini*.

The next morning our job was to bury dead German soldiers but the lads during the night had, nevertheless, managed to get hold of the wine. As the hungover soldiers were digging the graves for the Germans, several small bulls rushed into the yard, who knows from where. The diggers left behind the guns they had with them for the salute and scarpered![53]

The 15th re-grouped at Hammerstein on 26 February with the Kampfgruppe Hämel to their right. Contact had been lost with the French Charlemagne Division, supposed to protect the left flank. The next morning, with air support, Russian tanks bypassed Hammerstein and overran Klein Küdde and Gross Küdde, forcing Divisional HQ into retreat again. New defensive lines were drawn by the 34th Regiment between two lakes, Vilm and Dolgen.[54]

53 Rubess, *Brīnumainā Kārtā*, pp.79–80.
54 Klein Küdde and Gross Küdde are now Gwda Mala and Gwda Wielka and the lakes are Jezioro Wielimie and Dolgie.

One man who was there, Legionnaire Žano Mūsiņš, reflected in his diary on rapidly-changing situations on the ground.

> Our patrol goes over the river and a few miles further, on the other side of the forest, there is a main road, where we hear traffic. We catch a Russian supply wagon and grab a few items before we are spotted by their cavalry unit and we have to disappear back into the forest. Our luck holds: they do not follow us into the forest.
>
> The next day, early in the morning, Russian artillery opens up and in the distance we can see many tanks accompanied by infantry. In short shrift our defence line and bunkers are in shambles and we are forced back. After moving back during the night, in the morning we are far away from Landeck II. It is not long before the Russians have found us and attack again. We withdraw and leave the Russians behind. We move towards Gross Küdde. When we get there we stop for a break. We get our first supply of food and, of course, also some sleep...
>
> Something has gone wrong, because early the next morning Russian tanks appear in our village and give us hell! We are scattered [to the] winds and it is every man for himself! Quite a few manage to escape to Neustettin where our Division's HQ was but soon the tanks follow us and chase further on and on.
>
> The next day I was sent with a message for Colonel Vīksne about our unit, but he could not be found and nobody knew where he was. I returned to my unit, but on the way back I was told by men from the 32nd Regiment that my very close friend from Liepāja had been killed in the battle for Nakel. He was my girlfriend's brother.
>
> Another day. We are moving further, I do not know where, but we are on the move. There's no news of any fighting. We are billeted in a Polish farm. The people are very kind, knowing what they think of Germans. Obviously they know that we are Latvians. Next day we take up positions between two lakes. Our lads manage to catch two Russian soldiers. They tell us that any Latvians the Russian army catch they shoot! It is nice to know! We have to withdraw further away, otherwise we will be surrounded. We pull back four kilometres to another village and stay there the night.[55]

I finish reading out the diary to him as we sit in his kitchen.

VH: This sounds very dramatic. What was it like?
ZM: Hell. They were blowing seven bells of shit out of us. It's like being fired at by artillery, shooting straight into our Army groups. You've got nowhere to go. At the time they were practically in a horseshoe around us. We were more or less encircled, almost, but we got out. We lost quite a lot of people. Neustettin – that's there as well.

55 Diary of Žano Mūsiņš, given to author.

VH: When you say you lost a lot of people, what do you mean? To machine gun
  fire, shelling?
ZM: Put simply, we were in a panic. Out.

He gestures with his arm.

Every man for himself. You couldn't do *nothing* any more. There was like a wave
of fire coming onto you, and what can you do? You just take off. At that time
we were damned disorganised after Landeck. We were all in tatters. There was
very little cohesion in the unit. It was every unit for themselves. We lost half a
company at the time – about 60 or 70 people. I'm one of the lucky ones who got
out. God knows what happened to them. Wherever they were, I don't know. I've
never met any of them ever since. It was sheer hell.

The worst bit was that there was no connection any more with the German
command groups so we didn't know where we were, where anything was: you
were more or less on your own. And of course the tanks didn't joke. If you're
in open country you can't take the tanks on, but once you're in the woods or
in a village the tanks don't come near you, because the Germans did have the
Panzerfaust and if a tank got hit by a Panzerfaust it was gone. And we had them,
but you had to be within 50 metres to hit a tank with a Panzerfaust. To get close
to a tank you had to be where the tank can't see you, and if you got caught out
in the open you didn't have a chance.
VH: Did you take any tanks on?
ZM: No. I personally never had a chance.
VH: Would you have done?
ZM: Oh yes. Because at that time it was survival. Although I was really a
  machine gunner, with an MG-42, shooting about 1,000 rounds a minute.
  It was wicked: like a broom. The only trouble was you ran out of ammunition very quickly, and if you fired a long burst you'd start to run out, and
  there was only so much you could carry. So we tended to fire in short bursts
  and then you could do better. They [the Red Army] were just like a big wave
  of people, like in prehistoric times.[56]

The Latvians dug in on the west coast of Lake Dolgen, defending the divisional
HQ at the village of Sparsee [Spore], which was still full of civilians. But then seven
Russian tanks suddenly appeared, causing panic. Colonel Janums sent two reserve
companies to strengthen defences along the south side of the village and deal with the
tanks. Two were quickly knocked out and another four destroyed by German units
and artillery. The surviving tank retreated and the Latvians moved out of immediate
danger, but things were not going well.

Legion historian Arturs Silgailis' detailed notes of the time show how chaotic
things were:

56 Žano Mūsiņš, interviewed by author, transcribed.

The disintegration of the German Army became more and more obvious at this time and resulted in premature retreats and the discarding of weapons. The 34th Grenadier Regiment replenished their heavily-depleted weapons with arms discarded by the French SS Division Charlemagne … The combat strength of divisional units was minimal. Many of the men were still wandering about in search of their units. The 33rd Grenadier Regiment had a combat strength of only 100 men. The fate of its two battalions was still unknown at this time.[57]

Latvian reserves had been gathered in Hammerstein as the Soviets pressed west and were sent to strengthen positions near Lake Vilm and Sparsee. Among them was Arturs Grava:

We were issued with rifles that could be loaded one cartridge at a time – we didn't have other weapons. I swapped mine for a modern gun that had been left somewhere. My group was put into positions on the south-east corner of the lake. On the night of the 26–27 February I was in a patrol north of our position when there was an unexpected Russian attack. My group retreated west, while I only had a route northwards open to me. I attached myself to some Latvian artillery unit, which, having shot off its three shells, moved further north.

The units that had retreated westwards – and there were many of them – bumped into bigger Russian forces and turned back. I met my own people near Sparsee, north of the lake. News arrived of seven tanks approaching. The Germans organised resistance and the Latvians were allotted to a sector that had to be defended. When the tanks appeared, they didn't come directly towards us but crossed our field of fire about half a kilometre in front of us. One tank was shot up by Latvian artillery. The change of position for the Germans turned into disorganised fleeing, it seemed, for fear of being cut off. The Latvians also left their positions.

Together with another Latvian (I don't remember his name), transporting two injured Legionnaires (Lerks in a wheelbarrow and Primaks holding onto my shoulder) we went over a small river bridge, almost as the last to cross. A few more Germans followed us, but they weren't able to help us. When night came, my colleague went to look for help and I was left with the injured. He found help – a Polish farm-worker with a horse and cart. We quickly drove on, in the dark.

I did meet my unit again, but the company commander, Over-Lieutenant Pommers, kept me with his leadership group at Elfenbusch station as liaison with the Germans on the other side of the tracks. Between us there was an approximately 200-metre-wide undefended gap. The nearest German group had settled into some high-up Party member's house and they accepted me in a friendly way. They treated me to smoked sausage that they found there, showed me the latest

57 Silgailis, *Latvian Legion*, pp.175–176.

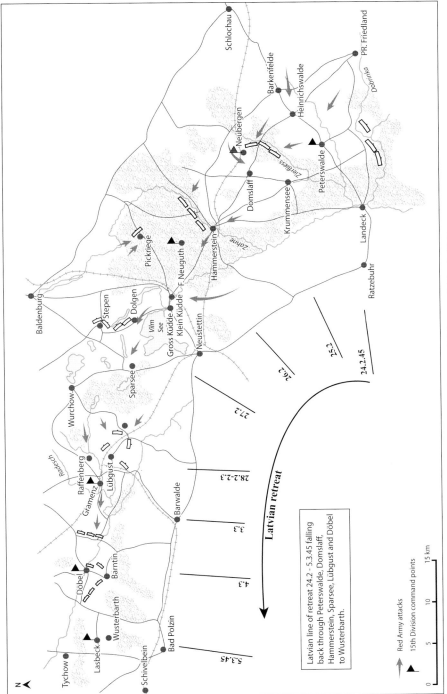

The retreat to Lübgust, 24 February–5 March 1945.

Latvian line of retreat 24.2 - 5.3.45 falling back through Peterswalde, Domslaff, Hammerstein, Sparsee, Lübgust and Döbel to Wusterbarth.

Latvian retreat

Red Army attacks

15th Division command points

0   5   10   15 km

room decorations – portraits of the ruling men, with their faces hung upside down. In those days I didn't know who they were, but I didn't see the Führer.

When I went to the Germans a second time, they laughed and told me about when the owner of the house arrived. He had a real go at them, because he had only given them permission to stay in the hallway.

Near to the station was a German armoured train, which was attacked by a Russian bomber. As I was watching the duel through the station window, something exploded and my face was caught by bits of broken glass. Over-Lieutenant Pommers sent me to the first aid post, where they patched me up with plasters.

At the first aid post I was with five or six Germans, who were discussing an event that you wouldn't have believed in normal times. I don't know how it started, but during the event, the soldiers had refused to follow the officer's orders. The officer threatened to shoot them, when one of them grabbed an automatic rifle and called out: *'Schiessen Sie, dann sehen wir wer besser kann!'* ['Go on, shoot, then we'll see who's better at it!']

I don't know how the incident ended, only later I was amazed that so many of the witnesses were at the first aid point at the same time.[58]

By early March 1945, the German grip on Pomerania was shattered. The Second Army was falling back to Danzig and Gotenhafen to hold the ports as long as possible to keep the mass evacuation of Operation Hannibal going. The east wing of the Third Panzer Army was in disarray, with units across the region trapped or taking heavy casualties. Military discipline was breaking down, with a wave of refugees fleeing west ahead of the Red Army.

Retreating through Klein Küdde, Lake Vilm and Sparsee, and then losing contact with each other around Kussow and St Elfenbusch, the 33rd and 34th Regiments met up in Gut Lübgust [Lubogoszcz], where Janums sought out a command post in the manor house.

The division has assigned me Marienhohe as the command post but when I try and get there the car sinks into the mud, so we're very happy when we get back onto a cobbled road. I have to look for a better command post, and by the main road is the Lübgust manor house. In recent days I've noticed a lot of command posts – some better, some worse. Under the present circumstances it's not really important because usually we billet ourselves there for one, maybe two days. So in choosing a command post I don't really think about the comfort side of it, but only how useful it will be to me.

This time I chose the manor house, because it's situated in the middle of the defence district and next to a good road. We arrive there at dawn. It's noticeable how big the building is and how solidly built. There are barns, sheds, even a brewery and distillery. All these buildings sit in a large arc

---

58 Memoirs of Arturs Grava, sent to author 20 July 2022, trans. Aivars Sinka.

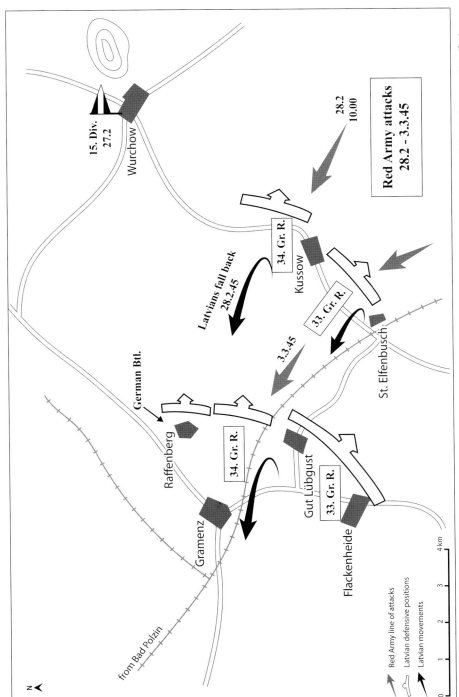

Lübgust detail, 28 February 1945. At the end of February–early March 1945, the 15th Division was in positions around Gut Lübgust and Raffenberg.

surrounding the manor yard, at the north end of which is an impressive two-storey manor house.

There are cows in the dairy, pigs oinking – but not a single person around. All the buildings seem abandoned and empty. When I try to open the massive oak front door I realise that you can't do that with just one hand – the gates open slowly and solemnly, with little noise. With my HQ officers, we go into the enormous hall. My attention is immediately drawn to the rolls of carpet sewn into cloth. In the corner are a number of pieces of luggage, put there for departure. It seems that not everyone has left the manor house.

Janums describes a 'very wide and ornate staircase' leading upstairs from the hall, but he's looking for a room on the ground floor to use as a command post. He opens some smaller doors off the hall to find exactly what he's looking for.

...a study, fairly simple but with everything an office needs. A writing desk with a telephone, a couple of leather club armchairs and an elegant fireplace in the corner of the room. It seems to me this room is exactly right for a command post! I don't need to worry that any one of my companies will be short of space in this manor house because it's so big, so I leave the allocation to my HQ commander Captain Akermanis and Adjutant Lieutenant Ešis and special operations commander Lieutenant Bušmanis.

We get to work organising a communications network for this position. Telephones ring, messengers come and go, everybody's busy and so a number of hours in the morning go by. About 11:00 an enemy attack started in the region where our 34th Regiment was.

Looking through a telescope in the study I can clearly see the enemy artillery explosions and the soldiers from the 34th retreating in the direction of Raffenberg. In the last days I've seen this scene many times, but my squadron's northern flank is wide open.

Janums continues:

I was watching the battle unfold so closely I didn't notice a German officer come into the room. By the time I did he was close enough to introduce himself as the owner, Captain Baron Rohr. In front of me was a slim-built 45-year-old German Army Captain. He stood silently for a while, as though looking for words, then gasped: 'Tell me Squadron Leader, sir. What should I do now?'

Having said that, he looked at me full of doubt, as if looking for help. I understood this man now wants to hear the impossible – that we will hold this manor house and also the whole Bolshevik wave will stop and his manor from birth and all his wealth will be saved. I take him to the window and show him the enemy shells already exploding in the north. I tell him that the whole German army is in retreat and my squadron will not be capable of holding this position very long. Within a day we will be on the retreat – and later on that day or the day after, this manor house will fall into enemy hands.

I tell him – therefore – to take whatever's necessary and get to the other side of the Oder river as soon as possible. As I say these words the officer seems to sag as if having received a heavy blow, like a person who has had his final hopes destroyed. Then he leaves the office. Baron Rohr departed that afternoon.

After he'd gone Captain Akermanis reports that in the cellar are to be found large quantities of bread, dried meat, smoked sausage, various conserves and jams and tinned food. Most importantly, the cellar is full of French wines and spirits of different sorts. Some are fifty or more years old. He ends his report by saying: 'Squadron Leader, sir. We'll wash our feet in the wine that's younger than ten years old!'

His demeanour tells me that he's already tried out some of the older wines. My men haven't had proper food for more than a week. We've managed with tins of this and that which could be found in the cellars of every abandoned farmhouse, but we haven't seen bread for a long while. Therefore the news that tonight we'll get bread is a great temptation. But my attitude to the usefulness of wine and brandy in these conditions makes me think slightly differently.

A second battalion commander has just arrived to see me, and I have to brief him about the defensive positions he is to take up, so it seems to me the wrong time and place to be tasting the brandy. I give an order for the cellar to be locked and a guard put on the door. Drinks are not to be given to anyone. Every company has to send their own cart to collect. I order the bread, meat and sausage to be divided between the units proportionate to the number of people. Tonight will I hand out a fifth of a bottle of cognac and half a bottle of wine to every man.

Captain Akermanis goes off to sort out the distribution of food. After he has left I dictate the defensive orders to the squadron which are written down by Lieutenant Bušmanis. Finishing the orders, I have to show where the Company HQ is located. With the front so risky I want to keep that separate from Regimental Command so I order that it should be at Zuch Manor.

About an hour later Captain Akermanis reported back to the command post to confirm that the company had moved out to its new position. It was past 22:00 when the Colonel had finished giving all the necessary orders for the next day. By then silence had descended on the frontline. But Janums had forgotten one thing: what had happened to the wine cellar keys and who was guarding the door? As he mulled over his plan for the next day, that thought suddenly returned.

Lieutenant Bušmanis is still fiddling around by the table. Stopping in the front of the fireplace I think over all the orders and commands that I've given. I don't think I've forgotten anything. I remember how Captain Akermanis said goodbye very sincerely. I don't think he will have forgotten to take the HQ

Company's share of the wine with him, but what's happened to the distribution of food? And who has got the keys to the wine cellar?

Akermanis didn't say anything about that to me and I want to sort it out. I think that some of the other HQ officers might know something about this, so I go off to find out where they've disappeared to the whole evening. When I open the heavy padded doors from the study, the sound of singing comes towards me from the cellar.

On the upper floors too men are singing, stamping time with their feet. I climb up the stairs and look in a bedroom. The furniture is ornately-carved mahogany, but the room itself looks as if a battle has happened here. There are vast numbers of empty bottles scattered all around. In one bed, with his muddy boots on a red velvet counterpane, lies a soldier, supine. His companion is sleeping in the next bed: he has crawled under the duvet so that just his muddy feet can be seen poking out from under the sheets.

The sight in the second room isn't any better. It's clear the cellar has been drunk dry: tonight, my boys are drunk. After all the work I've done today I wouldn't have minded a glass or two myself but every bottle is empty. There's not much point in going any further. It's clear that my HQ is not capable of any work tonight.

Returning to my office I report what I've seen to Lieutenant Bušmanis, and we agree that tonight we will stand guard for our men. I sit at the table and study the map, looking at the roads leading to the Oder and the crossing points.

My musings are disturbed by Lieutenant Bušmanis who has found some nuts and a full box of nicely-made wooden pipes. That's a valuable find and could be useful for my men. We put them to one side. Lieutenant Bušmanis tells me the whole manor house is beautifully decorated with antique furniture, carpets and works of art. It looks as if it's an abandoned castle. I look around later and find ornate wooden carvings, silver, paintings and a guest book listing the dinner parties held here, who came and what they ate. It's a shame to think that all this will be ruined tomorrow or the day after when the Red Army comes through. I go back to my maps and study the routes to the Oder so that I don't have to think about the vandalism that's going to happen here.

Janums' final sentence sums up the enormity of the challenge and the danger ahead.

It seems to me that the enemy must already be much closer to the Oder than we are.[59]

The Latvians headed north-westerly to the Baltic coast, across the thrust of the Soviet offensive. Spring had reached Pomerania, and the roads were a sea of mud, clogged with military vehicles and refugees. Trucks and cars that broke down or were in the way were pushed off the road. Survivors from units badly mauled in the Red

---

59 Janums, *Mana Pulka Kauju Gaitas*, pp.227–230. Trans. Daina Vītola.

Legionnaire Arturs Grava, who was wounded at Gut Lübgust on his first day in action. Photographed age 97 at *Jani* celebrations in the United States, midsummer 2022. (Picture: Aivars Sinka)

Army offensive joined their ranks, among them the French Charlemagne and the Pommern Division, but death and disaster were never far away.

Four days before his 98th birthday, former Legionnaire Arturs Grava joined a Zoom call from his home in Cleveland, Ohio, to be interviewed by the author about his war service.

> AG: I was wounded on my first day in action, 3 March 1945. That was at Gut Lübgust, about 32 kilometres [20 miles] west of Wilmsee. I was in a building on the very edge of Lübgust on a nightwatch, and at first light in the early morning the Russians started bombarding us. Shells hit the building I was in, so we pulled back and in the rubble of a house we saw a few Panzerfausts. About an hour later the Russians approached with a tank – one tank – and our company didn't have any Panzerfausts so I crawled back and retrieved one of them. The Sergeant took it from me and shot at the tank but missed, but the tank was scared to come any closer. There was an exchange of fire – nothing major, really – and after an hour, maybe two, I was hit in the elbow with a bullet, and that was the end of my war experience.
>
> VH: Which elbow? Right or left?
>
> AG: Left.

He rolls up the left sleeve of his shirt and lifts it to the camera to show the scar.

> AG: The bullet went right through my elbow but I was very, very lucky. Later in the hospital they told me the bullet went right between the bones but my arm is perfectly alright. It was stiff for a while. I got first aid right on the spot, then I walked four kilometres to another place but that was being closed and would not accept anyone. So I walked to the next one, seven

Legionnaires of the 34th Regiment Latvian Legion in the Ostenheide Forest. In the parade hat: Captain Leitmanis. (Picture: Latvian 'Green Books' [*Latviesu Karavirs Otra Pasaules Kara Laika*] vol. 6.)

kilometres away, reached that and they were also in the process of closing as the Russians were approaching.

I got a lift on a – I don't know what it was, a supply cart? – and went a few kilometres with them but then I got off because they were going in a different direction and started walking again. I travelled a little distance by car, and reached Belgard. There was a new first aid facility there, just established, and I was the first patient. I spent the night there, and then the next day they took me by car to a train and the train took me in the direction of Kolberg.

I don't know how, but the Russians stopped the train, disconnected the engine or something, but the tanks left us alone the next day and during the night me and several Germans got off the train and walked into Kolberg, about ten kilometres or so. We reached there in the morning.[60]

On the evening of 6 March, with the road at Grossin cut, the column diverted into the Ostenheide forest to rest. They split defensive duties between the various units. The 34th Regiment guarded the western edge of the forest, the 33rd took the south-western edge, the Pommern division was assigned the south-eastern side with the

60 Interview with author, 20 July 2022.

Charlemagne division to the east. But chaos ensued. Legion historian Arturs Silgailis wrote:

That night for some unknown reason panic broke out among the men of the Pommern and Charlemagne divisions, and they destroyed their heavy weapons and took flight in a westerly direction. Corps commanders received messages that both divisions had been annihilated so ordered the rest of the corps to destroy their heavy weapons and retreat. This reached all units except the 33rd Grenadiers, which replenished its stocks of weapons from those left in the forest.

The next day the artillery battalion returned to the woods and recovered three of its guns, some horses and signalling equipment and as night fell, moved onto the refugee-packed roads again for an overnight journey to Broitz, reaching there in the early hours of the following morning.

At noon the journey continued through Borntin, Wangerin and Gumtow to Zedlin heading for Horst on the Baltic Sea. The artillery units were told to destroy the three guns they had rescued from the forest, dump their ammunition and blow the bridge at Borntin.[61]

An account in the Latvian Legion 'Green Books' official history of the aftermath of that moment in the Ostenheide Forest offers an insight into the type of commander Karl Burk was. He split the division into smaller units and told them to try and reach Stettin, where they could cross the Oder. The final part of the order was that all motor vehicles and injured men were to be left behind. In an account dealing with the experiences of the 15th Fusilier 'Recce' Battalion, the Legion official history notes:

That was the maddest order that the Recce Battalion received throughout the course of the fighting. The battalion commander understood that something was wrong with the Divisional leadership.[62]

The order was ignored. This account of the Ostenheide Forest comes from the Legion's official history, and was translated by Arturs Grava:

On 6 March, around midnight, when darkness covered the forest of Ostenheide, an order was received from the Division to destroy everything, retaining only three two-horse carriages from each battery for the transportation of the wounded. The battalion carried out this order, making all cannons and wagons useless.

There was confusion and alarm at the staff of the battalion when the order was received. The adjutant of the battalion, Lieutenant Ģērmanis, was assigned the task to verify this order; he received a confirmation from the commander

---

61 Silgailis, *Latvian Legion,* pp.179–180.
62 Unknown author, Latvian 'Green Books', vol. 6, p.203.

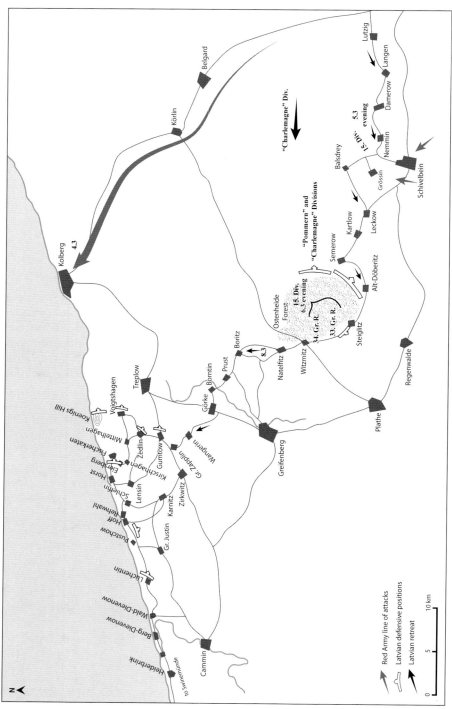

The retreat to the Baltic coast 5–13 March, 1945.

of the Division elaborating that the cannons are not to be blown up, only to be made useless. The breechblocks and sight units were removed and buried or scattered in the forest.

Later, on 7 March, the order at the staff of the Division turned out to be hastily given (it had come from the Army or the staff of the Corps). The commander of the Division received a new order – to attempt the restoration of the cannons. This was only partially successful as only one cannon was restored to battle readiness. The 1st Battery also recovered two abandoned wagons, a considerable number of telephones, and 18 horses. Also the 2nd and 3rd Batteries recovered a few wagons and horses.

In the early morning of 7 March, the entire battalion, now as infantry, assembled in the north-west corner of Ostenheide Forest to begin the march to Witmitz, then on to Natelfitz and Borntin. The enemy was not seen during the march. The battalion had these horse-drawn wagons:

> 1st Battery: three two-horse wagons and kitchen
> 2nd Battery: three two-horse wagons
> 3rd Battery: four two-horse wagons.[63]

On a sunny afternoon in Fenstanton in the Cambridgeshire countryside seven decades later, I show Legionnaire Jānis Urpens a map showing the retreat of the 15th Division in the early weeks of March 1945, which includes detail of the positions around the Ostenheide forest and afterwards.

> Yes, that must be the road we used. We went as far as about 20 kilometres from Kolberg but we didn't go into Kolberg because the Russians had got ahead of us, so we went into Horst.[64]

The German frontlines were in disarray. Survivors of the routs at Körlin and Belgard regrouped on the Baltic coast at Horst and Hoff with those heading west and trying to avoid the siege at Kolberg.

Imants Jansons was one of those men. His unit of sappers were often nearly trapped and constantly pursued, with Russian aircraft spotting and harassing them. Fighting was often at very close quarters and the only food supply was from foraging at farms. Entire nights were spent on the march west. The roads were littered with equipment abandoned along the way: artillery pieces, wagons full of uniforms, tents, bicycles, motorcycles, accordions and worn-out boots, all dumped where soldiers rested and decided to lighten their loads. Food had become the uppermost concern in the soldiers' minds, second only to the pain in their feet. Jansons wrote on 8 March 1945:

63 Freivalds, *The Latvian Soldier*, p.227. Trans. Arturs Grava.
64 Interview with author.

The bottoms of my feet are hurting like mad and I am barely strong enough to stand, let alone walk. During the day and evening it isn't so noticeable, but towards the morning it is like torture. Before sleeping I change the socks and shoes on my aching feet. They steam like sweat running off a horse's back after a run. The skin is soft and red. There are small blisters. I tie a silk cloth to the soles and put the socks and shoes back on. The next second I am in a deep, deep sleep…

It is twilight when we are awakened and ordered to prepare to march again. My soles are fiercely painful. On taking my first steps it is necessary to limp, for it feels like I am stepping on hot coal or needles … Every step is immeasurably painful. I can walk only by dragging my feet on the ground.[65]

On the morning of 10 March, Soviet planes attacked Jansons' platoon as they destroyed a bridge connecting two villages through a swamp. Later, linking up with wounded soldiers returning from hospital, they heard that the Russians had broken through to the coast and they were surrounded. A German unit headed out to try and break through the encirclement: fierce fighting was heard shortly afterwards.

Later that day, the Latvians managed to force the road open and German planes air-dropped food and ammunition. They marched past large summer houses on the outskirts of the town showing recent signs of clashes with the Red Army, with fallen soldiers still lying in the road and their horses dead alongside them. The enemy was not far away and the shelling and mortar fire was constant, so the Latvians climbed down from the cliffs and the forest to move along the beach, close to the sea. As the sun set, there was more contact with the Soviets and the 2nd Platoon's messenger had his leg shot off almost to the knee. Jansons wrote:

We tie it off tightly with a towel so the injured man doesn't bleed to death. We put him on a blanket and quickly carry him back. He feels the pain and with each step he moans and curses loudly. We even get angry, for carrying him is extremely difficult. It's quite surprising how heavy such an injured person can be. There are five or six of us carriers and all of us out of breath. Finally a refugee takes him on his wagon.[66]

On 11 March the sappers were transferred to the seaside town of Horst. There they would become part of another last-gasp escape – the breakout west along the Baltic coast to Dievenow. In Rīga 75 years later, historian Valdis Kuzmins takes my notepad and draws a squiggly line down the centre of the page.

65 Jansons, *Manu Dienu Gramata*, pp.161–162.
66 Jansons, *Manu Dienu Gramata*, p.169.

The station at Kolberg [Kołobrzeg]. (Picture: Jim Donnelly/Anaxa Images)

This is the road to the sea, right? This comes after Jastrow, Flederborn, Landeck and Kamin and ends with the Latvians and Germans keeping that channel open along the coast so they can escape to the west. But that's only possible because of the break-out at Domslaff along that road, and the death of one of the most able and promising Latvian commanders, Eižens Bonoparts.[67]

67 Interview with author, 27 November 2019, Rīga.

17

Kolberg

The top of the lighthouse in Kolberg – Kołobrzeg to visitors today – offers a fantastic view across the city's rooftops and landmarks. From here I can see where so much dramatic history played out in March 1945 when the city was one of Hitler's *Festungs*, or Fortresses, holding back the Red Army for grim life. The story of the encirclement and battle for Kolberg is one of the most gripping and tragic encounters on the Eastern Front.

To my left and right a wide belt of sandy beach stretches along the coast in both directions as far as the eye can see, dotted with sun loungers and volleyball courts. Cafés and ice cream carts ply a busy summer trade. A strip of trees separates the beach from the town with a sequence of ornamental parks to rest, chat or pass the time.

Modern day Kołobrzeg is a spa town, a destination for beach holidays and camping; for rest, relaxation, medical treatments and recuperation. The railway drops passengers right in the centre of town, a matter of metres from the shops and restaurants lining the approaches to the harbour. The lighthouse stands at the head of a jetty stretching out into the vast blue-grey expanse of the Baltic Sea. It's a great place, but like so many towns along this coastline, it has a dark past.

As March 1945 dawned, Nazi Pomerania was crumbling piece by piece, shattered by the power of the Soviet offensives west and north. Ports, cities, important towns, main roads and railways were being lost by the day. The rapid Russian thrust to the coast cut off German forces to the east, leaving the sea as the only way out.

Every German ship available was pressed into service for the mass evacuation of Operation Hannibal. The thousands of lives lost when the MV *Wilhelm Gustloff* was torpedoed off Stolp [Słupsk] at the end of January 1945 did not deter desperate refugees and wounded soldiers from pressing onto any available deck space in the hope of getting away from this hellish endgame.[1]

---

1   In his 2012 book *In Titanic's Shadow – the World's Worst Maritime Disasters*, David Williams quotes calculations by Gustloff authority Heinz Schon putting the number of passengers and crew on board as 10,582. (Chapter 10: *No Roses on their Graves*). The loss of life is estimated at between 9,343 and 9,600, of whom almost 5,000 were children. See pp.31–36 of *100 Days* for John Toland's gripping and terrifying account of the sinking of the *Wilhelm Gustloff*.

Kolberg seen from the lighthouse. (Picture: author)

View from the lighthouse at Kolberg to the east. (Picture: author)

The lighthouse at Kolberg was a focal point for the evacuation from the port. Badly damaged in the battle for the city, it was quickly rebuilt afterwards. (Picture: author)

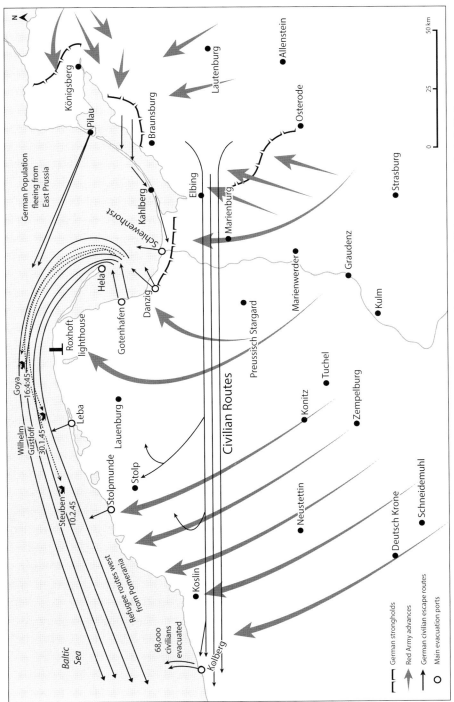

Operation Hannibal and the flight of the German population. Exodus towards the Baltic ports, particularly Kolberg.

Neither did the loss of another 4,500 lives deter people, when a second cruise liner, the SS *General von Steuben* was torpedoed by the same submarine, S-13, ten days later. The ship went down within 20 minutes with 2,500 wounded soldiers, 800 civilians, nurses, crew and military personnel on board, as well as an unknown number of refugees from Pillau. Around 650 on board survived, with the *Steuben's* torpedo boat escort T-196 rescuing 300 people from its decks as it sank.[2]

Kolberg offered hope however slim, so tens of thousands of civilians and soldiers alike flocked there. The city had been declared a fortress at the end of 1944, anticipating a Soviet offensive in early 1945, but when the vastly-experienced new commandant Colonel Fritz Fullriede arrived on 1 March 1945, he found it ill-prepared, packed with refugees fleeing from the east, and the station full of trainloads of people trying to escape. A veteran of action in Poland in 1939, on the Eastern Front, with the Afrika Korps and in Italy, Fullriede quickly took control of the situation.

A perimeter was thrown around the outskirts of the city with a shell of defensive strongpoints. A series of fallback positions to the sea inside that perimeter defended access to the harbour and quayside, meaning civilians could be ferried until the last minute to two destroyers lying in deeper waters. From there, the lucky ones could be shipped to Swinemünde. The area around the jetty and the lighthouse could be held until the end and still – hopefully – there would be an escape route by sea.

Fullriede moved just in time. Three days later the 1st Guards Tank Army reached the coast on either side of Kolberg, cutting it off. The only way out now for the 68,000 refugees and 3,300 soldiers trapped inside the Soviet ring was by sea.

The fight for Kolberg lasted from 4–18 March. Defending the city were men from the German Third Panzer Army, the remains of the Charlemagne Division and some units of the Latvian 15th Division, including around 1,500–2,000 unarmed men. Their weapons included about 60 artillery guns, 18 tanks and an armoured train, Panzer Zug 72A. The evacuation operation centred around refugees being transferred from the quayside at Kolberg to the two destroyers, *Z34* and *Z43*, which bombarded Soviet positions at key moments.[3]

The Red Army attacked the city from six different directions. The first strike on the morning of 4 March was thrown back and the job of taking the city was handed to the Polish 1st Army. One Latvian soldier there was Harijs Valdmanis, an ambulance driver and medical administrator operating from a base on the outskirts of the city. We speak by phone on his 95th birthday.

> I was in Kolberg for almost a fortnight. We came in on 4 March and then we couldn't get any further because the Soviets cut off the way west, so we stayed. Myself and a colleague with a motorbike were sent ahead to check out the way. We went up to the gates of Kolberg and there were some people building tank traps, so we went back and said the road was OK. So our company went into Kolberg – then it turned out we couldn't go any further.

2   Kieser, *Prussian Apocalypse*, pp.120–121.
3   Duffy, *Red Storm on the Reich*, pp.232–234.

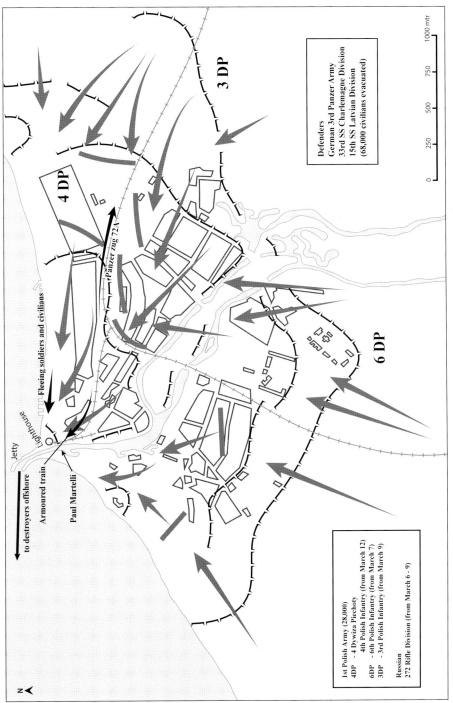

Festung [Fortress] Kolberg, 4–18 March 1945. The Polish 1st Army offensive.

3 DP

4 DP

6 DP

Panzer zug 72A

Jetty

to destroyers offshore

Armoured train

Lighthouse

Fleeing soldiers and civilians

Paul Martelli

N

Defenders
German 3rd Panzer Army
33rd SS Charlemagne Division
15th SS Latvian Division
(68,000 civilians evacuated)

0   250   500   750   1000 mtr

1st Polish Army (28,000)
4DP   - 4 Dywizia Piechoty
          4th Polish Infantry (from March 12)
6DP   - 6th Polish Infantry (from March 7)
3DP   - 3rd Polish Infantry (from March 9)

Russian
272 Rifle Division (from March 6 - 9)

I didn't see very much of Kolberg itself because our trucks were parked outside the town and myself and three other guys were staying put with the [ambulance] cars in the park. The rest of our company was somewhere in the city in a school, but we were camping all the time, looking after our trucks and cars. Then one day we got the message that we were being taken out by ship: I think it was 14 March. We were taken out on a German warship. First small boats took us to the warship anchored outside the harbour, the warship took us to Swinemünde, and then we started walking.

As I remember it was quite peaceful. We were not troubled with anything. There must have been some attacking because one of our company guys was killed at the school building. He had just been outside and there came *granat-casters* – a *granat* [mortar] in a pipe – but I can't remember much fighting. I remember a plane high up in the skies but there was no bombing. That's how I remember it.

I was never in the city itself, and we heard about our colleague afterwards. It was a *granat* that killed him, not in a massed attack.[4]

The experience of many others in and around Kolberg was that it was far from peaceful, especially in the later stages of the siege. With roads, railways and railway stations choked with people trying to flee, the local population panicked when they met Red Army troops. Horst Wegner, a civilian, was walking to Kolberg with his family when Russian tanks appeared.

The infantry sitting on top of the tanks started to shoot wildly all over the place. My father got shot right through his thigh … The Russians … [Mongolian troops] had huge scars and pockmarks on their faces, and they were draped in jewellery – they wore watches up to the elbows. They came in and pulled out anyone wearing anything military – a military coat, for example. They were taken behind the barn, shoved against a wall and shot.[5]

A steady stream of retreating soldiers and refugees heading west was moving along the beach, with Legionnaire Jānis Čevers among them.

We were in Kolberg. That was a nasty place. The Russians were inland from the sea front and we were retreating along the coast. There was quite a steep hill and there were thousands and thousands of civilians, prisoners, Germans, Latvians retreating, moving along the beach. It was total chaos.

4   Interview with author, 05 October 2018. After the war, Mr Valdmanis moved to Oslo in Norway and lived the rest of his life there. He was one of two surviving Legionnaires to attend the unveiling of the 'Beehive' memorial to the Latvians at Camp 2227 at Zedelghem in Belgium. The other was Laimonis Ceriņš, who died in 2020.
5   Blatman, *The Death Marches*, p.75.

Three or four German ships were shelling the Russians, hammering them on top of the cliff so they couldn't get their heads up. We moved along the coast there for about 40 kilometres.[6] It was hit and miss, running and fighting from town to town. We weren't very strong. We didn't have any artillery or anything. It was coming to the end of the war. We didn't even have guns for a while – we had to give them to the Germans. There were stacks and stacks of dead German soldiers and dead civilians. We were fighting, running; fighting, running. We didn't stay in Kolberg – we just went through it.

All I remember is running for my life. Falling over dead bodies. Running for my life. Watching the German ships shooting, hammering the Russian soldiers, firing non-stop. Everyone was trying to escape to the west. We weren't fighting, just trying to escape. Thousands of people, keeping going. Dead bodies, everywhere. The Germans were firing at the Russians but some shells were falling short and landing on us.[7]

Among the defenders of Kolberg were a few hundred men of the Charlemagne Division, survivors of a series of catastrophic encounters with the Red Army which had left around half their once 7,000-strong volunteer force dead or missing in less than a month.[8]

The 350 Charlemagne men who escaped Kolberg were sent to defend Berlin in the dying days of the war. Four were awarded the Knight's Cross for their courage but most were killed there or shortly afterwards when captured. Those who survived Kolberg were sent to Siberian gulags. In less than a year, 52 had died of malnourishment, dysentery or pneumonia.[9] On the final day of the war, 13 Charlemagne men were captured in Bavaria by the Americans and handed over to the 2nd Free French Armoured Division. They were promptly shot as traitors by a firing squad.

Paul Martelli survived, and his account of what happened in Kolberg is gripping and terrifying in equal measure. A teenage SS soldier in a unit of volunteers described as 'fanatical Nazi-sympathisers', Martelli's memoirs paint a vivid human picture of the desperation of the final days in Kolberg.[10]

Martelli arrived in Kolberg on 6 March 1945 after a series of fights between his unit and Soviet forces advancing on Körlin. In his memoir *On the Devil's Tail*, Martelli describes seeing Russian soldiers silently crossing the Persante river camouflaged as

---

6   Horst is known for its cliffs.
7   Interview with author, Derby, UK.
8   Trigg, *Hitler's Gauls*, p.125.
9   Trigg, *Hitler's Gauls*, p.127.
10 From transcript of Reuters news report 18 March 1998 on possible German pension payments to Nazi war criminals, quoted in Trigg, p.164. Some critics say Martelli's book is 'opaque' and lacks firm and verifiable facts, though the accounts of Korlin and Kolberg are not singled out for criticism and do date accurately. While critical, reviewer Rafe McGregor at The History Net.com considers Martelli's writing 'rich, visceral and authentic' (see <https://www.histo-rynet.com/book-review-on-the-devils-tail-by-paul-martelli-with-vittorino-dal-cengio.htm>).

Frenchman Paul Martelli wrote a dramatic account of the last days of Kolberg as a member of the Charlemagne SS Division. He later joined the French Foreign Legion. (Picture: courtesy of Helion & Company)

young pine trees so they could creep forward blending in with the bushes and trees on the other side before attacking the French positions.

Sent forward as a scout, Martelli spotted them just in time and raised the alarm moments before a frenzied Soviet attack. This reached to within a few metres of their main positions before being thrown back by mortars and machine gun fire. That night, short on ammunition, hungry, tired and with their coats stiff with ice, they fell back north to Kolberg – an experience exactly matching that of the Latvian Legionnaires nearby.[11]

At sunset the next evening they stopped to rest in a village, where they were fed and looked after by locals. Martelli fell asleep, to be woken in the early hours (04:00)

---

11 P. Martelli and V. Dal Cengio, *On the Devil's Tail – in Combat With the Waffen SS on the Eastern Front 1945 and With the French in Indochina 1951–54* (Warwick: Helion, 2018), pp.85–95.

by warning shouts of tanks approaching. Soldiers and villagers alike gathered in the square hurrying to escape.

> Now the creak and squeal of tanks moving in the distance could be heard above the hubbub. That metallic screeching would make anybody's blood run cold, including my own; they would enter the village in a few minutes. The streets were choked with women and children, old folks walking. Some were on bicycles and others, panting, pulled overladen handcarts – all were abandoning their homes.

The French SS formed up in columns to move to Kolberg, escorting the civilians through what Martelli calls 'apocalyptic scenes': airfields and aeroplanes on fire, the flames igniting ammunition already in the guns. Rows of new Panzers were parked waiting for the fuel that was burning at the airfield. Rumours swept the column that the 2nd Belorussian Front and the 1st Guards Tank Army had broken German resistance at Köslin, with horror stories of attacks by Polish partisans and T-34 tanks ploughing into columns of civilians and crushing them under their tracks.[12]

Martelli tells how he stopped to take his boots off, fell asleep and became separated from his unit. When he woke up he pressed on towards Kolberg, narrowly missing death twice: first when he was strafed by a Russian fighter and then again when a T-34 spotted him on the road and accelerated towards him spraying bullets. He hid in the forest until it moved on, but discovered a gruesome scene further along the road.

> There were two wrecked trucks and shapes lying on the road ahead. I unslung my rifle ready to fire but there was no movement so I continued to walk towards them. As I drew closer, the horror of the scene gradually unfolded. The snow and water in the ditch were red with blood. The larger shapes were the body parts of horses, still warm, that had been blown to pieces.
>
> Amongst these were the dismembered bodies of humans. Soldiers lay side by side on the edge of the ditch, comrades to the end. Children, their tiny bodies torn by machine gun fire, in death held onto their mother's necks with their tiny arms; a last embrace. The limbs of children protruded from under the bodies of some of the women – they had sacrificed their lives in a pitiful attempt to save them. The scene was familiar to me: it brought to mind the massacres of refugees I had witnessed as a child in France.
>
> *Wars*, I thought, *are all the same in the end – an orgy of death and fear.*[13]

Martelli reached the outskirts of Kolberg on the afternoon of 6 March to find thick tree trunks blocking the road into the city with MG-42 and Panzerfaust positions set

---

12 Martelli, *On the Devil's Tail*, pp.103–104.
13 Martelli, *On the Devil's Tail*, p.106. As an eyewitness account this is horrifyingly vivid, raw and believable but Martelli's lack of verification undermines his account. Revisionism, whitewashing of Nazis and portrayals of Soviet cruelty are other factors to consider.

up behind them. The only food he could find when he reached his unit was bread and margarine. The next morning the men were re-designated as a police unit to manage civilians during the evacuation, with pregnant women, children and the wounded or sick given priority.

Among the recent arrivals was wounded Legionnaire Arturs Grava, who reached Kolberg after walking and getting lifts after being hit by a bullet in the elbow at Gut Lübgust on 3 March.

> AG: I was put in a temporary hospital in a hotel on the eighth floor. As soon as I arrived in a side room, a shell exploded in the roof above my head. The ceiling came in and I couldn't stay there, so I went downstairs to some official place and they gave me permission to go aboard to leave for Swinemünde. Someone saw that I was kind of limited – with just one arm, tying your shoelaces is very difficult – but I went anyway.
>
> When the soldier asking for permits saw me [trying to get it out of my pocket one-handed] he got impatient. I was searching in my pockets and he just waved me through and said: 'Go.'
>
> So I got on the ship and I reached Swinemünde the next morning.
>
> VH: You were lucky.
>
> AG: I was very lucky, I admit that. Had the bullet been a few millimetres on one side or another I would have lost my arm. A few centimetres the other side, I would have lost my life.
>
> Our position [in Gut Lübgust] was completely encircled. I don't know anybody who got out of that.[14]

The Russian artillery was very accurate, constantly adjusting to the movements of the guns defending Kolberg and the infantry moving forward to the frontline, so the French SS were ordered to search for spies. Suspicion fell on the *Ostarbeiter*, Russian prisoners working for the Germans, but then they were tipped off about voices speaking Russian coming from a basement, where the prisoners were not allowed. The French surrounded the building, readying themselves for a fight and instructed a Russian-speaking colleague to demand the men inside come out … only for four Latvian Waffen-SS men to open the door with their hands in the air.[15]

Born in France in May 1929 of German-Italian parentage, Martelli was just 15 during the siege of Kolberg. Some consider *On the Devil's Tail* a subjective, descriptive account of war: others may feel his eye for detail, whatever its intention, conveys the human horror of moments like this. Around 10 March, while the hunt for the spies alerting Soviet artillery to defensive positions was still underway, Martelli describes how he stalked and destroyed a T-34 which came close to his position, crawling to within 30 metres of the tank in the street.

---

14 Interview with author, 20 July 2022
15 Martelli, *On the Devil's Tail*, p.115.

I swallowed hard before rising to my right knee, positioning the tube of the Panzerfaust under my armpit and tried to stay calm as I followed the simple firing procedure. I squeezed the trigger with my thumb. A cloud of white smoke enveloped me and an instant later, I heard the dull smack of the warhead as it struck the tank, then a loud bang. A rocket of flame shot from inside the tank lighting up the whole street. Hot fragments of metal rained down around me … I had achieved this alone – a fifteen year-old David against a metal Goliath.[16]

By night Martelli's patrols checked the documents of everyone venturing into the streets. Those whose documents were not in order were treated as spies and taken to headquarters for questioning. If they could not explain themselves, they were shot. By day civilians were moved from the city centre to landing stages at the harbour and loaded into patrol boats and barges which took them to the destroyers waiting offshore.

The situation was by now becoming desperate. The Russians had cut the water supply off and refugees and soldiers alike were beginning to suffer from dehydration. Wehrmacht troops in their late forties and fifties, suffering from dysentery, thirst and lack of sleep, waited for the Russians with MG-42s and Panzerfausts in shoulder-deep foxholes.

On 12 March, the 4th Polish Infantry attacked again, supported by tanks and artillery. Both sides took heavy casualties. Loudspeakers broadcast messages urging the Germans to surrender but two offers were rejected by Fullriede.

In fresh attacks the Polish took the barracks, part of the railway station and Salt Island in the central harbour area. Sometimes fighting hand-to-hand against vast numbers of troops supported by tanks, artillery and flamethrower teams, the Germans fought hard to hold the quayside: the only possible escape. The armoured train Panzer Zug 72A fought on until it was destroyed on 16 March. By then the Germans were barely hanging on to anything other than coastline. The stronghold in the fort near the lighthouse would be the final point of resistance.

The plan was for as many civilians and soldiers as possible to make a dash for the harbour while the remaining soldiers left alive covered the last boats out. The Legion's Catholic chaplain Kazimirs Ručs, a survivor of the carnage on the road to Landeck two weeks before, was one who got out:

> We ended up on a boat taking us to the big destroyers. You had to time your move so you ran across when the ship was raised on a swell. If not you were done for. How many of our lads were pushed into the sea by the Germans already on the boat trying to save themselves? But I made it, and the next morning the big ship docked in Swinemünde.[17]

Paul Martelli was one of the last men out of Kolberg:

16   Martelli, *On the Devil's Tail*, pp.118–119.
17   Ručs, *Dzīve ar Dievu*.

Kolberg harbour looking from the lighthouse towards Stettin [Szczecin], the sea route to safety. The quayside was packed with civilians waiting to be ferried to destroyers waiting in deeper water, which were shelling the Soviets to hold them back. (Picture: author)

The jetty at Kolberg harbour looking out to the Baltic Sea. (Picture: Jim Donnelly/Anaxa Images)

We ran through rubble-strewn streets, a landscape of devastation littered with burning trucks, smashed wooden carts, carcasses of dead and half-charred horses and the corpses of civilians and soldiers.[18]

After loading their wounded into patrol boats with Russian tank shells, mortars and Katyusha rockets exploding around them, Martelli was among the last men left defending the harbour. His small group of SS took up positions in nearby houses to stop the oncoming Poles storming the area. Every time a patrol boat docked at the pier they would rake the Polish lines with gunfire as the boat loaded. When the artillery found the range and began to shell them, they fell back to the pier and set up a makeshift defence post which held out against full-frontal attack until the order came to abandon their positions and head for the jetty. There, about a hundred German soldiers were waiting to board the patrol boat.

We ducked low as we ran towards the landing stage and the gangway to the boat. At the moment of laying foot on the deck I turned for a last look: a squad of German soldiers from various units had reached our barricade and a handful of SS soldiers were firing from their positions on the beach, the last dozen or so men left ashore … We were the last Waffen-SS from the Charlemagne to leave Kolberg.[19]

The transfer from patrol boat to the merchant ship *Kolberg* took place in surging seas, with soldiers being swept into the water by crashing waves. The transfer operation was suddenly abandoned as Martelli waited to cross the planks, and he leapt from the patrol boat onto the deck of the merchant ship at the last minute. The *Kolberg* set out for Swinemünde, arriving the following afternoon. Early the next morning, at 06:30 on 18 March, *Z43* was the last boat out with the rearguard.[20]

Kolberg was liberated by Polish troops later that day, followed by a ceremony re-enacting General Haller's 'Wedding to the Sea' of 1920. A monument commemorating this marriage stands alongside the lighthouse where these dramatic moments played out.

The liberation of Kolberg was one of the most intense operations for the Polish 1st Army in the war so far. Of the 28,000 Polish soldiers involved in the battle, 4,004 were casualties, including 1,266 dead. The Germans lost 2,300 men.[21]

Kolberg was a lucky escape for around 2,000 Latvian men from the Latvian 15th Division supply chain units who had been disarmed and held there in the uncertain days following Flederborn and Landeck, when the Nazi command temporarily replaced the Latvian officers with Germans.

---

18 Martelli, *On the Devil's Tail*, p.133.
19 Martelli, *On the Devil's Tail*, p.140.
20 Here issues of verification are problematic. An *MS Kolberg* could not be found in searches by the author of shipping records online relating to Operation Hannibal.
21 Kochanski, *The Eagle Unbowed,* p.518.

The memorial to the Marriage to the Sea at Kołobrzeg. (Picture: author)

Having lost touch with the 15th Division, Legion commander Rudolfs Bangerskis only heard about their situation in late February. He sent intelligence officer Paul Grube to investigate, then demanded the Latvians be withdrawn from Kolberg. On 12 March they were switched out and an SS punishment battalion took their place.[22] Meanwhile, the bulk of the 15th Division further south could bypass Kolberg and head instead for Horst.

Fullriede's defensive strategy at Kolberg, the force of the resistance offered and the efficiency of the evacuation operation meant 68,000 refugees were evacuated to Swinemünde, earning him a Knight's Cross from Hitler a week later.[23]

Kolberg was devastated. The city's website recalls the damage:

> The city was in ruins. The damage was estimated at 85–90 percent. The water supply, power plant and gas plant were not working. Churches and most public buildings suffered. All shore facilities in the port were destroyed. Few buildings survived in the spa area. There was only one intact bridge on [the river] Parsęta. The rest were blown up by the Germans.
>
> There was not a single intact house in the centre. Only burned-out shells of houses were still standing. There were dead bodies in the streets, [and] the stench of decomposing bodies. Such a world was seen by those who came here to settle down and make their own lives. It was only when the militia was created that the public felt safer. Like mushrooms after the rain, restaurants, cafes, bars, grocery and industrial stores sprang up on the ground floors of the burned-out houses. There was no shortage of food and vodka. Trade flourished, including the black market.[24]

The noted Eastern Front commander General Erhard Raus looked back on events in Kolberg in memoirs written in American captivity. Fullriede had arrived in the newly-designated 'fortress' in a Fiesler Storch to find, as he put it: 'the fortress was absolutely defenceless.' When Raus mentioned this to Hitler, he was promised 12 anti-tank guns immediately, to be sent from the factory in Spandau to Kolberg by rail. Hitler was not aware that the single-track railway line to Kolberg was blocked and Soviet tanks were a matter of hours away.

Fullriede was 'forced to pick his defence force and his weapons from the streets.' Damaged tanks, anti-aircraft [flak] guns and anti-tank guns were lined up to face the oncoming Red Army men; fighters from the Kriegsmarine and Luftwaffe joined the remnants of forces which had found their way to the coast. Despite their desperate attempts to defend the city, Fullriede's force could not hold out beyond four days of full-blooded attacks from all sides, and the garrison was evacuated by the German Navy as the net closed in.

22 Latvian 'Green Books', vol. 6, pp.317–324 (translated).
23 Duffy, *Red Storm on the Reich*, p.235.
24 Kołobrzeg town website at <http://www.Kołobrzeg.pl/epoki-historyczne>, accessed 26 July 2020.

Raus wrote:

> It was difficult to imagine why Hitler decided this former small coastal fort should be defended, unless for historical reasons. In modern times, however, the events that occurred in Napoleon's day could not possibly be repeated.[25]
>
> Nonetheless, the Russians appeared to be impressed by the glorious past of the city, because their approach was slow and hesitant. The first Soviet attack was delayed for two days, until 14 March, but the defensive tactics employed by the garrison soon revealed their weakness, and after only a few days, on 18 March, the enemy captured the city. Most of the entirely-improvised garrison had to be rescued by the Kriegsmarine.[26]

Modern Kołobrzeg is a vibrant city by the sea. It's full of tourists, many of them German, enjoying time at the coast, having spa treatments and eating and drinking in the many restaurants. By the lighthouse, where the fighting was so desperate, two topiary sea horses in an ornamental park decorate approaches to the harbourmaster's house.

It's raining on the first morning that I'm there with my photographer friend Jim, so we jump into an electric golf buggy, the vehicle the council allows guided tours to use. Our driver is Konrad, a 19-year-old from the town who is doing this as a summer job between his studies in Poznan. A million tourists come to Kołobrzeg every year, he says, as he wipes the rain off the plastic sheeting across the front of the vehicle and teaches us the correct way to pronounce the town's Polish name: 'Kow-wob-jeg.' He gets behind the wheel and starts to drive.

> When the Soviets came here, this was like a German city.[27] The old German name for it is Kolberg. They came here and as the whole city was freed, they crushed it, bombed it, burned it down. Then they gave the people somewhere to live. It wasn't the best times.
>
> I'm too young to know about the war, but my grandmother was a young girl at the time, just a little girl. The Russians hit her in the head and left her in a ditch. They also shot her father – killed him – and left her for dead by the side of the road. But she managed to survive. She died four years ago [in 2014]. When she died, part of history died. Young people now don't know a lot about those times. They don't bother about it. Too many horrible things.
>
> There are a lot of German tourists, and a lot of the older people [here] went to work in Germany, so they needed to know German. Now young people my age are learning English, but every day I am speaking German on these city trips. It's my main source of money.

25 The 1807 defence of the besieged city by Prussian forces.
26 Erhard Raus, *Panzer Operations – the Eastern Front Memoir of General Raus, 1941–1945*. Trans. Steven Newton (Cambridge, Mass., Da Capo, 2003), p.330.
27 In the 1932 presidential election, Adolf Hitler won 44.97 percent of the vote. Details at <http://www.Kołobrzeg.pl/epoki-historyczne>.

The German officers' casino in Kolberg, now the Fregata café, Kołobrzeg. (Picture: Jim Donnelly/Anaxa Images)

We drive through an area of spa hotels, where certain sections of Polish society, such as farmers, have their own deals for treatment. We pull up at the Fregata, a café, restaurant and wedding venue that used to be a casino for German officers. It's now a ballroom and banqueting hall perfect for wedding receptions, overlooked by a balcony once used by the casino overseer to check play.

Next door stands the original Post Office, for sale for the past four years but bound by regulations about what alterations any new owner can make to it. Konrad points to a small park nearby.

> That's the old Adolf Hitler Platz, and in the centre of it there is an old German monument, an eagle like a German eagle. When the city became Polish again they just changed the plate on it and kept the eagle as a Polish eagle ... but it looks really, really German!

We turn down Armia Krajowa Road, named after the Polish resistance army which fought the Germans after the war and whose members were deported and even executed during the Soviet occupation as 'obstacles to Communism.' Konrad says:

The eagle at what was Adolf-Hitler-Platz in Kolberg [Kołobrzeg]. (Picture: author)

Almost all the buildings on this road were destroyed during the war. This road is named after the Armia Krajowa. They were fighting for Polish independence and thought that when the Soviets came things would be easier. But the Soviets came and were even worse than the Nazis – they tried to kill them all or put them in jail until they died.

My grandfather was a partisan. My father told me stories about how the Russians said: 'If you're a partisan then just surrender and tell us. We'll forgive you and you can be free.' So my grandfather surrendered, and they put him in jail for many years. Eventually there was an amnesty and they let him out.

We pause first at the city cathedral and then the Rathaus [Town Hall]. Konrad tells us that almost every building in town was damaged in the war. He stops the buggy on a bridge across the river: this was full of vehicles destroyed in the fighting, he says.

For an hour Konrad drives us round the city in the rain in his plastic-sheeted golf buggy, shouting into my recorder above the noise from the wet roads. We drive alongside canals moving logs to the harbour, across several bridges and around the harbour; past his former secondary school that was once a German pilot school. In Soviet times it was a stables, now it is a school again. Nearby, a former barracks has been converted into apartments.

The Germans called Kolberg 'The City of Roses' but the Nazi times brought ruin and destruction. As the years go by, the siege of Kolberg 1945 is blending into its past history. Rebuilding began in 1956 and Kołobrzeg today is a bustling, busy place … but like a replica.

The history isn't hidden. There are memorials to what happened here, there's an excellent museum with weapons and vehicles from 1945, and the city is friendly and welcoming with fresh, clean sea air: a far cry from March 1945. Konrad tells us more about his city tours with German visitors.

I do the same tours with the Germans as I am doing with you. I tell them the same things. But they say: 'We are Germans. The people who did this were Nazis. The Nazis did it – not us.' [28]

---

28 Guided tour, recorded with permission, August 2018.

A Soviet T-34 tank at the Kołobrzeg Museum. (Picture: author)

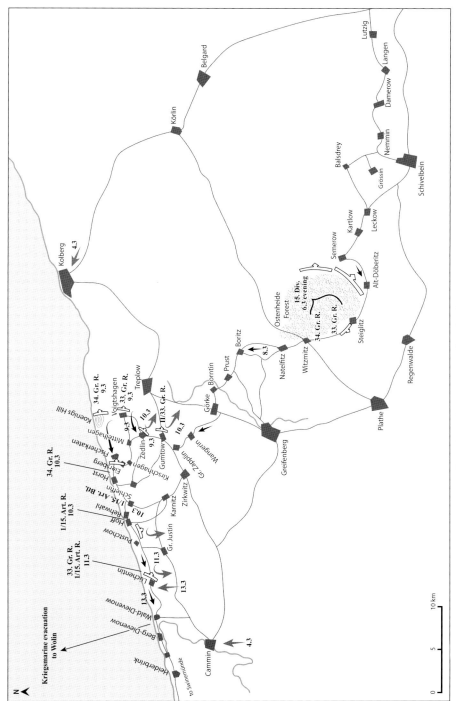

Escape along the Baltic coast March 1945, from Horst to Dievenow.

18

Escape Along the Coast: Horst to the Oder

The Latvians reached the coast on 9 March 1945. They were tired, battered and hungry but still the Russians were ahead of them. They took up positions in the hills at Voigtshagen and Koenigs Hill and made a plan to clear the way ahead. Colonel Janums had developed special teams for overcoming resistance in difficult situations, Legionnaire Žano Mūsiņš remembered.

> He had a special group of men in that unit. We used to call them 'The Cut-throats.' They would shoot you with a smile on their face. They always had their machine guns hanging across their chest. You didn't mess with them because they were those sort of blokes.

He blows his cheeks out.

> They were mad. Don't ever tangle with them! And they were his front units. One of the hills here...

He looks at the map and points to a hill on the coastline east of Horst [now Niechorze] marked Koenigs Hill.

> I wonder if that's the hill where the Russians had already pushed in and they'd got their tanks on top of the hill and we couldn't get past them. Old Janums took his 1st Company, those Cut-throats, and said: 'Lads, could you move them?' And that was it.
> All they did was spread out in the usual well-trained manner. Down, roll, up, run. Boom, boom, boom. In half an hour the tanks were gone. They all carried Panzerfausts and everything. They were a real unit. I wouldn't ever have liked to face them ... they were a real Hell's unit, and that's why Janums liked them. Whatever it takes.

He laughs.

I really admired them. I don't think I'd have had the guts to do that. They probably had about six Iron Crosses each. They were maniacs! I don't know what they did after the war. Maybe they were all locked up…[1]

The Latvian soldiers had covered considerable distances each day to stay ahead of their Soviet pursuers. Some were veterans of such punishing conditions, having fought in Russia. Others were new recruits with little experience of the physical and mental extremes a soldier can be exposed to. Jānis Čevers was an experienced hand.

There was one time in Poland when we were encircled and we had to go across a river at night because of the Russians. We got wet through. We crossed the river and there were dugout holes there, not man-made, that we got into. We stayed there and about 500 metres away, maybe less, among some trees was the Russian front. We saw a captain come out with a loudspeaker and start talking: 'Come to us. Give yourselves up. You are surrounded. For you the war is over.'

Then a lot of the youngsters tried to make a run for it across the field to capitulate to the Russians. I don't know who shot them – Russians or Germans or Latvians – but they were running out of the line to capitulate! That made them deserters. Not many of them made it, but quite a few did try. One German officer said to me: 'Well, *we* stay here. It's our best chance to get out of this encirclement in darkness.' And get out we did.

The Russians were behind us and also ahead of us, so we had to cross the river. We waded across in the dark. There was one German officer crossing the river on a horse. He got hit by a Russian bullet and he fell off the horse into the water. There were a lot of shots, all around, going all over the place. I was about 20 metres away. He was in the middle of the river and suddenly just fell.

That was also the first time I experienced the Katyusha, the 'Stalin Organ' rocket launcher on a lorry. We got in the forest and we heard it going 'zig, zig' – the 40 barrels. The explosions weren't that big, like hand grenades, but they could wound and kill a soldier. We were running through the forest to get away and the Russians were firing Katyushas at us, which were landing all around us.[2]

Physical fitness and determination were key to survival, he remembers.

We were travelling 20 kilometres a day, all along the Baltic coast. That was the difference between farmers' boys and city boys. The city boys couldn't keep up, they couldn't walk any more. Their feet were bleeding. When they took their boots off they couldn't get them back on. The city boys, we had to leave them.

1   Interview with author. Eižens Bonoparts, who fell at Domslaff, was the commander of the 1st Company.
2   From 1942, American Studebakers supplied under Lend-Lease were used as a chassis for the Katyusha rocket launchers.

There was no first aid or nothing. I never saw the Red Cross or anything in the frontline after Jastrow.

But when we got away from the fighting we settled down in country houses, estate homes in Poland. They were big farms and the living quarters had leather seats. There was no more food supplied; we had to look after ourselves. We found chickens, and cows that hadn't been milked, and when cows haven't been milked they make a terrible noise. We knew that the Poles hung their sausages in the chimneys for smoking, so that's the first place we went when we came to a new house. We'd shoot a pig or something.[3]

In Cambridgeshire, Janis Urpens pours me another cup of tea and laughs when I say he's not the first veteran to tell me the first thing he did was check the chimneys of German farmhouses for sausages.

Of course it wasn't funny at the time. There was a very great shortage of food. I think we were more like skin and bone. There was no supply – you ate what you could find. I remember I had five days without any food at all, but I was still running.

It was a very severe winter. Crossing a small lake I broke through the ice and I just managed to get out. Somehow. I had a very big winter coat and that kept me floating. Somehow, with a rifle helping, I managed to get out. I'm probably very lucky.[4]

In the kitchen of his house in Coventry, I read extracts of his war diary back to Žano Mūsiņš to see what else he might say about that time. There's the story of a very near miss.

Early in the morning the Russians attack us with force and force us to withdraw in a hurry because they got behind our line of defence. We pull back a mile or so and make another stand, but we have been bypassed by many tanks on our left and we have to move back quickly. A bullet hits my rifle and it cannot be used any more. Surprisingly I have no injury or harm but the bottom of my trench coat is in tatters!

I look up and raise my eyebrows. He nods several times and then smiles.

Somebody up there was looking after me. How come I never got any bullets anywhere, don't ask me. That's the closest I came to getting hit.

There was a burst of machine gun fire. You should have seen my greatcoat. It was all ripped to bits. It can't be any closer than that! The section of the butt where you carry your rifle – where the bolt is? The bullet went through there and knocked the rifle out of my hand. I picked it up and tried to pull the bolt back but it was jammed solid. And the greatcoat was in tatters from the machine gun

---

3   Interview with author, Derby, UK.
4   Interview with author, Fenstanton, 2019.

fire. It must have been a burst of bullets because if it had been hand grenades there'd have been splinters of shrapnel everywhere. My trousers were in tatters below my knee.[5]

Gunārs Rozens and his 100-strong group of Legionnaires had left Stargard at the end of February after being stranded there, expected to defend a town with no weapons.

> We want to get back to our own units. Some [men] simply wander away. The rest of us, at an opportune moment, travel on. On 28 February we arrive in Bütow. From there we are sent to Schlawe [Sławno], where we are billeted in a school on the outskirts. We spend about six days there. There are 89 of us.
>
> When the Russians attack Schlawe, we are roped in to defend it. Old, unusable rifles are handed out. We are forced to retreat. When we leave Schlawe there are 34 of us left. Oberjunker Kugrens was killed in Schlawe.

The Russian thrust to the Baltic coast had cut the German Second Army off in the north-east, leaving the only way out to head east to Danzig and Gotenhafen and hope for a seaborne evacuation. Towns were falling quickly to the Russian attack. With western routes blocked, Rozens and his group of Legionnaires headed 34 kilometres north-east, eventually reaching Stolpmunde [Ustka].

Until this point in the war the town had been a popular seaside resort and spa town, as well as a busy cargo harbour and ferry terminal for travellers heading to East Prussia. Now it was choked with thousands of refugees trying to escape west. Even here there was no escape for Rozens.

> On 7 March, we – the remaining 34, under the leadership of Sergeant Mangulis – make our way to Stolpmunde port. As we are all wounded, we receive permission from the commandant to leave by ship. When we arrive at the quay, the Russians begin to attack, firing on the port and the town. There are no ships in the harbour. A speedboat leaves in a tremendous hurry and some manage to jump aboard. I think Sergeant Mangulis did too.
>
> The rest of us left, I think about 20, manage to get away from Stolpmunde by the coast road. We know the only way out of the siege is by sea, therefore [the choice is] Gotenhafen or Danzig. We are left with no leadership, so make our own way in that direction. Not far away the Russian army is following us and a few villages ahead have already been taken; we have to make huge detours.
>
> We can't get into any buildings, everywhere is full of German soldiers, food is impossible to come by, so we go on almost without stopping. Whilst walking along the side of the road, one of our group is hit by a trailer and badly wounded in the thigh, losing a big chunk. We manage to put him in a German army car. What happened to him after that I don't know.[6]

5   War diary of Žano Mūsiņš, interview with author.
6   Memoirs of Gunārs Rozens, Latvian War Museum archive.

Słupsk town hall, 2018. (Picture: author)

The logistics of this episode are difficult to imagine. An estimated 33,000 refugees fled west through Stolpmunde before it fell to the Red Army on 8 March.[7] In the city of Stolp further inland [now Słupsk], the arrival of Soviet soldiers triggered a wave of suicides among those fearing brutal treatment and reprisals. Support for the Nazi Party in Pomerania had rocketed from virtually nothing in 1928 to 56 per cent in the Landtag state elections of March 1933, and there was plenty of reason for Nazis to be fearful as evidence of their crimes was systematically uncovered.[8]

In Słupsk today monuments stand to 800 victims of 'Nazi bestiality' between July 1944 and February 1945. These people died repairing railway tracks and carriages

7   Ustka town website at <http://visit.ustka.pl/odkrywaj-ustke/historia-miasta/#historia-miasta> translated, accessed 02 May 2020. The town was under military command until August 1945, when a new Polish administration took over and an influx of Polish settlers began. The Germans remaining were deported to the west in December that year: in November 1946 the town was renamed Ustka.

8   A. McElligott, *Rethinking the Weimar Republic: Authority and Authoritarianism 1916–1936* (London: Bloomsbury, 2013). Table 7.2 quoting <http://www.gonschior.de/weimar/Preussen/Pommern/Uebersicht_LTW.html>.

in *Aussenarbeitslager* [outdoor labour camp] Stolp, a sub-camp of Stutthof.[9] Another memorial – *The Monument of the Executed Labourers* – stands in a park in the city's Southern Woods. This is dedicated to 22 forced labourers murdered by the Nazis on 7 March 1945, the day before the Red Army liberated the town.[10]

Refugees who could not get away faced being consumed in the horror. A German signals officer escaping from Lauenburg [Lębork] watched Russian tanks shelling a convoy of refugee vehicles carrying women and children. They had become stuck in the snow amid the carnage all around. He described how the tanks then drove along the road 'crushing everything under their tracks.'[11]

For civilians in towns across Pomerania the situation was highly unpredictable and often very tense. Decisions had to be made whether to stay and face an uncertain future, or leave and head west. Either choice was fraught with risk. Derk Steggewentz, a veterinarian for twenty years in Schlawe, lying on the Wieprza river eight kilometres west of Stolp, bought train tickets so his wife Annie could leave with their son Gerda. She refused to go.

> She didn't want to leave me on my own. The future was very uncertain. No-one knew what was going to happen, especially when the Russians came. The closer the Red Army got to Schlawe the more stories we heard about the violence used by the Russian soldiers, especially against civilians. Often I started thinking about plans as to how to send Annie and Gerda away: first a car, then a horse and carriage – but still Annie refused to leave.
>
> I was thankful I didn't have to send her in freezing weather and snow and take the risk of being kicked off the road by a crowd going west, or even worse, that she would be robbed in the middle of nowhere by people who work for the Nazis who didn't care about the civilians but only about themselves.
>
> Three days before the Russians came we sent Gerda to Confirmation (the ceremony affirming Catholic belief) attended by many dear friends. We could talk openly because the Nazis had all left. When we switched on the radio for a short time we heard the words: 'Fights in the region of Schlawe.'

Within days life as they knew it would be changed forever. Their house would be ransacked, they would have left Schlawe and the foreman Grundels would be lying dead in the garden.

9   Memorial at Kollataja Street to the 800 prisoners from Stutthof who died, online at <https://sztetl.org.pl/en/towns/s/38-slupsk/116-sites-of-martyrdom/50765-monument>; details of conditions at Stolp camp at US Holocaust Memorial Museum online at <https://www.ushmm.org/online/camps-ghettos-download/EncyclopediaVol-I_PartB.pdf p1425>. accessed 26 July 2020.

10 Slupsk town website at <http://www.slupsk.pl/kultura/>, translated, accessed 26 July 2020 and W. Stefaniec, *History of the Concentration Camp in Pictures* online at <GP24.pl> dated 08 December 2008 at <https://gp24.pl/historia-obozu-koncentracyjnego-w-obrazkach/ar/4372183&prev=search>, translated, accessed 06 May 2020.

11 Duffy, *Red Storm on the Reich*, p.193, quoting German signals officer Husemann.

384 THE ROAD OF SLAUGHTER

Around 3 March, near Schlawe we could hear single shots being fired from time to time. A big part of the society had run away out of fear of the Russians, in groups, into the forests. I phoned the town council for instructions about what to do at work, in the butchery, with the live and slaughtered animals – in this case, pigs. I managed to get hold of somebody who said that the Mayor and all the prominent Nazis had long since left, and no instructions had been left as to what to do.

At about 14:00 Grundels the foreman asked me to come downstairs. Waiting there was an SS officer, who ordered me to poison all the meat that was left in the butchery in order to contaminate it for the Russians. I told him I wouldn't do it because many civilians were still here. What would happen to them if even one Russian soldier died from the poisoned meat? There would be no mercy for them.

This SS man cursed and said he would hang me. He left, warning me he would be back, and it will not be good for me if I haven't poisoned the meat by then.

I knew he was telling the truth as they had already hanged many people who hadn't done what they were told. In these disturbing weeks of war, we could see how the mask of cultural and respectable people was slipping from this Nazi SS man. It was clear they were just bandits.

Half an hour later two Wehrmacht officers called, asking if they could use the phone to ring through the positions of two heavy guns. They managed to make the connection with their formation. At this moment Annie came with cold drinks. The soldiers were surprised: 'Who's this?' they asked. Then they said that we had to leave this solitary piece of land.

We decided to run. Everyone packed up their backpack, taking only a few small things, for example a bottle of cognac – whatever we could grab in the rush. That evening, during a blizzard, we got into our car. The house was empty. Sometime later the Grundels came back, and that had fatal results as they became victims of the Russians. I found their corpses later in the garden, and every time when I was sneaking into the butchery, I could see their dog in the same place.

Petronka, the secondary school teacher, was told to collect and bury the dead. Miss Scharfer had said goodbye the day before. I don't know where she had planned to go. I heard later that her body was found in the Wieprz river. Shortly before we left for Stolp Gerda dug out and took with him his favourite presents from confirmation: a little travel alarm clock which he had hidden in a tin and buried in the garden. Later this alarm clock was left in Stolp.

During the night journey to Stolp we could only drive east because the road west was cut off. There wasn't a live soul on the road – nobody. When we reached the first houses in Stolp on 6 March, the car broke down on Immelman Strasse, now Grodka Street. A friend of my wife used to live there, an Evangelical priest called Renka, who looked after the other priests. We found their house empty, but he appeared soon after, alone. He had put his wife and children on the boat at Stolpmünde [Ustka].

With typical black humour he gave us his house, all his belongings and a large number of cigarettes. He was a captain and had been ordered to take the Russian prisoners west. We ate the rest of his food supplies and then slept in his bed. Our new DKW car, which had done only 7,000 kilometres, was left on the street. Renka told us that a doctor we knew in Schlawe was in charge of loading hospital trains going west. I phoned him. He gave us a place on the train, but the destination of the train was unknown. No-one knew where it was supposed to be going. I didn't want to be captured with my wife and child in the middle of nowhere, so I refused the place.

During the phone call the doctor told me there was a man we used to work with at the city council in Stolpmünde who was organising the evacuation and had 3,000 places. I called him and explained my situation. 'I have a son and a wife. Can you help us?' I asked. He said: 'Sorry, but I don't have any space for your wife.' At that moment, we didn't have any choice but to stay. 'If we have to be captured, let it be here,' I thought, 'where there are no Nazis and we have no enemies.' Later, we might find a chance to survive here in Schlawe.

By 7 March, the number of people in Stolp had tripled, from 50,000 to 150,000, including many elderly people and children, healthy and sick, heading west in blizzards, dragging little trolleys and sledges behind them, without any firm destination – just west. Steggewentz busied himself trying to attract as little attention to his family as possible.

I was removing the chairs and stuff which would bring Russian attention to Captain Renka's house, especially his uniform hanging just next to the entrance. There were Nazi pictures on the wall and so on. Next night there was a lot of shooting and fighting nearby, so we spent the night in the cellar. We were listening to the sounds of battle approaching, but after single shots from machine guns and shelling from artillery fire, there was nothing.

In the early morning, at dawn, I said goodbye to Annie and Gerda and went to check out the position. I was walking along empty streets in an empty town on the way to Ulicka Street. On the way I bumped into armed Russian soldiers going carefully along the houses. They took me to their commander who asked me in German about anti-tank blockades and about the airfield. I couldn't tell them anything, so they started threatening me with guns and took my watch and cigarettes. One of them looked at my leather boots and said: '*Du soldat!*' – 'You are a soldier!'

They told me to go, and to walk away with my hands up. I was waiting for them to shoot me in the back, but it didn't happen. I went round the corner, took off my boots and went back to my family. I said the Russians were very nice people because they didn't shoot me. We wanted to wait until the Russians came, and then go to Schlawe.

Later that day we heard a loud cannonade of shots, and some Russians dropped into our cellar. Then they began checking our house. I was still hopeful that we could trust them. I went upstairs where I met an officer with a red band around his cap. I explained that I was a veterinary doctor and I wanted to go to Schlawe. Could he give me a pass? He wrote something on a piece of paper and I went back to the cellar.

We packed up our backpacks and when we came out of the cellar this officer was standing nearby. He saw my wife and took the piece of paper back from me and told us to go back to the cellar.

A while later I sneaked out of the basement and saw this officer in the kitchen grab the tablecloth and pull it off the table [sending] everything that was on it [to the floor]. He was completely drunk. So we sneaked out and started walking down the road to Schlawe, despite the blizzard. Many times we were stopped and searched…

Luckily when we got to Warszkowka that evening a big formation of Russian soldiers arrived at the same time. Because of that we didn't go to the butchery, where very likely we would have met the same fate as the poor Grundels. We went along the road Birkenweg in the direction of the mill at *Kuckucksmühle* [Cuckoo Mill] where we had a friend. We stayed with him for a few days, hidden in the hay barn. Very often the Russians came with candles and matches, searching for women. They couldn't find us, and by some miracle the hay didn't catch fire.

After a few days the men left the barn and the women stayed hidden. The oldest women were lying next to the door, the youngest at the back, but made to look older. The next weeks were a time of a wave of suicides.[12]

The town of Demmin – then in Pomerania, now part of Mecklenburg-Vorpommern in Germany – is most notably associated with a wave of mass suicides – said to be in excess of 1,000 people – both before and after the Red Army captured it. The German journalist Beate Lakotta compiled an estimate of the number of suicides in Pomerania and Germany in towns such as Neustrelitz (681), Neubrandenburg (600), Stolp (1,000) Lauenburg (600), Malchin (500) and hundreds in Teterow, Rostock, Penzlin and Burg-Stargard Gustrow and Bad Doberan – as well as 4,000 in Berlin alone.[13]

Each death was an individual tragedy, wrote Derk Steggewentz.

My friend and I found two teachers, Miss Muller and Miss Krebs, who had hanged themselves from a tree in the garden, and my friend's parents were lying dead under the tree. My colleague Dr Schartz shot his wife, his daughters, his grand-daughters and himself. A few weeks earlier he had been full of happiness

12 From the memoirs of Derk Steggewentz: *Marzec 1945,* pp.279–285 from Sroki, J. (ed): *Mój los był tylko jednym spośród wielu milionów … Powiat sławieński w roku 1945 Wspomnienia dawnych mieszkańców [My fate was only one of many millions … Sławno County in 1945: Memories of former inhabitants].* Trans. Janusz Korona. (Sławno: Margraf, 2008).
13 Lakotta, B. Article: 'Tief vergraben, nicht dran ruhren' ['Bury it deep, don't touch it'] in *Der Spiegel* (trans.) 05 March 2005. Also online at <https://en-academic.com/dic.nsf/enwiki/11708193>.

Postcard of Horst. Undated, but featuring the wicker sun chairs that are a feature of the northern Baltic coastline. (Picture: public domain)

when the Nazi authorities let his daughters and grand-daughters go by car west, as soon as he could get petrol. Quickly he organised some fuel, but when he went to the office to get his permission, they took his petrol. The result was the death of the young women and children. What's that compared to the life of a Nazi who wants to save his own?[14]

What was left of the Latvian 15th Division gathered on the Baltic coast west of Kolberg and east of the Oder. Among them were Jānis Čevers, Laimonis Cerinš and Žano Mūsinš. Their eyewitness accounts add dramatic and very human details to the limited military accounts of what happened here. The Germans attempted to form a bridgehead between Hoff and Horst for a rescue by sea, led by Hans von Tettau, who reached the coast four days after breaking out of an encirclement at Schivelbein on 5 March. Von Tettau had been surrounded near Regenswalde and lost radio contact with HQ. This was re-established on 6 March and he was ordered north to the coast west of Kolberg. Instructions and orders were transmitted to him by a Fieseler Storch spotter plane, which had to detour far out over the Baltic in order not to be shot down.[15]

The remnants of military units shattered by the Red Army in western Pomerania joined von Tettau: French from the Charlemagne Division, the Latvians of the 15th Latvian SS and stragglers from various units defending the Pomeranian Wall. There

14 Memoirs of Derk Steggewentz.
15 Guderian, *Panzer Leader,* p.338.

were also tanks from the Panzer Division Holstein, which had suffered heavy losses in Stargard and then Kolberg.[16]

The remnants of the Charlemagne Division reached the coastal village of Horst on the evening of 9 March. They were given the task of protecting a convoy of several thousand refugees as the German forces broke out west along the coast to Dievenow. The escape was brutal and bloody.

> In the mass of tightly-packed refugees the constant mortar and machine gun fire from Russian positions caused absolute mayhem. The dead and wounded lay in heaps. Again and again it was down to the French SS grenadiers to charge forward and clear out nests of Russian soldiers pouring fire into the would-be escapers.[17]

When the rescue by sea from Horst that he had been hoping for did not happen, Von Tettau was stranded on the Baltic coast, so he planned a breakout along the coast west to Dievenow [Dziwnów], a collection of small villages and seaside resorts at the mouth of the Oder. The mainland was linked to Wolin island and Usedom by bridges, and was just a short journey by boat. A small German seaplane base and airstrip also operated there.

Kriegsmarine sailors put up a vigorous defence of the bridgehead at Dievenow, proving themselves deadly against Soviet armour with the Panzerfaust. On 7 March, a mass tank attack ended with 33 out of 34 T-34s destroyed. In a second attack the following day, 36 were destroyed.[18]

The breakout from Horst was timed to start at 22:00 on 10 March. Von Tettau gathered the strongest force he could on a narrow front along the cliffs of the Baltic shoreline. Holding the cliffs would create a safety corridor along the coast below for the thousands of soldiers and civilians there. Colonel Janums took charge of the Latvians in positions east of Horst. Artilleryman Laimonis Ceriņš was part of his squad.

> LC: After Neustettin we moved on to Horst, west of Kolberg. There was an order to go on to Kolberg from the German divisional commanders but Colonel Janums ignored it. The Russians were already ahead of us. We had to go the other way. A chap came and told us to get away to the seaside to fight the Russians. Forget about Kolberg. Our supply unit went first, a few days before that. Some of them got out on a German ship. We were told what was happening there. We lost quite a lot of men there.
>
> VH: So you've been wounded, moved to Horst ... how did you get there?

16 Samuel W. Mitcham, *The Panzer Legions: A Guide to the German Army Tank Divisions of WWII and their Commanders* (London: Stackpole Books, 2007), p.236.
17 Trigg, *Hitler's Gauls,* pp.122–123.
18 Guderian, *Panzer Leader,* p.338.

LC: On foot. Very slowly. Every day. We stop, have to watch, take position, just in case the Russians come.[19]

The Latvians were close to exhaustion after being in continuous action for several weeks – sometimes heavy, some skirmishes – with no regular food supplies, little shelter and long-distance marching day after day, sometimes through the night. As Jānis Čevers describes, men were losing the will to live.

We were zigzagging in and out from the Baltic coast: along the coast, thirty kilometres inland, back on the coast. There were not many big battles any more, but we were fighting a little bit and marching with no sleep. We were absolutely exhausted. In one particular instance the whole company just flopped down in one field. One man said: 'I'm so tired that I don't care anymore if I wake up alive. I just want to sleep.' And then we all dropped off to sleep.

If the Russians knew our situation they could have had all of us. The Russian planes came very low over the field hammering us with machine guns and woke us up. Then we ran! But the feeling of the sleep was unbelievable. We had to leave a lot of them behind because they couldn't walk any more. I didn't take my boots off until the capitulation.[20]

Žano Mūsiņš and I are still looking at the map of the area west of Kolberg, trying to get our bearings. Mr Mūsiņš says:

About this time, when we came to this area, we had the order to go to Kolberg but Janums diverted us down this way...

He gestures to the west, in the direction of Horst.

ZM: Some units went to Kolberg and got trapped and smashed to bits. When we arrived there [at Horst] we were all right but the Russians cut us off when they broke through to the coast, so we had to push them back. We pushed them back about two to three miles [around four kilometres]. The coast there has a very high bank, high dunes, so we walked along the coast, right by the water-side. The only way the Russians could reach us was by chucking some shells down there. One exploded nearby and it hit one of our corporals, Augstkalns. Only light injuries on the ankle, though. We got caught in the open and there's no defence against aeroplanes in the open. We just lay down in ditches or what-ever you could find. The plane went over twice and sprayed us with machine guns. I've got a feeling this was an English plane.

19 Interview with author, Derby.
20 Interview with author, Derby.

Flat out: an exhausted soldier of the 33rd Infantry Regiment of the 15th SS Division during the retreat in Pomerania. (Picture: Latvian War Museum LKM 5-13983/1504-FT1-2)

We look at a picture of an exhausted soldier from the 33rd Regiment flat out in the snow in what looks like a blizzard, head back, in Arturs Silgailis' book about the Latvian Legion. I ask Mr Mūsiņš if he recognises the feeling.

ZM: Yes. That's about what it was.

VH: That guy lying down looks like he's dead.

ZM: That's what we were like. Any time you had a break you would just lie down, catch your breath, put your feet up. Because your life depended on your feet.

VH: And marching through the night, you're trying to put distance between yourself and the tanks ...

ZM: Yep.

VH: You're marching at three or four miles an hour. And the tanks are doing, say 10 miles an hour [5–6 kilometres per hour against 16 km/h.]
  You're marching for your life, aren't you?

ZM: You are marching for your life. We were marching for our lives. It came to it that sometimes you march on the road in a column. You hold onto the belt of the man in front. You all march in a line. And if there was a bend in the road ... well, you were all sleeping while you walk. If the man leading walks and falls into a ditch the whole unit just follows him and they all fall down in a pile! Because everybody was asleep.
  It's fantastic. I never, ever knew that people could march while sleeping. You are pushed so far that your body will move physically while your mind is resting. And it just switches off.[21]

For the first two weeks of March 1945, the Legionnaires lived on food from airdrops. The days were long and demanding. Often they had to break through Soviet encirclements then act as a rearguard for a more general withdrawal. The 33rd fought a bloody battle with the Red Army at Zedlin [Sadlenko] on 10 March repulsing an attack by tanks and infantry in savage hand-to-hand fighting.[22]

The Russians shelled Zedlin until the smoke from the town was so thick the Latvians couldn't see the enemy approaching. A sudden Soviet attack forced the 1st Company out of the town but they quickly counter-attacked and, in fierce house-to-house fighting, regained control.[23] The 2nd Company held its positions. German accounts of the battle along the coast put the Soviet strength in the region as twelve infantry divisions, one tank corps, one cavalry corps and one mechanised brigade.

In heavy fighting the escape route along the shore was secured, even though the enemy knew about the situation in the narrow gap and tried in all ways to cut it off. While involved in the battles, the 15th Latvian SS Division inflicted the following losses on the enemy: 3,700 fallen (counted), 25 tanks shot-up with Panzerfausts, two tanks destroyed by direct artillery hits, 102 automatic rifles and 80 various captured vehicles.[24]

This account of events on 10 March from the 'Green Books' was translated by Legionnaire Arturs Grava.

With the arrival of darkness, the regiment was ordered to begin withdrawal from the front at 20:30, leaving the covering units in positions until 22:00. The regiment retreated to Fischerkaten-Horst where it received further orders.

---

21 Interview with author, Coventry, UK, August 2018.
22 Silgailis, *Latvian Legion,* p.180.
23 Latvian 'Green Books', vol. 6, p.48.
24 *Landeszeitung fuer Mecklenburg und Nachbahr gebiete*, 10 March 1945, reproduced in Latvian 'Green Books', vol 6, p.51, translated.

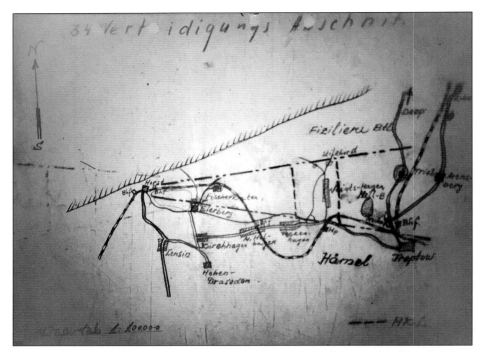

Hand-drawn sketch showing Latvian positions in the area around Horst, taken from the War Diary of the 15th SS Division in the Latvian National Archive, Rīga. Author's visit, November 2019. (LNA ref: A1588/49-51, file 296-1-32)

The regiment was ordered to reach Hoff by 10:00. The regiment began its march at 08:00, moving west along the north edge of Horst. Along the seashore, dispersed German soldiers and wagons were moving in droves without interruption. The wounded were laid down on the shore, waiting for transportation. A few warships were seen in the sea, shelling the enemy occasionally.

At Hoff, the Artillery Battalion of the 15th Division was in positions. Here, the Sapper Battalion of the division, led by First Lieutenant Jansons, was attached to the regiment.

The direction of the retreat was Rehwal-Dievenow. The retreat was accomplished along the seashore through an approximately 1.5 kilometre-wide gap. Russian assault units attacked frequently; the movement was hindered by enemy artillery and mortar fire. The forests were full of army units and civilian refugee columns. The Russians inflicted heavy losses on them. Captain Ezernieks of the regiment staff was seriously wounded. Units of the regiment were separately involved in battles to secure the left flank. At times, the rear of the Division also had to be covered.

During the retreat, the regiment passed the 33rd Regiment which stayed in the rearguard of the Division. On 13 March, one of the best battle officers of

Latvian Legionnaires move west from Horst towards Dievenow along the Baltic Sea coastline.
(Picture: Latvian Legion 'Green Books')

the regiment, First Lieutenant Tēraudiņš, lost his life; also the commander of the Sapper Battalion, First Lieutenant Jansons, and several non-commissioned officers and enlisted men.[25]

In the national archives in Rīga, scrolling through the microfiches of the 15th Division's war diary, I find a map. It's drawn by hand, in pencil. I look at it more carefully and realise it's a plan of Latvian positions before the breakout from Horst. This is probably the original. Laimonis Ceriņš was part of that escape:

It was like a resort where people spend their holidays. We had to keep them back from the seaside because otherwise we'd have been cut off. From about 10:00 until night we had to keep them away from the seaside. We were lucky. There were only fifty of us, so we did some things to make the Russians think there were more of us. It was a bushy area, so what do you do to make the enemy think there are more of you?

Our experienced frontline commanding officer Lieutenant Herberts Žagars who led the attack said: 'OK, we start shooting and we all start shouting *"Urrāh! Urrāh! Urrāh!"* and they will think there are a lot of us and they'll keep their distance.' It worked for a while, and it was OK. We pushed them back. We lost only two men from the 50. These men were reliable frontline men with experience on the Russian front, and they were also from the same area as me

25 Author unknown, Latvian 'Green Books.' Trans. Arturs Grava, sent to author 20 July 2022.

Gun crew of the 15th Artillery Regiment in position near the Oder river, March 1945, possibly at the Dievenow bridgehead. (Picture: Latvian 'Green Books')

– the Valmiera region. There were also men who'd come from the 19th Division. Probably they were wounded and had been sent to Germany to recover.[26]

On the evening of 10 March, the 33rd Regiment moved to the coast at Hoff [Trzęsacz]. By now the artillery battalion was down to just 70 men and the only artillery piece they had was the gun they pulled out of the Ostenheide Forest. They took positions in the woods at Pustow and stopped several Russian attacks before running out of ammunition. Then both the Charlemagne and the 33rd Regiment fought their way through to Berg-Dievenow, arriving there on 12 March.

Laimonis Ceriņš explained how they got away:

> Late evening, everything is dark, it's quiet and there's the smell of gunpowder and smoke. Me and another fellow were given an order to go with a report to headquarters, which was slightly back. On the way we found the 15th Division's supply lorries, which were being damaged, as there was no chance of getting them out. I talked to the drivers, you see, and they told me.

---

26 Interview with author, Derby, UK. Žagars' family came from the same area as Mr Ceriņš, between Liepa and Cesis. Their family homes were about six miles (10 kilometres) apart. Žagars became a prisoner of the British in Denmark and was later a CIA agent. (See his 1958 interrogation at <https://www.cia.gov/library/readingroom/docs/ZAGARS%2C%20HERBERTS_0043.pdf>.)

Soldiers of the 33rd Regiment of the Latvian 15th SS Division pictured during the escape from Horst along the Baltic Sea coastline to Dievenow in March 1945, with refugees. Left: First Lieutenant Konrads and Captain Akermanis. (Picture: Latvian Legion 'Green Books')

When we got to headquarters, everyone's gone. So we went back and started moving west along the coast, and we met Colonel Janums and his men at probably one o'clock in the morning. Everyone was very tired so we just lay down wherever we wanted, but with bushes all round you never know who is coming. So the Colonel says he wants to meet all the senior officers from Captain upwards to discuss what to do. And we want three volunteers to keep guard. I was one of them. The next day we got to Dievenow, and we got one or two bombs from the Russians.[27]

Behind them, along the coast to the east, the rest of the 33rd Regiment commanded by Major Augusts Alksnītis acted as a rearguard, setting up blocking positions in the seaside village of Luchenthin [Łukęcin] to protect the bridgehead at Dievenow. What had been an idyllic sandy beach fringed with woods became a scene of devastation. Legion historian Silgailis says of this time:

By the dawn of 12 March the flow of humanity had subsided and the seashore presented a horrendous sight. The entire coast was littered with destroyed and abandoned wagons, motor vehicles, corpses and dead horses.[28]

27 Interview with author.
28 Silgailis, *Latvian Legion,* p.181.

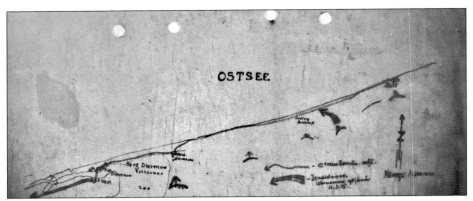

Sketch of the final positions during the escape from Dievenow, March 1945. From the 15th
Division War Diary at the National Archives, Rīga. (Picture: author)

One German, Sergeant Borgelt from Third Panzer Army headquarters, arrived in
time to witness the operation, and reported mass attacks by Soviet infantry being
beaten back while mortar shells exploded on the beach among the refugees. He wrote:

> Never had I seen so many bodies – civilians, German and Russian soldiers – but
> especially the Russians in great heaps, lying this way and that way on top of one
> another. Between the corpses were strewn dead horses, the overturned carts of
> the refugees, bogged-down military transport, burned-out cars, weapons and
> equipment ... I saw mothers cast their infants into the sea because they could
> carry them no further.[29]

Amid heavy fighting and considerable losses on both sides, the Germans retreated to
a belt of defences on the Strait of Narrows and held it while evacuating their troops
to Wolin. At Dievenow the German Navy ferried 6,000 soldiers and 26,000 refugees
to the island of Wolin on 11 March alone. The operation was completed by the end
of the next day.[30]

The 33rd Regiment were left in their positions until that night, and had to get
across the Oder river to Wolin Island or be cut off. Laimonis Ceriņš was the last man
out.

29 Duffy, p.198, quoting Borgelt, in Paul, W., *Der Endkampf um Deutschland 1945* (Esslingen,
    1978), pp.160–61.
30 Dziwnówek town website, online at <www.dziwnow.pl> and Duffy, p.198. Among the Polish
    officers involved in the assault on the final German fortifications of Klein Dievenow [now
    Dziwnówek] was the future Communist dictator of Poland, Wojciech Jaruzelski, a second
    lieutenant in a reconnaissance unit in the 5th Infantry Regiment. When the fighting ended,
    the victorious Poles staged another Wedding to the Sea ceremony on 15 March. A monument
    to the Polish soldiers who fought here was erected in 1975.

Near evening, Colonel Janums said: 'Look. We have to move across the river.' In the far distance we could see the bridge, a couple of kilometres away. He said: 'We're here. They're there. We're going over the bridge and blowing it up. But we have to keep a guard until 22:00 in case the Russians come.'

There was no time to think about danger. It was very quiet, and we were lucky to get out of it. Another 50 men. By the riverside there were bullrushes growing. We found three or four boats. Only one was good enough to cross that wide river. It was dark and the water from the sea was pushing inwards.

VH: There was a current?

LC: Yes. That's a dangerous thing. You can't just go straight across. Nobody knew how to do it. One man had been paddling little boats in Rīga. Anyway, the officer says: 'Come on. Ten men, get in, go across, come back again.' So they go but the boat doesn't come back. We were shouting…

He looks at me.

Dirty words! But then it does come back and we jump in, push off. I was the last into the boat. My foot was the last on Pomeranian land. That was 12 March. By that time the Russians had already taken Stettin, but they didn't move on, so we had the chance to get to Wolin, to the two islands there. And then from there you can get across to the mainland.

We made our way across to Suckow and then south-west to Neubrandenburg, where we were from 23–30 March. Then Furstenburg. That was the most rest we had. From there we had to dash to the west, as far as possible.[31]

Legionnaire Brunis Rubess had been with Janums in Dievenow, and returned from an errand to find both the Colonel and his unit gone.

Slowly the Russians took over the whole of Pomerania, and there was only a small piece of land left by the sea to the east of the Oder. When, as regularly occurred, I turned up at the divisional *štābs* [HQ] with a report from Janums, the *štābs* had disappeared (they had scarpered). Now I was by myself, separated from my unit in the Dievenow seaside.

I started to walk along the beach, hoping to catch Janums' regiment, whose objective I knew – the bridge over the Oder. In the same direction, in enormous chaos, walked groups of soldiers, farmers with carts, women with children … Now and again the odd shell exploded because the Russians were just a few kilometres from the dunes.

About halfway, I was grabbed by German gendarmes, who were sending stragglers (lost sheep) straight to the fighting to keep the Russians away from the seaside. As some of these soldiers are Latvian, I am given the job of interpreter. Soon however, there's a need to carry a young lieutenant from the battlefield.

31 Interview with author, Derby.

A bullet had grazed his head. The injury wasn't life-threatening, but it bled like hell.

With the lieutenant on my shoulders I went back towards the sea, where help was available. When a German car took the lieutenant, I'm left by myself again, covered in blood from head to toe. For the remainder of my journey, no-one was interested grabbing a lost sheep and sending it to fight against the enemy! I was saved.

In Dievenow I met soldiers from the regiment. One of them had found tins of fish. Great, but there was a shortage of bread. We found a place to sleep, a hut by a kindergarten. When we woke up, we discovered that the hut was a crispbread 'knaeckebrot' warehouse. That was a big, big stroke of luck. An even bigger stroke of luck was getting over the Oder bridge. The Red Army was near Stettin, just a few kilometres to the south.[32]

The battle for Pomerania – for the Latvians at least – was over. Hans von Tettau reached Dievenow on 12 March with a force of 20,000 soldiers from various units. The Korpsgruppe von Tettau at the time of the breakout included elements of the 163 Infanterie Division, 402 Infanterie Division, Einsatz Division Bärwalde, Einsatz Division Pommerland, Panzer Division Holstein, the 15th Latvian SS and Battalion Fenet of the 33rd SS Charlemagne.[33]

It was something of a multi-national army fighting for their lives, and there was no doubting the bravery of the men. As Legion veteran and historian Visvaldis Mangulis wrote of the 15th Division:

> In 50 days it marched 600 miles [965 kilometres], and fought 12 Soviet infantry divisions and a tank corps.[34]

There were also in the region of 30,000 refugees who had attached themselves to von Tettau's group for protection and owed their lives to him. Von Tettau's distinguished service was recognised with oak leaves for the Knight's Cross he won in 1942. Colonel Janums was awarded the German Cross in Gold for his outstanding leadership and personal bravery.[35]

32 Rubess, *Brīnumainā Kārtā*, pp.82–83.
33 L. Gladysiak, *The Korpsgruppe Von Tettau and the Breakout from Niechorze* [Horst] online at <https://www.infolotnicze.pl/2012/05/23/grupa-korpuna-von-tettau-wyamanie-spod-miejs-cowoci-niechorze/>. Dated 2012, translated, accessed 20 June 2019.
34 Mangulis, *Latvia in the Wars of the Twentieth Century*, p.147.
35 Guderian, *Panzer Leader*, p.338, Traces of War website at <https://www.tracesofwar.com/persons/19521/Tettau-von-Hans.htm> and Gladysiak, *The Korpsgruppe Von Tettau and the Breakout from Niechorze*. Janums' decoration from Silgailis, p.181.

In the Mārtiņa Beķereja café in Rīga Old Town, military historian Valdis Kuzmins is giving me his thoughts on the escape along the coast. To him it is the final part of a bigger story.

It all started on 24 February when the 15th were not far from Landeck. The Russian First Belorussian Front decided to break Pomerania, and they launched a huge attack north to the sea with tanks, cavalry, infantry – lots of them. That was a proper breakthrough. All troops in this area were cut off from the German mainland, and Janums' account is very good on how his regiment broke out of many towns, like the battle of Domslaff, when the commander Eižens Bonoparts launched an attack with his 1st Company to break out and open up this road to the sea. That was the first place when it might all have been 'done'. Horst and Dievenow are just the last part. The lifeline is the road to sea.

Every day along this road might have been your last day. There were German units, Latvian units, French units – living in German castles, all over the place – and Horst and Dievenow were just the last part. The Russians reached the sea and said: 'That's it. All German forces are cut off. They're done.' And they started to plan the next moves: taking Kolberg, getting to the Oder.

The Russians under-estimated the will of these units to break out – on foot; day in, day out. They simply walked to safety, and they were helped at that last part because although the Russians controlled the sea and could shoot at the sea, there was a high cliff and a sandy beach, so the Latvians and hundreds and thousands of civilians walked along the beach in the dead ground close to the cliff where the Russians shells couldn't hit them.

It's heartbreaking: Germans carrying their toddlers or pushing them in prams 50 kilometres with shells landing everywhere and soldiers shooting randomly. Those guys were 20 years old and their hearts were made of stone, seeing those scenes on the beach.

I have never read a German account of this Horst and Dievenow action, but I would suspect that though there may have been 50 Latvians there sounding like 200, there were probably 50 Germans next to them and 50 French next to them and then another 50 Germans. So there may have been only 50 Latvians but actually 200 men were fighting.

He stirs his coffee and looks at me.

That's the problem of only having accounts from one unit. They only write about what's happening to them. The soldier typically only knows about the next treeline, not the big picture. Horst and Dievenow are just the end of this messy road, the road to the sea. On the way you have the breakout at Domslaff on 24 February in which one of the very gifted commanders – Eižens Bonoparts – was mortally wounded. So yes, Janums gets away, but not everyone does.[36]

36 Interview with author, Rīga, 27 November 2019.

Important sections of the research into the episodes experienced by the Latvians in Pomerania were translated for this book by Aivars Sinka, the Anglo-Latvian head of Daugavas Vanagi, the Legion veterans' organisation. He is the son of Juris Sinka, who came to the UK as a wartime refugee, was educated at Oxford and worked for BBC Monitoring at Caversham translating Cold War Soviet radio transmissions.[37]

Mr Sinka is among many Latvians horrified by the 'SS' stigma hanging over men who had little choice whether to fight:

> Apart from a core of seasoned fighters, who had either been conscripted in 1943 or had volunteered in 1942, the men of the Latvian 15th Division were mostly raw recruits: teenagers with no combat experience and hardly any equipment, let alone weapons. According to the Catholic chaplain Kazimirs Ručs, there were 15,000 schoolboys in Pomerania, taken from the final draft in summer 1944 and reinforced by at least 700 RAD students, who had been working in labour camps in Germany to earn the right to study. Another 4,000 16 and 17-year-olds were sent to Germany as Air Force 'helpers'.
>
> All of this is a war crime, carried out by the Nazis against the citizens of Latvia – a war crime that is so far uncompensated and largely uncommemorated. Sadly, this is often in case the sensitivities of the West are offended. To try to put the moniker of 'SS' on these victims of Nazi and Soviet war crimes is neither correct nor just, but is typical of the Soviets, their successors and their 'useful idiots', and replicated in the untruths used to justify the Russian invasion of Ukraine in 2022.
>
> The Latvians were usually forced to be the first and last lines of German defence. Throughout the campaign, they were always under-armed. Their officers, like Vilis Janums and Jūlijs Ķīlītis, were veterans of the First World War and the Latvian War of Independence, and saw it as their job to protect their men. On balance, and in the face of Nazi attempts to sacrifice them and Soviet attempts to destroy them, they bore this responsibility with honour.
>
> There is ample evidence of the tactics of the Germans – to let others do the fighting. I am shocked at the willingness of SS commander Adolph Ax to sacrifice Latvian lives by his dithering and inept command, ironically earning himself a Knight's Cross at Landeck. I wonder how modern military strategists might assess his decisions?
>
> At Wallachsee, after wasting a whole day unable to decide what to do, he refused Colonel Janums's offer to clear the Soviets from the road and, instead, fatally weakened his rearguard by pulling the 48th SS out of Flederborn to attack Wallachsee.
>
> This decision not only weakened the defence of the town but also signalled to the Soviets that they were pulling out, resulting in the death of hundreds of Latvian soldiers and refugees trapped on the road. Ax wanted Janums and the

---

37 Elected to the post-independence Latvian parliament for the right-wing *For Fatherland and Freedom* party, Juris Sinka was a vigorous defender of the Legion.

33rd Regiment on his flank to protect him from attack from the east without any regard for the wagon train behind him. Some have criticised Janums for following this order, but I'm not sure he had the choice. Ax didn't appear to have considered the need for a vanguard or to secure the high ground on his left between Flederborn and Landeck.

By the time Ax gets to Landeck he has failed to maintain communication with his different units and has totally lost the trust of his officers and soldiers, with yet more fatal consequences. It's no wonder he lost his job a couple of weeks later, but, if you take Colonel Janums's account at face value, Ax still had time for one more crime against the Legionnaires. In a decision that, in my view, bordered on the vengeful, and only one week after Flederborn and Landeck, he sent Janums and Ķīlītis and almost all the remaining combat-capable Latvians to Kamin on 11 February.

They were told it was a 'quiet sector', but marched 40 kilometres straight into an attack by the Soviet 162nd Guards division with tanks and substantial amounts of artillery. They were sent there to replace a German battalion: sacrificed, I would say, to save German lives. As German units were fleeing without informing the Latvians, Ax and his number two Pape ordered them to fight to the last man, but Janums ignored that and fought his way out of the encirclement. Ax's behaviour in blaming the Latvians when he was replaced as commander was disgraceful.

What we do see here is courageous leadership against the odds, in terrible weather, while having to follow German orders and facing danger on all sides. The constant encirclement is exhausting, but the Latvian officers kept them going through break-out after break-out, culminating in the escape along the coast to Dievenow to cross the Oder.

It's clear that a plan is forming: to get across the Oder and surrender to the Americans and British, if possible. They know they can't trust the Germans and surrendering to the Russians means either death or Siberia. Those who made it to the West are the founders of the global Latvian diaspora, and it's fascinating to see this wider picture of their experiences emerging.[38]

What happened to those who did survive the Pomeranian bloodbath is the subject of the author's forthcoming books.

To the south-east of Berlin, Colonel Janums abandoned his positions and dodged both Russians and Germans to lead his 900-strong battle group to safety through the forests to surrender to the Americans at the Elbe. The diary of adjutant Major Edvins Bušmanis tells a gripping and almost hour-by-hour account of their escape.

The men of the 'Recce' Battalion, considered the best fighters, were split off and sent to defend Berlin to the death – in effect, sacrificed for Hitler. The diaries of two Latvian survivors, Pēteris Krievs and Jānis Auzans, tell vivid, graphic stories of the bloody endgame in the city.

---

38 Aivars Sinka, email correspondence with author, May 2022.

The 4,500 men remaining after the 15th Division was split on 19 April 1945 were sent to Mecklenburg, where their officers refused to throw their lives away in 'suicide positions' at Nienhagen and marched west to Schwerin to surrender to the British and Americans.

Most of the 4,000 Latvians sent to Danzig were killed or taken prisoner, but three men made it to the west: Ēriks Rudzītis, interviewed by the author at the age of 93, Harijs Blezūrs and Augusts Spilners, whose Latvian diary has been translated by his daughter, Nora. They tell of frightened poorly-trained conscripts being mown down at the front, with a Nazi noose waiting for anyone whose nerve failed. Most of the men who crossed the Oder never returned to Latvia.

They became the Lost Legion. The comrades they left behind may still be lying in the towns and villages in Poland where they fell, in the German war cemetery near Szczecin or, as at Ślesin, mixed up in graves with their Red Army foes, and unremembered.

Appendix I

Sites for possible further investigation

A number of disturbing stories have emerged from this research. Not all can be immediately confirmed, but all warrant further investigation.

1. The Jastrowie to Lędyczek road (Jastrow to Landeck): how many did die here, and who were they?
2. Lędyczek: stories of the 'NKVD-style' execution of 600 Latvian RAD recruits at a barracks here with shots to the back of the neck.
3. Immenheim: stories of hundreds of Latvians found dead. 100 unarmed prisoners shot dead by the Red Army.
4. Ogardy (then Wugarten): Mass rape and murder.
5. Wilmsee: mass rape and killing of 400 female Latvian RAD recruits.
6. Neuheim (Dąbrówka Nowa): Latvian soldiers bulldozed by tanks and survivors massacred. Testimony of Ernests Šperliņš.[1]
7. Flatow: nine 15th Division prisoners shot.

---

1 In July 2010, the Pomost Association and the Society of Friends of the Pomeranian Military Museum recovered the remains of 51 Latvian and two German soldiers from a grave in Dąbrówka Nowa [then Neuheim]. Four months later, 20 skeletons were exhumed from two graves at the edge of a field in Kosovo, halfway between Nakło [then Nakel] and Mrocza [then Immenheim]. The way the skeletons were arranged suggested they were thrown into a ditch. The dogtags were in such a poor condition it was impossible to identify the bodies on-site. Next to the skeletons, several buttons, two combs and the remains of a German helmet were found. All the remains were re-buried at the German Soldiers' Cemetery in Stary Czarnowo in the West Pomeranian Voivodeship.

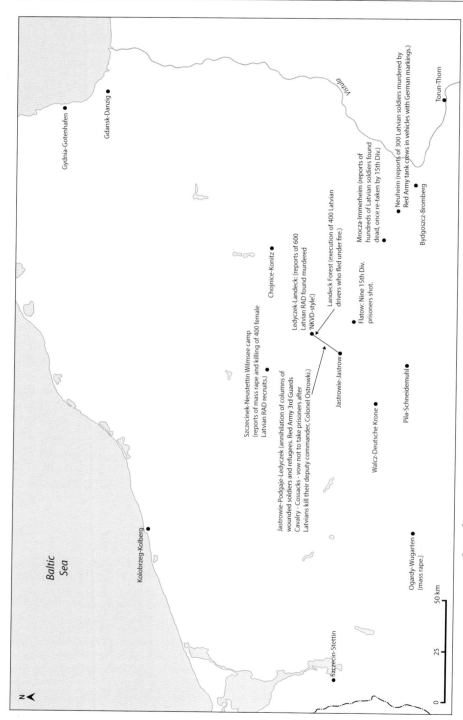

Sites of reported atrocities in Pomerania against Latvians by Red Army and NKVD.

Appendix II

Timeline of main events Jastrow to Landeck 30 January–4 February 1945

Before the 15th Division arrives in Jastrow on 30.1.45	The 15th Division, retreating as the rearguard from the Flatow direction, is not only being pursued by Russian/Polish forces from the east, but the Russian Cavalry Corps has also swept around Jastrow towards Ratzebuhr and Landeck. Landeck is being fought over between German and Soviet forces, so the 15th Division is effectively cut off. Just before this, on 27–28 January, the '*tross*' (wagon train) of the 32nd Regiment of the 15th had been ordered north ahead of the retreat. At this time, Ratzebuhr came under pressure from Russian tanks. Though some straggling units suffered losses, they successfully passed through Jastrow, Flederborn and Ratzebuhr. Jastrow is defended by the German 51st and 59th infantry regiments, together with other assorted German units. The 51st Regiment's 1st Battalion is taking up positions either side of the road between Jastrow and Schneidemühl on the west bank of the Küddow, while the 2nd is at Betkenhammer, approximately five kilometres south of the town. The 59th is in positions on high ground 1.5 kilometres north-east of Jastrow. At Flederborn, the 48th SS (Dutch/German) regiment have recaptured and are defending the town, which changes hands twice. They are under attack by Polish forces from the east and in imminent danger from being cut off from Ratzebuhr by Russian tanks. The road between Jastrow and Flederborn is under pressure from the enemy.
30.1.45–31.1.45	All the units of the 15th Division (plus assorted German units) come together in Jastrow. The initial order is to hold Jastrow to the last man. That is then changed on the next day to attempt a break-out. There are about 800 injured in Jastrow. As the trains are no longer running, the injured have to stay with the Division transport. Hundreds of 15th Division drivers are pressed into service as soldiers, while paramedics and clerks take over the driving of lorries, ambulances and horse-drawn carts.

31.1.45 Jastrow	Major Elster leading a German unit *Festungs-Gr. W. Btl. 22* is given orders to be responsible for the all-round defence of Jastrow, while Colonel Janums is charged with the inner defence ring around the town. Janums, with the 33rd Regiment, must defend Jastrow as long as possible, together with the Joachim battle group and the two battalions of the 51st German infantry regiment assigned to him. However, the regiment's *štābs* (HQ) is to report directly to Divisional commander Ax. Janums believes that this 'artificial' reporting line is so that the commander of the 51st wouldn't have to report to him. The Divisional HQ, non-combat units, the Divisional transport and the injured wait for the road to Flederborn to be cleared. Meanwhile, led by Ķīlītis, four battalions (three of the 34th and the remaining battalion of the 32nd) are ordered to break through to Flederborn.
Jastrow-Flederborn	The four battalions set off at about 14:00. The battalion of the 32nd, led by Major Alksnītis is in the rearguard. The German 48th are defending Flederborn from Polish attack.
	At the rear of Alksnītis' battalion is the battalion doctor Pauls Dzintars, who, after hearing fighting ahead, witnesses hundreds of soldiers – many of them the drivers who had been pressed into service – fleeing eastwards away from the fighting but towards where the Polish units are. He hears gunshots from that direction.
Flederborn	Ķīlītis approaches Flederborn in the evening and comes across the rear of the Polish attack. The Polish units are routed by the 34th.
	Ķīlītis arrives at Flederborn in the dark after the fight with the Polish and bringing 96 prisoners. The defenders of the town aren't expecting him and a brief 'friendly' firefight takes place between the 34th and 48th with some losses on the Latvian side. Ķīlītis then enters the town and hands over the prisoners to the German officers. The 48th supply additional ammunition to the 34th.
	Alksnītis has been ordered to attack Strassforth (about two kilometres south-east of Flederborn) before entering Flederborn. After hearing from a prisoner that the village is defended by two battalions of Polish soldiers and having lost the element of surprise, Alksnītis postpones the attack and goes into Flederborn.
1.2.45 Jastrow	At 10:00 the commander of the 2nd Battalion of the 51st informs Janums that around 1,000 enemy soldiers coming from the south-west have crossed the Jastrow-Betkenhammer road near the railway crossing and gone into the wood south of Jastrow. Shortly after that, the commander of the 1st Battalion of the 51st Regiment also informs Janums that small enemy units are bypassing their defensive positions. Janums sends a scouting patrol to check on the validity of this information, which reports upon its return that they haven't found any enemy soldiers in the wood and that there are no footprints in the snow to indicate that 1,000 soldiers had entered the forest.

	At 13:00, the commander of the 2nd Battalion of the 51st arrives at Janums' headquarters and informs him that the enemy had attacked Betkenhammer in great force at 12:00 and the battalion is retreating towards Schonwald. Janums orders Lazduzieds with a battalion made up of two companies to counterattack in the direction of Schonwald-Betkenhammer and renew the earlier positions. Janums orders the 2nd Battalion of the 51st to secure the counterattack by blocking the road Jastrow-Deutsche Krone 2.5 kilometres south-west of Schonwald and maintain constant communication with Janums' attacking battalion. When Lazduzieds reaches the railway viaduct north of Schonwald, he meets the 2nd Battalion of the 51st retreating towards Jastrow. Lazduzieds points out to its commander that he has been ordered to secure Lazduzieds' flank. The German battalion commander refuses to carry out the order. Janums orders Lazduzieds not to carry out the attack but take up positions near Schonwald. He notifies the Divisional commander of the situation and the German commander is relieved of his position.
1.2.45 Flederborn	By 04:00 on 1 February, Ķīlītis has swapped out the 48th with his own men and has them in place in defensive positions.
	At some point on 1 February, he asks the Germans what has happened to the Polish prisoners.
Jastrow-Flederborn	Soviet units take the positions held by the German 59th Regiment, north of Jastrow, west of the Flederborn road. Ax orders the Recce battalion to retake the positions, while the 59th is ordered to provide a reserve north of Jastrow.
	Starting at 13:00, on the afternoon of 1 February, the Recce Battalion (with one German infantry and one mortar company allotted to them) fight their way up the railway line from Jastrow, reaching and clearing Tiefenort for the first time by 19:00, then taking up positions.
	Ķīlītis says that the night of 1 February in Flederborn was relatively quiet.
	Evening of 1 February, 48th commander Paul Massell is killed just before entering Flederborn.
2.2.45 Jastrow	02:00: the German 51st retreats in disarray from positions south of Jastrow. Janums orders the Joachim battle group to replace them in their positions. The Joachim battle group delays its attack, meets resistance and then falls back to the edge of Jastrow.
	06:00: two companies of the 2nd Battalion of Janums' 33rd Regiment fight off two attacks in the southern sector of Jastrow. At 10:30, after the third attack, the enemy takes the viaduct and the companies fall back to the railway station.
Jastrow-Flederborn	At 03:00, after the Recce battalion has re-taken the heights, the German 59th Regiment are ordered back into those positions, while the Recce battalion moves back to Jastrow for rest.
	At 07:00, the enemy attacks again at Tiefenort and the 59th retreats in disarray. The Germans at Tiefenort call for help and the Recce Battalion comes out again from Jastrow and retakes Tiefenort at 09:00 on 2 February.
Flederborn	In Flederborn on 2 February, Ķīlītis repulses two attacks relatively easily, while heavy artillery fire resumes.
	On 2 February, the 48th sets out towards Ratzebuhr but fails to meet objectives: Ķīlītis believes the loss of Massell is part of the reason.

Jastrow-Flederborn	10:00: Ax and the HQ leave Jastrow, with the Joachim battle group as the vanguard. The German 51st leaves with them, against orders (they should have remained in Jastrow, reporting to Janums). The transport column with the injured follows behind the other units.
Flederborn-Wallachsee	When Ax gets to Flederborn, Ķīlītis advises him to move on through before the artillery barrage. The road is still blocked south of Wallachsee. The column sets off from Flederborn with a German unit and an 88mm gun battery in the vanguard. The column reaches Wallachsee at about 23:00, but can go no further as the road is blocked by an enemy strong point, including an anti-tank gun. The units waiting in the forest for the road to be cleared come under sniper fire.
	The rear of the column is stuck on the road (it seems not all had even reached Flederborn by the time of the midnight artillery barrage).
Jastrow	Janums sets up three covering positions for the retreat, grouped in depth towards Flederborn: the first on the south-west side of Jastrow; the second on the south-west side of a wood north-east of Jastrow; and the third by Tiefenort.
	After receiving the order to hold Jastrow as long as he can before retreating towards Flederborn, Janums decides to hold on until darkness. The Soviets take the railway station in the afternoon.
	At 17:00, Janums starts the retreat from Jastrow and last units leave by 22:00.
Jastrow-Flederborn	As the last units leave, Janums goes up to the Divisional HQ, which is still in Flederborn, where he is surprised that the transport column is not moving forward. Ax orders him to turn around and retake Jastrow to provide space for manoeuvre. Janums refuses on the grounds that this is impractical. Ax changes the order to instead take up defensive positions around Tiefenort. Ax orders the mechanised transport column of the Supply Regiment to clear the road towards Landeck.
	At 22:00 Janums' HQ company replaces the Recce Battalion at Tiefenort. The remains of the Recce Battalion are presumed to be going into Flederborn.
Flederborn	At 22:00, the Division's Artillery Regiment enters Flederborn. The situation is so cramped and the enemy so near (1 kilometre) that only direct fire across open sights is possible. The gunners are instructed to cover the rearguard positions of Janums' units, but can only partially do this because of lack of ammunition.
	During the night, the 34th is ordered to be the rearguard at Flederborn. Everyone else is to leave. At midnight the town comes under a blaze of shellfire. The commander of the 34th Regiment, Vīksne, writes: 'At Flederborn the division was surrounded. The order to break out was not given, they promised to free us by breaking in. After three heavy days, we nevertheless received the order to break out. On the day of the breakout I received a serious head wound.'
3.2.45 Wallachsee	At 07:00, Ax is still stuck at Wallachsee. Janums reaches the Divisional HQ there, where he is surprised that, despite having been there since midnight, Ax and the HQ leader Wulff have done nothing to facilitate the breakthrough. Janums asks Ax permission to organise the breakthrough, which he receives.

Flederborn	The battle around Flederborn flares up. The enemy attacks from the south, west and east.
	Lieutenant Bonoparts' company, of Janums' 33rd Regiment, having arrived during the night, is ordered not to withdraw from Flederborn with the regiment, but to stay to prevent the enemy from deeper penetration.
Wallachsee	Ax countermands his order to Janums and instead decides that the 48th should attack Wallachsee. Janums is ordered instead to move forward on the right flank of the column, staying within 1.5–2 kilometres of the road. Janums gathers his men and waits in the forest by a clearing for the delayed attack by the 48th on Wallachsee to start.
Flederborn	The 48th is given the order to leave Flederborn and secure the road at Wallachsee. The carts of the regiment and the division are not able to leave Flederborn until the 48th has taken Wallachsee. At Flederborn, at dawn, the 48th starts to move out. The Russians and Poles see this and increase their attacks to press into the village.
	Having noticed the 48th leaving Flederborn, Soviet tanks now arrive in the village. Ķīlītis carries out a fighting retreat, house by house. As he retreats, Ķīlītis has the fighting at Wallachsee in front of him and the sound of the tanks behind. Once the tanks in the village feel secure, they start to shoot up the rear of the column, which has been left to fend for itself. Ķīlītis and his men pass the shot-up column and reach Wallachsee just as the fighting there ends. They can hear the tanks following behind.
	Lieutenant Bonoparts leads his 23 men into a counterattack through the burning village. The enemy sustains heavy damage, and as a result of this counterattack, the pull-back is successful.
Wallachsee	On his own initiative, Lieutenant Bonoparts and three men with four Panzerfausts advance to the hills west of Wallachsee. The enemy, however, has pulled back to houses in Wallachsee. The company launches an attack on the village with the support of 'a weak German unit.' They launch eleven counterattacks between 09:00–15:00.
	By about 12:00, the attack on Wallachsee is carried out successfully. The 48th attacked from the west, while Latvian units attacked from the road. Two previous attacks on the enemy position had failed. The transport on the road starts to move again.
Wallachsee-Landeck	After the attack on Wallachsee by the 48th has started, after 11:00, in line with his orders, Janums with his men go through the forest parallel to the road and cross the frozen Küddow river approximately two kilometres east. Going through the forest, they approach the Dobrinka river, looking for a place where there is a gap in the line. After their recent experiences, Janums wants to avoid a fight if he can and makes use of the flexibility he has been given to vary his direction to the right or to the left. After crossing the Dobrinka, they push on in the direction of Wusters. By late evening they reach Krummensee. The regiment only has 650 men left. (Meeting Janums a few days later, Ķīlītis describes Janums as having broken through on his own initiative out of his disgust at the behaviour of the Germans).
	The Artillery Regiment has pulled out of Flederborn and joined the column on the road, leaving two guns behind for cover. The head of the column is held up at Wallachsee because of infantry fighting in front and on both sides of the road.

	The breakthrough at Wallachsee has come too late for many. By lunchtime, the tail of the transport column still hasn't started moving and is completely stuck (possibly just north of the Flederborn crossroads) as the renewed attack on Flederborn begins.
	At about 12:00, there is a panic on the left side of the road and behind and the entire column moves 2–3 kilometres further up the road. As a result, on the road past Wallachsee, opposite an open space to the left of the road the Division's column gets stuck, with three lanes. Two Russian tanks appear on the left side of the column at Wallachsee and cause panic in the covering infantry units on the left side: they hastily retreat to the main road, leaving the left flank of the column completely open. The Russian tanks advance to the plateaus on the left side and, unhindered, begin to shell and machine-gun the compact masses on the road. This situation causes renewed panic in the column and results in great losses of humans, horses and various materials, as the whole compacted column has to move under shellfire through the completely open stretch of road opposite Wallachsee. Many artillery units are lost and there are many soldiers killed and wounded, with dead horses and equipment left on the road. There are not enough artillery munitions left to return fire at the Russian tanks. The surviving part of the column is squeezed in the forest on a 1.5 kilometre stretch of road between Wallachsee and Landeck, with its head about 1.5 kilometres from Landeck. During the course of the entire march from Flederborn to Landeck, the road was covered by well-sighted enemy artillery, tank and infantry heavy weapons fire. At the same time, the head of the column took light and heavy infantry weapon fire from the eastern side of the road. Artillery Regiment infantry protect the column on both sides of the road while the attack on Landeck takes place.
Landeck	Ķīlītis follows the edge of the forest until he reaches the road just in front of Landeck. The road has been blocked again. He sees the leadership of the Division standing around, not knowing what to do. He decides not to get involved, but to go through the forest and find a place to cross the river and get past the enemy.
	The enemy had blocked the road just in front of the bridge into Landeck with fire from height 118, just to the left of the road and machine gun nests near the bridge. At the same time, from the other side of the roadblock, KGs Hämel and von Bargen had pushed the Soviets out of Landeck to take the bridge over the river, from where they launched attacks to the rear of the Red Army.
	On the road south of the enemy blockage, Wulff tries to organise a full-frontal attack to the bridge, at the same time as the Russians are being pushed from the Landeck side. Wulff has trouble in getting fighting units to the bridge to force entry to Landeck. Accounts describe well-armoured German units going up the side of the road with no-one to give them orders, while Ķīlītis and Janums are in the forest with their units to the east of the road and many other soldiers are trying to shelter in the forest from Katyusha attacks.
	Major Alksnītis of the 32nd writes: 'We can't get into the town. We are located between the Flederborn-Landeck road and the Küddow river. The enemy fires with mortars and machine guns and tanks are also active. With gruelling effort, the men were got forward for the attack on the Landeck bridge.'

	The last stretch close to Landeck is captured in an assault by all available soldiers of the Division, including the 32nd Regiment, dislodging the Russians from the plateaus west of Landeck. Major Rubenis, commander of the 32nd Regiment, is killed leading his soldiers in the final assault.
	The attack (at about 15:00), is finally successful but at great cost, including the loss of Wulff, Rubenis, the commander of the Artillery Regiment Captain Eglītis and many men. Three Legionnaires sacrifice themselves, setting up an anti-tank gun on the road to destroy the last Russian positions. Kazimirs Ručs holds battlefield services where soldiers had fallen, including for Wulff.
	At the same time as the fight for the Landeck bridge, Ķilītis engages in a short firefight with an enemy unit near Adlig Landeck manor house, east of the Landeck road. As this is going on, the news arrives that the bridge has been freed and they disengage and run to the bridge to cross into Landeck.
Evening of 3.2.45 Landeck-Krummensee	The 15th Division reaches Landeck and goes through to Krummensee for rest. The medical transports with the injured had largely got through, as had the motorised transport, but most of the horse-carts didn't get through. Many of the soldiers had frostbite, many were sick.
After 3.2.45 Jastrow-Landeck	The break-out of the 15th Division to Landeck has disrupted the attackers' plans, stopping the Soviet attack in this direction. In response, parts of the 3rd Shock Army's front reserves are concentrated in this sector, formed into three corps.
13–24.2.45 Jastrow-Landeck	The surrounded German garrison at Schneidemühl breaks out (in various documents the numbers in the breakout are stated between 2,000–20,000 while Russian documents say 10,000). The road that these units take is almost the same as the Latvians between Jastrow and Landeck. The German soldiers move through the woods along the Küddow river. At that time all three corps of the 3rd Shock Army are there. The remaining seven divisions of the Shock Army were put at battle stations. However, the German soldiers, who set out in five columns to the east of Jastrow, had split into small units and each night, until 24 February, they came across the front in the Landeck area.

Timeline compiled by Aivars Sinka.

Appendix III

Timeline of the 32nd Regiment, its 3rd battalion (III/32) and the court martial of Major Siliņš

Sturmbannführer [Major] Mārtiņš Siliņš has the distinction of being the only Latvian commander court-martialled during the Second World War. Born 26 June 1900 in Krape parish near Jaunjelgava, he commanded the III Battalion of the 32nd Regiment from November 1944.

At some point in late January 1945, he led a group of between 20 and 50 men – his battalion *štābs*, or staff – from the Jastrow-Flederborn area via Ratzebuhr to a pre-arranged rendezvous point in Neubrandenburg instead of fighting alongside the Latvian column on the road to Landeck. On 17 March he was made acting regimental commander, then shortly afterwards was arrested and court-martialled for frequent changes of command post and cowardice in the face of the enemy.

He ended the war attached to the 32nd Regiment staff and later came to the UK, settling in Bradford, where he died on 30 April 1973. The eulogy at his funeral was given by a captain of the 1st Cavalry Regiment, where Siliņš served from 1924.[1]

The 32nd Regiment suffered very heavy losses throughout the period in Pomerania and its experience demonstrates the German technique of placing the Latvians in 'suicide positions' (Immenheim, Kujan) and ordering them to fight to the last man, while also picking off groups and units to reinforce certain areas (such as Danzig). This timeline details their journey across modern Poland and charts how the regiment was whittled down and scattered.

---

1 Axis History Forum, online at <https://forum.axishistory.com/viewtopic.php?t=126237> and Londonas Avize, 18 May 1973, online at < http://periodika.lv/periodika2-viewer/?lang=fr#panel:pp|issue:220100|article:DIVL305|page:5|block:P5_TB00014>.

5–8 August, 1944	After the disaster at Mozuļi Manor, the process of re-forming the 32nd Regiment of the 15th Division starts. Between 5–8 August 1944, 650 new conscripts (boys born 1925–26) join the regiment from the conscription commissions in Valmiera and Brenguļi (under Hāzners and Cubins). There are rumours and opposition to being sent to Germany and the officers do their best to calm the situation. They are formed into four companies. More boys are picked from Cēsis on 9 August. The conscripts are taken to Rīga, but are not told their ultimate destination.	J. Cubins memoir (A. Krīpēns Archive - Latvian War Museum)
10 August–19 January	On 10 August, the boys are loaded on to the ship *Donau*. With them are other conscripts, the HQ of the 15th Division and some German soldiers. The ship is overloaded. There are many on the quayside to see them off. They reach Neufahrwasser near Danzig on the afternoon of 12 August. On 27 September, they reach their training base at Stuednitz-Sommin. Latvian officers are sent on courses and temporarily replaced by German officers. Latvian officers return in November. SS runes on uniforms for the Division are replaced by the Latvian symbol of the rising sun.	J. Cubins
19 January 1945	670 men and 4 officers under Captain Jānis Lanka are sent to Courland as reinforcements for the 19th Division. Note: it had originally been planned to send a whole regiment made up of one battalion from each of the three regiments in Pomerania. However, because the 19th Division needed soldiers and instructors, rather than officers, it was decided a volunteer battalion was needed instead. The men were 'well-armed' and given winter clothes and boots. The battalion went to Danzig by train and embarked for Latvia. (According to GB6, the battalion was accompanied to Danzig by the adjutant of the 32nd, Lieutenant Zaķis). According to Jānis Melderis's *6,000 Latviešu Virsnieku Likteņi Otrā Pasaules Kara Gados* [*The Fate of 6,000 Latvian Officers During WWII*], the battalion was called the 32nd Grenadier Regiment Reserve Battalion.	GB6, p.67 and p.82 J. Zaķis (Krīpēns Archive) J. Melderis *6,000 Latviešu Virsnieku Likteņi Otrā Pasaules Kara Gados* (p. 299)
21–22 January	The remaining soldiers of the 32nd are formed up to be sent to the front in two battalions: I (led by Major Alksnītis) and III (led by Major Siliņš). Together, there are 39 officers, 234 instructors and 1,490 soldiers (together 1,763 men). The first battalion (I/32) has four companies (1st, 2nd, 3rd, 4th). The third battalion consists of four companies: the 9th, 10th, 11th and 12th.	GB6, p.67
22 January	456 men of the II battalion (II/32) are left in the training camp at Studnitz: Major Šmits with eight officers, 73 instructors and 375 men. Therefore, it is assumed that 1,307 went out to battle on 22 January 1945.	GB6, p.68

23–31 January *(11th Company of III/32)*	The 11th company of the III/32 were delayed in getting to the front because of lack of transport, left behind at Bruss. They are then ordered under Lieutenant Ceberis to go to Lobesent, south-east of Vandsburg, which they reach on 25 January and are put under the command of the local German Commandant. All is quiet until 27 January, when a battalion-size attack is made by the enemy at 14:00. The unit suffers heavy losses. They fall back into Vandsburg, make contact with the division and retreat towards Flatow in a blizzard. At the village of Kleschin, the company destroys the first enemy unit to attack. They beat off several further attacks. On 30 January they receive the order to disengage from the enemy and go to Jastrow, where they join up with the rest of the division and are assigned to Janums' 33rd Regiment. There are only 30 men and one officer left.	GB6, p.79
23–24 January	Alksnītis with the 3rd and 4th Companies of the I/32 is sent to the Nakel front to fight on the flank of the 34th Regiment. The rest of the regiment arrives in Immenheim.	GB6, p.70
24 January	All units that are left in the training area retreat, unarmed, towards Danzig, including the II/32. The 490 men of the II/32 are now under an unnamed replacement commander (Major Šmits is given command of another unit in Danzig).	GB6, pp.232-233
25 January	The commander of the 32nd Regiment, Lieutenant-Colonel Pauls Celle, is relieved of his command due to a nervous breakdown (although the order does not mention that). Major Rubenis is put in charge of the 32nd Regiment. The handover to Rubenis may have already happened a day or two earlier. Hāzners writes in 1963: 'Celle handed the regiment over on 23 January (maybe it was the evening of the 24th) to Rubenis in my presence when we were already at the front, when we were already surrounded by tanks. Celle had completely lost his head and was already talking incoherently.'	GB6, p.71 Vilis Hāzners letter to Krīpēns 13.9.63 (Krīpēns archive)
25–26 January	Contact is lost with Alksnītis and his two companies and also with Siliņš and the III/32. The 1st and 2nd companies of the 32nd under Rubenis are thrown into battle to retake Schlossen (between Nakel and Bromberg) which fail. Repeated orders are sent from Divisional command to retake Schlossen. The HQ company of the 32nd Regiment is fighting left of that position, together with a company of the recce battalion, and successfully takes Strelau [Strezelewo], which is between Schlossen and Bromberg. After a number of counterattacks by the Russians, and suffering heavy casualties, they fall back.	GB6, pp.71–74

26 January	By the morning of 26 January, these companies of the 32nd (1st, 2nd, and HQ) are almost cut off. About half the men are lost. Around 12:00, the enemy has broken the line of defence and a number of enemy tanks are already operating behind the line. The units suffer losses and retreat, breaking through towards Immenheim. During this retreat the 32nd's HQ Company is mauled again. They reach Immenheim towards evening, arriving in small groups. The regimental command point has been attacked by enemy tanks and the regimental HQ is scattered. Major Rubenis is lightly injured by shrapnel. During the battles fall Captain Bremšmits, vice-Lieutenant Brikmanis, Oberleutnant Lapiņš and Lieutenant Apinis of the HQ company are missing in action, while Lieutenant Dukāts is concussed. The remaining men are formed into a battle group under Lieutenant Zaķis.	GB6, pp.71–74 J.Zaķis
26 January	The 3rd Battalion of the 32nd (III/32), without its 11th Company (which had stayed in Bruss), was held up in Konitz due to lack of transport. It is ordered on 26 January to report to the 33rd Regiment, to resist the enemy at Schlaufensee.	GB6, p.77
26 January	At 08:30 the III/32 under Captain (later Major) Siliņš is put under the command of Janums, who orders them, together with the 3rd and 4th companies of the 33rd, to attack Hauensee.	VJ, pp.155–156
26 January	16:00: Janums goes to find the 32nd as there is no news from Siliņš. As the enemy has taken the edge of the forest at Gruenhausen, Siliņš has held back the attack, not wishing to attack in daylight without artillery support. Janums allows him to put off the attack until daylight has gone and provides instructions as to how to deploy his men. At nightfall, the battalion attacks successfully and so prevents the encirclement of Janums' group.	VJ, p.156
Movements of Regimental wagon train 26 January–20 February (the tross of III/32)	After the heavy battles of 25–26 January, the regimental *tross* (wagon-train) is reformed at Immenheim. The men are ordered to leave Immenheim quickly for Vandsburg, then to leave Vandsburg on 27 January for Flatow, where 40 carts and 120 men are added to the *tross*. Halfway to Flatow, the *tross* is stopped by gendarmes, who, in the name of the local commandant, take away 40 men and some carts to work on local defence. They go through Flatow (night of 27–28 January), then Jastrow, Flederborn and Ratzebuhr before the Red Army encirclement cuts the road. The *tross* reaches Ratzebuhr on the evening of 30 January but pushes straight on, because Ratzebuhr is threatened by the Russians. They follow minor roads to get to Beerenwalde (again some soldiers are taken for defence duties). Here, also, they are joined by some divisional transport units (12 men and four carts). Then they travel to Bad Polzin, Regenwalde, Gollnow and over the Oder to Poerlitz, aiming for Neubrandenburg (which is where scattered Latvian units are supposed to gather). Once they get to Stettin, they discover that the Latvians had to gather in the Neustettin-Hammerstein area instead. The *tross* enters Hammerstein on 20 February.	GB6, pp.80–82

27 January	Janums instructs Siliņš to hold his positions until 06:00 and then to fall back to Immenheim and be under the command of the regimental commander of the 32nd (Rubenis).	VJ, p.159
27 January onwards	At some point between 27th–30th January, Major Siliņš and his štābs (HQ) become separated from the III/32, either because of the fog of war or intentionally by Major Siliņš. It is not clear how many men were involved: Siliņš's adjutant, Kļaviņš writes that the battalion HQ 'plus a small leftover of the battalion' (likely to be between 20–50 men) turned up later on 7 February in Neubrandenburg. Siliņš is still in charge of the battalion on 27 January, but according to Alksnītis' entry for 30 January, Major Rubenis is reported as being in charge of III/32. The official history states: 'The battle experiences of the III/32 were similar to those of the rest of the division, experiencing the same tragedy as the whole regiment and the whole division. This battalion though, since Immenheim, was more under the command of Major Rubenis than battalion commander Major Siliņš, who often changed the location of his command points and communicated badly with his units.'	Alksnītis (A. Krīpēns archive) GB6, p.77
27 January	By the time Alksnītis, the commander of I/32, has retreated to Immenheim he has only about 60 men left. Alksnītis takes over command of the group formed by Zaķis.	GB6, p.74
27 January	Janums and the 33rd is ordered to retreat to Immenheim which is under Russian attack. There, he finds only a rearguard led by Alksnītis with remnants of the 32nd. The Divisional HQ and everyone else has already retreated to Klarashohe.	VJ, p.160
27 January	Alksnītis with the remnants of the 32nd, plus support from a German company and an anti-tank gun, is given the task to block the road to Vandsburg. They successfully overcome and break up a Soviet column of 400–500 men, which was marching from Immenheim. After this, again, Alksnītis only has around 60 men left.	Alksnītis
27 January	Meanwhile, the III/32, together with the 33rd and 34th Regiments has taken up positions south of Zabartowo (south-east of Vandsburg).	GB6, p.74 Alksnītis
28 January	In darkness, the units of the Division retreat through Runowo to Sypniewo and then take up defensive positions (south to north) from Dreidorf to Sypniewo. The III/32 Battalion takes up positions on the right flank, while Alksnītis and his men take position at Ruden (west of Dreidorf). The regimental commander Major Rubenis arrives as well.	GB6, p.74
29 January	Alksnītis gathers together the scattered remnants of the 32nd Regiment at the customs house four kilometres east of Kujan. He sends out patrols.	GB6, p.74

30 January	Wulff (the 1a of the Division) orders Alksnītis with the remains of I/32 to take up a rearguard position on the north side of the road to Flatow (four kilometres east of Flatow) and Rubenis with the remains of III/32 to do the same on the south side of the road. These orders are given with the threat that if anyone retreats into the town, they will be shot. Meanwhile, Wulff, Ax and the divisional HQ retreat to Flatow.	GB6, p.74
31 January	Alksnītis has about 80 men under his command, which grows as stragglers arrive. The Russians attack the positions of the 32nd twice. 14 Russian tanks arrive behind a screen of trucks but do not attack directly, only fire from 400m, and do not do much damage.	GB6, p.75
31 January	Alksnītis, who is in charge of 'the remains of the 32nd Regiment', is assigned to the 34th Regiment for the retreat from Jastrow.	VJ, p.170
1 February	That night the units of the 32nd pull back from their positions outside Flatow and retreat to Jastrow through Gursen. Alksnītis forms up all the men of the 32nd into four companies of 60 each. The march to Flederborn begins, leaving Jastrow at 14:00. There is fighting with Polish forces as they approach Flederborn. They remain in Flederborn until 3 February.	GB6, p.75
3 February	Retreat from Flederborn takes place at approximately lunchtime. Units rush in a panic towards Landeck after the road is freed at Wallachsee, where it had been blocked by intensive mortar and machine gun attacks. But when they get to Landeck, the road is blocked. It proves difficult to gather units together to attack Landeck bridge, where it is likely that the 32nd, led by Rubenis, leads the assault. Eventually, the road into Landeck is opened up. Major Rubenis is killed in this attack, leading his men. Janums says of Rubenis, who had been an 'honourable' battalion commander for him: 'This man, who had waded through Russia's swamps, fell on 3 February leading his regiment in attack by Landeck.' Alksnītis says: 'All the units are mixed up all over the place. It's very hard to keep hold of them. All are rushing northwards. When we reached Landeck it turned out that the German Scheibe group was there but that the Russians were in the southern part of the town. We can't get into the town. We are located between the Flederborn-Landeck road and the Küddow river. The enemy fires with mortars and machine guns and tanks are also active. With gruelling effort ("*ar lielām mokām*") the men were got forward for the attack on the Landeck bridge. We took the bridge. Our forces entered Landeck.'	GB6, pp.75–6 VJ, p.153 Alksnītis

4 February	Alksnītis, who has gathered together approximately 160 men from the 32nd Regiment, moves to Peterswalde, where he receives reinforcements (three companies: one from Lieutenant-Colonel Rušmanis' regiment and two from Lieutenant-Colonel Meija's regiment). Alksnītis and all of these men are transferred into the 33rd Regiment. In his report, Alksnītis says: 'The Latvian men didn't fight any worse than the Germans, despite being less-well armed and equipped.'	GB6, p.76 Alksnītis
10–12 February	The survivors of the 32nd, plus the reinforcements are sent as part of the 33rd under Janums to positions at Kamin – effectively suicide positions. Janums, ignoring orders, successfully breaks out of the encirclement on 12 February.	GB6, p.34
7–19 February	Lieutenant Kļaviņš of the III/32 relates that 'on 7 February, the battalion štābs and the diminished remains of the battalion arrived in Neubrandenburg and gathered at the assembly point for Latvian soldiers. We found, already ahead of us, many Latvian officers and other soldiers. We stayed here until 19 February. Then we left for Stettin. With the battalion štābs were four officers and 280 instructors (NCOs) and soldiers.' NB: Because of the nature of the Neubrandenburg unit (see below), many or most of these 280 are likely to have been attached to the battalion from the stray soldiers who were found at the Sammelstelle der Lettischen Legion. Siliņš receives news of his promotion from Captain to Major while at Neubrandenburg.	GB6, p.77
January–April 1945	The 'Sammelstelle der Lettischen Legion' [Assembly point of the Latvian Legion] was created in Neubrandenburg from the beginning of 1945 as a unit for soldiers who had either lost their units or were returning from hospital, so they had a place where they could gather and find out where they should go. There were similar places in Latvia (Rīga, Liepāja, Ventspils). This was initially under the command of Captain Lietuvietis but from March 1945 under Captain Meiers. In March, an order came from Himmler for 300 soldiers to be sent to Danzig. Meiers and the unit's doctor (Dr Auškaps) replied that there were no fit soldiers available as all were injured. The Sammelstelle afterwards moved to Flensburg and then Hamburg. Right near the end of the war, when there were many injured Latvians being treated in Denmark, an over-eager Doctor Siliņš in Denmark would send soldiers who had recovered from their wounds to this unit (by now in Flensburg) for sending to the front. The doctors in Flensburg made sure that they were marked down as unfit and sent them back to Denmark.	GB9, p.463 Cubins

| 19 February – 6 March | Lieutenant Kļaviņš relates how the III/32 travels to Stettin (21 February), Neustettin (26 February), Bulz, Belgard (27 February), Trepkow (3 March). On 4 March, going through Cammin, Major Siliņš goes missing and Lieutenant Cubins takes command. On 5 March they reach Dievenow, where they are disarmed. Siliņš rejoins the battalion and they reach Neuendorf. On 6 March they start in the direction Misdroja-Swinemünde. Siliņš again disappears, but this time with the only copy of the unit's orders. This could be problematic for the unit, so they manufacture their own orders ('*Marschbefehl*') and travel through Swinemünde to Mullen, arriving 6 March. | GB6, p.77–78

Cubins |
|---|---|---|
| 7–20 March | The III/32 travels through Anklam to Freiberg, arriving 8 March). They then travel to Basov and onto Georgendorf (10 March). On 12 March Major Siliņš reappears in Georgendorf. They then go to Balwitz (13 March) and Wanzkee (14 March), where they meet the remains of the regiment's *tross* (wagon train). Then they move to Leppin, arriving there on 20 March. | GB6, p.79 |
| 10 March | The II/32 reach Danzig. There are 4,144 men in total in the Danzig region, including 490 of the II/32. | GB6, p.83 |
| 19 March | The 32nd has been ordered to assemble at the Neuhof, Wanzka, Rollen-Hagen region, where it is to be under the command of Major Siliņš. By 19 March, 449 32nd Regiment troops have arrived at the assembly point. | Extract of Divisional orders (Krīpēns Archive) |
| 20 March | Major Siliņš is ordered to the Divisional HQ, together with his adjutant Lieutenant Kļaviņš. Both are kept under house arrest in Burg Stargard. Kļaviņš is released on 31 March after interrogation. Siliņš is charged with changing his command point regularly and of cowardice in the face of the enemy. Kļaviņš continues: '…and that, also, was the only case in the history of the 15th Division where an officer was court-martialled (though many were threatened with that) and he was relieved of his command.' | GB6, p.79 |
| 24 March | The 32nd Regiment is re-formed under Lieutenant-Colonel Osvalds Meija. After reinforcements from construction units the regiment numbers reach 1,600 in the first week in April. | GB6, p.86 |
| 1 April | Kļaviņš returns to his regiment on 1 April. | GB6, p.79 |
| 4 April | The largest group of the II/32, under an unnamed replacement commander, is reported to have arrived in Swinemünde (from the encirclement at Gotenhafen) made up of 3 officers, 61 NCOs and 336 soldiers. They are under the command of the German naval pioneer commando (Kdo Marine Festungs-Pi Stab.). They are unarmed and without transport. The men likely make it back to the Division, somewhere west of the Oder. | Extract of Divisional orders (Krīpēns Archive) GB6, p.234 |

9 April– May	Some elements of II/32 (the HQ soldiers) are trapped in Danzig, with other Latvian units. They participate in a failed counterattack on 9th April. On the night of 5–6 May they are evacuated to the Hela peninsular (where they are in a group of 37,000 soldiers). Some other Latvian soldiers are there too. The prisoners march out after the capitulation in national groups (Latvians in the rearguard) and first meet the Russians on 11 May. There is a final parade taken by a German general on 12 May, with the Latvians led by Major Šmits and Lieutenant-Corporal Rebergs.	GB6, p.84
30 March –19 April	The remains of the 32nd move to Lychen and Rutenberg on 30 March, undertaking training and digging anti-tank ditches. Bangerskis visits the regiment on 13 April. Covert plans are made by the Latvian officers to retreat westwards and surrender to the western Allies. Major Siliņš is returned to the regiment in the second half of April, joining regimental HQ without any specific role.	GB6, p.79
19–28 April	Oberführer Burk orders that any soldier caught drunk, refusing orders or guilty of violence is to be shot. The retreat that had been covertly planned by the Latvians is disrupted by the order to form the Janums battle group for the defence of Berlin. 507 officers, NCOs and men of the 32nd are transferred to Janums for this purpose and the remaining weapons are given to these men. Alksnītis, Cubins and the 1st Battalion become part of the breakout by Janums, marching around Berlin. Cubins covers the final break through the German lines with his machine gun. They are prisoners of the Americans by 28 April.	Extract of Divisional orders (Krīpēns Archive) Jānis Cubins memoir, (Krīpēns Archive)
27 April	Final order to the 32nd Regiment is issued: the regiment is ordered to retreat, setting off shortly before midnight. They set off, with the 13th Company providing cover with whatever weapons were left. By now reduced to about 900 men, they march for a number of days, with short breaks. At one point they come across Russian tanks, but bypass them using forest roads. The Russian tanks had taken a parallel road to the north, where a Latvian construction unit had been walking three hours before and became the victims of these tanks (a few escape to tell the tale to the 32nd). The men of the 32nd, using the excuse that they are unarmed, evade requests by local commandants to take up defensive positions. On the night 1–2 May, they get through the Schwerin-Wismar narrows and at 14:00, at Dambek village, they come across a motorised Canadian unit. The Canadians take the Latvian officers' revolvers and order them to proceed westwards.	Extract of Divisional orders, (Krīpēns Archive) GB6, draft materials (Krīpēns Archive)

After marching about 30km following a Latvian flag, they reach Damlok village, where they rested for two days. At Damlok, there is an unpleasant incident, which angers the soldiers and badly impacts discipline. Lieutenant-Colonel Meija, with his adjutant Štrauchs and two messengers, takes a cart with supplies and abandons the regiment. Captain Kronis saves the situation, calming things down and keeping the men together as a unit. After Damlok, on 4 May, the men continue marching westwards, to get further away from the Russians. An American military police unit stops them, calls in a couple of tanks and surrounds them 'like real prisoners.' Telescopes and other military-related items are confiscated and they are marched further westwards under guard.	GB6, draft materials (Krīpēns Archive)

Key:

GB6: Volume six of the 11-volume official history of the Latvian Legion *Latviesu Karavirs Otra Pasaules Kara Laika*: [*The Latvian Soldier During World War Two*] known as 'the Green Books', GB9: volume 9.

VJ: Vilis Janums' autobiography, *Mana Pulka Kauju Gaitas [My Regiment in Battle]*.

Krīpēns Archive: documents, memoirs, correspondence, orders and records held in the Arvīds Krīpēns archive at the Latvian War Museum, Rīga.

Timeline researched and assembled by Aivars Sinka.

Appendix IV

Combat report for deployment of the Hämel Regiment for the period 26 January–12 March 1945

Dated 27 March 1945, and discovered during the research for this book in the 15th Division War Diary held at the National Archive, Rīga.

15. WAFFEN-GREN. DIV. der SS (LATVIAN. NO.1)
APPENDIX NO. 00-155. to
WAR JOURNAL NO.6.
APPENDIX VOLUME NO.1.
ORIGINAL COPY
Abschrift!
Rgt. Hämel – Gef.St. 27.3.45

Combat report for deployment of the 'Hämel' Regiment
for the period 26.1–12.3.45

In accordance with the orders of SS-Obergruppenführer Steiner from 26.1.45, the Gefechtsgruppe 'Scheibe', under the command of SS-Sturmnannführer Scheibe, was formed out of the ULB[1] of II.6germ. SS-Pz. Korps Hammerstein and parts of Rgt 49.II Steinborn, SS-Flakbatterie 54, Hammerstein, drafting officers from the Officer Training Company of the SS-Pz. Korps, Bärenwalde.

> Order of Battle: Gefechtsgruppenstab (Staff)
> Kampfgruppe Hämel
> Kampfgruppe v. Bargen
> Flakbatterie 54
> Strength: 20 / 61 / 540 [officers/NCOs/enlisted men]

---

1 Überlebende: survivors.

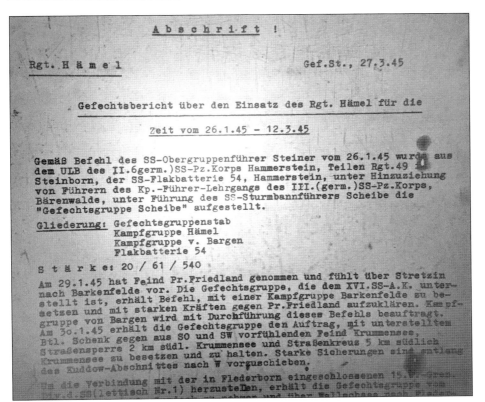

The Hämel Regiment report is stored on microfiche within the 15th Division war diary in the National Archive in Rīga. (Picture: author)

On 29.1.45 the enemy took Pr. Friedland and advances towards Barkenfelde via Stretzin. The Gefechtsgruppe, which is assigned to the IVI. SS-A.K., receives orders for a Kampfgruppe to occupy Barkenfelde and to reconnoitre Pr. Friedland in force. Kampfgruppe von Bargen is tasked with the execution of this order. On 30.1.45 the Gefechtsgruppe is ordered to occupy Krummensee, roadblock 2km south of Krummensee and the crossroads 5km south of Krummensee and to hold them against the enemy approaching from the SE and SW. Strong fortifications along the Küddow Sectors are to be pushed forward to the W.

The Gefechtsgruppe receives orders from the Corps to take Landeck and push on through Wallachsee and Flederborn in order to link up with the 15.W-Gren. Div d. S (Lettisch Nr. 1) which is encircled at Flederborn. Reconnaissance shows that Landeck is heavily occupied by the enemy. After an attempt to take Landeck with a reinforced company fails, Kampfgruppe Hämel, along with the subordinated Kampfgruppe v. Bargen, which is sent from Barkenfelde following mopping-up operations there, receives orders to take Landeck and establish a strong bridgehead on the western bank of the Küddow. Landeck is taken in a night attack on the night of 1-2.2 and in the face of heavy enemy resistance a small bridgehead is established on the western bank of the Küddow. An operation to expand the bridgehead on 2.2. fails. On 3.2.45 the enemy attacks the Landeck Bridgehead and the southern part of Landeck several times with strong forces. Attacks are mopped up with the exception of a small incursion into the southern part of Landeck. At 15.00 the first elements of the 15. W.-Gr. Div. D. SS (Lettisch Nr. 1) reach own [our] lines having broken through from Flederborn. This development is exploited to expand the bridgehead.

Page 2:
Rgt. 48, elements of J.R.59, as well as Kampfgruppe Küchler are subordinated to Gefechtsgruppe Scheibe. The Gefechtsgruppe's defensive front covers: Försterei[2] Hardelbruch, along the Küddow up until Landeck and along Dobrinka to the E until the river crossing 1500m south-west of Brützenwalde. The Gefechtsgruppe is reinforced with heavy weaponry: Flak-Kampftrupp 661 (Hptm. Troll) and I./SS-AR 15 (Lett. Nr. 1.).

To expel the enemy incursion into Adl. Landeck an attack is arranged for 7.2. by Div. Gruppe Ax using Rgt. Gruppe Janums: the attack fails.

New Order of Battle for Gefechtsgruppe Scheibe:

Gefechtsgruppenstab
Kampfgruppe Hämel
Flak-Bttr.54
Btl. Schenk
Rgt.48 (*General Seyffard*)
Teile. J.R.59
Kampfgruppe Küchler
I./SS-AR. 15 (Lett.Nr.1)
Flak-Kampfgruppe 661

With a strength of 99 / 595 / 2239 was subordinated to the Gruppe Ax with defensive responsibility for the sector described above. The following, relatively quiet period is used to strengthen and expand the positions and to carry out intensive reconnaissance and shock troop activities. With the detachment of elements of the 15. W. Gr. Div. (Lett.Nr.1) from the Gefechtsgruppe on 10.2.45 the Gefechtsgruppe is assigned to the 32.J.D. Despite the complete absence of heavy weapons – detachment of the I./SS-AR. 15 (Lett.Nr.1) and Flak-Kampftrupp 661 (Troll) from the unit – the Gefechtsgruppe defends a sector of front 17km long with a strength of 78/443/1761.

Due to developments in the situation at Konitz, the state of readiness at the front is relaxed[3] and, after being reorganised several times, an extension of the sector is

2   'Forest Ranger', presumably woodland.
3   *Auflockerun* = loosening up, also implies relief. Unclear if this means that certain units were removed from the frontline for rest or if the units became more dispersed as a result of widening the front.

carried out, bordered on the right by Först Hardelbruch, and as far as[4] Grievenwal on the left (2 km east of Kappe). Support with heavy weaponry is supplied by the I./ AR.68, which is directed to work with the Gefechtsgruppe. To simplify the chain of command the Gefechtsgruppe is reorganised and henceforth includes Rgt. 48 and Rgt. Hämel. This is likewise a period of relative calm (enemy action is restricted merely to activity from artillery and shock troops), during which the Gefechtsgruppe pushes ahead with the expansion and reinforcement of positions with utmost urgency and carries out intense shock troop and reconnaissance activities.

On 15.2.45 the I./48 is relieved by the FEB 32. FEB 32 is relieved on the 16.2. by Kampfgruppe Pomrehn 15.W.-Gr.Div. (Lett.Nr.1). On 16.2.45, as a result of the withdrawal of the ULB of the III. (Germ) SS-Pz.Korps, the Gefechtsgruppe is reorganised into Rgt.48, Kampfgruppe Pomrehn and Btl. Schenk. SS-Sturmbannführer Hämel assumes command of the Gefechtsgruppe. The Gefechtsgruppe is directly subordinated to the Geh.Kdo. des XVIII (Geh.) A.K.

Page 3:
On 20.2.45 units are redeployed along the line due to the order being given to withdraw the I./48 and the command staff of Rgt. 48. Btl. Schenk, which was deployed at the Dobrinka sector in the area of Kappe, is relieved by W.Gren.Rgt. 33 and takes up the positions of the I.48 in the Landeck Bridgehead. The Schw.J.G.-Zug 48 remains with the Rgt., referred to henceforth as Hämel. The Rgt. is subordinated to the 15.W.G.Div. (Lettisch Nr. 1) after its arrival but retains command over the units in the sector held until this point, including the W.Gr.Rgt.33 and Kampfgruppe Pomrehn, until such a time as the Div. Staff or the 15.W.Gr.Div.(Lettisch Nr.1) headquartered in Krummensee is operational. New front for the Rgt. Hämel: left wing Dobrinka-Übergang 1500m south-west of Prützenwalde, right wing Landecker Mill excluding Rgt.Gef.St. Forstamt Landeck. Nothing to report in this sector until the 24.2.45.

Due to the enemy incursion in the neighbouring division the withdrawal of the front to the Zier-Fließ[5] sector is ordered by division command. The dissolution of the Landeck Sector takes place without pressure from the enemy. However, after taking up the new position, there follow heavy enemy attacks, which are contained on the counterattack by the depth of the HKP. On the evening of the 26.2.45 the order is given for a further withdrawal to the Breitenfeld-Falkenwalde – later Breitenfeld-Hammerstein - Line. Disengagement from the enemy and movement from the Zier-Fließ sector to Hammerstein on the night of the 25–26.2 takes place without pressure from enemy action. The Rgt. is tasked with the defence of Hammerstein. Expanded[6] *Volkssturm* positions in S, SE, N and NE Hammerstein are occupied as of 07:00. During the afternoon a heavy attack with infantry and armour on Hammerstein

---

4   Unclear, but presumed to be excluding Grievenwal.
5   Known to the Latvians as Zierflies brook.
6   Unclear what exact state these positions were in, and the extent to which the *Volkssturm* built on them.

takes place. The enemy, attacking from the S and NE, succeeds in breaking through the Rgt.'s positions and rolling up the line. Links to the left and right are lost. After the units regroup at the forest edge 2km west of Hammerstein and links are established with Rgt.34 on the right wing, the Rgt. takes up new positions. In accordance with instructions from Division this holding position is abandoned, and a new position occupied on the Railway Line/Crossroads Klein Küdde – Südspitze Dolgensee – Ostufer Dolgensee Line. The enemy continues to attack the new positions while the unit regroups and at dawn on the 27.2 succeeds in establishing a foothold and forces the Rgt. to withdraw its lines to the Pommeranien Positions between Dolgensee und Vilmsee. Over the course of the day, Btl. Schenk, which became separated from the main body of the Rgt. during the combat, fights its way back along the Dolgensee to Sparsee. In the afternoon the enemy launches a heavy attack with armoured support and by evening succeeds in advancing to Sparsee, where Btl. Schenk is stationed. The Btl. receives orders to establish and hold a defensive position on the heights just to the south-east of Sparsee. Hptm. Schenk holds the occupied position until 2230.

The Rgt. has suffered heavy casualties amidst the fierce fighting of the past few days. Further elements of the Rgt have become separated and dispersed. The fighting strength of the Rgt. is extremely low. Since the Rgt. is not capable of taking up new positions on the Kussow-Buchwald Line at present strength, the Division Training School detachment is subordinated to it. This new defensive position is occupied until 0400 on 28.2. During the morning the enemy attacks Kussow from the S with infantry, cavalry and armour. The enemy succeeds in pushing back our positions. In the meantime, Btl. Schenk rejoins the Rgt. and constructs a new position on the heights just north of Kussow which is held against all enemy attacks.

Page 4:
Btl. Herwig is deployed at the road junction Buchwald-Wurchow-Schofhütte-Wurchow in the face of enemy approaching from the SE and NE and suffers heavy losses in the course of the enemy attacks. The Btl. is withdrawn and redeployed on the heights 1 km W of the road junction. Over the course of heavy fighting Buchwald is lost to the enemy; new positions are taken up just to the W of Buchwald. The Rgt's newly gained position, with open flanks on the left and right, is held until the Div. gives the order to retreat to Ernsthöhe in the Bublitz-Gramenz line. There, the Rgt. receives orders to occupy Hill 132,500m to the W of Raffenberg along with 1 Kp. Training School detachment and secure it against enemy encroachment from the E. The remainder of the Rgt. is then to take up accommodation in Hasendanz. Since the Training School detachment only has a weak-strength platoon available, Hptm. Herwig receives orders to occupy this position as well.

On the 2.3, Raffenberg, which has in the meantime been built up into a defensive base, is attacked and overrun by the enemy. Raffenberg is retaken with a counterattack, inflicting heavy casualties on the enemy. The Rgt's positions were then strengthened and expanded. On the 3.3 the enemy attacks the neighbouring unit to the left in force and breaks through at the crossroads at Ernsthöhe. Heavy enemy attacks on own positions at Raffenburg are repulsed. Due to the new situation in the neighbouring unit the Rgt. is forced to deploy the Rgt. reserve and all available forces from the Rgt. staff on the heights just to the north of Hansendanz to eliminate the threat of the flanking manoeuvre from the N. Own positions are held against continuous attacks by the enemy. In order to prevent the Rgt. from being outflanked, the order is given to withdraw to the heights of the Gramenz-Bublitz railway line, and later to Steinburg-Burgdorf. However, with the enemy aiming to penetrate further into the neighbouring unit on the left, the Steinburg-Burgdorf line is not occupied, but rather the Rgt. receives orders to take up new positions on the heights at Villmow-Gr. Krössin. Since a further order to withdraw reaches the Rgt. too late, the enemy succeeds in rolling up the Rgt.'s positions from the open left flank with infantry, cavalry and armour. Own losses are high. The Muttrin-Döbel line is occupied by the remnants of the Division Training School and the subordinated Pionier Btl.; the remainder of the Rgt. is immediately deployed in the defence of the Zadtkow-Straßenkreuz line 1500m south-west of Zadtkow.

The Division Training School is forced back from Muttrin by enemy attacks over the course of the afternoon and is then redeployed to reinforce the new positions on the Zadtkow heights.

On the 4.3, 18:00 the Rgt. receives orders to make preparations to break out, commencing on the night of the 4–5.3. (The enemy had succeeded in encircling large, friendly forces through rapid advances from the S towards Kolberg and in the direction of Belgard). On the 5.3, 0100, the Rgt. begins the march to the assembly point at the crossroads 3km S of Wusterbarth, The route of the march ordered for the breakout: Lutzig – Sesritz – Damerow – Nemmin – Krössin – Stargordt – Labuhn – Woldenburg. The Rgt. reaches Balzdrey in a day march undertaken at the edge of the Div., which is forced to turn N by strong enemy action from Schivelbein, and continues the march to Teltzkow on the night of the 5 and 6.3. After a short rest the march is resumed via Kartlow, Berkenow towards Alt-Döberitz. The intention to regain the original route of march via Labuhn from here must be abandoned due to…

Page 5:

…reports of enemy forces being received, according to which Labuhn is heavily occupied by the enemy and following the independent decision of the Rgt. Kdr. the Rgt. reaches the woodland 3km east of Witzmitz as the vanguard of the Div. with the intention to immediately move beyond the Plathe-Korlin road. By personal order of the Div commander however, the unit is instructed to halt and rest in these woods. The Rgt. moves into the area of the Foresters' Lodge, 2.5km east of Witzmitz as the Div. Reserve.

On the afternoon of the 7.3 the Rgt. receives orders to form a defensive perimeter around Witzmitz. The Rgt. Kdr. is appointed combat commander for Witzmitz. Positions are held in accordance with orders until 8.3, 03:00 against weaker enemy reconnaissance sorties. Having carried out this order Rgt. marches to Brotiz via Natelfitz in order to take over new defensive assignments there in positions to the W and SE. The Rgt. leaves these positions in the evening in order to take up position in a bridgehead on the Rega at Borntin. In accordance with orders from Div., at 0030 on 9.3 the Rgt. disengages from the enemy and, screened by a rearguard, reaches the assembly area of the Div. in a forced march via Klätow, Gumtow, Zedlin. As part of efforts to establish a strong bridgehead the Rgt. receives orders to take up a defensive position on the western edge of Vockenhagen-Bhf. As of 8.3.45. I.Btl. Belgard (Vaniek) is subordinated to the Rgt. for the execution of this task. During the afternoon, the forward defences are attacked from the NE by the enemy and pushed back to HKL. The Rgt.'s own section of line is held against all enemy attacks. During the night, the order is given to occupy the new Mittelhagen-Drosedom line with instructions to break away from the enemy on 11.3 and, leaving behind a strong rearguard detachment, to reach the Div. assembly area (woodland 1.5km east of Rewahl). At 09:30 the Rgt. receives orders to advance along the coast as the vanguard of the Div. in order to breakthrough towards Dievenow. Rgt. reinforced by 1 Kp. Pioniers, the advance commences at 11:00 and, with heavy defensive screening to the S, the Rgt. reaches East Dievenow in the evening, where it finds quarters.

On 12.3 the Rgt. is dissolved. All Wehrmacht personnel released from the unit are then combined, as with Btl. Vaniek, into the Btl. Herwig. The remnants of the former *Kampfgruppe* Scheibe with a strength of 9 / 2 / 54 are subordinated to the 15. W.-Gr. Div. (Latvian Nr.1), in order to be reassigned to the III (Germ.) SS-Pz.Korps upon reaching the area where they are to be quartered.

F.d.R.[7]
Gez.:[8] Wawarter
SS-Hauptsturmführer u. Adjutant

Gez.: Hämel – SS-Sturmbannführer u. Kommandeur
F.d.R.d.A.[9]
[signature]
Leutnant (01)

---

7   *Für die Richtigkeit* [law]: commissioned by.
8   *Gezeichnet*: signed.
9   *Für die Richtigkeit der Abschrift*: certified as a true copy.

Bibliography

Interviews

Author interviews with Legionnaires Jānis Čevers, Laimonis Ceriņš, Žano Mūsiņš, Ēriks Rudzītis, Talis Iskalns, Ziedonis Āboliņš, Jānis Urpens, Henry Vītols, Harijs Valdmanis, Pauls Vanags.
Refugee memories: Aina Urpens, Sarmite Ērenpreiss-Janovskis

Archive material

Brombergs, A., *Latviju Enciklopedija (The Latvian Encyclopedia)*, vol. 34 (Stockholm, 1952). Accessed from de-classified CIA files at <https://www.cia.gov/library/readingroom/docs/>.
Hämel, H., Regiment Hämel after-action report, dated 27.03.1945, included in the War Diary of the 15th SS (Latvian Legion) in the National Archives, Rīga. Appendix No. 00-155. to War Journal No. 6. Appendix Volume 1. Trans. Tom Fane
Krīpēns, Arvīds, documents, memoirs, correspondence, orders and records held at the Latvian War Museum, Rīga. Trans. Aivars Sinka.
Kubicki, A.,'My Memories of the War in Nakło' in *Zeszyty Historyczne Muzeum Ziemi Krajeńskiej nr 5* (Historical Notebooks of the Krajeńska Museum, 2015)
Museum of the Second World War, Gdańsk. *Liberation and Destruction* exhibition, *Crimes Against the Population* exhibition, Museum of the Second World War, Gdańsk. (Online at <https://muzeum1939.pl/>)

Books

Ardanowski, J.K., and Sztama, P., *Z Głębokości Wołam Do Ciebie … Tragedia kobiet pochodzenia żydowskiego, więzionych i mordowanych w podobozach KL Stutthof w okolicach Torunia w ostatnich miesiącach II wojny światowej. [I call you from the depths]* (Brodnica: Wszechnica Edukacyjna i Wydawnicza Verbum, 2014)
Bassler, G., *Alfred Valdmanis and the Politics of Survival* (Toronto: University of Toronto Press, 2000)
Beevor, Antony, *Berlin – The Downfall 1945* (London: Viking-Penguin Books, 2002)
Bessel, R., *Germany 1945: from War to Peace* (London and Sydney: Pocket Books. Simon and Schuster, 2010)

Bessel, R., *Life in the Third Reich* (Oxford: Oxford University Press, U.S.A.; 2nd Revised edition, 2001)

Bettina Birn, R., and Riess, V., *Revising the Holocaust* in The Historical Journal, 40, I. (Cambridge: Cambridge University Press, 1997)

Blank, R., Fings, K. and Echtemkamp, J., *Germany and the Second World War Vol IX–1* (Oxford: Clarendon Press, OUP, 2008)

Blatman, D., *The Death Marches – the Final Phase of Nazi Genocide* (Cambridge, Massachusetts and London: The Belknap Press of Harvard University Press, 2011). (Originally published as *Les Marches de la Mort*, 2009)

Blood, P., *Hitler's Bandit Hunters: The SS and the Nazi Occupation of Europe* (Lincoln, NE: Potomac Books, University of Nebraska Press, 2007)

Borowski, T., *Last Blood on Pomerania – Leon Degrelle and the Walloon Waffen SS Volunteers, February – May 1945.* (Warwick: Helion, 2016)

Buggeln, M., *Slave Labor in Nazi Concentration Camps* (Oxford: Oxford University Press, 2014)

Buttar, P., *Battleground Prussia – the Assault on Germany's Eastern Front 1944–45* (Oxford and Long Island, NY: Osprey Publishing, 2010)

Campbell, C., *Target London: Under Attack from the V-weapons During WWII* (London: Hachette UK, 2012).

Clark, A., *Barbarossa* (London: Cassel, 2000)

Clark, P., *The Death of East Prussia – War and Revenge in Germany's Easternmost Province* (Chevy Chase, MD: Andover Press, 2013)

Clough, P., *The Flight Across the Ice – the Escape of the East Prussian Horses* (London: Haus Publishing, 2009)

Davies, N., *Heart of Europe – the Past in Poland's Present.* (Oxford: Oxford University Press, 2001)

Davies, N., *Europe at War 1939–1945: No Simple Victory* (London: Pan Books, 2007)

Duffy, C., *Red Storm on the Reich: The Soviet March on Germany, 1945* (New York: Da Capo Press, 1993)

Ethell, Jeff., *Ta 152 – Monogram Closeup 24.* (Sturbridge, Massachusetts: Monogram Aviation Publications, 1990)

Figes, O., *The Whisperers: Private life in Stalin's Russia* (London: Penguin, 2008)

Forbes, R., *For Europe: The French Volunteers of the Waffen-SS* (Mechanicsburg, Pennsylvania: Stackpole Military Series, 2010)

Freivalds, Caunītis, Bērziņš, Kociņš and Hāzners (eds), *Latviešu Karavīrs Otra Pasaules Kaŗa Laikā [The Latvian Soldier During World War Two],* vols 1–11 (Västerås, Sweden: Ziemeļblāzma, 1979)

Fritz, J. and Anders, E., *Murder of Polish POWs at Podgaje (Flederborn),* February 1945 in *The Second World War and Latvia: Events and Consequences 1940s–1960s.* Research of the Commission of the Historians of Latvia, 2011, and reports of conference 'Extermination of the Latvian Army, 1940–41' (Rīga: Zinatne, 2011)

Gatrell, P., and Baron, N. (eds), *Warlands: Population Resettlement and State Reconstruction in the Soviet-East European Borderlands, 1945–50* (Berlin: Springer, 2009)

Glantz, D., and House, J., *When Titans Clashed – How the Red Army Stopped Hitler* (Lawrence, KS: University Press of Kansas, USA, 1995)

Goldsworthy, T., *The Waffen-SS in Allied Hands, Vol 1 – Personal Accounts From Hitler's Elite Soldiers* (Newcastle upon Tyne: Cambridge Scholars Publishing, 2018)

Great Soviet Encyclopaedia, The. Various volumes. (London: Macmillan, 1974)

Grīnvalds, J., *Kā es Redzēju tās Lietas [As I Saw Those Things] The Diaries of Jānis Grīnvalds.* Trans. Aivars Sinka (Rīga: Preses nams, 2002)

Guderian, H., *Panzer Leader* (Middlesex, UK: Classic Penguin, 2000). Originally published in 1952 by Michael Joseph

Hastings, M., *Armageddon: The Battle for Germany 1944–45* (London: Pan Books, 2015). Originally published by Macmillan, 2004

Janovskis, G., *Pie Tornas.* Trans. Daina Vītola (Vasteras, Sweden: Ziemeļblāzma, 1966)

Jansons, I., *Manu Dienu Gramata [The Book of my Days]* (Australia, self-published by Zaiga Jansone, 2017)

Janums, V., *Mana Pulka Kauju Gaitas [My Regiment in Battle]* (Sweden: Daugavas Vanagi, 1978)

Jones, M., *After Hitler: The Last Days of the Second World War in Europe* (London: John Murray, 2015)

Kažociņš, I., *Latviešu Karavīri Zem Svešiem Karogiem 1940-1945 [Latvian Soldiers Under Foreign Flags]* Trans. Aivars Sinka (Rīga, Latvijas Universitātes žurnāla 'Latvijas Vēsture' fonds, 1999)

Kieser, Egbert, *Prussian Apocalypse – the Fall of Danzig 1945.* Trans. Tony Le Tissier. (Barnsley: Pen and Sword Military, 2011). Originally published in German as *Danziger Bucht 1945. Dokumentation einer Katastrophe* (1978)

Ķīlītis, J., *"Es karā aiziedams…" Mani raksturīgākie piedzīvojumi Otrā pasaules karā [I Go to War: My Most Characteristic Adventures in WWII].* Trans. Aivars Sinka. (Self-published, Ottawa, Canada:1956)

Klotiņš, A., *No Zobena Dziesma – Roberts Zuika un viņa vīru koris karā, gūstā un trimdā [From a Sword, a Song – Robert Zuika and his male-voice choir in war, captivity and exile]* Trans. Aivars Sinka. (Rīga: Zinatne, 2013)

Kochanski, H., *The Eagle Unbowed: Poland and the Poles in the Second World War* (London: Penguin; 6th edition, 2013)

Kochavi, A.J., *Confronting Captivity: Britain and the United States and their POWs in Nazi Germany.* (Chapel Hill, NC: University of North Carolina Press, 2011)

Kovtunenko, Lieutenant Rolands, *Battle at More – a Participant's Account of a Battle Against Overwhelming Odds.* Trans. Colonel Janis Viksne (Rīga: Timermanis and Vejins, 2009)

Leitītis, J., *Pulkvedis Vilis Janums. Raksti, Stāsti un Atmiņas,* Trans. Aivars Sinka (Toronto: Daugavas Vanagi Central Committee, 1986)

Longerich, P., *Holocaust: The Nazi Persecution and Murder of the Jews* (Oxford: Oxford University Press, 2010)

Lumans, V., *Latvia in World War II* (New York: Fordham University Press, 2006)

McElligott, A., *Rethinking the Weimar Republic: Authority and Authoritarianism 1916–1936* (London: Bloomsbury, 2013)

Maciejowski, M., *Zbrodnie Niemieckie na Pomorzu Zachodnim I Ziemi Lubuskiej Popelnione w Latach 1939-1945 w swietle sledztw prowadzonych przez Oddzialowa Komisje Scigania Zbrodni przeciwko Narodowi Polskiemu w Szczecinie* Chapter XI. (Warsaw: Instytut Pamięci Narodowej – Komisja Ścigania Zbrodni przeciwko Narodowi Polskiemu [Institute of National Remembrance – Commission for the Prosecution of Crimes against the Polish Nation], 2013)

Mangulis, V., *Latvia in the Wars of the 20th Century*. (Princeton Junction: Cognition Books online at <http://old.historia.lv/publikacijas/gramat/mangulis/09.nod.htm#345>, 1983)

Martelli, P., and Dal Cengio, V., *On the Devil's Tail – in Combat with the Waffen SS on the Eastern Front 1945 and with the French in Indochina 1951–54* (Warwick: Helion, 2018)

McDowell, L., *Hard Labour: The Forgotten Voices of Latvian Migrant 'Volunteer' Workers* (London: Routledge, 2013)

Merridale, C., *Ivan's War – the Red Army 1939–45* (London: Faber and Faber, 2005)

Meler, M., *Jewish Latvia: Sites to Remember. Latvian Jewish Communities Destroyed in the Holocaust*. (Tel Aviv: The Association of Latvian and Estonian Jews in Israel, 2013)

Merritt Miner, S., *Stalin's Holy War: Religion, Nationalism, and Alliance Politics, 1941–1945*. (Chapel Hill, NC: University of North Carolina Press, 2003)

Mitcham S., *The Panzer Legions: A Guide to the German Army Tank Divisions of WWII and their Commanders* (London: Stackpole Books, 2006)

Mitcham, S., *German Order of Battle: Panzer, Panzer Grenadier, and Waffen SS Divisions in WWII* (London: Stackpole Books, 2007)

Mitcham, S; Mueller, G., *Hitler's Commanders: Officers of the Wehrmacht, the Luftwaffe, the Kriegsmarine, and the Waffen-SS*. (Lanham, MD: Rowman & Littlefield Publishers, 2012)

Newton, S., *Panzer Operations: The Eastern Front Memoir of Generaloberst Erhard Raus* (Cambridge, Mass., Da Capo, 2003)

Nichol, J. and Rennell, T., *The Last Escape – the Untold Story of Allied Prisoners of War in Germany 1944–45*. (London: Penguin, 2003)

Ochman, E., *Post Communist Poland – Contested Pasts and Future Identities* (Abingdon: BASEES/Routledge series on Russian and East European Studies, 2013)

Palmer, A., *The Baltic – a New History of the Region and its People* (New York: Abrams Press, 2007)

Paul, W., *Der Endkampf um Deutschland 1945* (Esslingen, 1978)

Pencz, R., *For the Homeland: The 31st Waffen-SS Volunteer Grenadier Division in World War II* (Mechanicsburg, PA: Stackpole Military History Series, 2009)

Plavnieks, R., *Nazi Collaborators On Trial During The Cold War: Viktors Arājs and the Latvian Auxiliary Security Police* (London: Palgrave Macmillan, 2018)

Polmar, N. and Allen, T., *World War II: the Encyclopedia of the War Years, 1941–1945* (New York: Dover Publications Inc., 2012)

Rubess, B., and Ikstena, N., *Brīnumainā Kārtā: Stāsti par Bruņa Rubesa Trim Mūžiem* [The Autobiography of Brunis Rubess]. (Rīga: Nordik, 1999)

Silgailis, A., *Latvian Legion* (San Jose, CA: Roger James Bender, 1986)

Silins, L., *Latviesi Stuthofas Koncentracijas Nometne 1942–1945* (Rīga: Latvijas Universitates zurnala Latvijas Vesture fonds, 2003)

Snyder, T., *Bloodlands – Europe Between Hitler and Stalin* (London: Vintage, 2010)

Sruoga, B., *Forest of the Gods* [English edition] (Vilnius: Vaga, 1996)

Swain, G., ed. Terry Cox, *Against the Grain* (London: Routledge, 2018)

Thorwald, J., *Defeat in the East* (Canada and the US: Bantam Books, 1980)

Toland, J., *The Last 100 Days.* (London: Arthur Barker Ltd, 1965)

Trigg, J., *Hitler's Gauls: The History of the 33rd Waffen-SS Division Charlemagne* (Hitler's Legions Book 1) (Stroud, Gloucestershire: The History Press, 2009)

Vajda, F. and Dancey, P., *German Aircraft Industry and Production, 1933–1945* (Warrendale, PA: Society of Automotive Engineers, 1998)

Waite, C., *Survivor of The Long March: Five Years as a POW 1940–1945* (Stroud: Spellmount, 2012)

Weale, A., *Renegades* (London: Random House, 2002)

Williams, D., *In Titanic's Shadow – The World's Worst Merchant Ship Disasters* (Stroud: The History Press, 2012)

Zaloga, S.J., *V-2 Ballistic Missile 1942–52* (London: Bloomsbury Publishing, 2013)

Articles

Baltic News Network, 06.02.2015, announcing death of Roberts Zuika at <https://bnn-news.com/brilliant-conductor-roberts-zuika-passes-125147>

Ceran, T., 'The Economics of Extermination' (02 March 2020) <https://przystanekhistoria.pl/pa2/tematy/obozy-koncentracyjne/62142,Ekonomia-i-Zaglada-Podobozy-KL-Stutthof-w-okolicach-Torunia-1944-1945.html>

Ciechoński, T., 'They Commemorated the Victims of the German Jewish Camp' (13 June 2017) <https://Toruń wyborcza.pl/Toruń/7,48723,21956357,upamietnili-ofiary-niemieckiego-obozu-dla-zydowek-zdjecia.html>

Czyzykowski, P., 'Schneidemühl Fortress 1 – Warfare' (undated) <www.dawna.Piła.pl> at <https://www.dawna.Piła.pl/czytelnia/twierdza_Piła_01.php>, accessed 26 July 2020

Dzintars, Pauls, trans. Daina Vītola, *Daugavas Vanagi Mēnešraksts*, Nr 5 (01 September 1999) <periodika.lv>.

'Festung Schneidemühl' in *Weapons and Warfare*, <https://weaponsandwarfare.com/2015/12/10/festung-Schneidemühl/> accessed 19 June 2019

Fritz, J. and Anders, E., *Mord dokany na polskich jencach wojennych we wsi Podgaje (Flederbon) w lutym 1945 r.* [Murder of Polish prisoners of war in the village of Podgaje (Flederborn) in February 1945.] Extract from English summary, pp.185–186 from *Studies in the History of Eastern Europe and the Baltic States* in Europa Orientalis 3 (2012)

Gladysiak, L., *The Korpsgruppe Von Tettau and the Breakout from Niechorze* <https://www.infolotnicze.pl/2012/05/23/

grupa-korpuna-von-tettau-wyamanie-spod-miejscowoci-niechorze/>, translated: accessed 20 June 2019

Hewitt, N., 'Operation Hannibal 1945: the Germany Evacuation that Dwarfed the 'Miracle of Dunkirk',' BBC History Extra, (20 February 2020) <https://www.historyextra.com/period/second-world-war/operation-hannibal-germany-dunkirk-what-happened-rescue-mission-soviet-troops-what-was-how-many-died/>

Klimowicz-Sikorska, M., 'SS Men were Punished in Gdańsk' (22 February 2010) <https://www.trojmiasto.pl/wiadomosci/W-Gdańsku-karano-SS-Mannow-n37085.html>

Kossert, A., *Endlosung on the Amber Shore: the Massacre in January 1945 on the Baltic Seashore – a Repressed Chapter of East Prussian History* (London: The Leo Baeck Institute Yearbook, 49–1, 2004) at <http://muenchow.cms.udel.edu/images/Palmnicken1945.pdf>

Krzemiński, J., 'Poland's Expensive Highways' (05 February 2020) <https://www.obser-watorfinansowy.pl/in-english/polands-expensive-highways/>

Kubicki, A., *My Memories of the War in Nakło in Zeszyty Historyczne Muzeum Ziemi Krajeńskiej nr 5* (Historical Notebooks of the Krajeńska Museum, 2015)

Laikrasts Latvietis, Nr 132, (16 February 2011) <http://www.laikraksts.com/raksti/raksts.php?KursRaksts=1077>

Landeszeitung fuer Mecklenburg und Nachbahr Gebiete, (10 March 1945), reproduced in Latvian 'Green Books' vol. 6.

Kuzmins, V., 'The 15th Division of the Latvian Legion in the Fight on the Velikaya River (1 March–14 April 1944): A Case Study in Maintaining Fighting Power' (undated) <http://www.karamuzejs.lv/~/media/karamuzejs/documents/raksti/Valdis%20Kuzmins%20-%20The%2015th%20Division%20of%20the%20Latvian%20Legion.ashx>

McGregor, R., Review of Martelli, P. *On the Devil's Tail*: for The History Net.com <https://www.historynet.com/book-review-on-the-devils-tail-by-paul-martelli-with-vittorino-dal-cengio.htm>, accessed 28 May 2021

Maciejowski, M., *Zbrodnie niemieckie na Pomorzu Zachodnim I ziemi lubuskiej popelnione w latach 1939–1945 w swietle sledztw prowadzonych przez Oddzialowa Komisje Scigania Zbrodni przeciwko Narodowi Polskiemu w Szczecinie* [German Crimes in Western Pomerania and the Lubuskie Region Committed in 1939–1945 in the Light of Investigations Conducted by the Branch Commission for the Prosecution of Crimes Against the Polish Nation in Szczecin] (Szczecin: IPN, 2013)

Molenda, T., *Characteristics of the Pomeranian Position West of Krzyż Wielkopolski*. From the website Wielkopolski Historiaczyne at <https://wielkopolskahistorycznie.pl/2020/07/11/pozycjepomorskie/> citing Miniewicz J., Perzyk B. *Wał Pomorski*, 1997. (Warsaw: MBP Publishing House, 2020)

New York Times: 'Poles symbolise union with sea' (13 February 2020) <https://timesmachine.nytimes.com/timesmachine/1920/02/13/118261587.pdf>, accessed 21 January 2020

Orski, M., ed. Aharon Weiss, 'The Jewish Camp at Brusy-Dziemiany', *Yad Vashem Studies*, Volume XXII, (1992)

Plavnieks, R., 'Justice Behind Propaganda: Soviet Prosecutions of the men of the Arājs Kommando', *Latvijas Vēstures Inst.tūta Žurnāls*, Nr. 4 (1997), quoting 'The Arājs Commando Member as Seen in the KGB Trial Files: Social Standing, Education, Motives for Joining It, and Sentences Received' (Viksne, 2001). In: *Holokausta Izpētes Problēmas Latvijā*. (Rīga: Latvijas vēstures institūta apgāds, 2015)

Raus, Erhard, *Panzer Operations – the Eastern Front Memoir of General Raus, 1941– 1945*. Trans. Steven Newton (Cambridge, Mass., Da Capo, 2003)

Reimann, M., 'In One German Town, 1,000 People Killed Themselves in 72 Hours', *Timeline.com* (07 October 2016) <https://timeline.com/demmin-nazi-mass-suicide-44c6caf76727>, accessed 09 June 2020

Ručs, K., *Dzīve ar Dievu: prelāts Dr. Kazimirs Ručs, garīdznieks, latgalietis, latvietis trimdā atmiņas*. [*Life with God: Prelate Dr. Kazimirs Ručs, clergyman, Latgalian, Latvian in exile: memories.*] (Rīga: Madris, 2004)

Rule, R., 'Leon Degrelle – Traitor of Belgium' in *Warfare History Network*, (09 January 2019) <https://warfarehistorynetwork.com/daily/wwii/leon-degrelle-traitor-or-war-hero/>

Ruņģis, A., 'Uz Tām Prūšu Robežām' [excerpt] from *Latvija Amerikā*, Nr.27 (07 July 2001)

Sprūde, V., *Fake News: Latvian Legionnaires Burnt Polish POWs Alive* (undated) <http://okupacijasmuzejs.lv/en/history/independent-latvia/fake-news-latvian-legionnaires-burnt-polish-pows-alive>, accessed 26 July 2020

Sprūde, V., 'Ko Liek Pārvērtēt Leģiona Arhīvs' in *Latvijas Avize*, (24 February 2007) <http://lpra.vip.lv/leg_arh2007.htm>, accessed 13 May 2021

Sroki, J (ed), *Mój los był tylko jednym spośród wielu milionów … Powiat sławieński w roku 1945 Wspomnienia dawnych mieszkańców* [*My fate was only one of many millions … Sławno County in 1945: Memories of former inhabitants*] Trans. Janusz Korona. (Sławno: Margraf, 2008)

Stefaniec, W., *History of the Concentration Camp in Pictures*, <GP24.pl> (08 December 2008) <https://gp24.pl/historia-obozu-koncentracyjnego-w-obrazkach/ar/4372183&prev=search>

Steggewentz, D., *Marzec 1945* from Sroki, J (ed); (2008) pp.279–285. *Mój los był tylko jednym spośród wielu milionów … Powiat sławieński w roku 1945 Wspomnienia dawnych mieszkańców* [*My fate was only one of many millions … Sławno County in 1945: Memories of former inhabitants*] Trans. Janusz Korona. (Sławno: Margraf, 2008)

Strods, K., *Garīdznieks karavīra zābakos. Ieskats Kazimira Ruča gaitās latviešu leģionā* [*A chaplain in soldiers' boots: Kazimirs Ručs' journeys with the Latvian Legion*] (2019) <https://www.lsm.lv/raksts/Dzive--stils/vesture/garidznieks-karavira-zabakos-ieskats-kazimira-ruca-gaitas-latviesu-legiona.a314341/>

Traces of War <https://www.tracesofwar.com/persons/19521/Tettau-von-Hans.htm>, accessed 13 May 2021

Zeszyty Historyczne Muzeum Ziemi Krajeńskiej Nr 5 (Historical Notebooks of the Krajeńska Museum, 2015)

Zychowicz, P., 'Tajemnica mordu w Podgajach. Jedna z największych polskich zagadek II wojny *światowej* [The Mystery of the Murders in Podgaje. One of the greatest Polish riddles of WWII].' *Do Rzeczy,* (19 April 2019) Trans. Janusz Korona, accessed 26 July 2020 <https://dorzeczy.pl/historia/100018/Tajemnica-mordu-w-Podgajach-Jedna-z-najwiekszych-polskich-zagadek-II-wojny-swiatowej.html>

Websites

Alchetron.com at <https://alchetron.com/Heinz-Hämel>
Axis History Forum at <https://forum.axishistory.com>
British Commonwealth Forces War Records website at <https://www.forces-war-records.co.uk/european-camps-british-commonwealth-prisoners-of-war-1939-45#Oflag>
Bydgoszcz city tourism website <https://visitbydgoszcz.pl/en/explore/what-to-do/2522-exploseum>
Bydgoszcz Diocesan website, translated, at <http://diecezja.bydgoszcz.pl/2009/02/21/wicbork-wniebowzicia-nmp-i-apostoow-szymona-i-judy-tadeusza/>
'Camps in Germany 1945-1951 for refugees from Baltic countries' Online exhibition at <www.archiv.org.lv/baltic_dp_germany/?id=12&lang=en>
Centralny Oboz Pracy w Potulicach (1945-1949), a report for the project *Potulice – jedno miejsce, dwie pamięci* [*Potulice - one place, two memories*] at <http://www.geschichtswerkstatt-europa.org/media/projekte/Die Broschure.pdf>
<Dawna.Piła.pl> on Schneidemühl quoting interview with Piła district museum historian Marek Fijalkowski at <http://www.forum.dawna.Piła.pl/viewtopic.php?f=12&t=521&start=25> (2005)
Der Spiegel online: Lakotta, Beate article at <https://www.spiegel.de/spiegel/spiegelspecial/d-39863564.html>
Dziwnówek, History of; online at <https://www.dziwnow.pl/asp/pl_start.asp?typ=14&menu=31&strona=1&sub=4&subsub=30>
Exploseum, Bydgoszcz at <http://www.exploseum.pl/>
Exploseum: Former German explosives factory turned into interactive museum [press release 01 February 2016] at <https://ec.europa.eu/regional_policy/en/projects/poland/exploseum-former-german-explosives-factory-turned-into-interactive-museum>
Forum Bydgoskiego Stowarzyszenia Miłośników Zabytków 'Bunkier' at <http://forum.bsmz.org/viewtopic.php?f=9&t=284>
Gmina Sicienko administrative pages at <https://www.sicienko.pl>
Kołobrzeg [Kolberg] town website at <http://www.Kołobrzeg.pl/epoki-historyczne>
Konflikty.pl history website at <www.konflikty.pl> quoted on Piła history forum at <http://www.forum.dawna.Piła.pl/viewtopic.php?f=12&t=521&start=25>
Katyn massacre: <https://poland.pl/history/history-poland/katyn-massacre-basic-facts/>
Lacplesis.org: Russian Front bunker story at <http://lacplesis.org/WWII/Latviesu_Karaviri_Volchovas_Fronte/Latviesu_Karaviri_Volchovas_Frontes_Sektora.pdf>
Latvian Legion webpages at <https://latvianlegion.org/index.php?en/accused/Hāzners/level-00-case.ssi> Ref: Hāzners, Vilis

<Latviesi.com>: recollections of Imants Balodis

<Lettia.lv>: specialist Latvian history website at <http://www.lettia.lv/en_a_legionari-nirnberga.html>

<Konflikty.pl> website *Wal Pomorski at Schneidemühl*: online at <www.konflikty.pl>

Muzeum Ziemi Waleckiej at <www.MuzeumWałcz.pl>

<Periodika.lv> online archive for Daugavas Vanagi contemporary newspaper reports, at <http://periodika.lv/periodika2-viewer/view/index/>

Piła: destruction statistics from Carl von Ossietzky Universität, Oldenburg webpages at <https://ome-lexikon.uni-oldenburg.de/orte/schneidemuehl-Piła>

Piła: historical forum <www.dawna.Piła.pl> including Miniewicz, J., and Perzyk, B. (1997) on *Wal Pomorski* at <http://www.forum.dawna.Piła.pl/viewtopic.php?f=12&t=521&start=25>

Piła: Polish Central Statistical Office 2012 population report on Schneidemühl expulsions at <https://stat.gov.pl/cps/rde/xbcr/gus/p_population_in_poland_size_and_structure_30062012.pdf>

Polish Genealogical Society of America website at <https://pgsa.org/polish-history/translated-descriptions-of-polish-villages-and-provinces/poznan/>

Słupsk town website at <http://www.słupsk.pl/kultura/>

Stutthof Museum website at <http://stutthof.org/historia/>

The Destruction of Königsberg website at <https://canitz.org/index.php/the-destruction>

Traces of War website: <https://www.tracesofwar.com/persons/21310/Ziegler-Joachim.htm>

—— <https://www.tracesofwar.com/sights/111055/Mass-Grave-Soviet-Soldiers-Cmentarz-Komunalny-nr-2.htm>

—— <https://www.tracesofwar.com/sights/5445/Soviet-War-Graves-Cmentarz-ul-Wybickiego.htm?

UNESCO World Heritage Centre online: the medieval town of Toruń at <https://whc.unesco.org/en/list/835>

War History Online at <https://www.warhistoryonline.com/world-war-ii/>

Warfare History Network website at <https://warfarehistorynetwork.com/daily/wwii/leon-degrelle-traitor-or-war-hero/>

<Wartimeguides.blogspot.com> – testimony and tours of Second World War-related locations in Toruń, Poland, by guides Hania and Pawl Bukowski at <http://wartimeguides.blogspot.com>

Worldwar-two.net – article <http://www.worldwar-two.net/events/operation-hannibal/0/ events/operation-hannibal/0/>

Złotów town website. 'A Postcard from Złotów' at <https://www.Złotów.pl/A_postcard_from_Złotów.html>

Index

PEOPLE

PLACES

MILITARY UNITS

GENERAL TERMS

Also by this author

Fire and Ice: the Nazis' scorched earth campaign in Norway (The History Press, 2014)
Blood in the Forest: the end of the Second World War in the Courland Pocket
    (Helion, 2017)
Up Against the Wall – the KGB and Latvia (Helion, 2019)

www.vincenthunt.co.uk